A HISTORY OF
GEORGIA

A HISTORY OF
GEORGIA

BY

BONNIE LONDON

CLAIRMONT PRESS
Montgomery, Alabama

BONNIE BULLARD LONDON is a graduate of Sullins College, The University of Georgia and Georgia State University. She has taught in grades K-twelve, with a concentration in eighth grade Georgia History in the Atlanta City Schools. She has also been an instructor with the Governor's Summer Honors Program. In addition to working as a supervisor in language arts and social studies, Bonnie has served as an elementary principal in the Atlanta City Schools and the Clarke County School District. She has worked as a consultant for the Northeast Georgia RESA, and for the Georgia State Department of Education. Presently, Bonnie is president of London Limited, an education consulting firm. She has authored a number of articles and student workbooks in the areas of Georgia Studies and Language Arts.

ACKNOWLEDGMENTS: *A History of Georgia* is the result of the collaborative efforts of many people. Special recognition is given to Helen Richardson, Fulton County Schools, Barbara Mathis, Clarke County Schools, Pat Van Gorder, Clarke County Schools, along with Marguerite Bullard and Norma McNair. In addition, thanks is given to the Savannah Historical Society, the Research Department of the Clarke County Regional Library, University of Georgia Library, the Department of Archives in the Atlanta City Schools, and to the manuscript readers throughout the state for their diligent work and excellent suggestions. (See list on page 597)

Editor: Sarah Epley Sims

Assistant Editor: Faye Andress

Photo Research: Robin McDonald

Design: Robin McDonald

Printed in the U.S.A.   OPQRSTU-0594   ISBN 0-9623319-4-5

INTRODUCTION

Above: One of Georgia's most famous citizens is memorialized at the Martin Luther King, Jr. Center. ***Front cover:*** *Georgia's state capitol is covered with sixty ounces of gold from Dahlonega.* ***Page i:*** *The Georgia state flag flying over the capitol.* ***Page ii:*** *Reflections distort skyscrapers in downtown Atlanta.* ***Page iv:*** *Azaleas bloom around the Glynn County courthouse in Brunswick.* ***Back cover:*** *The Taliaferro County courthouse in Crawfordville.*

ALL TOO OFTEN, history is seen as a group of boring facts and dates. It is actually an adventure story filled with tales of other people in other times—but people just like you. As you read this book and work through the student activities, keep asking yourself these questions: What will history books in the future say about me and my generation? How do events that happened ten, twenty, or one hundred years ago affect my life today. How can what I do now affect the future of my brothers and sisters and even my own children or grandchildren? In the end, you too, will be featured in the next part of the adventure story.

—*Bonnie Bullard London*

Top left: Relaxing on Little St. Simons Island, one of Georgia's "Golden Isles." Top right: The ever-changing skyline of Atlanta. Above: Spring at Callaway Gardens near Pine Mountain.

TABLE OF CONTENTS

Top left: A living history demonstration at Ft. King George State Historical Site, Darien. ***Top right:*** Russell Dam on the Savannah River. ***Above:*** Fall at Cloudland Canyon State Park in north Georgia.

UNIT I

A STATE AND ITS BEGINNING

? B.C. - 1663

Geography is the study of the earth as home for man
— Grammar School Geography
Alexis Frye, 1902

L ONG BEFORE MAN lived in the state of Georgia, the sun, wind, rain, snow, and ocean currents were preparing the land to receive its first inhabitants. It was a long process lasting millions of years, a process of change that continues even today.

An awareness of the geography of an area is essential to understanding how our state was settled and has continued to grow and prosper through the years.

It was, in large part, the geography of the region that enticed prehistoric Indians to settle here and become part of Georgia's ancient history. These early people set the stage for the drama that was to follow.

The 681-square-mile wilderness area of the Okefenokee Swamp is the largest protected fresh water swampland in the United States. The area is virtually unchanged since prehistoric Indians roamed the area. The Seminole Indians called the swamp E-cun-fi-no-can, meaning "Trembling Earth."

CHAPTER ONE

GEORGIA: SOMETHING FOR EVERYONE

To be short, it is a thing unspeakable to consider the things that bee seene there, and shal be founde more and more in this incomparable land, which never yet broken with plough yrons, bringeth forth all things according to his first nature wherewith the eternall God indued it.. . . [It is] the fairest, fruit fullest, and plesantest of all the world.

— French Explorer, Captain Jean Ribault 1562

CAPTAIN JEAN RIBAULT praised the area many call the "Empire State of the South." He described a place with a mild **climate**, many natural resources, and different kinds of land regions from the mountains to the coast. Ribault had traveled along the Georgia coast seeking a new home for his shipload of French Huguenots. Despite the kind words in his description of our state's geography, Ribault did not settle in Georgia.

To understand the history of Georgia, one needs to know its geography. The term geography comes from the Greek word *geographia*, and means "earth's description." Geography is the science of studying the earth as the home of humans. It helps

Opposite page, left to right: The St. Simons Island lighthouse, built in 1872; the old style beauty of Savannah with azaleas in bloom; plentiful rainfall and rich soil provide abundant and diverse crops. Right: Atlanta's skyscrapers.

Measuring 315 miles from north to south, and 250 miles from east to west at its widest point, Georgia is home to 6.4 million people.

answer such questions as why Indians lived in certain places, why early **settlers** moved to particular areas, how the location of a town affects its **economy**, and why department stores carry certain kinds of clothing.

LAND AREA AND LOCATION

Georgia is one of the ten fastest growing states in the country, and there is room enough for that growth. There are 58,910 square miles of land and 854 square miles of inland water in Georgia. In land area, it is the largest state east of the Mississippi River. Its greatest length is 315 miles, and its greatest width 250 miles. Georgia has almost as much land as all the New England states combined. It is larger than England and Wales together, and there are only twenty states in the United States with more land area.

The exact location of Georgia is between 30° 21' and 35° north latitude, and between 80° 50' and 85° 36' west longitude. One way to describe Georgia's location is to say that, along straight lines, Honolulu, Hawaii, Rio de Janeiro, Brazil, and Berlin, Germany are all equal distances from Atlanta. The geographic center of the state is eighteen miles southeast of Macon in Twiggs County.

There are 159 counties in the state. The largest is Ware County with 907 square miles, and the smallest is Clarke County with 122 square miles. Georgia is in the southeastern part of the United States. It is bordered by the Atlantic Ocean on the east, Florida on the south, Tennessee and North Carolina on the north, South Carolina along the Savannah River, and Alabama on the west.

The elevation of the state begins at sea level along the eastern coastline and rises to 4,784 feet at Brasstown Bald in Towns County in northeast Georgia.

Do You Remember?
1. How did Captain Jean Ribault describe Georgia?
2. How many square miles of land are in Georgia?
3. Where is the geographic center of Georgia?
4. What is the smallest county in the state? Largest?
5. Which states border Georgia?
6. What is the highest elevation in the state? Lowest?

GEORGIA WATERWAYS

Georgia's waterways provided transportation to trading posts for the Indians and landing sites for the **colonists.** Today, the Atlantic Ocean and inland rivers, lakes, and streams are used for recreation, to make electricity, and as ports for trade and tourism.

Sunset marks the end of another day along St. Simons beach—one of Georgia's "Golden Isles." The island was called ASAO by the Indians.

Above: Georgia's 100 miles of coastline is the center of tourism and recreation. Below: The salt marsh on Little St. Simons Island is home to a rich variety of water life.

THE ATLANTIC OCEAN

Georgia has more than 100 miles of coastline on the Atlantic Ocean, beginning at the Savannah River and going to the St. Mary's River. Some parts of the coastline serve as wildlife refuges, and others as commercial fishing and shrimping centers. There are harbors for the coming and going of luxury cruise ships, and miles of recreational beaches which draw tourists from far and near.

Geologists think the coastal area was once part of seven barrier island **systems.** Thousands of years of erosion resulted in one barrier island system. Now, the barrier shoreline is a chain of eight islands that are separate from the mainland. Cumberland and Ossabaw islands are protected from development by the Environmental Protection Agency. Others, including Jekyll and St. Simons, have become summer vacation retreats known for their luxury homes and estates. The entire system, with its sunshine and bright sandy beaches, is called "The Golden Isles."

Between the barrier islands and the mainland is a four to six mile band of salt water marshes covering a total of 450,000 acres. At

least one-third of the salt marshes along the Atlantic coastline are in Georgia. The marshes, protected by the government, are home to many kinds of water life. A marine biology laboratory sponsored by the National Science Foundation is located there. Sidney Lanier pictured the beauty of the area in his poem "The Marshes of Glynn," when he wrote, "Ye marshes, how candid and simple, and nothing-withholding and free."

Many inlets and creeks lead inland from the ocean and provide excellent fishing and crabbing. They were a hiding place for pirates during the seventeenth century when Spanish and English trading ships traveled along the coast. Pirates, such as the infamous Blackbeard, attacked the ships and took goods for their own use or for resale on the illegal market.

There are also sand ridges along the coast. These ridges were formed by the continuous beating of ocean waves. Coastal Indians used them as trails. Those trails became the route of present-day highways within the coastal plain. Seaport bluffs and ridges were the sites of early towns, including Savannah and Darien.

Top: *The marshes of Glynn.*
Above: *The Sidney Lanier Bridge spans the major entrance into the port city of Brunswick.*

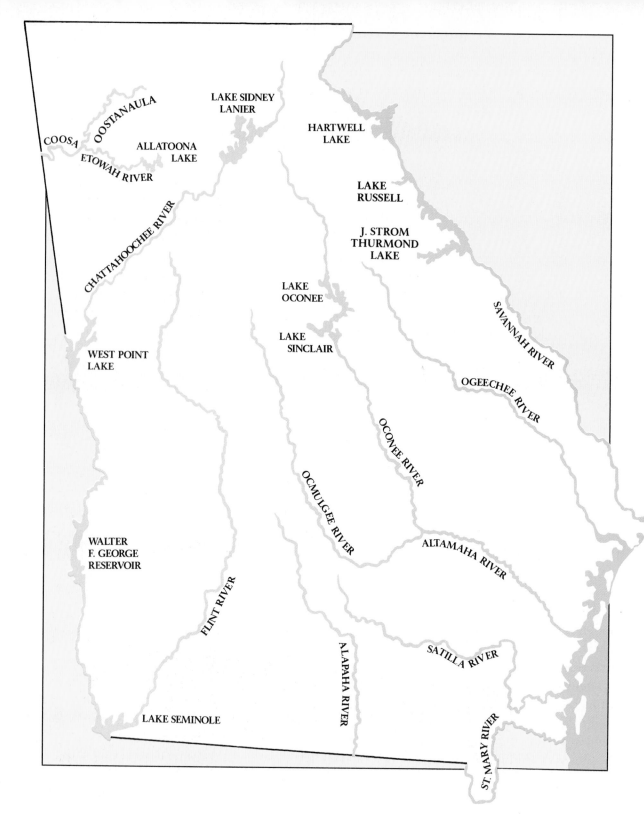

COOSA

OOSTANAULA

LAKE SIDNEY LANIER

HARTWELL LAKE

ALLATOONA LAKE

ETOWAH RIVER

LAKE RUSSELL

CHATTAHOOCHEE RIVER

J. STROM THURMOND LAKE

LAKE OCONEE

SAVANNAH RIVER

WEST POINT LAKE

LAKE SINCLAIR

OGEECHEE RIVER

OCONEE RIVER

OCMULGEE RIVER

WALTER F. GEORGE RESERVOIR

ALTAMAHA RIVER

FLINT RIVER

SATILLA RIVER

ALAPAHA RIVER

LAKE SEMINOLE

ST. MARY RIVER

8   A HISTORY OF GEORGIA

RIVERS

Georgia has twelve principal river systems. The Savannah, Ogeechee, Altamaha (which combines the Oconee and Ocmulgee rivers), and Satilla rivers flow directly into the Atlantic Ocean. Western rivers, including the Chattahoochee and Flint, become a part of the Gulf of Mexico. In the northern part of the state, the Etowah and Oostanaula rivers form the Coosa River, which flows through Alabama into the Gulf. The Alapaha, located in south Georgia, flows across the Georgia-Florida border.

The Savannah River

By the time Hernando de Soto reached the Savannah River in 1540, Indians had traveled the 314-mile-long waterway for many years. They called it the "Isondega," meaning "blue water." Many of their villages were located along its banks. Today the state has two major seaports in its eastern basin: Savannah and Brunswick.

Opposite Page: Over 20,000 miles of rivers and streams crisscross the state providing navigable water routes, hydroelectric power and numerous recreation areas for Georgians. Below: As the gateway to the Atlantic, the Savannah River port is Georgia's largest seaport. Ships from around the world stop here to deposit or take on cargo.

Hartwell Lake
One of six lakes managed by the United States Army Corps of Engineers, Hartwell Lake is located on the Savannah River seven miles east of the city of Hartwell. The lake boasts a 960 mile shoreline, 4 marinas and 3 state parks making it a favorite recreational area.

Above: Barges can travel the Chattahoochee River from West Point Lake south to the boundary of Georgia and Alabama. *Right:* The Eagle and Phenix Cotton Mill dwarfs a fisherman on the Chattahoochee River in Columbus.

Along the border of South Carolina, it spreads into three lakes: J. Strom Thurmond Lake (formally called Clark Hill Lake), Lake Russell, and Hartwell Lake.

The Chattahoochee River

The Chattahoochee River flows 436 miles from the foothills of the Blue Ridge Mountains to the Gulf of Mexico. Part of it is the southern section of the border between Georgia and Alabama. The Chattahoochee is one of the oldest rivers in the Southeast, and was known to the Cherokees as the "river of the painted rock." Major cities along its banks include Gainesville, Atlanta and Columbus. Lake Lanier, West Point Lake, and the Walter F. George Reservoir are part of the Chattahoochee's winding path.

Other Rivers

The 265-mile-long Flint River runs parallel to the Chattahoochee from College Park, near Atlanta, until it empties into Lake Seminole at Bainbridge. In northwestern Georgia, the

Located in the southwestern corner of the state where Georgia, Florida and Alabama join, 5,000-acre Lake Seminole is known throughout the region as a prize lake where the state fish of Georgia, the largemouth bass, can be caught.

Above: The ninety-mile-long Altamaha (pronounced All'-ta-ma-haw) River, was claimed by France, Spain, and England during the days of exploration in the early 1700s.
Right: The 150-mile-long Ocmulgee River begins where the South, Yellow, and Alcovy rivers join at Lake Jackson. It winds through the middle of the state and joins the Little Ocmulgee and Oconee rivers to become the Altamaha River.

Cherokees traveled the Oostanaula and the Etowah rivers to the Indian village of Chiaha, the site of present-day Rome. Chiaha, known as the "Head of the Coosa," had a trading post and post office.

The Ocmulgee and Oconee rivers meet near Hazlehurst and Lumber City. They then flow into one of Georgia's most powerful rivers, the Altamaha. This muddy river is rich in fish and fertile swamps. It empties into the Atlantic Ocean near the coastal city of Darien.

These major waterways have been important to the **social, political,** and **economic** growth of Georgia.

Named for the Etowah Indians who lived along its banks from about 1000 A.D. to 1500 A.D., the Etowah River flows from the Blue Ridge Mountains in Lumpkin County to Rome.

Do You Remember?
1. What name is given to the barrier islands off the coast of Georgia?
2. Why are Georgia's rivers important?
3. What are three major rivers in Georgia.

GEOGRAPHIC DIVISIONS

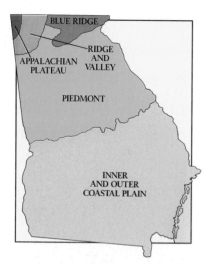

There are twenty-four physiographic (natural characteristics of the earth's surface) patterns in Georgia. These natural divisions differ both in area and in their land base, which may be limestone, clay sediment, shale, or marsh. However, there are enough similarities among the twenty-four patterns that they can be combined into five major physiographic regions: 1) the Ridge and Valley Region; 2) the Appalachian Plateau; 3) the Blue Ridge Region; 4) the Piedmont Region; and 5) the Coastal Plain Region.

THE RIDGE AND VALLEY REGION

The Ridge and Valley Region has low open valleys and narrow ridges which run parallel to the valleys. Elevation ranges from 700 to 1,600 feet above sea level. The region runs from Polk and Bartow counties northward to Chattanooga, Tennessee. It is known for textile and carpet manufacturing. The region is surrounded by the Piedmont Region to the south, the Appalachian Plateau to the west and the Blue Ridge Region to the east.

Below: The Ridge and Valley land region is a heavily forested area with rich fertile soil. ***Opposite page, top:*** The hydroelectric power dam on Lake Allatoona in Bartow County.

THE APPALACHIAN PLATEAU

The Appalachian Plateau, also known as Lookout and Sand mountain plateaus, is a small region in the northwestern corner of the state and includes Dade County and part of Walker County. The plateau is made up of two flat-topped mountains that drop into Lookout and Chickamauga valleys. At the base of both steep mountains are almost vertical cliffs 200 to 300 feet in height.

Spread: As part of the Appalachian Plateau, Lookout Mountain is located along the border between Tennessee and Georgia. **Inset:** *Called the "Grand Canyon of North Georgia," Cloudland Canyon is located on the east side of*

Above: Hundreds of trails siding along Georgia's Blue Ridge Mountains lure hikers from all regions of the state. *Above right:* Peaks rising from 2,000 to almost 5,000 feet above sea level provide a picturesque view of the tree-covered mountains. The rivers flowing through the region provide much of Georgia's hydroelectric power.

THE BLUE RIDGE REGION

The Blue Ridge Region is a hundred miles wide and has an area of about two thousand square miles. The highest and largest group of mountains in Georgia is in this region. These mountains are important to the rest of the state because they are the first barrier to warm, moist air rising from the Gulf of Mexico. When that air makes contact with the high mountains, it cools. The rain or snow which results provides water for the entire state. Here, precipitation can exceed eighty inches per year. Brasstown Bald, the highest peak in the state, is in this region. The Blue Ridge Region contains a large percentage of the state's forest land. It is also known for its recreational opportunities.

Above: Once a sleepy little community called Terminus, Atlanta is the business center of the Piedmont Region, the most heavily populated area in Georgia.. ***Opposite page:*** Containing thirty-one percent of the state's land area, the rich red earth of the Piedmont Region provides acres of fertile farmland.

THE PIEDMONT REGION

The Piedmont Region begins in the mountain foothills of northern Georgia and goes to the central part of the state. It has gently sloping hills and valleys in the north, flatlands in the south, and most of its soil is Georgia's well-known red clay. About one-third of the state's land area and one-half of the population are in the Piedmont Region. It was the cotton belt of antebellum days. Today it is known for the production of wheat, soybeans, corn, poultry and cattle. Business and industry also flourish throughout the area.

A marina on St. Simons Island. The Outer Coastal Plain area is a popular recreational site for fishing and sailing enthusiasts alike.

THE COASTAL PLAIN REGION

The Coastal Plain Region is about three-fifths of the state. It is divided into the Inner Coastal Plain and the Outer Coastal Plain. The inner plain has a mild climate, a good supply of underground water, and is the major agricultural region of the state. Its soil varies from limestone to clay. The Vidalia Upland has become world famous because of the unique sweet onions which grow there.

The outer plain does not have drained soil to provide fertile farmlands, but it is the center of **naval stores** and pulp production in the state. Along the coast, the deep harbors and barrier islands offer recreational facilities, seafood gathering and processing industries, and major shipyard ports.

Above left: *Tree farms can be seen throughout the Inner Coastal Plain. They help preserve Georgia's richest national resource and prevent damaging soil erosion.* ***Left:*** *Vidalia onions are so popular that a Vidalia Onion Festival is held each May.* ***Above right:*** *The seafood industry is vital to the Atlantic Coastal Plain. Shrimpers use heavy nets to harvest the state's most valuable catch.*

Okefenokee Swamp
The Outer Coastal Plain is best known for the 681 square mile Okefenokee Swamp. This swamp is home for alligators, hundreds of bird species like the great egret pictured below, and many other kinds of animal and plant life.

THE FALL LINE

The Coastal Plain Region is separated from the Piedmont Region by a natural boundary known as the fall line. This line runs from Columbus on the western side of the state, through Macon and into Augusta on the eastern side. Other cities located on the fall line are Milledgeville, Roberta, Thomson, and Warrenton. The fall line is the point at which hilly or mountainous lands meet the coastal plain. Rivers and creeks flowing from the rocky hill country cut deep channels in the softer soil of the plains. This drops the elevation and creates waterfalls. Indians, early settlers, and traders found the waterfalls an excellent power source and built settlements there.

Do You Remember?

1. What are the names of Georgia's physiographic regions?
2. What distinguishes the Outer and Inner Coastal Plains?
3. Which region is in the northwestern corner of Georgia?
4. In which region is the Okefenokee Swamp located?
5. In which region would you find a lot of carpet outlet stores?

Above: The fall line separates the Piedmont Region from the Coastal Plain. Top: Fall line waterfalls provide a source of power for numerous textile mills like this one in Columbus.

THE RED OLD HILLS OF GEORGIA

General Henry R. Jackson

The red old hills of Georgia! My heart is on them now;
Where fed from golden streamlets, Oconee's waters flow!
I love them with devotion, tho' washed so bleak and bare—
How can my spirit e're forget the warm hearts dwelling there?

Chorus:

The red old hills of Georgia! My heart is on them now;
Where fed from golden streamlets, Oconee's waters flow.

I love them for the living—The gen'rous kind and gay;
And for all the dead who slumber within their breast of clay.
I love them for the bounty, which cheers the social hearth;
I love them for their rosy girls—the fairest of the earth.

The red old hills of Georgia, where, where upon the face
Of earth is freedom's spirit more bright in any race?
In Switzerland and Scotland each patriot breast it fills,
But sure it blazes brighter yet among our Georgia hills.

And where, upon their surface, is heart to feeling dead?
And where has needy stranger gone from these hills unfed?
There bravery and kindness for aye go hand in hand,
Upon your washed and naked hills—"My own, my native land."

The red old hills of Georgia! I never can forget;
Among life's joys and sorrows, my heart is on them yet;
And when my course is ended, when life her web has wove;
Oh, may I then beneath those hills lie close to them I love.

Located in Stewart County near Lumpkin, Providence Canyon covers 3,000 acres and is the result of erosion that began only 150 years ago. The canyon is a Georgia state conservation park.

CLIMATE

Geography influences where people live, what crops are grown, and which industries develop. Climate is equally important. Climate refers to the kind of weather a region has over a period of time.

TEMPERATURE

As a result of Georgia's latitude and longitude, the climate is usually humid and moist. In most places, summers are hot and winters are mild. However, there is a narrow band across the north Georgia mountain region which has warm summers and moderately cold winters.

The highest temperatures in the state usually occur in July, and the coldest readings are normally in January. The average temperature for the year is sixty-five degrees. However, the mercury can fall below zero in the northern sections and rise above one hundred in the middle and southern regions of the state.

PRECIPITATION

Precipitation, usually in the form of rain, ice, or snow, is vital to Georgia's economy. Snow, which generally falls only in the mountain regions, melts to provide a water runoff into streams and lakes. Rainfall aids the growth of crops and forests. In a normal year, Georgia receives an average of forty to fifty-two inches of rain in central and southern regions and sixty-five to seventy-six inches in the northern mountains. July is the wettest month of the year, and October is the driest.

During the last half of the 1980s, Georgia, like many other parts of the country, experienced a severe drought, with rainfall far below average. Scientists disagree about the exact causes of Georgia's drought conditions, but the results concern everyone. Lack of rain lowers lake levels and underground water tables. There is not as much water to use in the production of hydroelectric power. Businesses, industries, and home users are all affected by having less water. Shortages of rainfall also mean fewer water-connected recreational opportunities.

Drought periods limit agricultural production, so there is less harvest to sell to farmers' markets, food production companies, and grocery stores. Droughts also cut back the growth of grain for livestock. This affects beef, dairy, and poultry farms.

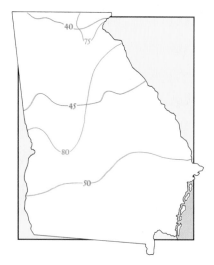

This map shows average annual temperatures around Georgia. Red lines indicate summer (July) temperatures; blue lines indicate winter (January) temperatures. Floyd County registered a record low temperature for Georgia of -17 degrees on January 27, 1940.

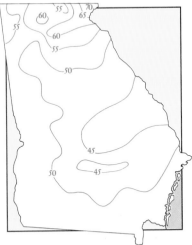

Above: This map shows average annual precipitation around Georgia (in inches). *Left:* The winter months in the northwest Georgia mountains not only provide beautiful natural sculptures, but are also essential in providing water runoff into lakes and streams as winter turns to spring.

To Georgia's economy, snow means much more than a day out of school for students. Rain means more than carrying an umbrella. Rain and snow mean economic survival.

WINDS

Winds influence the overall weather pattern of Georgia. Air masses which begin over the Gulf of Mexico and the Atlantic Ocean control summer's warm months. The winter months are controlled by air masses that start in the polar regions of Alaska and Canada. Wind patterns can bring moderate weather, or intense storms in the forms of tornadoes and hurricanes.

TORNADOES

When warm moist air mixes with a rapidly moving cold front, severe thunderstorms are possible. In the southeastern United States, these storms can produce tornadoes, particularly during April and May. Tornadoes are swirling funnels of air which move in a line from southwest to northeast. They sometimes cause extensive property damage, injuries, and loss of life.

HURRICANES

Hurricanes are produced by warm, moist air over tropical oceans or large bodies of water, such as the Gulf of Mexico. They are more likely to occur during August, September, and October. Hurricanes often measure several hundred miles wide, with winds from seventy-five to two hundred miles an hour. Coastal areas may suffer damage from both strong winds and high tides. Georgia's most damaging hurricane came ashore in Savannah on August 27, 1893. The winds were recorded at only seventy-two miles an hour, but one thousand people died from flying debris, or other storm-related causes. There was at least ten million dollars' worth of property damage. However, this type of destruction is unusual for Georgia.

Hurricanes are given names from a list drawn up yearly by the National Hurricane Center in Miami, Florida. The center chooses one name, either male or female, for each letter of the alphabet. When a name is assigned, the position of its initial letter in the alphabet matches the number of the storm. For example, the most damaging hurricane to hit Georgia in the last fifty years was the fourth hurricane of the year, Hurricane David, which struck Savannah on September 4, 1979.

Springtime in Georgia not only means budding flowers and trees, it also means tornado weather. These funnel shaped storm clouds can move up to 300 miles per hour and cause substantial destruction to life and property. Here, a new funnel descends from a storm cloud.

Do You Remember?

1. What is the average annual amount of rainfall in Georgia?
2. What months are considered the "hurricane season"?
3. How are hurricanes named?
4. When do the greatest number of tornadoes occur?
5. What is one word which describes Georgia's climate?
6. What is the average annual temperature in Georgia?

GEORGIA WILDLIFE

With enough land, different physiographic features, and a moderate climate, Georgia is a natural home for wildlife.

MAMMALS

Over forty **species** of mammals are found in Georgia. One of them, prized by hunters and naturalists alike, is the white-tail deer. It was almost extinct by the early 1900s but, because of careful management, the deer can now be found in all 159 Georgia counties.

Squirrels, opossums, raccoons, and rabbits live all over the state, and foxes can be seen in most sections. Bobcats are usually found in the forest mountain regions or in swamps. Wild hogs make their home in coastal plain river swamps, along with beavers, otters, and minks.

GEORGIA BIRDS

Georgia is a year-long home for 170 species of birds, including robins, cardinals, blue jays, thrashers, woodpeckers, and wood ducks. Two hundred other species feed and nest in the state during spring and fall migrations. One of the most popular visitors is the ruby-throated hummingbird. Thousands of people place feeders of sugar water in their yards each year hoping to attract the shy, tiny visitors as they **migrate** to South America.

Above: Few animals surpass the grace and beauty of one of Georgia's most plentiful animals, the white-tail deer. As the only deer native to the state, the white-tail can run 30-35 miles per hour and jump over an 8-foot barrier. *Left:* Raccoons are masked, meat-eating mammals, often found around Georgia's many lakes and streams searching for clams or frogs. Contrary to popular belief, the raccoon does not intentionally wash its food before eating.

Right: Named Georgia's official state bird in 1935, the brown thrasher lives in deep underbrush and is known for its rich, loud songs. It helps Georgia farmers by dining on grasshoppers, caterpillars and worms. Below: The national emblem of the United States, the bald eagle generally nests near water.

There are also many game birds in Georgia. Quail, doves, ducks, and wild turkeys are the most popular with hunters. Georgia has joined at least forty- two other states in classifying the bald eagle as an endangered species. Hunting eagles is strictly forbidden by law. The state funds a program to feed the young eaglets until they are ready to live on their own. Even so, the bird is so close to extinction that, in 1989, there were only three natural bald eagle nests in the state.

REPTILES AND AMPHIBIANS

Forty species of snakes live in Georgia. All but six are harmless. These are valuable to the state's agriculture because they eat undesirable rodents. Poisonous snakes include the copperhead, cottonmouth, coral, and three types of rattlesnakes.

The Coastal Plain Region, particularly swampy areas such as Okefenokee, is home to the American alligator. Alligators grow to an adult length of six to twelve feet. They are protected by the **federal** government from unauthorized killing.

There are twenty-seven varieties of turtles in Georgia. The famous loggerhead sea turtles live on the barrier islands off Georgia's coast. Visitors to a stream, marsh, or pond can easily find some of Georgia's other amphibians. The state is a natural home for twenty-four types of frogs, four species of toads, and thirty-six kinds of salamanders.

FISH

There are 500 species of fish, including six types of bass, in the state's fresh water lakes, streams, and marine waters. Shrimp, mollusks and crabs live off the coast and in the salt marsh regions.

The alligator is Georgia's largest reptile and lives among the twenty-one islands that make up the swamp area of Okefenokee.

Do You Remember?

1. What protected animal was near extinction but can now be found in all 159 Georgia counties?
2. What are two game birds found in Georgia?
3. What Georgia bird is on the endangered species list?
4. What poisonous snakes are native to Georgia.
5. How many fish species live in Georgia's waters?

Below: *The grand and stately live oak, seen here in Reynolds Square, Savannah, is the official state tree of Georgia. The live oak, which can grow to fifty feet in height, is often covered with gray Spanish moss.* **Opposite page, above:** *Rare plum-leaf azaleas are found at Providence Canyon. While the Cherokee rose is the state flower, azaleas have the distinction of being the official wildflower.* **Opposite page, below:** *A type of daisy, the black-eyed susan is common throughout the state.*

A part of Georgia's natural beauty is in its rich assortment of trees and vegetation.

TREES

Forests cover about seventy percent of the state. Short-leaf pine, and hardwoods, such as red oak, hickory, and maple are usually found in the northern part of Georgia. Live oak, turkey oak, gum, willow oak, and elm trees dot the countryside. Cypress grows in the Okefenokee National Refuge and Wilderness Area. Longleaf pine, southern magnolia, and dwarf palmetto grow well in the southern part of the state.

One of the most popular trees is the wild dogwood, which flowers in the spring. It is currently an endangered tree due to an incurable disease spreading into the state from Florida.

PLANTS

Azaleas, wild roses, and black-eyed susans can be seen all over the state. Shades of red and plum-colored rhododendron add bright color to north Georgia woodlands.

Fifty types of plants are protected by the 1973 Wildflower Preservation Act. They include such plants as pink lady's slipper, large flowered skullscap, and the rare Oconee bells (found in the Clayton area). Fringed campion grows along the Flint and Apalachicola rivers. An interesting protected plant is the hooded pitcher plant, which eats insects.

Do You Remember?
1. How many Georgia plants are protected by law?
2. What tree is endangered because of disease?
3. What plant is found only in the Clayton area?

CHAPTER REVIEW

Summary

To understand Georgia's history, one needs to know its geography. There are 58,910 square miles of land and 854 square miles of inland water in the state. There are 159 counties in Georgia. Only Texas has more. Besides the 100 miles of water on its eastern coast, Georgia has twelve main river systems. Some important rivers are the Savannah, Ogeechee, Chattahoochee, Altamaha, and Flint.

The five physiographic regions of Georgia include: 1) Ridge and Valley 2) Appalachian Plateau; 3) Blue Ridge; 4) Piedmont; and 5) Coastal Plain. Georgia's climate is humid and moist. Summers are hot and winters are usually mild, except in the mountain region, which tends to have warm summers and fairly cold winters. Rain and snowfall is forty to fifty-two inches in central and south Georgia and sixty-five to seventy-six inches in north Georgia. Much of Georgia's economy depends on its mild climate. Hurricanes can affect the coast between August and October.

Georgia has many wild mammals, birds, snakes, turtles, and fish.

People, Places, and Terms

Identify, define and/or state the importance of each of the following.
1. geography
2. barrier islands
3. hurricane
4. fall line
5. extinct
6. tornado
7. precipitation
8. climate
9. Brasstown Bald

The Main Idea

Using complete sentences, respond to each of the questions.
1. How does Georgia's climate influence the movement of industrial plants from the northern states to Georgia?
2. Describe the location of the Outer Coastal Plain.
3. Name three major Georgia waterways and describe the importance of each.
4. How does the Piedmont Region differ from the Appalachian Plateau Region?
5. Where are the "Golden Isles" located?

Extend Your Thinking

Using complete sentences, respond to each of the questions.
1. Why would you visit Georgia's Blue Ridge area?
2. How does the average rainfall in Georgia affect you?
3. Why is the study of geography important in studying the history of Georgia?
4. Why is it necessary to provide protection for the bald eagle?

Looking Ahead

During the time Hernando de Soto was traveling through Georgia searching for riches, he found the land, climate, and animal and plant life much as it is today. As you read Chapter Two, you will learn:
➤ what Georgia was like millions of years ago.
➤ about the culture of Georgia's early people.
➤ how we learn about these early people.
➤ about Spanish explorer Hernando de Soto's exploration in Georgia.

DID YOU KNOW . . .

. . . The deepest cave in the United States is located in Georgia? A part of the Pigeon Mountain Wildlife Management Area, Ellison's Cave is 586 feet deep and is located in Walker County.

. . . Decatur County has the longest cave in Georgia? Climax Cave is 12 miles in length and is one of 380 caves in the state.

. . . It is 1,051 miles around the state's physical boundaries?

. . . Georgia is represented as the third listing in the U.S. Postal Service Zip Code Directory? The "ABAC" listing is home of Abraham Baldwin Agricultural College in Tift County. (Aaron, Kentucky and Aarousburg, Pennsylvania occupy the first two listings).

. . . St. Mary's was the first place in Georgia to have historical markers with both braille and raised letters?

. . . St. Catherine's Island (above), located in Liberty County and covering over 25,000 acres, was once the home of the Indian Chief Gaule. It is also the location of Georgia's first settlement founded in 1566 by the Spanish. In later years, Button Gwinnett, one of Georgia's signers of the Declaration of Independence, bought the island as his home.

. . . Georgia's coastal salt marshes and deep rivers provide a home for sturgeon? In 1986, a female sturgeon weighing 496 pounds, with 100 pounds of roe, was caught in Georgia. The catch was worth over $3,000.00.

. . . On August 28, 1941, St. George, in south Georgia, made the state's record books when eighteen inches of rain fell in seventeen hours?

. . . On June 24, 1952, Louisville recorded a record high temperature of 112°?

. . . Macon received a record snowfall of 16.5 inches in February 1973?

CHAPTER TWO

THE LAND AND ITS EARLY PEOPLE
? B.C. - 1670 A.D.

There were . . . many very magnificent monuments of the power and industry of the ancient inhabitants of these lands. . . . I observed a stupendous conical pyramid, or artificial mound of earth, vast tetragon terraces, and a large sunken area, of a cubic form, encompassed with banks of earth; and certain traces of a larger Indian town, the work of a powerful nation, whose period of grandeur perhaps long preceded the discovery of this continent.
— Description of the findings of Quaker botanist William
   Bartram, while visiting the area near Wrightsborough in 1773.
   (Wright, Max E., Georgia's Indian Heritage, 1988,
   W.H. Wolfe Associates.)

ANY STUDY OF HISTORY depends primarily on written records which have been kept over the years. Systems of writing are only 5,000 to 6,000 years old, and nothing was written about Georgia until European explorers came to this land. The period before written records were kept is called "prehistory" or "prehistoric." The exact dates of prehistoric events are not known. However, what we can discover about them is important to the study of Georgia.

Small arrow points, like the one shown in this picture, were used by the Etowah tribe. They were made from stone, wood, or deer antlers.

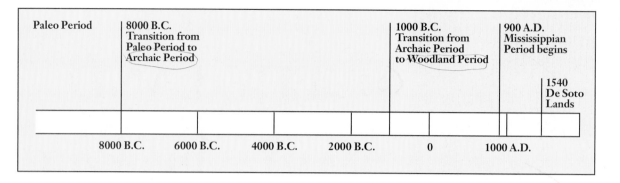

Paleo Period	8000 B.C. Transition from Paleo Period to Archaic Period			1000 B.C. Transition from Archaic Period to Woodland Period	900 A.D. Mississippian Period begins	
						1540 De Soto Lands
	8000 B.C.	6000 B.C.	4000 B.C.	2000 B.C.	0	1000 A.D.

Opposite page: During prehistoric times, over 500 million years ago, most of what we now know as Georgia was under water. The sea was filled with strange looking creatures unknown to us today.

GEORGIA AS IT WAS MILLIONS OF YEARS AGO

If you were to describe Georgia as it was millions of years ago, what would you say? If you guessed that most of Georgia was covered with water, you would agree with many geologists (scientists who study the origin, history, and structure of the earth). There is evidence which indicates that, except for a narrow band of land dotted with volcanoes that ran through the upper coastal region, Georgia was totally under water. You would also agree with geologists if you said that, at one time, Georgia was south of the equator. According to the Continental Drift Theory, geologists believe much of the earth's present land area was once joined together. They think movement far below the earth's surface caused the land to rise above the water. Some of the movements were like volcanic eruptions, and created mountains. While the movement was taking place, the continents very slowly separated from each other. They drifted, over several million years, to where they are now. Water drained away from the land, and the earth began to look much as it does today.

ANCIENT CREATURES

We are able to learn about plant and animal life that lived before written history by studying fossils. Fossils are traces or remains of once living organisms. They include such things as skeletons, footprints, and prints of leaves. Some of the oldest fossils are those of sea creatures.

Trilobites are among the most numerous prehistoric fossils. The trilobites were small one to six inch arthropods, or animals with jointed limbs, which had shell-like hardened skin covers. Their bodies were jointed, and they had many legs and feet.

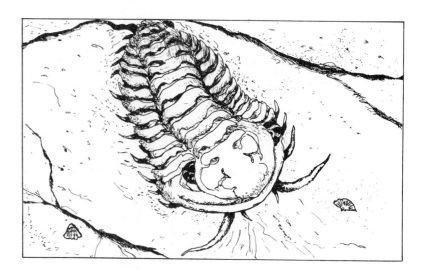

Right: Resembling a modern insect with compound eyes, the trilobite is thought to have existed up to 600 million years ago. Their only living relative is the horseshoe crab. Below: A great shark, the charcharodon, had a skeleton made of cartilage and a tough skin with small, toothlike scales. As today, the shark had no natural sea life enemies.

Trilobites wriggled their bodies as they walked along the sandy bottom of the sea. From the shape and location of their fossils, it can be guessed they could swim. They probably moved their legs rapidly while bending their bodies up and down. After swimming for several feet, they went back to the sandy sea floor.

The seas once contained hundreds of varieties of now extinct fish, including the ancestors of present-day sharks and sawfish. Many ancient sharks were small in size, like the sand sharks near our beaches today. There were also charcharodon sharks. These included great white sharks like the one in the movie "Jaws."

One of nature's slowest mammals, the giant ground sloth was easy prey for prehistoric Indians. The extinct saber-tooth tigers, on the other hand, were vicious members of the cat family with long protruding "eye teeth." The baby mastodon, shown in front, grew to elephant size.

Paleontologists (scientists who study fossils) have identified another type of prehistoric shark: the megalodon. Megalodons were possibly the most dangerous sea creatures that ever lived. Some of them were forty feet in length, and had teeth up to eight inches long. Fossils of sharks' teeth can still be found on Georgia's beaches.

Scientists have also learned that many land animals roamed through the hills and plains of Georgia. In Glynn County, fossils have been found of prehistoric horses, tapir, deer, and giant mammoths. Fossils of large rodents, such as rats (called southern bog), lemming, and the red-black vole, were found in Wilkes County. There is evidence that bison, white-tail deer, and mastodons, an ancestor of elephants, lived in the state. In Barrow County, fossil remains of ground sloths have been uncovered. The giant ground sloth was often larger than a modern elephant. In 1950, a mammoth tooth was found in Bartow County.

Do You Remember?
1. Where do scientists think Georgia was originally located?
2. What fossils were found in Wilkes County?
3. What fossils were found in Glynn County?

Born in Genoa, Italy in 1451, Christopher Columbus was an adventurer who sought fame and fortune. On Friday, August 3, 1492, an expedition of 87 men sailed west from Spain on the Santa Maria, *commanded by Columbus; the* Pinta; *and the* Nina. *Land was not sighted until October 12. Certain he had reached the East Indies, Columbus called the native inhabitants Indians.*

When Christopher Columbus explored the New World in the late 1400s, he found people with dark eyes, straight black hair and light brown to reddish-brown skin. Their faces were large, with jaws that stuck out and small chins. Columbus thought he was in the East Indies, so he called the people Indians. Today most historians think Columbus was wrong on two counts. First, he was not in the East Indies. He was on the North American continent, most likely in the area of the Bahamas. Second, the Indians he thought native to the New World are believed to have come from Asia to North America some 20,000 to 40,000 years before Columbus began to explore.

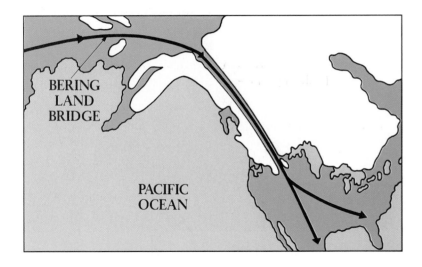

*Left: Plants, animals and, later, man used the Bering land bridge to cross over from Asia to the United States and Canada. This crossing continued until about 10,000 years ago when the glaciers began to melt, flooding the land bridge. **Below:** Born in 1908, Willard Frank Libby won the Nobel Prize in Chemistry for his development of a method of radiocarbon dating.*

HOW WE LEARN ABOUT GEORGIA'S EARLY PEOPLE

Studying rocks and fossils can tell us much about the land and animals during prehistoric times. To learn about the people, we depend on archaeologists and anthropologists.

Archaeology is a science which deals with the study of artifacts to learn about the life, people, and customs of early times. Artifacts include anything made by humans, like tools or weapons. Archaeologists dig into the earth and remove such items with great care.

Sometimes archaeologists can tell about how old a prehistoric site is because they know when particular tools, weapons, or pottery were used. They may also choose to use the Carbon 14 test to help date things they find. This test, discovered by Dr. W. F. Libby, is quite complicated, but the idea behind it is simple. Radioactive carbon is in all living things. When an animal or plant dies, it begins to lose this carbon at a known rate. By learning how much carbon is left in the remains, scientists can tell, within about 200 years, when it lived. The Carbon 14 test can also be used to date artifacts like clothing or written records.

Anthropology is the scientific study of how human cultures began and developed. Culture has to do with how a certain group of people behaved at a given time in history. Anthropologists sometimes study fossils and artifacts to find out how groups of people lived. For example, there are many types of projectile points. By studying a particular point, looking at its type, size,

Anthropologists who study the origin, development and behavior of man seek to find answers about the six different cultures who lived in the Ocmulgee area from 8000 BC to 1717 AD. Today, the Ocmulgee Mounds in Macon are a 683 acre reserve that continues to reveal the mysteries of earlier cultures.

markings, and what it is made of, anthropologists can guess what size animals were killed with the point. Working together, geologists, archaeologists, anthropologists, and other scientists help us understand prehistoric cultures.

Scientists think, during the Ice Age, the sea level was much lower than it is today. There is evidence that a land bridge connected Asia and America across what is now the Bering Strait. It is thought that bands of people crossed the land bridge in search of game for food.

Projectile points, remains of camp sites, and other evidence indicate that, when the food was gone in one area, the people moved to another. In this way, they came to what is now Georgia.

What archaeologists have learned about prehistoric times is not identified with **tribes**. Instead of having names we know, such as Cherokee or Creek, early Indians are identified by cultural periods. No two cultures were exactly alike, and changes took place slowly. People learned from those who lived before, discovered new things, and taught what they knew to their children. Archaeologists have grouped prehistoric people in the following cultures:

Cultural Period	From	To
Paleo	?	8000 B.C.
Archaic	8000 B.C.	1000 B.C.
Woodland	1000 B.C.	900 A.D.
Mississippian	900 A.D.	1600 A.D.

PALEO PERIOD (? - 8000 B.C.)

Early people can sometimes be identified by the projectile points they used. A projectile is a weapon, such as an arrow, spear, or dart, which is moved by a power source, such as a bow or the human arm. Most Paleo points were made of stone. Other stone tools of this period were knives, and scrapers used for cleaning hides.

Remains of their dwelling places indicate that Paleo Indians lived in groups of twenty-five to fifty people. Hunters used long wooden spears to kill large animals such as mammoths, bison, ground sloths, and mastodons for food. Archaeologists have also found large numbers of animal bones at the bases of cliffs. This leads them to believe that, at times, Indians chased the animals over the cliffs to kill them.

There have been only a few Paleo sites found in Georgia. Because these Indians moved around, they did not leave many ar-

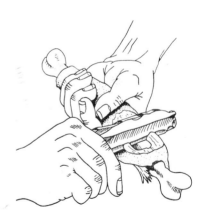

Top: The mammoth was one of the Paleo Indians' major sources of food.
Above: The unifacial knife was used to cut meat.

tifacts in any one place. Archaeologists have found artifacts from the Paleo period in the Savannah River area, the Ocmulgee River area, and at Albany, on the Flint River.

ARCHAIC PERIOD (8000 B.C. - 1000 B.C.)

The Archaic period included three distinct time spans: early, middle, and late. During the early Archaic period, from about 8000 B.C. to about 5000 B.C., Indians still hunted large game. However, these animals slowly became extinct. This may have been because the climate grew warmer, or because too many of them were killed. Whatever the reason, Archaic Indians began hunting smaller game, including deer, bear, turkey and rabbit. Hunters made their spears and points smaller. The people also began to eat reptiles, game birds, and fish. The early Archaic Indians invented useful items, such as choppers, drills, and chipping tools made from deer antlers.

Archaeological evidence indicates that Archaic people moved each season. During the fall, they lived where berries, nuts, and fruits were plentiful. In summer, they moved to good fishing locations. They also migrated during spring and winter. The moves were always for the same reason: to find food for the tribe.

Some of the stone artifacts found in Georgia are made from rock not often found in this state, but common in other parts of the country. This led archaeologists to think there was some trading among different groups or tribes of Indians.

Geographers tell us that by 5,000 B.C., when the middle Archaic period began, the area grew warm and dry. Water levels along rivers and the coastal areas moved back, and the Indians began to

Left and below: Points made by Archaic Indians had notches on the side which were attached to smaller spears than those used by the Paleo Indians. These spears were thrown like a javelin to hunt animals such as deer and bear. When spear points were broken during a hunt, they were chipped into smaller points and used again.

eat shellfish, such as mussels and clams. Finding more food meant the people did not need to move as often. There is evidence that several small groups joined together to establish camps. Scientists have found hooks made from animal bones which came from this period. These hooks were sometimes on the ends of long spears, which were weighted in the middle with polished stones. Hunters could throw the weighted spears long distances.

A common artifact from the late Archaic period (4000 B.C. to 1000 B.C.) is the grooved axe. Indians made this tool by putting a stone axe head on a wooden handle. **Excavations** of late Archaic settlements indicate that axes were used to clear trees and bushes around the camp. The Indians saved seed to plant in the next growing season. Therefore, it is thought that **horticulture** began in the late Archaic period.

By 2500 B.C., the climate had become cooler and wetter, much like the climate of Georgia today. Water filled rivers, streams and lakes, and Archaic Indians depended on shellfish for most of their food.

On Stallings Island, a few miles above Augusta on the Savannah River, archaeologists discovered a mound of mussel and clam shells. It was 512 feet long, 300 feet wide, and 23 feet higher than the depth of the river. Also at the Stallings site were remains of burial grounds, fire hearths, pipes, axes, shell beads, bone pins and needles, bone hooks, and many different projectile points. Because of these discoveries, historians think late Archaic Indian villages were more permanent than those of any group before them.

The way food was prepared also changed. Pottery shards, or pieces, dating from the Archaic period indicate that clay con-

tainers were used for storing, cooking, and serving food. Archaeologists think learning to make and use pottery may be one of the greatest contributions Archaic people made to Indian culture.

Other archaeological finds help us understand the lives of Archaic people. A grinding stone found in Fayette County may have been used to crush nuts into a type of flour. Scientists believe the Indians used a nutting stone found in Coweta County to hammer nuts and get the meat and oil from them.

WOODLAND PERIOD (1000 B.C. - 900 A.D.)

Evidence suggests that during the Woodland period several hundred families began banding together as a tribe. They lived in villages and built huts in which to house themselves.

The Indians used small trees and bark to build the dome-shaped huts. They stuck the trees into the ground on one end, then bent them forward at the top and tied them together. They then wove sticks in and out between the trees to form walls. Sometimes the Indians covered the sides of their huts with cane mats or tree bark. They made roofs of grass or pieces of bark. They left a small opening in the top of the hut so smoke from cooking fires could get out. Woodland people put fiber mats on the dirt floors for sleeping and sitting.

Hunting became easier during the Woodland period when the bow and arrow came into use. Arrow points were made out of stone, shark teeth, or deer antlers. Fishing, hunting, and gathering nuts and berries remained important ways of getting food. However, the people also grew such things as squash, wild greens, and sunflowers.

Woodland Indians learned to make pottery last longer. They found clay along river banks and mixed it with sand. They rolled the mixture into strips and coiled the strips on top of each other into the shape they wanted. The Indians then made the clay smooth with a rock and water. They used wooden paddles to make designs on the pottery. After the clay containers dried in the sun, they were baked in a hot fire. The containers were then hard enough to use for cooking.

Elaborate religious **ceremonies** were introduced during the Woodland period. These ceremonies were spread through trade among different tribes. The Hopewell culture in Ohio had many of the same ceremonies Georgia Indians used.

During this period, the Indians built cone-shaped burial mounds for the dead. They adorned bodies with necklaces, bracelets, rings, and copper or bone combs. When Woodland Indians were buried, their families and friends put special funeral pottery, tools, tobacco pipes, and weapons in the graves with them. These artifacts cause archaeologists and anthropologists to think this group of people believed in some type of life after death.

Above: A Woodland arrow. Below: Life for the Woodland Indians centered around hunting. Deer provided venison for food, hides to be tanned for buckskins, intestines which were dried and used for thread and bow strings, and the antlers which were sharpened into spear points.

ROCK EAGLE MOUND

The Rock Eagle Mound in Putnam County is of stone in the shape of an eagle or buzzard dating back to the Woodland period (1000 B.C. - 900 A.D.) It measures 120 by 102 feet and its purpose is a mystery.

Examine the picture carefully and answer the following questions:

1. In what period was the eagle mound made?
2. Why do you think the eagle or buzzard was important to the people?
3. There are several skills you learn in school today that the Woodland Indians had to know in order to build the rock mound. Name some of these skills.

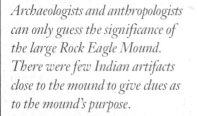

Archaeologists and anthropologists can only guess the significance of the large Rock Eagle Mound. There were few Indian artifacts close to the mound to give clues as to the mound's purpose.

MISSISSIPPIAN PERIOD (900 A.D. - 1600 A.D.)

The Mississippian culture is considered the highest prehistoric civilization in Georgia. The period gets its name from the fact that the first things learned about the culture were from excavated villages along the Mississippi River. It is sometimes called the Temple Mound period, and was a time when the people lived in villages, farmed, and were very religious.

There are ten major Mississippian archaeological sites in Georgia. From them we learn much about how the Indians lived. For example, we know the people grew most of their food. Maize, or corn, beans, pumpkins and squash were all planted together in hills. They also grew tobacco to use in ceremonies. Mississippians planted in different fields each year so the soil would stay fertile. They prepared the land with stone or bone hoes and digging sticks.

Mississippian Indians began to dress and fix their hair differently. Clothes were less simple, and they wore beads and ear ornaments. Sometimes they painted or tattooed their bodies. They also began wearing feather headdresses.

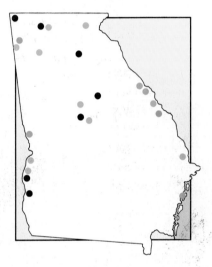

Villages grew, and several thousand families might live in a single settlement. They built centers for religious and **tribal** ceremonies and as a home for the priest-chief who was the head of the village. The villages were often protected by **moats** and **palisades.** In some Georgia villages, guard towers have been found 100 feet apart along the palisades, indicating the need for defense against tribal enemies.

Excavations at Ocmulgee National Monument near Macon led to the discovery of a large ceremonial lodge built of red clay in the shape of a circle. It is about forty-five feet across, and has a six-inch-high bench around the inner wall. The bench, divided into forty-seven sections, is believed to have been for seating tribal nobles. There is a large eagle-shaped clay platform with seats for the priest-chief and two assistants. A fire pit is in the center of the floor. Archaeologists and anthropologists think the lodge was probably used for both religious and village ceremonies and meetings.

Excavations at Etowah, near Cartersville, and at Kolomoki, in Early County, have uncovered elaborate flat-topped mounds. The forty-acre Etowah site has seven of these pyramid shaped mounds. One is fifty-three feet high and has steps leading to the top. A number of graves have been found along the base of a single

*Top: The Ocmulgee ceremonial earthlodge used for meetings and religious activities is considered to be one of the oldest buildings in the country. **Above:** This map shows the distribution of prehistoric Indian sites in Georgia. Green dots represent Paleo sites, red dots are Archaic sites, black dots are Woodland sites and blue dots are Mississippian sites.*

*Above: The Etowah Indian Mounds located three miles from Cartersville were home to the Etowah Indians from 1000 AD to 1500 AD during the Mississippian period. **Opposite page, below:** These stone statues belonging to the Etowah Indian tribe were believed to represent their images of god and were treated with great reverence.*

mound, and other bodies have been discovered in the tops of the mounds. Bodies were dressed in fine clothes. Beads and feather or copper headdresses were placed on them. Some of the intricately designed copper headdresses weighed almost a hundred pounds. Carved marble statues have been found at some burial sites.

The Kolomoki site in Early County covers over 300 acres. One of the temple mounds is about 50 feet high, 320 feet long, and 200 feet wide. With the tools available to them, it took a long time and many workers to build these mounds.

About 1300 A.D., something mysterious happened. The people left the villages, and there is nothing to tell us where they went. Did disease wipe out whole settlements? Did tribal enemies kill all

the people in the villages? Did family units decide to migrate to other areas and become part of a new tribe? Since this was before written history, we may never learn what happened to the Mississippian people.

Do You Remember?
1. What is an archaeologist? What does an anthropologist study?
2. What is the difference between artifacts and fossils?
3. Which cultural period is considered the highest stage of prehistoric Indian civilization?
4. What is at least one thing that separated the Archaic period from the Woodland period?

THE EARLY HISTORIC PERIOD

In 1540, Spanish **explorer** Hernando de Soto arrived in Georgia. With him were over 600 men and a number of horses and other animals. They marched north from Florida into the southwestern part of Georgia, close to present day Albany. As De Soto and his army moved across the state, they wanted one thing: to find gold.

When De Soto arrived in Georgia, the Indians saw white men and horses for the first time. De Soto had only a small number of men to face thousands of Indians, but his weapons were better. His army had the **harquebus** and crossbow, and **lancers** on horses. The Spanish also wore plated armor, through which Indian arrows could not go.

During De Soto's search for gold in Georgia, thousands of Indians were killed by his soldiers. Many more Indians died from diseases brought to the New World by the Spanish and other explorers. Some historians believe almost half the Indian population died from measles, smallpox, influenza, and whooping cough.

De Soto's expedition into North America was a failure. He found no gold or treasure. Most of his army was lost to starvation

Above: *A skilled swordsman, horseman, and explorer, Hernando de Soto had little trouble enlisting young Spaniards to travel with him to Florida in search of gold.* ***Right:*** *De Soto's soldiers, called "Conquistadores" or "Conquerors," along with eight priests, a large number of slaves, horses, food, and battle-trained dogs, made up the expedition force that traveled through Georgia in 1540.*

Spanish forces under Don Pedro Menendez de Aviles founded the first European colony in the United States in St. Augustine, Florida in 1565. His first job was to run off the French who had tried to settle at the mouth of the St. John's River.

and disease, and De Soto himself died somewhere along the Mississippi River. However, his march through Georgia changed the lives and culture of the Indians forever.

De Soto was followed by many other European explorers, most of them from Spain, France and England. These **nations** established settlements in Georgia and competed with each other and with the Indian tribes for control of the land.

In 1565, Spain sent Captain General Pedro Menendez to begin a **colony** in St. Augustine, Florida. The following year, the Spaniards moved up the coast to St. Catherine's and Cumberland islands. They named the region Gaule (pronounced Wallie) for the Creek Indians living in the area. About thirty men were left to establish the first Spanish post on Georgia soil. Missions were later established on St. Simons Island and at Sapelo at the mouth of the Altamaha River.

When the English settled Charles Town in 1670, and as French pirates conducted raids against the missions, Spanish control was in jeopardy. During the coming years, the English, French, and Spanish all fought to control the "Debatable Land."

Do You Remember?
1. What was DeSoto searching for in Georgia?
2. Where was the region called Gaule located?

CHAPTER REVIEW

Summary

The first settlers in our country are believed to be Asians who came to North America over a land bridge across what is now the Bering Strait. Descendents of those early settlers can be divided into four distinct prehistoric civilizations: Paleo, Archaic, Woodland, and Mississippian. Archaeology and anthropology show how each group helped the ones that followed it.

In the 1540s, Spanish explorers came to Georgia. The most famous of them was Hernando de Soto, who came in search of gold. He was followed by French, English, and other Spanish explorers.

People, Places, and Terms

Define, identify, or explain the importance of the following.

1. carbon dating
2. projectiles
3. culture
4. tribe
5. archaeology
6. anthropology
7. Bering Strait
8. artifacts
9. fossils
10. Hernando de Soto
11. prehistory

The Main Idea

Using complete sentences, answer each of the following questions.

1. What was the length in years of the Archaic period? Which was longer, the Woodland or the Mississippian period? Was the Archaic period longer or shorter than the Paleo period?

2. List one characteristic other than agriculture which was different in each of the four major Indian periods.

3. Compare and contrast methods of obtaining food within each of the prehistoric periods.

Extend Your Thinking

Write a short paragraph to answer each of the following questions.

1. What do you think could have happened to some of the Mississippian tribes that disappeared?

2. In which of the four periods would you have most liked to live? Explain your answer.

Map Skills

Use a Georgia map of counties to complete the following activities.

1. Mark and label the location of the Ocmulgee, Etowah, and Kolomoki Indian mounds.

2. Using different shading, shade each county in which remains of the four Indian cultures have been found. Make an appropriate legend for your map.

Looking Ahead

Establishing a colony in the place we now call Georgia was a difficult task. It was also a time of excitement and adventure. In the next chapter, you will discover:

➤ how a prisoner named Robert Castell influenced James Oglethorpe.

➤ what life was like on the ship *Anne* as she traveled through rough seas.

➤ why lawyers were not allowed to settle in early Georgia.

➤ why the founder of Georgia, James Oglethorpe, left the colony when it was considered a failure.

DID YOU KNOW...

... A spear point found in Colquitt County is dated about 8,000 B.C.?

... Copper-covered puma jaws were found in one of the Mississippian Indian burial grounds? According to one Indian legend, the jaws represented an animal that had preyed on the Indians. These bones had been used in a ceremonial burial.

... Indian axe heads were made by taking a pebble and chipping crystalline stone into a desired shape? It took several hours to make an axe head.

... There are over 275 types of soil (below) found in Georgia as a result of thousands of years of changes in land formation?

... In Brunswick, there is an oak tree (above) estimated to be over 900 years old? This would mean it was a young tree in the year 1,000, more than 700 years before James Oglethorpe arrived in Georgia.

... When Hernando de Soto's army traveled through the Indian villages in the area now known as Georgia and South Carolina, they sometimes allowed their horses to eat a year's supply of the Indians' corn in several days?

... The largest single nugget of gold found east of the Mississippi was discovered in White County? It weighed 25 1/2 ounces which, in today's market, would be worth over $10,000.

... Paleo people thought poisonous plants had evil spirits who hated people?

... Paleo people believed that all things, such as rocks, the sun, rivers, and wind, had spirits or souls?

AN ADVENTURE INTO A NEW LAND

1733-1783

Progress is the activity of today and the assurance of tomorrow.
— Poet Ralph Waldo Emerson

THE SETTLEMENT PERIOD in Georgia lasted for fifty years. It began in 1733 when the first English colonist set foot on Georgia soil and lasted until 1783 when the Treaty of Paris was signed ending the American Revolution. During that period, Georgians found and built a new home in the wilderness, fought in a war against former friends, neighbors and relatives, and started the process of building a new government called the United States of America.

It was an adventure filled with excitement, danger, disappointment, and hope for a better tomorrow.

Named in honor of the only son of England's King George III, Fort Frederica was built by James Oglethorpe in 1736, as a fortified defense against invading Spanish troops. The fort was near the site of the Battle of Bloody Marsh. Today, visitors can walk among the ruins at St. Simons Island and imagine Oglethorpe strolling on the grounds of his home, Orange Hall, which was close to the fort.

CHAPTER THREE

THE THIRTEENTH COLONY

1663 - 1752

The air is always serene, pleasant and temperate, never subject to excessive Heat or Cold. [The soil] is impregnated with such a fertile Mixture which will . . . produce almost every Thing in Wonderful Quantities with very little Culture.

> — James Oglethorpe describing Georgia to prospective English colonists.

E NGLAND DEFEATED the Spanish Armada in 1588. This gave her undisputed control of the seas and encouraged exploration. Like most Europeans, the English believed there were large amounts of gold, silver, and exotic foods in the New World. They thought the country who claimed this new land would become even more powerful.

ENGLISH COLONIAL EXPANSION

Over the hundred years before James Oglethorpe landed at Yamacraw Bluff and established Savannah, England had begun twelve colonies along the Atlantic coastline. From the founding of Jamestown in 1607, the colonists faced many hardships. They were often hungry and sick, or at war with Indians. The French and Spanish also bothered them by trying to take English territory for themselves. However, the English did not give up. They had strong reasons for settling the new land.

England ruled the seas after defeating the Spanish Armada in 1588.

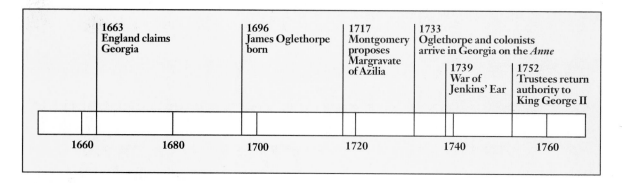

CHAPTER OUTLINE

1. English Colonial Expansion

2. A Dream Becomes a Reality

3. Building a New Home

Among the colonists, the reasons were as different as the people. Some came to Maryland, Rhode Island, and Massachusetts so they could have religious freedom. A few felt a spiritual "calling" to bring Christianity to the Indians. Others wanted adventure and the chance to make a new start. Almost everyone thought that, with hard work, they could have a better life.

England hoped to establish a system of **mercantilism**. Among the things she had to buy from other countries were cotton, forest products, tobacco, and some foods. Under a system of mercantilism, her colonies would produce such raw materials and ship them to England. There, English citizens could use the raw materials to make finished goods, such as furniture, clothing, tools, and sugar. England could then sell these items to other nations and strengthen her own economy.

England was also interested in defense. As each colony was settled, it had to be protected from the French, Spanish, and Indians. This need led to the settlement of the area we know as Georgia.

On April 26, 1607, approximately 104 hearty English settlers sailed down a river they named the James River, after King James I. A few days later they chose a piece of land by the river to build the first permanent colony, called Jamestown.

GEORGIA BEFORE OGLETHORPE

In 1566, Spain began establishing missions along the Georgia coast. The purpose of the missions was both to convert Indians to Christianity and to spread Spanish contact from Florida to the Carolinas. Spain moved out of the region, known as Gaule, by 1686. However, more than one country thought the land was theirs.

England first claimed Georgia in 1663, but it was not until 1717 that they tried to settle it. Sir Robert Montgomery wanted to create the "Margravate of Azilia." His dream was to have "the most delightful country of the universe [where] coffee, tea, figs, currants, olives, rice, almonds and silk..." would be produced for English markets. Montgomery proposed to settle an area which lay west of the Savannah River and ran to the Altamaha River. He promised to give land, gold, silver, and precious stones to those who would move to this "paradise."

Montgomery's plan seemed good, but there was not enough

A Plan representing the Form of Setling, the Districts, or County Divisions in the Margravate of Azilia.

Above: Posters recruiting settlers for the Jamestown Colony filled Great Britain with a sense of adventure and excitement. *Left:* Sir Robert Montgomery, who, in 1717, proposed a Georgia settlement called Margravate of Azilia, envisioned a settlement with intricate homesteads and pasture land surrounded by fifty-three heavily fortified gun turrets.

financial backing to carry it out. After a few years, Montgomery's dream of a "future Eden" died.

In the years that followed, there were several other proposals to settle the area for England. None were successful until the late 1720s, when James Edward Oglethorpe began to talk of a colony for the "working poor."

JAMES OGLETHORPE — HUMANITARIAN AND REALIST

James Edward Oglethorpe, born in London in 1696, was a member of an influential family. He was well educated and wealthy. He cared greatly about people in trouble, and tried to find ways to help them. Oglethorpe became a member of Parliament's House of Commons in 1722.

During that time, England was faced with many problems. There were more people than there were jobs. Many citizens, including some well-known ones, could not pay their debts. Laws concerning debtors were strict and harsh. Those who could not

Opposite page: As a man who possessed the virtues of kindness, compassion, and leadership, James Oglethorpe was a commendable choice to lead the settlers to their new home. *Left:* Well-known British painter and engraver William Hogarth was arrested for failure to pay his debts. Many of his paintings made fun of the contradictions of luxury and poverty in British society. *Above:* Oglethorpe was shocked at the inhumane treatment of debtors he visited in prison and wanted to pass laws to help the indebted.

Not only were thousands arrested each year for not paying their debts, but many were charged a fee for being in jail. The death of his friend, Robert Castell, while in debtor's prison led Oglethorpe to demand prison reforms.

pay went to jail. One of those so jailed was Oglethorpe's friend, architect Robert Castell.

Oglethorpe was on a committee studying the prisons when he learned that Castell had died of smallpox. Oglethorpe was angry because people who could not get jobs and pay their debts had to go to jail. He was also upset because he felt there had been no need for his friend to die in a dirty prison. Oglethorpe worked to get laws passed which both improved prison conditions and let thousands of prisoners go free.

Letting people out of prison did not help them. There were no jobs for them and, without work, they still could not pay their debts. Dr. Thomas Bray, a clergyman and active humanitarian, proposed that a colony be founded to help these people.

Bray died before his proposal was acted on. However, James Oglethorpe, Lord John Percival, and nineteen other men outlined a plan which promised a fresh start in the New World to "unfortunate but worthy individuals."

Do You Remember?
1. For what reasons did England want to settle new colonies?
2. What had the Spanish begun along the Georgia coast?
3. What was Sir Robert Montgomery's dream?

A DREAM BECOMES REALITY

In the summer of 1730, Oglethorpe's group of twenty-one men asked King George II for a tract of land on the "southwest of Carolina for settling poor persons of London." The group knew England's reasons for beginning new colonies, so they proposed ways to carry out England's goals. The new settlement could defend the southern Carolinas from Spanish Florida. It could also provide protection from the French, who were pushing east from the Mississippi.

Oglethorpe's group listed economic reasons for the proposed settlement. France and Spain made money trading with the Indians who lived between the Atlantic Ocean and the Mississippi River. England could share in this. Oglethorpe and his supporters also said the new colony could produce silk, cotton dyes, and wine: three items England was importing from France, Russia and Spain. They promised to send spices and semi-tropical fruit to England. English merchants were pleased with the idea of getting a good supply of raw materials while, at the same time, having a new market for their manufactured goods.

Georgia, like other American colonies, would offer religious freedom to Protestants who were being mistreated by the Catholic Church in Europe. Too, the King liked the idea of more land and greater power for England.

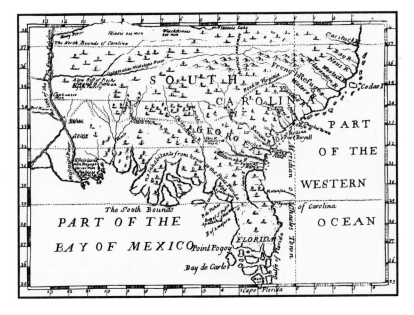

Left: This 1733 map was the first map of Georgia. It was used as part of the advertising campaign to entice settlers to seek a new home in the colony. *Above:* King George II of Great Britain was anxious to settle the region named in his honor in order to add wealth to England and as a defensive buffer for the South Carolina colony.

On June 7, 1732, King George II gave a **charter** to Oglethorpe's group as twenty-one "**trustees** for establishing the colony of Georgia," and taking care of it for twenty-one years. The grant covered an area of "all vacant land between the Savannah and the Altamaha Rivers extending from the Atlantic Ocean westward indefinitely to the South Seas" (the Pacific Ocean).

GEORGIA'S CHARTER

The charter had six thousand words and many limits. The King stated that the trustees could not own land, hold political office, or be given money for their work. "Papists" (Catholics), blacks, liquor dealers, and lawyers could not become colonists. Catholics were excluded because of a long-standing division between the Catholic Church and the Church of England. Blacks were not admitted so as not to introduce **slavery** to the colony. The trustees feared settlers would not work if liquor was permitted. They did not trust lawyers to allow colonists to settle their differences out of court.

The colony belonged to the Crown, so the trustees were to get instructions from King George II. They could pass no laws unless the king agreed. The trustees worked around some of the rules

Above: The seal of the Trustees of Georgia. The cornucopia stands for "plenty" and was used to indicate that money would be made from the settlement of Georgia. The two figures with the water jars represent the Savannah and Altamaha rivers. Below: A nineteenth century map showing the area covered by the original charter.

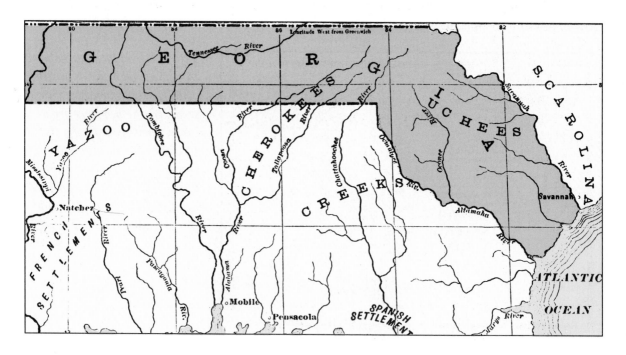

by not having a governor and by using **regulations** instead of laws.

In allowing settlement of the colony, King George limited the trustees' authority, made them managers for a definite period of time, and said they could make no profit. In spite of the limits, excitement grew as the trustees developed the "Georgia Plan for Colonization."

PREPARATION FOR THE VOYAGE

A search began to find settlers for the newest colony. Newspapers told of a land with mild temperatures and rich soil. They offered those who were chosen a new start in life. Sir Robert Montgomery had described it as the "most delightful Country of the Universe." This was widely accepted as fact. Clergymen preached sermons, wrote religious books, and raised a great deal of money by talking about the goodness of the proposed colony.

The trustees talked with applicants and planned for the voyage and settlement. Unfortunately, debtors and former prisoners did not get to go. This meant the humanitarian reasons for the proposal were all but forgotten. Only a few of those chosen had ever been in debtors' prison, and no one got out of jail to make the trip. All who applied were carefully checked on. Those chosen were promised fifty acres of land, tools, and enough food for one year. Potential colonists who could pay their own way were given five hundred acres of land and could take ten **indentured servants.**

In exchange, colonists had to agree to the following: a) each man was to defend the new colony against all enemies; b) land given to colonists could not be sold and no money could be borrowed on it, but it could be passed on to a male heir; c) each colonist was to receive seeds and agricultural tools, and was to use them in cultivating the lands of the new settlement; d) colonists were to use a portion of their land to grow mulberry trees; (It was hoped that silkworms would eat the leaves and make cocoons for the production of silk. The silk was to be shipped to England and used as cloth for the latest fashions.); e) Each colonist was to obey all regulations established by the trustees.

Even though the agreement was strict, the fever of settling in the new colony grew. On October 24, 1732, the chosen settlers met to receive instructions for their voyage to Georgia.

A great deal of hope was placed on the small silkworm. If it could flourish in Georgia, it would provide Great Britain with large quantities of silk to trade with other countries.

THE VOYAGE ON THE SHIP *ANNE*

When the settlers gathered on the London docks, they were both excited and a little afraid of the adventure ahead. Historians do not agree on the exact number of men, women, and children who traveled from England to Georgia, but between 114 and 125 people left London on November 17, 1732. The voyage to the New World took eighty-eight days.

Besides its passengers and crew, the *Anne* carried sheep, hogs, ducks, geese, and several dogs. There is no record of the ship being uncomfortable, but it was probably crowded with people and their belongings. Food was simple, mostly salted pork and peas, or dried beef and sweet pudding. Bread and hard cider were served with meals. There were few fresh vegetables other than carrots and onions. Fish were caught and cooked whenever possible.

Ships like the Anne *were sturdily built to make the Atlantic crossing from England to the colonies.*

Only two deaths were reported on the trip, both of them infants. The passengers spent their days playing games, talking together, and planning what they would do when the voyage was over. Finally, land was sighted and the *Anne* docked at Charleston, South Carolina. She stayed in Charleston one day, then put in at Beaufort, South Carolina. The passengers waited there while Oglethorpe and his staff searched for a permanent settlement site. The place decided on was about eighteen miles from the mouth of the Savannah River.

Before the *Anne* could set anchor, Oglethorpe had to make friends with the Yamacraw Indians through their chief, Tomochichi. Oglethorpe went to the trading post in the Yamacraw village to find an interpreter. The trading post was operated by John Musgrove and his wife Mary, who was part Indian and part English. Oglethorpe offered John Musgrove about 100 English pounds a year to interpret for the Indians and settlers. John agreed to act as interpreter, but Mary soon took over for him. With Mary's help, Oglethorpe and Chief Tomochichi established a close friendship which lasted until the chief's death in 1739.

On February 12, 1733, Chief Tomochichi allowed the *Anne's* passengers to land on sandy Yamacraw Bluff overlooking the Savannah River. The settlement they established was the thirteenth English colony in the New World. Georgia's citizens were added to about 654,950 other colonists spread from Massachusetts through the southern Carolinas.

Left: *When Tomochichi, Chief of the Yamacraws, met James Oglethorpe, leader of the settlement, little did they know they were to become life-long friends.* **Above:** *Chief Tomochichi is pictured here with his nephew who was probably the chief's sister's son. Notice the intricate designs on the chest of the chief.*

Do You Remember?
1. What were some reasons England wanted to settle Georgia?
2. What land was included in the original Georgia charter?
3. To what rules did the first colonists have to agree?
4. What Indian chief was a friend to the Georgia settlers?

BUILDING A NEW HOME

The group put up four large tents for shelter. After that, they began getting the land ready for planting, and preparing timber to build permanent homes. Most of the settlers had lived in the city and were **artisans** or tradesmen. They were not used to hard physical labor. Within two weeks, however, the first permanent homes were being built. The settlers were welcomed with gifts of food and farm animals from their Carolina neighbors.

Oglethorpe had no title, and only limited power, but he was accepted as leader of the colony. During the early months of settlement, he got grants of land and made treaties with the Indians. He had a small fort built on the bank of the river, and trained a **militia** to defend the settlement. Oglethorpe gave advice to local leaders, and encouraged the new colonists. He also worked with Colonel William Bull and surveyor Noble Jones to design the future city of Savannah. The basic pattern of this first planned city in the colonies was after a design by Robert Castell, Oglethorpe's friend who had died in a British debtors' prison.

The plan was for Savannah to have four squares. On the north

Right: Making silk from silkworm cocoons was a lengthy process.
Above: During the summer of 1739, the Creeks, Cherokees, and Chickasaws met at Coweta, (near present-day Columbus) the war town of the Creek Confederacy, to discuss war between the French and the Indians. Oglethorpe traveled 200 miles to talk to the tribes, enhancing the peaceful ties between the settlers and the Indians.

and south sides of each square, there were twenty lots sixty by ninety feet. On the east and west sides, four larger lots were set aside for buildings such as churches or stores. The center of each square was for social, political, and religious gatherings. The squares were divided into blocks, which were called tithings, and wards. There were ten houses in each block and four blocks in each ward.

An examination of a present-day map of Savannah shows the influence of Jones, Bull, Castell, and Oglethorpe. Modern Savannah, with a population of over 146,000, is built much the same as the city that was planned over 255 years ago.

Peter Gordon, an upholsterer by trade, kept a journal describing the crossing of the Atlantic on the Anne *and providing us with the earliest view of the layout of Savannah.*

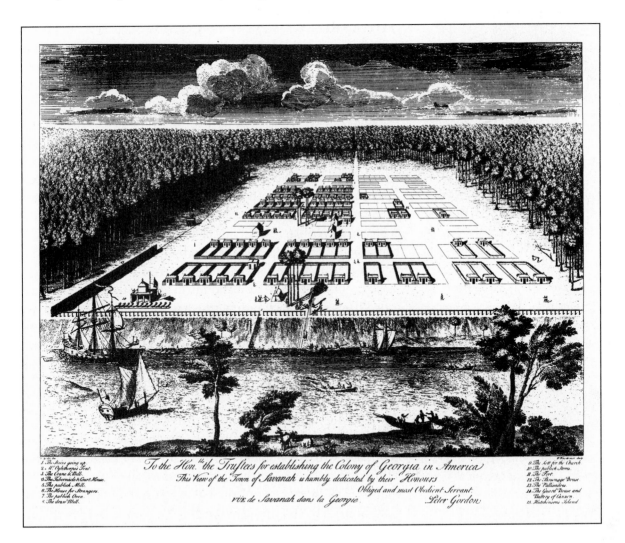

1. The Stairs going up.
2. Mr Oglethorpes Tent.
3. The Crane & Bell.
4. The Tabernacle & Court House.
5. The publick Mill.
6. The House for Strangers.
7. The publick Oven
8. The draw Well.

To the Hon.ble the Trustees for establishing the Colony of Georgia in America
This View of the Town of Savanah is humbly dedicated by their Honours
Obliged and most Obedient Servant.
rūe de Savanah dans la Georgie.   Peter Gordon

9. The Lott for the Church
10. The publick Stores.
11. The Fort.
12. The Brewage House
13. The Pallisadoes
14. The Guard House and
    Battery of Cannon
15. Hutchinsons Island

Each settler was expected to care for his house in Savannah, his five-acre garden plot on the edge of town, and his forty-five farm acres in the country. During the first months, the colonists cultivated mulberry trees to feed silkworms. They also built a sun dial for telling time, a **grist** mill, courthouse, water well, and bakery.

Work was done in spite of growing medical problems. Oglethorpe thought the use of rum caused the people to be sick. However, the scurvy, dysentery and fever were more likely caused by a lack of fresh vegetables, changes in the climate, poor sanitation, and hard physical labor. Forty settlers died in the first year. That number might have been greater if new colonists had not arrived.

THE ARRIVAL OF NEW COLONISTS

In July of 1733, when the sickness was worst, a ship carrying forty-two Jews landed in Savannah's harbor. The passengers asked to join the settlement. Since Catholics were the only religious group not allowed by the charter, Oglethorpe agreed. He needed to replace the colony's only doctor, who had died earlier. He also needed more able-bodied men in the militia. Because of the services of Dr. Samuel Nunis, the newly-arrived doctor, Georgia's first medical crisis passed.

In March 1734, Oglethorpe was planning to leave for England to report to the colony's trustees when more new settlers arrived. A group of German Protestants had been made to leave Catholic-controlled Salzburg. They were led by John Martin Bolzius, and asked to live in Georgia. Oglethorpe carried the Salzburgers to a place twenty-five miles from Savannah. There they began a town called Ebenezer, which means "the Rock of Help." They spoke a different language from the other settlers, so stayed mostly to themselves. However they worked hard and were busy colonists. In 1736, because the land was marshy, the Salzburgers were moved to Red Bluff on the Savannah River. There they built another town called New Ebenezer.

When the Salzburgers were settled, Oglethorpe left for England. With him he took Chief Tomochichi, his wife, grandnephew, and five other members of the tribe. The English liked the Yamacraws and held parties and receptions in their honor. The Indians were presented to King George II and the Archbishop of Canterbury. His countrymen thought Oglethorpe was a hero, and

Fifty German Protestant families received an offer from the Trustees of the Georgia colony to come to the colony in 1734 to escape the religious persecution in their own country. By 1741, close to 1,000 Salzburgers had built homes in the new colony.

excitement about the newest English colony grew. The visit strengthened Indian-British relationships. Oglethorpe went back to Georgia with the full support of the trustees.

When Oglethorpe reached Savannah in early February 1736, there were three hundred new colonists with him. Included were another group of Salzburgers, some Moravians (a group of Protestants who banded together in Saxony, Germany in 1722), and two religious leaders, John and Charles Wesley.

During his visit to England, Oglethorpe was given a large amount of money from the trustees to use in making the **frontier** borders stronger. They also agreed with three new regulations he wanted to introduce. Oglethorpe first helped the Salzburgers move to Frederica on St. Simons Island. Then he began to present the three new regulations to Georgia's settlers.

CLAMOROUS MALCONTENTS

Oglethorpe's new regulations were not popular. 1) Buying rum was against the law, and alcohol could not be used in trading with the Indians. 2) Slavery was not allowed because Oglethorpe thought it caused landowners to be idle while, at the same time,

*Above: Reverend John Martin Bolzius. **Below:** Ebenezer, located upriver from Savannah, was the first home of the hardworking Salzburgers.*

The Trustees and the Indians

On June 28, 1734, Oglethorpe and his party of nine Indian guests, including Chief Tomochichi, reached London. The British wanted the assistance of the Indians in developing their enterprises in the colony, and entertained them with numerous parties and dinners during their stay. King George II even granted Oglethorpe's Indian guests a meeting at Kensington Palace. This group portrait commemorating the meeting of the Indians and the Trustees of Georgia was painted by Willem Verelst in 1736.

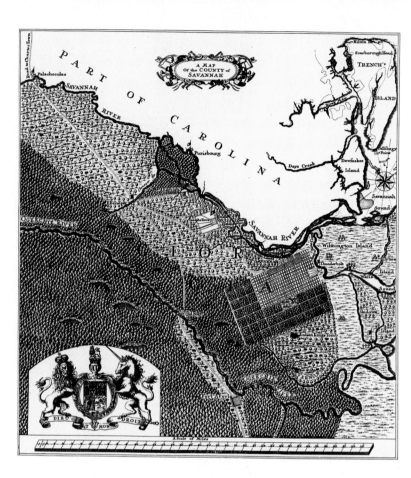

This map drawn in about 1735, shows the colony of Georgia in its first year. Notice the number of settlements that had grown outside the planned Savannah community.

made them want more land. 3) Trade with the Indians was to be watched carefully.

These regulations, added to the earlier one which said land could be passed on only through male heirs, began to divide the colonists. They were already facing economic hardships. Their mulberry trees were the wrong kind for producing large amounts of silk. The colonists were not able to grow hemp, flax, indigo, or grapes for wine. To make the discontent worse, their South Carolina neighbors, who had large amounts of land, slaves, and rum, were doing well. They were growing rice, cotton, and tobacco, and their success was due, in part, to the use of slave labor.

Scottish Highlanders, who had settled in Darien in 1735, and the German Salzburgers, were against slavery. However, growing numbers of English settlers wanted slaves. There was less and less support for trustees' regulations. Many Georgia settlers moved to places where they could live more as they wished. When Oglethorpe returned to Georgia after one of his trips to England, he found people upset all over the colony.

Oglethorpe, however, had little time to listen to the colonists. In the fall of 1739, a war broke out between England and Spain. England controlled Georgia's borders and Spain controlled Florida's. There seemed to be no way to keep the two groups from fighting.

THE SPANISH INVASION

Oglethorpe welcomed the "War of Jenkins' Ear." (The war was given this name because Spanish sailors were said to have cut off the ear of Robert Jenkins, an English seaman. The Spanish cut off Jenkins' ear to serve as a warning to British shipmasters smuggling goods off the Florida coast.) Oglethorpe wanted a reason to invade neighboring Florida. A troop of about 2,000 men, mostly Indians and Georgia and South Carolina settlers, was quickly organized. They tried to take major Spanish forts in Florida, particularly St. Augustine. However, a well-organized Spanish militia met Oglethorpe and his soldiers with a surprise attack on June 15, 1740. The Spanish won, and Oglethorpe's forces had to retreat to St. Simons Island.

During the next two years, there were numbers of attacks and counterattacks between the Spanish and English settlers, with

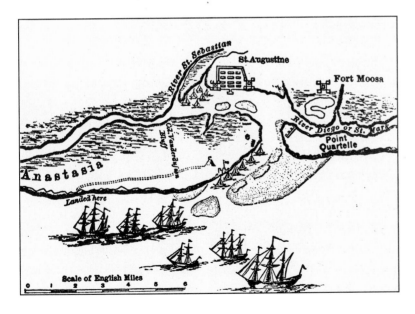

After England and Spain went to war in 1739, Oglethorpe led Georgia and South Carolina colonists in an attack on the Spanish colony at St. Augustine, Florida. However, the Spanish troops surprised the approaching colonists and forced them back into Georgia territory.

C.C.P.LAWSON

neither side gaining much ground. In July 1742, Oglethorpe got the opportunity he needed. His forces, assisted by the Scottish Highlanders, lay in wait in dense woods along the marshes on St. Simons Island. Spanish troops that came that way were caught completely by surprise and, in a minor skirmish, were beaten back across the Florida border. Even though the action was known as the Battle of Bloody Marsh, it was neither big nor very bloody. It did, however, mark the beginning of a safe southern frontier for the English.

After that battle, Oglethorpe tried a plan that worked. One of his soldiers had deserted and gone to the Spanish. Oglethorpe sent a note to the deserter by way of a released Spanish prisoner. The note, which was taken away from the prisoner by Spanish troops, said that British warships were on their way to begin a great battle against the Spanish settlers. These "warships" were really trading vessels which moved quickly to safe waters the first time they met the Spanish Navy. However, the Spanish troops did not know this and, since they thought they were outnumbered, chose to leave the area for good.

Opposite page: A stately man, Oglethorpe inspired his often ill-trained troops to follow him into battle. Left: The Battle of Bloody Marsh fought on July 7, 1742, between English colonists and Spanish troops occurred between the St. Simons lighthouse and Fort Frederica. The English victory with 650 men under Oglethorpe against 36 Spanish ships and several thousand troops helped secure the frontier boundaries against future Spanish invasions.

After serving Georgia for ten years, Oglethorpe left the colony in 1743 to return to England. Until his death in 1785, at the age of 88, Oglethorpe continued to work in many charities while living the life of a country gentleman.

THE END OF UTOPIA

In 1743, Oglethorpe was called to England to answer charges that he had not acted correctly when he failed to capture Spanish-held St. Augustine. Oglethorpe was cleared of the charges, but he did not return to Georgia. Instead, he remained in England, married a young heiress, and settled down to life as a patron of the arts.

William Stephens, the trustees' secretary, was named president of a colony filled with disagreement. Efforts to keep rum from being sold had been stopped in 1742. However, the people still wanted to own more land and have slaves. By 1750, this was allowed. The regulation against slavery was repealed, along with the one which allowed a colonist to own only 500 acres of land. When President Stephens retired in 1751, he was replaced by his assistant, Henry Parker. Although President Parker died a year later, he was responsible for organizing the state's first militia. In the next three years (1752-1754), Georgia was led by President Patrick Graham. During his tenure, many settlers who had left under the rule of the trustees returned to the colony. At about this same time, the English Parliament decided not to set aside enough money to take care of the colony's needs.

In 1752, one year before the charter's end, the trustees returned Georgia to the authority of King George II. A new era was about to begin.

A FINAL LOOK AT THE CHARTER COLONY

The idealistic vision of a utopian society which had been shared by the trustees of the colony was never fulfilled. Few debtors reached Georgia's shores and the colony was an economic failure. Many "malcontents" moved elsewhere, but the dissension in the colony continued. Rum was freely imported and slavery was introduced. Nearly one-third of the population of three thousand were slaves by the time the Georgia charter ended. Finally, the colony suffered from a lack of continuity in leadership. However, with all its failures, the colony had made progress.

During the twenty years under the original charter, 5,500 people had settled in Georgia. They had built new homes and started new lives. Although some left the colony to go elsewhere, they still made an imprint on the society and culture.

A large number of settlers were European Protestants who came to the colony to escape religious persecution. In Georgia, they were able to practice their beliefs without fear of punishment.

Treaties with the Indians and the elimination of the threat of Spanish invasion ended the necessity for British **military** protection. Georgia was a safe haven on the southern frontier.

There were also noteworthy religious, social, and political accomplishments in the colony's short history. Evangelist George Whitfield established the Bethesda Orphans Home in Ebenezer. The home served as a refuge for children without parents. Later the home was expanded into a school and renamed Bethesda House. The school provided a basic education for many of Georgia's future leaders. In Savannah, John and Charles Wesley had established the first Sunday School in America. They were also founders of the Methodist Church.

The court system, established during the early days of the settlement, was still functioning. By 1750, when the colonists gained outright ownership of the land, women were able to inherit property.

Perhaps the greatest accomplishment of the trustees of the colony had been their ability to enable the Georgia colony to sur-

Above: A dynamic preacher, George Whitfield arrived in Georgia in 1738 as a missionary. Below: The Bethesda Orphanage.

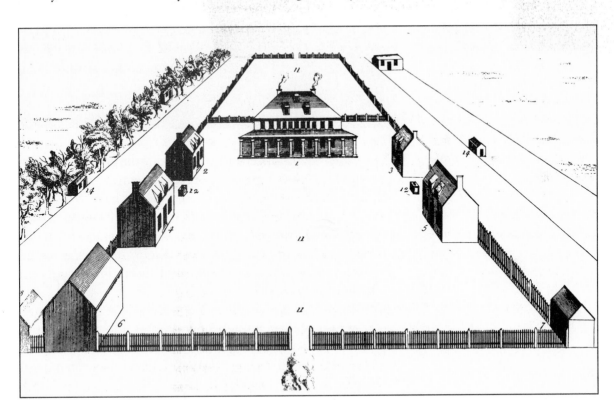

Right: Chief Tomochichi asked Oglethorpe to bring a minister to the colonies to serve his tribe. John Wesley, a young Church of England minister, volunteered. During his brief one-year stay, Wesley preached to the Indians and colonists. He conducted Bible study classes for the children every Sunday. Those classes are believed to be the first "Sunday School" held in the colonies. After returning to England, John Wesley and his brother Charles, founded the Methodist Church. *Above:* Charles traveled to the colony in 1736 with his brother. He also served as a missionary and for a brief period served as Oglethorpe's secretary.

vive the many hardships encountered during the first twenty years. The survival set the stage for Georgia to become a successful and profitable royal colony.

Do You Remember?

1. Why was Dr. Samuel Nunis important to Georgia's history?
2. What were the three regulations Oglethorpe introduced after his first trip to England?
3. When was the Battle of Bloody Marsh fought?
4. How was Robert Castell important to the settlement of Savannah?
5. How many years remained on the original charter when Georgia became a royal province?

OGLETHORPE

Henry Elliott Harman

*(On the unveiling of the Oglethorpe memorial
in Savannah, Georgia, November 1910)*

At last the centuries' slow, mysterious tread
Brings honor to the dead.
And Time, forgetting not his valor, grieves
And crown of laurel leaves.
The marble long has slept within its tomb,
Hidden in silent gloom,
But now it lifts its plaudits to the sky
For every passer by.
The tardy years were slow to place his name
On obelisk of fame,
But justice has her faithful memory kept
While men, forgetting, slept.
Yon waves that wash the broken shore-line dim
Still sing his requiem;
While slow Savannah's tide that passes by
Remembers with a sigh.
Each tall palmetto, leaning from the shore,
Looking the sea line o'er,
Holds tender memories of his name and weaves
A garland of its leaves.
This marble shaft now rises to command
That men may understand
How Virtue gives her sure reward at last
In measure full and vast.

*The Oglethorpe statue in Savannah's
Chippewa Square was sculpted in
honor of Georgia's founder by Daniel Chester French, who also sculpted
the famous statue of Abraham Lincoln in the Lincoln Memorial.*

Extend Your Thinking

   On a separate piece of paper, interpret the meaning of the poem,
"Oglethorpe."

CHAPTER REVIEW

Summary

Georgia was the thirteenth English colony established in the New World. King George II gave twenty-one trustees, including James Oglethorpe, the right to settle the colony in 1732. England hoped the new colony would defend her other colonies from the French, Spanish, and Indians. England also planned for the colony to produce and ship to her raw materials she had to buy from other countries.

Some settlers were looking for religious freedom. Others wanted adventure and the opportunity to make a fresh start in life.

James Oglethorpe led a group of 114 to 125 settlers to Georgia in 1733. When they arrived, they were helped by a Yamacraw chief named Tomochichi. Oglethorpe chose a settlement site near the mouth of the Savannah River. The settlers built their town in spite of hardships, which included starvation, scurvy, dysentery, and fever. Forty settlers died in the first year. During the first three years of Georgia's settlement, the original colonists were joined by Jewish settlers, German Protestants, Moravians, and other Englishmen, including religious leaders John and Charles Wesley.

The early settlers were not able to grow some of the crops they had promised to England. They were unhappy because rum and liquors were not allowed. They did not like the strict regulations on trading with Indians, and many settlers wanted to have slaves. To add to their problems, a war between England and Spain began in the fall of 1739.

Five thousand, five hundred settlers came to Georgia during the twenty years under the original charter. In spite of hardships, the people made progress. They signed treaties with the Indians, and ended threats of Spanish invasion.

Evangelist George Whitfield established the Bethesda Orphans Home in Ebenezer. John and Charles Wesley, founders of the Methodist Church, established the first Sunday School in America.

The court system, which was begun during the early days of settlement, was still in use. By 1750, when the colonists gained outright ownership of the land, women were able to inherit property.

Between 1750 and 1752, many things the colonists wanted were allowed. Rum could be sold, and the people could own slaves. The five-hundred-acre limit on land ownership was lifted. In 1752, one year before the charter's end, the trustees returned Georgia to the authority of King George II. Between 1743 and 1754, Georgia had three presidents: William Stephens, Henry Parker, and Patrick Graham.

Perhaps the greatest accomplishment of the trustees was that the Georgia colony survived the hardships of the first twenty years. That survival set the stage for Georgia to become a successful and profitable royal colony.

People, Places, and Terms

Define, identify and/or state the importance of each of the following.

1. John Wesley
2. clamorous malcontents
3. Robert Castell
4. mercantilism
5. James Oglethorpe
6. *Anne*
7. Dr. Samuel Nunis
8. Battle of Bloody Marsh
9. War of Jenkins' Ear
10. George Whitfield

The Main Idea

Write a short paragraph to answer each of the following questions.

1. Why did King George II want to establish the thirteenth colony? Compare and contrast these reasons with England's settlement of other colonies in the New World.
2. What were some of the failures of Georgia as a colony under the guidance of the trustees?
3. What were the accomplishments of the trustees' colony?
4. Why did many Georgia settlers want to introduce slavery into the colony?
5. Reread Oglethorpe's description of Georgia in the introductory section. In what ways do you feel the description was accurate or inaccurate? Explain your response.

Extend Your Thinking

Write a short paragraph to answer each of the following questions.

1. Would you have been willing to travel to the new colony? Why or why not? Explain what would have been the most exciting part of the trip for you? Describe what part of the settlement process would have been the most frightening for you?
2. In your opinion, were the "clamorous malcontents" justified in their feelings? Explain why or why not.
3. Suppose the regulations governing the colonies had been upheld. Would life in the colonies have been different? Explain why or why not.

Map Skills

1. Using a United States map, outline the original land area granted to Oglethorpe and the trustees.

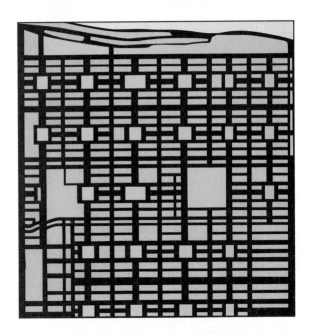

2. Examine the layout of the colony on page 77 and compare it with this street map of contemporary Savannah. How are the two plans similar? How are they different?

Looking Ahead

Georgia's settlers became more prosperous after Georgia was declared a royal colony. In Chapter 4 you will learn:

➤ why Georgia was slow to join the other colonies in declaring independence from England;
➤ how Georgia benefitted from the French and Indian War;
➤ how the Stamp Act and the Intolerable Acts led colonists to rebel against England;
➤ why the Sons of Liberty were important;
➤ about the Tories and Patriots;
➤ which three Georgians signed the Declaration of Independence;
➤ about two revolutionary war figures in Georgia's history: Colonel Elijah Clarke and Nancy Hart.

for the Governor of Georgia

CHAPTER FOUR

GEORGIA IN TRANSITION
1752 - 1783

The proposition is peace.... I propose, by removing the ground of difference, and by restoring the former unspecting confidence of the colonies in the mother country, to give permanent satisfaction to your people, and (far from a scheme of ruling by discord) to reconcile them to each other in the same act and by the bond of the very same interest which reconciles them to the British government.

— Edmund Burke, A speech written in March 1775 in defense of the colonies, and delivered to the House of Commons.

GEORGIA BECOMES A ROYAL COLONY

T HE SECOND PHASE of Georgia's development began in 1752, when Georgia ceased to be a **proprietary** colony and became a royal colony. The last part of the eighteenth century was a time of growth and development in all the colonies. New Jersey imported the first steam engine and Philadelphia hung the Liberty Bell. Benjamin Banneker, a thirty-year-old black man, put together the first clock made completely in America, and Benjamin Franklin invented bifocals. Transportation became easier as roads were paved in the northeastern colonies. Georgia, the youngest and poorest of the colonies, was ready for some of the prosperity enjoyed by the others.

During the two years before the first royal governor was appointed, some of the people who had left Georgia under the trustees began to come back. In 1752, colonists called Puritans migrated from South Carolina and bought 32,000 acres of land at Midway. These Puritans had slaves with them, and were growing

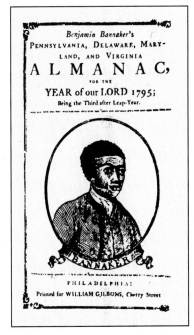

*Opposite page: Georgia's third royal governor, Sir James Wright, was responsible for the defense of the colony and for maintaining friendly relations with the Indians. **Top:** Edmund Burke, an influential member of Parliament, spoke out in favor of American independence. **Above:** Benjamin Banneker's almanac.*

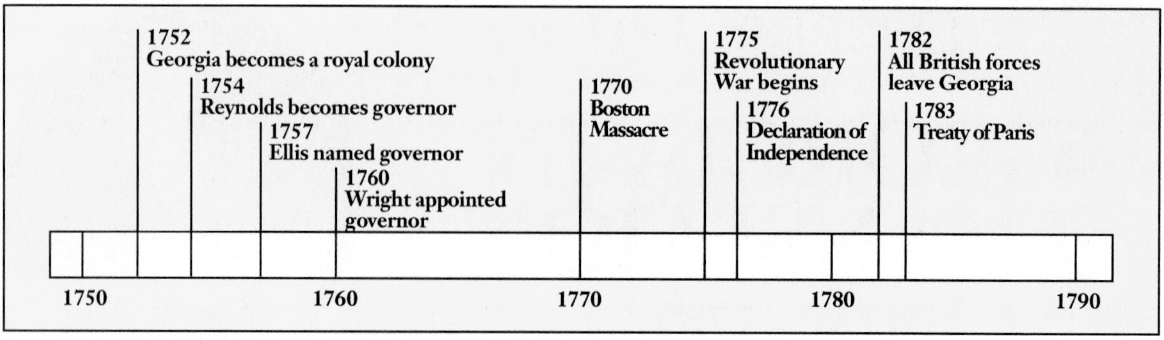

CHAPTER OUTLINE

1. Georgia Becomes a Royal Colony

2. Discontent in the Colonies

3. The Revolutionary War

rice and indigo in a short period of time. A port was built at Sunbury so they could ship their crops.

GEORGIA'S FIRST GOVERNOR AND FIRST GOVERNMENT

On October 1, 1754, Georgia's colonists cheered when John Reynolds, their first royal governor, arrived. Reynolds, a navy captain, introduced an idea Georgians had not tried before—self government.

The trustees had felt the first Georgia settlers were not able to govern themselves, so had not given them the right to vote, hold elections, or collect taxes. Governor Reynolds, on the other hand, wanted the colonists to help run the government.

A bicameral, or two-house, legislature was set up to represent the eight parishes of the colony. Each **parish** was both a church and a British government district. In order to vote, a settler had to own at least fifty acres of land. Those wishing to be in the lower house had to own no less than 500 acres of land to run for office. Members of the lower house could write and vote on bills before they became laws.

The King of England selected the members of the upper house. These men were wealthy, influential landowners. They were to advise the governor, approve land grants, make laws and, sometimes, act as judges in legal cases. Governor Reynolds also set up a court system. When the colonists had differences with each other, they went before the Court of Conscience, which was presided over by a local justice of the peace. Cases which could not be settled in the Court of Conscience could be carried to the Governor's Council.

GEORGIA'S FIRST ASSEMBLY

The new government met for the first time in 1755. They reorganized the state militia, and passed bills so roads could be built and repaired. The new legislature also drew up codes which restricted the rights of slaves.

For a while Governor Reynolds and the legislature worked well together. However, during one legislative session, members of the upper house would not agree to spend a large amount of money to improve the military defenses of the colony. Governor Reynolds became so angry that he stopped the meeting and sent the legislators home. During the months that followed, Reynolds tried to govern Georgia by himself.

Many Georgians did not like having their right to self government taken away. They wrote to King George II and complained. Other Georgians liked Governor Reynolds. There were arguments between those who thought he should leave and those who wanted him to remain. Finally, after two years, the group who wanted self government won, and Georgia's first royal governor was sent back to the British Navy.

THE MAN WITH THE UMBRELLA

In February 1757, the King chose Henry Ellis to take John Reynolds' place as governor. Governor Ellis had been to many places in the world. He was a naturalist and a scientist. It is told that he walked the streets of Savannah checking the thermometer which hung around his neck and taking notes of what he saw. He said Savannah was one of the hottest places in the world, and often carried an umbrella to protect himself from the sun.

Ellis learned quickly from Reynolds' mistakes. During his three years as governor, he brought together many different political groups. Ellis listened to the advice of the governor of South Carolina. He also depended on well-known and wealthy citizens to lead the colony. It was not long before the people were getting along better with each other.

THE INCREASE IN SLAVE LABOR

While Ellis was governor, large numbers of colonists migrated to Georgia from South Carolina and the West Indies. Many of these new settlers brought slaves with them, and the governor gave

Top: Beginning in 1754, Georgia had a new seal as a royal province. The front side of the seal depicted the province giving the King of England silk spun in the colony. *Above:* The coat of arms of King George II was engraved on the back side of the silver seal marking Georgia as a royal province.

them large amounts of land. By 1759, the population had grown from about 6,000 to 10,000, and included 3,600 slaves.

Not all Georgians wanted slaves in the state. The Highland Scots at Darien and the Salzburgers at Ebenezer believed that hard work by the white settlers would allow the same economic growth as would a system of slave labor. There were not many large plantations at that time, but the wealthy kept getting more land and talking about the need for slaves.

In 1759, Governor Ellis became ill and returned to England. The colonists were sorry to see him leave because they had made economic gains under his direction. There were more paying farms, and merchants had multiplied so colonists could buy the things they could not grow, such as cloth, sugar, farming tools, and seeds for planting.

GOVERNOR JAMES WRIGHT ARRIVES

In 1760, King George III appointed James Wright as Georgia's new governor. Wright had grown up in America and was, at one time, attorney general of South Carolina. He was loyal to the King, but he also wanted the colonies to do well. He believed that Georgia would continue to grow if large farms were even bigger, there was more trading done, and the western lands of the colony

Above: The original Georgia charter which prohibited the use of slave labor in the colony was soon forgotten as farmers from other colonies moved into Georgia bringing slaves with them. Shortly thereafter, slaves were imported into Georgia to work on the large farms. Right: During the French and Indian War, British Major General Edward Braddock was defeated attempting to force the French out of Fort Duquesne.

were opened to settlers. Wright agreed with the self-government Governor Reynolds had started, so the colonists were pleased with him.

A part of Georgia's growth during Wright's term of office took place after the French and Indian War ended in 1763. In that war, the British fought the French and the American Indians for control of land. After nine years of fighting, the British won. This meant Canada and all lands east of the Mississippi except New Orleans belonged to England.

Georgia did not take part in the war, but she was helped by it. The state's southern boundary was moved to the St. Mary's River. At the same time, the Indians gave up all lands between the Ogeechee and Savannah rivers north to Augusta. Later, the Indians also gave up the coastal land south of the Altamaha. All this land came under Georgia's control, and settlers began to migrate to the colony.

Ultimately the British were victorious in the French and Indian War. As a result, in 1763, King George III extended Georgia's boundaries, almost doubling the territory. The southern boundary of the province was now the St. Mary's River which separated Georgia from Florida.

The fortification of Fort Morris are long overgrown with grass and trees. Fort Morris was built in 1776 to protect the seaport at Sunbury.

The end of the French and Indian War also removed the danger of Spanish and French attacks along Georgia's land borders. Colonists could then settle inland instead of only along the coast.

GEORGIA CONTINUES TO GROW AND CHANGE

During James Wright's early years as governor, there were many changes. The town of Sunbury grew, and became the colony's official port of entry for ships arriving from other countries and colonies. Both houses of the general assembly worked together to promote Georgia's economic growth. Farmers were allowed to borrow more money, so they bought more land. The colony's first newspaper, *The Georgia Gazette*, was started in 1763.

Rice and indigo had become profitable crops. Enough silk was being produced so that, by 1767, almost a ton of it was exported to England each year. There were more schools, and the buying of books was at an all-time high. Many of the small frame houses were taken down and, in their place, two-story houses were built of wood or tabby, a mixture of lime, crushed shells, sand, and water. A number of the colonists spent their spare time working for charity or attending social clubs. The amount of owned land grew from one million to seven million acres.

However, there was another side to Georgia during Wright's early years. Many mothers died giving birth to children. Going to school was mostly for children in the upper economic class. Also, a group of what plantation owners called "undesirable people" migrated from Virginia and the Carolinas to settle in the middle and western parts of the colony. They became known as "Crackers." Historians do not know why they were called that. It might have been because of the cracking sounds of whips used on oxen or horses as this group went to market to sell their goods. It might have come from the cracking of corn as they prepared corn meal. Some say the term came from a Scottish word which meant "boasters." However it started, the term was meant as an insult. These settlers were thought of as people who did not obey the law and they were not welcome in the colony.

During this time, Governor Wright had other things to take his attention. There was no plan for defending the colony. Also, a growing number of Georgians who were not wealthy began to ask for a greater voice in government. They were not alone for, within a short period of time, their voices joined with others as the colonies began trying to gain **independence** from England.

Do You Remember?

1. Who was Benjamin Banneker?
2. Who was Georgia's first royal governor?
3. What was the Court of Conscience?
4. When did Georgia's first legislature meet?
5. How long was John Reynolds in Georgia?
6. In order, who were Georgia's three royal governors?
7. What was one thing Ellis accomplished as governor?
8. What was the name of Georgia's first newspaper?
9. Who were the Crackers?
10. When did James Wright arrive in Georgia?
11. What were two of Wright's accomplishments during the early days of his administration?
12. What was Sunbury?

Wormsloe, below Savannah, was the 750-acre estate of surveyor Noble Jones. Purchased in 1733, it is reported to be the oldest estate in Georgia. Today, Wormsloe is operated as a historical site by the state of Georgia. The name is supposed to be derived from the mulberry trees Jones planted on the estate for the silkworms.

DISCONTENT IN THE COLONIES

During the fifteen years before the American Revolution, many colonists began to dislike British rule. It is important to remember that, in 1760, Georgia was only twenty-seven years old. Virginia, on the other hand, had been a colony 153 years. As a royal colony, Georgia was enjoying economic, political, and social growth. She still needed financial and military help from England and did not want to damage her standing with the British.

ENGLAND TRIES TO CONTROL THE COLONY

When the American colonists complained, England passed some strict laws. The Navigation Act of 1763 said the colonies could use only British vessels to ship their goods. This was not a problem for Georgia. Most of her trade was still with England, and British ships often sailed to and from Georgia. However, the act meant that colonies who traded with several countries were no longer allowed to do so.

Owned by Peter Tondee, Tondee's Tavern was a favorite meeting place of the Liberty Boys. Some citizens called them "Liberty Brawlers."

In 1764, England's increased tax on wine and imported goods received very little opposition in Georgia. Most of the money Georgia needed for her government was given to her by Parliament, so she paid little tax to England. This was not true in the older colonies, and they became very angry about the new tax.

England passed the Stamp Act in 1765 to try to raise enough money to pay for the French and Indian War. This placed a tax on newspapers, legal documents, and licenses. A Stamp Act Congress met in Boston, Massachusetts to speak against British taxes.

The Georgia legislature was not in session at the time, so it did not send a representative to the Stamp Act Congress. A few Georgia citizens showed their dislike of the act on the day before it went into effect by burning an effigy of the stampmaster in the streets of Savannah.

On November 6, a group of Georgians came together to oppose the Stamp Act. They called themselves the Liberty Boys. Older Georgians called them the "Liberty Brawlers" because they met in local taverns. Tondee's Tavern in Savannah was a favorite meeting spot. However, the Liberty Boys were part of the larger Sons of Liberty, whose daring acts came to represent the spirit of the Revolution.

The taxes did not upset most Georgians very much, but the colony felt their effect. According to historical records, Georgia was the only colony which ever sold stamps. Only a few were sold, but Georgia's South Carolina neighbors spoke out with anger against her. Georgia's only newspaper, *The Georgia Gazette*, had to stop printing until the Stamp Act was repealed a year later.

Noble Wimberly Jones, the son of Noble Jones, was only ten when Georgia was settled. He openly supported the Patriots' cause and was an active participant in the raid on the powder magazine in Savannah in 1775.

GEORGIANS BEGIN TO REACT

During the next four years, many Georgians talked openly about their dislike of the strict new British laws. Between 1768 and 1772, members of the Georgia General Assembly spoke against the Townshend Act, which placed import taxes on tea, paper, glass, and coloring for paints. Later, they elected Noble Jones, a Patriot, as speaker of the general assembly without the approval of the governor.

Governor Wright became upset with the growing discontent. He tried to end the protests by doing away with the assembly. However, the people were not so easily silenced. Georgia was divided into two groups: the Tories who remained loyal to England, and the Patriots who joined others in the colonies to seek freedom from British rule.

Protests Increase

Georgia did not want to damage her standing with England, but protests against British taxes became more open in the other twelve colonies. "No taxation without representation" became a pre-revolutionary war cry. Since the Townshend Act had placed a tax on coloring for paints, the people stopped painting their homes. Because of the tax on tea, they quit drinking tea and turned to coffee.

On a cold day in March 1770, some people in Boston threw snowballs at British soldiers and called them names. The soldiers fired into the crowd, killing five civilians, including a freed slave named Crispus Attucks. Two years later, a group of northern colonists attacked and burned the British cutter, *Gaspee*, in Rhode Island.

By 1773, England had repealed the Townshend Act, except for the tax on tea. To protest the remaining tax, a group of Patriots dressed as Mohawk Indians boarded a British ship anchored in Boston Harbor and dumped its cargo of tea into Boston Bay. The

*Above: Crispus Attucks, a freed slave, was a familiar sight around the docks in Boston. On the 5th of March, 1770, as Attucks and a crowd of civilians faced a group of British soldiers, he urged the crowd to stand their ground. **Right:** As the gathering crowd taunted the British soldiers, a shot was fired, killing Attucks. Another soldier fired and by the time the smoke cleared, five people lay dead in the snow. The event became known as the Boston Massacre.*

British closed the port of Boston until the citizens of Massachusetts paid for the tea.

Massachusetts colonists were not allowed to have a town meeting without the agreement of their governor, who was also commander of the British troops. The operation of the court system was changed so that any British officials who committed capital crimes would be tried in England rather than by a court in the colonies. As a final punishment, the Quartering Act was passed, which meant the colonists had to house and feed British soldiers.

These new laws were called the Intolerable Acts. They were aimed at Massachusetts but, after they were passed, representatives of all the colonies except Georgia gathered in Philadelphia on September 5, 1774 for the First Continental Congress. At this congress, there were two major groups. One wanted to pull away from England and seek independence. The other wanted to make changes, but remain under British rule. If the colonists were not sure which group was right, they agreed on one thing. Something had to be done soon!

A COLONY DIVIDED

Anti-British feelings were growing in Georgia, but the people still seemed to care more about which parish would have the most power in the Georgia General Assembly. Because the colony still depended on England, they chose not to send a delegate to the

On April 19, 1775, 800 British redcoats met 70 minutemen (so called because they could be ready for battle in a minute) ranging in age from the early teens to the late 60s. Paul Revere had made his famous ride to warn the Patriots hours before. When the smoke of the battle cleared, eight colonists lay dead and only one British soldier was wounded. The British troops quickly left to meet the Patriots at Concord, a town 15 miles west of Boston.

First Continental Congress. However, one month before the congress, a group of Georgians met to discuss their reaction to the Intolerable Acts. After talking for a long time, they decided to send a resolution to England demanding that citizens of the thirteen colonies have the same rights as British citizens living in England. They insisted that the Intolerable Acts did not agree with the "Rights and Privileges of an Englishman."

The general assembly also decided to have a meeting in Georgia to talk about the growing upset over their ties with England. This meeting, called the Provincial Congress, was held in January 1775. Less than one-half of the parishes of Georgia were represented, and the meeting ended without much being done.

St. John's Parish, angry because the Provincial Congress had done so little, sent Lyman Hall as their parish representative to the Second Continental Congress. Hall attended the meeting in May of 1775, but was not allowed to vote as a representative of the colony.

Left: *Midway Church was located in St. John's Parish which included the settlements of Midway and Sunbury.* **Above:** *A member of the Midway Church Congregation, physician Nathan Brownson was a member of the continental Congress from 1776 to 1778 and served as governor of Georgia from 1781-1782.*

To show their support for the revolutionary cause, Patriots erected a liberty pole in front of Tondee's Tavern and held lively demonstrations aimed at gathering additional support from the colonists for independence from England.

WAR BEGINS

It took a long time for news to get around the colonies, so it was May before word reached Georgia that the Battles of Lexington and Concord had been fought in Massachusetts on April 19, 1775. Those battles, which marked the beginning of the revolutionary war, forced Georgians to take a stand. In just a few days, a group of radicals broke into the royal magazine in Savannah and stole 600 pounds of gunpowder. Other protests followed quickly.

Gunpowder for cannon used to fire salutes on the King's birthday was tampered with and would not explode. A liberty pole was put up in Savannah's public square. Tories, who were in favor of the King, were openly harassed. Guns were stolen from public warehouses and no one paid any attention to what the governor said. A "Council of Safety," made up of Patriots, prepared to form a new government.

Georgians called a meeting of the Second Provincial Congress for July 4, 1775. This group was not like the first congress; they were ready to act quickly. Five representatives were chosen to attend the Second Continental Congress in Philadelphia. The Council of Safety was told to raise money, buy war **materiel,** hold elections and, if needed, censor newspapers.

To show they meant what they said, the group officially seceded, or withdrew, from England. The Patriots had left Governor Wright without power. Wright was arrested in mid-January of 1776 by the Liberty Boys when he asked the Council of Safety to allow British vessels to purchase **supplies** from the colony. A month later, Wright escaped and fled to a waiting British warship, leaving the Council of Safety to govern the colony.

Do You Remember?
1. How long did the pre-revolutionary period last?
2. How old was Georgia in 1760, at the beginning of the pre-revolutionary period?
3. What was Georgia's reaction to the Navigation Act?
4. How did Georgia respond to the Stamp Act?
5. Who was Noble Jones?
6. What is the definition of "Patriot"?
7. What group was formed to protest the Stamp Act?
8. What was the colonists' slogan about British taxes?
9. What were the various Intolerable Acts passed for Massachusetts?
10. When did the First Continental Congress meet? Who was represented at that meeting?
11. What event forced Georgia to become actively involved in the American Revolution?
12. What was the Council of Safety?
13. Who were the Tories?
14. What happened to Governor Wright in January 1776? When did he leave Georgia?

On June 15, 1775, the Second Continental Congress created an official army naming George Washington as commander-in-chief of the colonial forces. Georgia's Washington County is named in his honor.

THE REVOLUTIONARY WAR PERIOD

THE DECLARATION OF INDEPENDENCE

The American Revolution began in April 1775 with the battles of Lexington and Concord, but it was three and one-half years before fighting took place on Georgia's soil.

The Declaration of Independence was approved by the Second Continental Congress on July 4, 1776. When it was officially signed on August 2 of that year, the names of three Georgians, Lyman Hall, George Walton, and Button Gwinnett, appeared on

*Georgia's three signers of the Declaration of Independence: **Above left:** Button Gwinnett was a merchant, politician, and, after the war, he served a two-month term as acting governor. That same year, he died from injuries sustained in a duel. **Above right:** George Walton, at age 26, was the youngest signer of the Declaration of Independence. Walton served as Georgia's governor twice. **Opposite page:** The third Georgia signer of the Declaration of Independence, Lyman Hall, became governor in 1783.*

the left side of the document right below the signature of John Hancock. This powerful document was written in three parts. The introduction, or Preamble, told how the colonists felt about democracy. The second part listed twenty-seven grievances against King George III and his government which caused the colonists to seek independence from England. The third part declared the colonies to be an **independent** nation for all future time.

POLITICAL CHANGES IN GEORGIA

Georgia joined the other colonies in celebrating the decision to be independent from England. Work was begun on a state **constitution.** Writing the new constitution was not easy. Conservative citizens wanted a government like the one already in place, with most of the power in the hands of a few wealthy landowners and merchants. The other, and more **radical**, group wanted

George Moodus

sweeping changes that would give all the people of Georgia a chance to govern themselves. The radical group, known as Whigs, won, and Georgia decided on a government based on the separation of powers and the rights of citizens to agree with how they were governed.

By May 1777, Georgia had adopted its first state constitution, and John Adam Treutlen had become governor. The parish system was done away with, and eight counties were formed. Chatham, Effingham, Burke, Richmond, Wilkes, Glynn and Camden were named for British subjects who had been in favor of the Revolution, and Liberty County was named in honor of American independence. On July 4, 1778, Georgians **ratified** the Articles of Confederation, which were to form the government of the United States of America. The Articles did not go into effect until January 1781, when Virginia and Maryland ratified them.

THE REVOLUTION IN GEORGIA

During 1777 and 1778, except for several unsuccessful attempts to capture British-held St. Augustine and parts of east Florida, Georgia was relatively quiet. However, British troops attacked Savannah in December 1778. A month later they took the port of Sunbury. Before long, Augusta was under **siege.**

In all three cases, the poorly armed and under-manned Georgia militia could do little to stop the British. Georgia fell again under British military rule and Governor Wright returned to Georgia to take charge of the government.

The Battle Of Kettle Creek

Finally, in February 1779, Georgia had a victory. A rebel militia group led by Colonel Elijah Clarke defeated an 800-man British troop at the Battle of Kettle Creek, about eight miles from Washington, Georgia.

The Battle of Kettle Creek was minor when compared to those fought in other parts of the country. It was, however, important to Georgia. The militia was able to take badly needed weapons and horses from the British soldiers, and the spirits of the Georgia militia were lifted by their victory. Georgia's success was short-lived, because the British won a major battle a month later at Briar Creek.

*Opposite page: Born in Austria, John Adam Treutlen, a Salzburger, was a member of the Georgia Council of Safety and the Georgia Provincial Congress. He defeated acting governor Button Gwinnett in 1777 and served as governor until January 1778. Treutlen County is named in his honor. **Above:** Elijah Clarke distinguished himself in the revolutionary war by defending Wilkes County against the British, Tories and Indians in fighting so intense that the area became known as "The Hornets' Nest."*

AUSTIN DABNEY

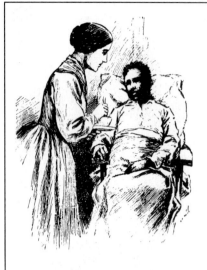

During his heroic fighting at the Battle of Kettle Creek, Austin Dabney was hit by a rifle ball which passed through his thigh. Dabney is given credit for saving the life of Elijah Clarke by giving the colonel a horse at Kettle Creek after his had been shot out from under him.

Although the Georgia militia was outmatched in both numbers and weapons, they showed fierce spirit. Clarke proved to be an able commander, and among those who followed him into battle at Kettle Creek was a revolutionary hero named Austin Dabney.

Dabney was freeborn, the child of one black and one white parent. He arrived in Georgia just before the Revolution with a man named Richard Aycock. Aycock, a white North Carolinian, was not known for his bravery. Instead of joining the Georgia militia, Aycock proposed that Austin Dabney take his place. After much discussion, Dabney was accepted. He proved to be an able soldier at Kettle Creek, and was wounded in action. A family named Harris cared for him while his wounds healed.

After the revolutionary war, veteran soldiers were given plots of land as part of the payment for their military service. Many did not want Dabney to get his veteran's share of land. Governor George Gilmer and some members of the Georgia legislature did not agree. They praised Dabney as a patriot and, after months of debate, he was given a valuable piece of land in Madison County. When he moved to his new home, Dabney took the Harris family with him. Together, they made the property profitable. Austin Dabney died in 1834, fifty-five years after the Battle of Kettle Creek.

Two Governments

As the fighting continued, Savannah remained under siege. In October, a four thousand man French fleet commanded by Charles Henri Comte d'Estaing tried to help Georgia retake Savannah from the British. Their attempts failed and, after a four-day battle, the French gave up the attack.

This left Georgia in the hands of two governments—one royal and one rebel. Each government tried to take charge of the state, but neither was very effective. The major battles were over, but guerrilla warfare was still going on in the back country of Georgia and South Carolina.

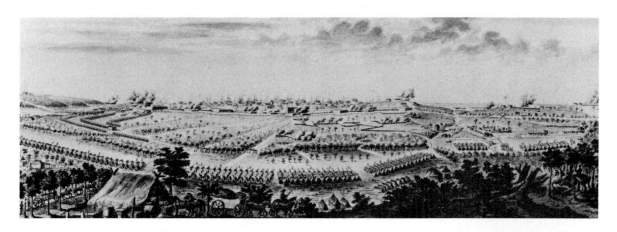

WASHINGTON LEADS CONTINENTAL ARMY

In June 1781, Georgia's militia was again under the command of Colonel Clarke. With the help of Continental troops, Clarke took Augusta from the British. General George Washington was commander of the Continental Army. French forces assisted when Washington's army faced British General Lord Cornwallis in October 1781, at the Battle of Yorktown, Virginia. The American forces won that battle, forcing Cornwallis to surrender.

Cornwallis did not know that British ships carrying 6,000 men were on their way to help him. They arrived just six days after his surrender. Had the French not delayed the landing of the British ships, the results of the American Revolution might have been different. By the spring of 1782, British forces in Georgia believed they could not defeat the Americans. They left Savannah, marking an end to the three-and-one-half year siege of that city.

The Treaty of Paris was signed by England, France, and the United States in September 1783. Independence was finally a reality. Battles and skirmishes on Georgia's soil were limited to eleven. However, Georgians could be proud of their part in the revolutionary war as the work of building a new country began.

Do You Remember?
1. Name the Georgia signers of the Declaration of Independence.
2. What was the purpose of the second part of the Declaration of Independence?
3. For whom were the original parishes of Georgia renamed as counties?

Top: British troops laid siege to Savannah in December, 1778. Governor James Wright returned to Georgia after the fall of Savannah. Above: An impulsive but brave French naval commander, Count Charles Henri d'Estaing, landed in Savannah on September 11, 1779 to help colonists regain Savannah. The attempt failed with heavy losses for the French and American troops.

NANCY HART

Called "the war woman" by the Indians, Nancy Hart is seen here on the Hart County Seal, with her rifle, in recognition of her brave stand against the Tories. The seal also shows the 1,900-foot-long, 17,900-foot-high dam located in Hart County on the Savannah River. Hart County is the only county in Georgia named for a woman.

During any wartime period, the exploits of heroes and heroines become part of the ongoing folklore of a nation. The American Revolution was no exception. Even though Georgia historians sometimes disagree about whether or not specific events took place, one woman is known as Georgia's most famous war heroine.

Nancy Hart, her husband Benjamin, and their eight children moved to Georgia around 1771 and settled twelve miles outside of the town we now call Elberton. Nancy was a tall, muscular woman who helped her husband operate their 400-acre farm.

As the revolutionary war escalated, loyal Tories of the area roamed the backwoods country harassing citizens. People became so frightened that Colonel Elijah Clarke took many women and children to the safety of Kentucky. Nancy Hart, however, was a headstrong, independent woman who refused to leave her home. Instead, she was loyal to the revolutionary cause, and became a noted spy for the American forces.

Legend has it that one day while Nancy was boiling lye soap, she saw a pair of eyes peering through a crack in her cabin. Before the intruder could make a move, Nancy threw a bucket of the hot soap into the face of the person outside. As he screamed in pain, she quickly tied him up and, the next day, took him at gunpoint to Colonel Clarke's headquarters, where he was executed as a British spy.

An event in 1780 is probably the most repeated legend. Colonel John Dooley, commander of a regiment at the Battle of Kettle Creek, was murdered by British soldiers. A few days later, five of these soldiers stopped at Nancy Hart's home and accused her of harboring a rebel soldier. They demanded that Nancy cook dinner for them. As the men ate, Nancy overheard their bragging remarks about the murder of Colonel Dooley.

Colonel Dooley had been a respected man in that territory, and Nancy, thinking quickly, brought out a jug of whiskey and offered

it to the soldiers. As they continued to drink, they did not notice Nancy motioning for her daughters to go to the woods and sound the alarm for help by blowing three times on a conch shell. Enjoying their drink and food, they also did not realize that Nancy was quietly taking their rifles as she served the men.

When Nancy pulled the third rifle away from the table, one of the soldiers looked up and yelled. The men rushed her and Nancy Hart calmly pulled the trigger killing one of them. She grabbed a second rifle and held the other soldiers at gunpoint until help arrived. Some reports say she may have killed two of the soldiers. After a quick trial, the remaining soldiers were hanged for the murder of Colonel Dooley. We may never know if the stories of Nancy Hart's courage are true. However, the legend of Nancy Hart remains an example of the revolutionary spirit of Georgia. Hart County and its county seat Hartwell, located in Northeast Georgia, are named in her honor. Hart is the only one of Georgia's counties named for a woman.

*Above left: Nancy Hart, the wife of a Wilkes County patriot, served at times as a spy for Colonel Elijah Clarke and at times on the battlefield alongside her husband. Unafraid of the possibility of her own death, she bravely fought the Tories, or Loyalists. **Above right:** The picture shows Nancy Hart blowing into the hollow conch shell. Why do you think this picture does not agree with the text?*

CHAPTER REVIEW

Summary

Georgia became a royal colony in 1752. Georgia continued to grow and prosper. Many people who had left the colony when it was under the rule of the trustees returned to the royal colony. A new group, Puritans from South Carolina, bought land and moved to Midway.

Governor John Reynolds was the first royal governor. He was followed as governor by Henry Ellis and then James Wright. During Wright's term, Georgia joined the other twelve colonies in declaring independence from England. The American Revolution soon followed. Beginning in 1775, British and American troops fought six years. For three and one-half of those years, Georgia was taken over by British forces. Several battles were fought on Georgia soil, including the Battle of Kettle Creek. Fighting ended in 1781, and the Americans won their battle for independence. The official end of the war came with the signing of the Treaty of Paris in 1783.

People, Places, and Terms

Identify, define or state the importance of each of the following.
1. James Wright
2. Stamp Act
3. Button Gwinnett
4. Sons of Liberty
5. Whigs
6. Intolerable Acts
7. Patriots
8. Second Provincial Congress
9. Elijah Clarke
10. Tories
11. Henry Ellis
12. Second Continental Congress

The Main Idea

Write a short paragraph to answer each question.
1. Why was Georgia reluctant to become involved in the revolutionary war?
2. Describe the three parts of the Declaration of Independence. Why was each part important?
3. Compare and contrast Georgia as an early colony with Georgia during the revolutionary war years.
4. Identify at least three causes of the American Revolution.

Extend Your Thinking

Write a short paragraph to discuss each question.
1. If you had lived in Georgia in 1772, would you have been a Patriot or a Tory? Defend your response.
2. Suppose the British ships had broken through the French lines before Cornwallis surrendered at Yorktown. What might have happened and how would it have affected you today?
3. Why do you think so few battles were fought on Georgia soil?

Map Skills

Which Georgia counties were renamed during the revolutionary period? Using a map of the counties of Georgia, shade each of these counties.

Looking Ahead

Chapter Five examines life in Georgia after the American Revolution. You will read how our present-day American system of democratic government came about. As you study the chapter, you'll learn:

- ➤ how the Yazoo Land Fraud brought scandal to the state;
- ➤ what sport was most popular with Georgians;
- ➤ how many Georgians obtained free land by the spin of a wheel;
- ➤ why Eli Whitney's visit to Georgia changed the South;
- ➤ how Crawford W. Long changed life for those who have to face surgery.

DID YOU KNOW . . .

. . . Henry Ellis, Georgia's second royal governor, died in Naples, Italy on January 21, 1800, at the age of seventy nine?

. . . The *Georgia Gazette* was in publication for only two years because of the Stamp Act?

. . . The signatures of Button Gwinnett, Lyman Hall and George Walton appear first on the Declaration of Independence despite the fact that Georgia was the last colony to join the revolutionary effort?

. . . An autograph of Gwinnett is one of the most expensive collector's autographs in the world priced at over $250,000.

. . . All three signers of the Declaration of Independence (below) from Georgia have counties named in their honor?

. . . Other Georgia counties named after revolutionary war heroes include Greene, Jasper, Lincoln, Newton, Paulding, Pulaski (named for Count Casimir Pulaski, (above) who died on the American side at the siege of Savannah), Washington, Wayne and Hart?

. . . George Walton, at age twenty six, was the youngest signer of the Declaration of Independence?

. . . Patriots in Massachusetts were called "Minutemen" because they could be ready to fight in a minute?

. . . At one point during the revolutionary period, the Georgia Liberty Boys wanted to hang Governor James Wright?

. . . Fort Frederica on St. Simons Island was the most costly British fort built in North America?

. . . Out of 282,000 men in the 13 colonies, George Washington never had an army numbering over 25,000?

UNIT III

THE NATION BECOMES UNITED

1783 -1838

We the People of the United States, in Order to form a more perfect Union, establish Justice, insure domestic Tranquility, provide for the common defense, promote the general Welfare, and secure the Blessings of Liberty to ourselves and our Posterity, do ordain and establish this Constitution for the United States of America.

— Preamble to the Constitution of the United States

The cost of freedom was high. In addition to losing farm crops, some revolutionary war soldiers returned home only to find that they had no place left to live.

THE FIGHTING WAS OVER, and the United States was a free country. However, in Georgia, years of hardship and change followed the Revolution. Many of her men had left their farms to fight, so there had not been much food grown. One of the first jobs of state government was to see that families in need had items such as flour and corn meal until they could plant and harvest a crop.

The paper money Congress issued during the war years was worth almost nothing. Prices of goods went up all over the United States. In some parts of the country, a pound of tea cost a hundred dollars. Soldiers, who had been promised twenty-two cents a day to fight in the Revolution, were not paid. Some sold their farms to try to settle debts.

Many of Georgia's rice and indigo plantations that had done well before the war were in ruins when it was over. When the British left Savannah toward the end of the war, 1,000 Loyalists went with

them. Together, they took thousands of British pounds sterling, and 4,000 to 6,000 slaves and indentured servants. The state had no money to pay its huge war debts, and few citizens had money to pay taxes.

There were questions about who owned land. Tories, who had remained loyal to England, had their lands taken away during the pre-revolutionary period. When the British were in charge of the state during the war, they returned land to the Tories. After the war, lands were again taken from them and given to former soldiers. In some cases, two or three families said they owned the same piece of land. It took time to decide which family would keep the land.

It was years before Georgia recovered from the Revolution. However, by 1787, Georgians had joined citizens of the other colonies in working toward founding a new nation.

The Second Continental Congress was in session at various times from May 10, 1775 through March 1, 1781 as lawmakers patiently, and sometimes in heated argument, hammered out the fine points of the nation's proposed new government.

CHAPTER FIVE

GEORGIA AS PART OF A NEW COUNTRY
1783-1820

Congress shall make no law respecting an establishment of religion, or prohibiting the free exercise thereof; or abridging the freedom of speech, or of the press; or the right of the people peaceably to assemble, and to petition the Government for a redress of grievances.

— Amendment I, Constitution of the United States

Above: The newly formed state of Georgia also boasted a new seal. On the front was a scroll of the Georgia Constitution. At the bottom were the Latin words, Pro bono publico, which meant "for the good of the public." On the reverse side of the seal the images signified the agricultural and commercial endeavors set forth for the state. Opposite page: James Madison, called the "Father of the Constitution." He became our fourth president.

GOVERNMENT IN THE NEW NATION

THE THIRTEEN STATES fought hard to become independent from England, but they were still not a united nation. The country was governed by the Second Continental Congress during the war years. In 1781, the Articles of Confederation and Perpetual Union were ratified. This provided a general government to bring about the union of the new states.

THE ARTICLES OF CONFEDERATION

Under the Articles of Confederation, the government had a unicameral, or single house, legislature. Each state, no matter what its size and population had only one vote in this legislature.

The Legislature had little power. It could declare war, coin money, establish post offices, and send or recall ambassadors to other nations. However, there was much the Legislature could not do. Most importantly, it could not **levy** taxes to fund a national

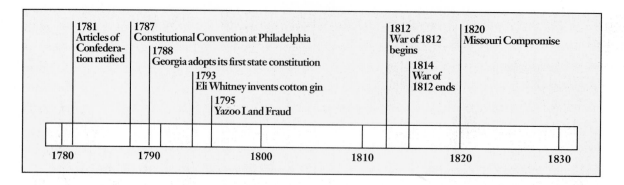

| 1781 Articles of Confederation ratified | 1787 Constitutional Convention at Philadelphia | | 1812 War of 1812 begins | 1820 Missouri Compromise |

1788
Georgia adopts its first state constitution

1793
Eli Whitney invents cotton gin

1795
Yazoo Land Fraud

1814
War of 1812 ends

1780   1790   1800   1810   1820   1830

government. Instead, it had to ask states for money. The states had spent a large amount to pay soldiers, buy weapons, and feed troops during the war. They had little left to give the national government.

The national Legislature also could not regulate, or control, the trade of goods between one state and another or between a state and other countries. Each state set its own **tariffs** for goods they shipped and, often, state tariffs were unfair.

Finally, the Legislature could pass laws, but could not set up a national court system to enforce them. The Articles of Confederation were not strong enough to make the thirteen separate colonies into one nation.

THE CONSTITUTIONAL CONVENTION

In the summer of 1787, fifty-five delegates, representing every state except Rhode Island, met in Philadelphia to revise the Articles of Confederation. This constitutional convention was a secret, "closed-door" meeting. Some people reported that raised, angry voices could often be heard by those outside. Several delegates went home before the convention completed its work. In the end, only thirty-nine men decided how to form the government under a constitution.

For four months, men who had led the nation during the Revolution were again called on to lead. George Washington was chairman of the convention. Alexander Hamilton and eighty-one-year-old Benjamin Franklin worked for government that was both strong and fair. James Madison, later called the "Father of the Constitution," drafted much of the final document. Delegates presented more than one plan. The group narrowed their choices to the Virginia Plan and the New Jersey Plan.

Left: *The first name on the new Constitution was that of George Washington. His leadership prompted his peers to elect him to serve as the first United States President.* **Top:** *Alexander Hamilton served on Washington's staff during the war. From 1789-1795, he served the new nation as secretary of the treasury.* **Above:** *Eighty-one-year-old Benjamin Franklin was the oldest and most famous member of the Constitutional Convention.*

The Virginia Plan

Governor Edmund Randolph of Virginia proposed what became known as the Virginia, or large-state plan. The plan provided for a bicameral, or two house, national legislature. Membership in the legislature would be based on the free population of each state. Members of the lower house would be elected by qualified voters. State legislatures would select members of the upper house. The legislature, or Congress, would choose the chief executive, make laws that affected all the states, and set up a system of courts.

The Virginia Plan would give the national government more power than the individual states. Representatives of smaller states thought the plan would give the states with the largest populations control of Congress.

Virginia governor, Edmund Randolph, proposed a plan at the convention that provided three separate branches of government. He also proposed that the number of representatives in Congress would be based on the population of each state. His proposal led to the present-day system of checks and balances in our form of government.

The New Jersey Plan

Some small states supported the New Jersey Plan, which would keep the government much as it had been under the Articles of Confederation. Under this plan, the legislature would be unicameral, and each state would have the same number of representatives in Congress. The plan was different from the Articles of Confederation in that it allowed Congress to tax the nation's citizens. The national government would also be able to regulate interstate and international trade.

THE GREAT COMPROMISE

For a while, it looked as though the convention would not be able to settle on a constitution. Finally, delegates from Connecticut took ideas from both plans and put them together in what was later called the Great Compromise. According to this plan: 1) The upper house of the legislature would be the Senate and would have two elected members from each state in the union; and 2) the lower house would be the House of Representatives and states would elect members to it based on their population.

Delegates to the convention agreed to this **compromise**, and the beginning of the new central government was in place. Differences among the delegates did not, however, end with the Great Compromise. They had to settle many details before the work of the convention was finished.

OTHER ISSUES OF THE CONVENTION

Southerners wanted to know how slaves would affect a state's population. After much debate, the delegates agreed that three-fifths of the slaves could be counted. This was known as the "Three-Fifths Compromise." For example, Georgia had about 29,500 slaves in 1790, so she could count 17,700 slaves in the state's official population. This increased both her number of members in the House of Representatives and the amount of her federal tax.

Another matter which convention delegates had to settle was how states would select members of Congress. The convention agreed that states would choose members of the House of Representatives by popular vote, and state legislatures would select senators. The President would be chosen by electoral votes. Each state would select the same number of electors as it had members of Congress.

States who had slaves wanted slave trading allowed for the next twenty years. They also asked for a national law which provided for the return of runaway slaves. The delegates agreed to these requests.

Another compromise had to do with a tax on exports. The delegates said they would not tax any products shipped to other countries.

One major matter the delegates worked on was how to divide power in the government. They decided to organize three separate branches of government: Executive (the President), Legislative (the Congress), and Judicial (the court system). They also agreed on a system of checks and balances. Each branch would have its own job to do, and would have a way to keep the other two from having too much power.

A PLAN FOR THE FUTURE

The delegates knew that, as the United States grew, the Constitution would need some changes. They made a way to amend, or change, the Constitution without having to rewrite it. Only a few years after the Constitution was written, ten **amendments**, called the Bill of Rights, were added.

With the work finished, the delegates signed papers that are the world's oldest written national constitution. Among them were Abraham Baldwin and William Few from Georgia.

Abraham Baldwin (top) and William Few (above) were two of Georgia's delegates to the Constitutional Convention. Both were signers of the Constitution.

George Washington served two terms as President of the new nation. Pictured here is Washington arriving for his second inauguration in 1793. While President, Washington sought to bring about unity at home and neutrality abroad. In 1797, he left government service and retired to his beloved Mt. Vernon in Virginia.

Only nine states had to ratify the Constitution for it to become official. By the end of 1788, eleven of the states had ratified it. North Carolina in 1789 and Rhode Island in 1790 were the last two states to ratify the Constitution. Georgia, the fourth state, adopted it on a cold Wednesday, January 2, 1788. It was an important beginning to a new year.

On August 30, 1789, George Washington became the first President of the United States.

GEORGIA ADOPTS A NEW STATE CONSTITUTION

The capital of Georgia was moved to Augusta in 1785. During 1788 and 1789, delegates met there to make changes in the state constitution. When they were made, the Georgia Constitution was very much like the one for the United States. The state would have a bicameral general assembly to include a senate and a house of representatives. Members would be elected by popular vote, and those members would select the state's governor.

Do You Remember?

1. When did the constitutional convention meet?
2. What were three powers the national Legislature did not have under the Articles of Confederation?
3. What was the New Jersey Plan?
4. What was the Virginia Plan?
5. What form of legislature did the Great Compromise suggest?
6. Why did southern states want the three-fifths compromise?
7. What other compromise affected slavery?
8. How did the delegates make sure the Constitution could be changed to meet future needs?
9. When did Georgia ratify the Constitution?
10. What Georgians signed the Constitution?
11. Where was Georgia's capital located?
12. Under Georgia's 1789 Constitution, how was the governor elected?

THE FEVER FOR LAND IN THE NEW NATION

While people were moving into the frontier areas of Georgia, the whole nation was growing. Thomas Jefferson became President in 1801. A few years later, the Louisiana Territory was bought from France for $15,000,000. Adding that land extended the United States from the Mississippi River west to the Rocky Mountains.

In 1808, the nation elected James Madison as its fourth President. While he was in office, the War of 1812 began between the United States and England. The war came about because the British kept trying to take American ships. She also would not allow trading vessels from America to reach French ports.

Many Americans blamed English citizens who lived in Canada for the growing number of Indian attacks on the new nation's frontiers. To some people, these two matters were excuse enough to go to war with England. What most Americans wanted, however, was to take Canada and make it a part of the United States.

Thomas Jefferson, author of the Declaration of Independence, continued to serve his country as Vice President under John Adams and as the nation's President in 1801. Jefferson was also an inventor, scientist, musician and architect.

The Battle of New Orleans was a stunning victory for the United States. Unknown to the two armies, the treaty to end the War of 1812 had been signed in Paris two weeks earlier. In this depiction, General Andrew Jackson commands American troops from his white charger.

Most citizens of the United States were not sure the war was wise, and were not prepared to fight. The war lasted about two years, with neither side making any headway. Both sides grew weary of the war and were glad to make peace. A treaty was signed in 1814, which restored everything to what it had been before the war.

The United States got no new land from the War of 1812, but she gained in other ways: 1) Older nations started to pay attention to the young country; 2) The separate states began to feel united into one nation; 3) Industry grew and, by 1815, the United States could supply many of its own needs, such as iron, textiles, wood, glassware, leather, and pottery; 4) The Indians had been defeated and pushed out of the northwest and southwest territories. This left the national frontier open for future growth. Near the middle of the century, all over the United States, there was a fever for land.

THE GREED FOR LAND IN GEORGIA

Before and during the revolutionary war with England, many Georgians were not sure if they wanted to be loyal to England or to the new nation. However, during the late 1700s and early 1800s, there was little question about what Georgians wanted. They wanted land!

During the settlement of the colony, much of the land which came from the Indians was given to settlers under the Headright System. Each white male counted as a "head" and could receive up to 1,000 acres. Parts of this system lasted until the early Twentieth century, but it was largely replaced by a land lottery. Land east of the Oconee River was distributed through the Headright System.

When public **domain** lands (land which belonged to the state or federal government) were opened for settlement, Georgia surveyed land lots of different sizes. This "lottery land" was located west of the Oconee River. For a small fee, any white male twenty-one years of age or older could buy a chance and, on the spin of a wheel, win land. Heads of households with children, war veterans, and widows were given extra chances in the land lotteries. Other states also had lotteries, and about thirty million acres of land were given away through them.

The Yazoo Land Fraud

Georgians' growing greed for land reached a peak in 1795 with the Yazoo Land Fraud. At that time, Georgia's western borders

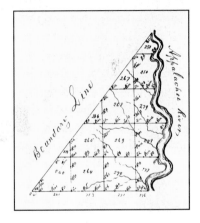

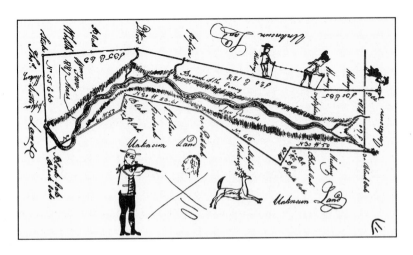

Pictured above is a survey plan of lottery lots in the portion of Baldwin County where Milledgeville is located. The plat (a map of the land area) shown at the left, is a layout of a headright grant. Boundaries were shown by naming the types of trees on the property.

were the Mississippi River and one of its **tributaries,** the Yazoo River, which was named for an Indian tribe. This included the states now known as Mississippi and Alabama. South Carolina and Spain thought they owned some of the same land, and had carried the matter to court for settlement.

However, before any settlement was made, four land companies worked on members of the Georgia General Assembly and Governor George Matthews. They offered stock and pieces of land if the assembly would pass a bill so the western lands could be sold. When the governor and assembly agreed, between thirty-five and fifty million acres of land were sold for a half million dollars: about one and one-half cents an acre. Before long, the public learned of this, and there were protests all over the state.

Newspaper articles were printed telling what the legislators had done. Grand juries met to look into both the law and the land sales. Many citizens called for the resignations of legislators involved in the Yazoo scheme.

As a result of public anger and pressure, the bill which allowed the land to be sold was repealed. The legislators involved were thrown out of office. All records of these land sales were burned in public at Louisville, which had become the state capital of Georgia in 1796.

Money from the land sales was returned to the state treasury. However, there were people who were not part of the original scheme, who had bought some of the land. These citizens wanted to keep that land, and it was nineteen years before all the claims were settled.

Above: George Matthews served twice as governor of Georgia. During his second term, he became embroiled in the Yazoo Land Fraud. **Right:** This map shows the disputed Yazoo lands in what are now the states of Alabama and Mississippi.

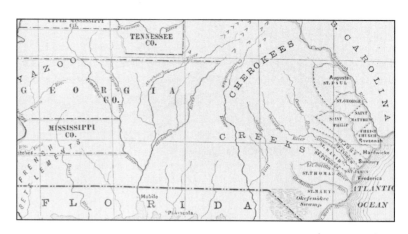

When news of the Yazoo Land Fraud became public, citizens were enraged. Land sale documents were seized and burned by a group of angry Georgians. A monument was later erected in Louisville to mark the site of the first permanent state capital of Georgia, and of the public burning of the Yazoo land papers on February 15, 1796.

GEORGIA CEDES WESTERN LAND

Georgia ceded its land west of the Chattahoochee River to the federal government for one and a quarter million dollars, making the river Georgia's western boundary. By 1814, Congress had agreed to pay over four hundred thousand dollars to settle Yazoo land claims. Georgia lost a large part of its land and a lot of money because of the Yazoo scheme. Several public officials were removed from office. To settle the land disputes, the government agreed to remove Indians who still lived in Georgia. This agreement led to a tragedy now known as the "Trail of Tears."

Do You Remember?
1. What was the Headright system?
2. What other method did Georgia state government use to distribute land?
3. What were three results of the Yazoo fraud?
4. Who could take part in Georgia's land lotteries?

Once the back-breaking job of picking cotton had been completed, the cotton had to be separated from the rounded seed pod, by hand. This was a very slow process requiring a lot of workers.

ECONOMIC DEVELOPMENTS IN GEORGIA

Cotton and tobacco were the major crops in Georgia after the Revolution. In the next thirty years, cotton would become "King" in the south. This would greatly change the lives of black and white Georgians.

COTTON GIN INVENTED IN GEORGIA

In 1793, Eli Whitney visited the home of Mrs. Catherine Greene Miller at Mulberry Grove Plantation near Savannah. Whitney, a friend of the family from New England, was a school teacher and an inventor.

As the story goes, Mrs. Miller asked Whitney to repair a broken watch, which he agreed to do. Not long afterward, a caller at the Miller home wished aloud for a machine to separate cotton fiber from its seed. Mrs. Miller, remembering the watch repair, asked Whitney if he could make a machine which could do the job done so slowly by hand.

After several weeks of work, Whitney presented a model of his cotton machine. He made the machine (later called a gin) with wire teeth on a turning cylinder. It could separate cotton seed, but the lint got caught in the wire teeth and stopped the machine from working. Several legends say that Mrs. Miller saw the machine's problem, took a clothes brush, and brushed the lint off the teeth. We do not know how much help Mrs. Miller really gave Whitney. However, before long, he had built a factory near Augusta and had a working cotton gin.

Cotton growers welcomed Whitney's gin. A worker could separate six or seven pounds of cotton seed a day by hand. Farmers who used the cotton gin could prepare about fifty pounds a day. Whitney's invention paid him well. However, he was poor when he died because there were so many lawsuits over the patent for the gin. The gin has been improved over the years, but the central working part is still much as it was in Whitney's original invention.

OTHER IMPROVEMENTS IN FARMING

Cyrus McCormick showed how to use the first grain reaper in Virginia. The reaper had wooden paddles fastened to the harness of a horse. As the farmer guided the horse through his fields, the

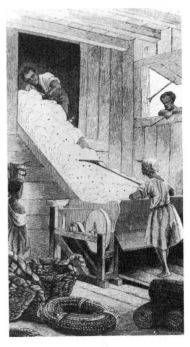

Left: *In addition to building the first cotton gin, Eli Whitney also established the first factory to assemble muskets, or guns, with interchangeable parts. This was the first known example of mass production in America.* **Top and above:** *The cotton gin (gin was short for engine) was cheap and easy to make, but it revolutionized the farming of cotton in the South.*

Cyrus McCormick (below) first demonstrated his grain reaper (right) at a local fair in the Shenandoah Valley of Virginia in 1831. He did not secure a patent for his reaper until 1834 when a competitor announced a similar invention. To help the farmers buy the machine that cut down the fields of wheat, McCormick allowed them to pay him on an installment plan.

paddles turned and cut the grain. Using it, a farmer could cut six times more grain in a day than with a scythe. The cotton gin and grain reaper led to larger and more profitable farms.

Improved ways of farming helped Georgia's economy become strong after the Revolution. However, an **inflationary** boom that suddenly ended caused the Panic of 1837. The **depression** that followed lasted into the early 1840s. During the depression years, many businesses failed, and many farmers and planters lost their land. Most banks did not have enough cash to pay out money that had been deposited with them. These were forced to close for good. At the height of the depression, only eleven banks were open in Georgia.

TRANSPORTATION

One important economic development during the early 1800s was the building of railroads. Before railroads were built, people rode on horses, boats, or stagecoaches. Freight was sent to market by riverboat ferries or wagon trains. Passengers could go to most Georgia towns from Savannah by stagecoach. Stagecoaches ran regularly from Savannah to Athens in the north and Brunswick in the south. A main stage line connected Augusta and Columbus by way of Macon, but the coaches could only cover thirty to forty miles a day.

Left: Before railroads, passengers ride on stagecoaches. *Above:* An early locomotive. *Below:* A map of Indian trails, which became roads used by settlers.

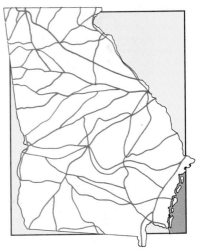

Many of Georgia's roads were stage trails cut where Indian footpaths had been. Roads in wet, swampy places had logs across them and were known as "plank roads." The federal government had some major highways built in the early 1800s. These roads were called turnpikes because they had toll gates known as "pikes." Travelers had to pay a fee at each pike to remain on the road. Among these turnpikes was the Old Federal Road. It was built in 1815 to run from Athens northward through Cherokee Indian territory into Tennessee. However, even the "good" roads were poor until the late 1800s.

Rail travel was, perhaps, the least favored means of transportation. In 1830, there were only thirteen miles of laid track. These belonged to the Baltimore and Ohio Railroad. By 1840, there were 3,300 miles of track. Most of this track belonged to the first state-owned railroad, the Western and Atlantic. The Western and Atlantic ran from Atlanta to Chattanooga.

Do You Remember?
1. Who was Eli Whitney?
2. Who showed how to use the first grain reaper?
3. Name two economic changes of the post-revolutionary period.
4. What were turnpikes?

THE ISSUE OF SLAVERY

Georgia's original charter in 1732 did not allow slavery. However, as land holdings grew in size, landowners needed help to work their fields. They asked the Trustees to allow them to import slaves and, not long before the Trustees left the state, they agreed.

The **institution** of slavery in North America began in 1619. A Dutch trader brought sixty blacks to Virginia to work in the tobacco fields. At first, blacks and some whites were indentured servants. They agreed to work for a time, usually five to six years, after which they could do as they wished. However, by the mid-1600s, there were laws that made indentured servants slaves for life.

SLAVE TRADING

People who traded slaves learned they could make a lot of money in this business. They began by going to Africa to get blacks to sell in the colonies. Traders tried to capture the strongest men and women in a village. In some cases, members of one African tribe would catch members of other tribes and sell them to slave traders for trinkets, blankets, or rum. There were also cases where a person who had broken a tribal law was sold as punishment. Sometimes, traders chained hundreds of Africans together and placed them in crowded ships going to the colonies. Some historians have said that at least one chained tribe chose to walk into the sea and drown rather than get on a waiting slave ship.

After Eli Whitney invented the cotton gin in 1793, farmers began to grow more cotton. They needed workers to plant, cultivate, and harvest this crop, so slave trading grew. Thousands of families were split up. Sometimes, even tribal kings whose families had ruled for hundreds of years were put in fields to hoe cotton.

Slave trading ships docked in places like New Orleans, Charleston, and Savannah. Traders led the blacks to auction blocks and sold them to the highest bidder. During the slave trading years, prices ranged from a few hundred dollars to over a thousand.

Once owners bought slaves, they moved them to their farms or plantations. Most of the slaves could not speak or understand English. Members of families and tribes were often sold to different owners. Since there were so many African tribal languages,

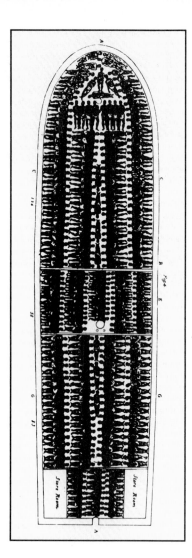

To make the slave trade even more profitable, ships like the one seen here wedged several hundred slaves into the hull of the vessel in inhumane conditions. This diagram of a slave ship was first published in 1789.

American slave ships like the Martha *increased in numbers as the trading of slaves became very profitable. The addition of slave labor made the plantations of the agricultural South more successful, allowing them to become larger.*

it was possible a new slave would not be able to talk with anyone who worked with him. It was thought this would help prevent slave uprisings.

SLAVE UPRISINGS

There were many more blacks than whites on large farms and plantations. Owners took care to see that slaves had no chance to rise up against their masters. It was hard for a group of slaves on one farm to get messages to groups in other places.

When a slave left his plantation, he either went with the owner or overseer, or had to have a pass. Passes stated where a slave could go and when he must be back, so secret meetings were almost impossible.

Laws, called Slave Codes, took away nearly all the rights of slaves. It was against the law for them to testify against whites, make any type of contact, hit a white, or carry a weapon. On some plantations, overseers counted hoes, pitchforks, and shovels at the end of the day so they could not be kept for use as weapons.

Slaves had little time to talk together. They were watched every day except Sundays, and on holidays like Christmas, New Year's Day, and the Fourth of July. Even some free blacks who owned slaves kept a careful eye on them. However, all the attention given by owners was not enough to stop some uprisings.

In 1800, the year Nat Turner was born, Gabriel Prosser

A preacher, Nat Turner, was known as a mild-mannered man who worked as a slave in Southhampton, Virginia. On Sunday, August 21, 1831, Turner led a small group of men through the countryside killing about 60 whites. For the next two months he hid in woods and swamps until his capture. He was taken to Jerusalem, Virginia and hanged on November 11, 1831.

gathered several thousand slaves. The plan was to attack Richmond, Virginia at midnight on August 30. A few hours before the planned attack, two slaves told their owners about the planned uprising. The owners reported it to the authorities. Prosser, not knowing he had been betrayed, was prevented from invading Richmond by an intense thunderstorm. He was arrested and executed along with thirty-four others.

Some reports say that, in 1822, Denmark Vesey, who had bought his freedom, gathered 9,000 slaves to take Charleston, South Carolina. However, he was betrayed and his plan failed. In 1831, Nat Turner led an attack in Virginia and killed more than sixty whites. Turner and twenty others were killed, but fear of uprisings spread.

POLITICAL IMPACT OF SLAVERY

The first serious disagreement between pro-slavery and anti-slavery forces was in 1819 and 1820. By the end of 1819, there were eleven slave states and eleven free states. The number of members a state had in the United States House of Representatives depended on its population. Population in the North was growing rapidly. Southerners were afraid that Northern states would soon have more influence in Congress. In 1820, as Maine and Missouri prepared to enter the Union, Congress tried to decide whether future states would be slave or free.

After much discussion, Northern and Southern congressional leaders reached an agreement. This Compromise of 1820 became known as the Missouri Compromise. Maine came into the Union as a free state. Missouri, which was part of the 828,000-square-mile Louisiana Purchase, was admitted as a slave state. The Compromise stated there would be no slavery north of 36° 20' latitude. This included any lands west of the southern boundary of Missouri. For the time being, the question of slavery was at rest, but it was only a temporary solution to the questions of slavery and territorial rights.

Do You Remember?
1. What did Georgia's original charter say about slavery?
2. What port in Georgia was used by slave-trading ships?
3. What were the Slave Codes?
4. What did Gabriel Prosser, Denmark Vesey, and Nat Turner have in common?

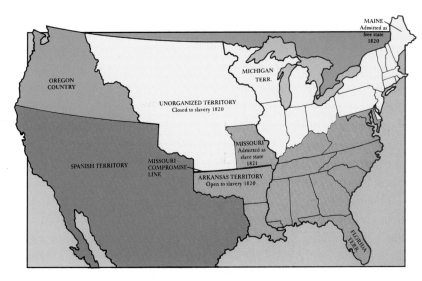

This map of the Missouri Compromise of 1820 shows the free and slave states after Missouri was admitted to the Union as a slave state. Maine was to enter as a free state at the same time. Both the North and South celebrated victory over the Compromise, but as Thomas Jefferson stated, the compromise was "a reprieve only and not a final sentence."

Top: As the frontier expanded, so did the number of settlements such as this one on the Chattahoochee River. *Above:* Frontier women had to be both brave and industrious, and most of what the frontier families had, they made for themselves.

LIFE IN GEORGIA AT THE TURN OF THE CENTURY

THE FRONTIER LIFE

There were two different sides to Georgia in the late 1700s and early 1800s: its towns and the frontier. Frontier Georgia was undeveloped land in the central and western parts of the state which had few settlers. Most of this land had been given away through the lottery system. Adventurers from settled towns, such as Savannah and Augusta, wanted the excitement of frontier life. Some frontier settlers migrated from other states. They came over rough ground on roads that were little more than trails cut through thick brush and forests. Many of these roads had been cleared by Indian tribes who once lived in the area. A map of Georgia's present-day highways compared to a map of early Indian trails shows how much alike they are.

During the early days on the frontier, trading posts located many miles apart were the only stores. Men were known for fighting, hard drinking, and hunting. Thirty years later, the frontier was dotted with farms, trading posts, taverns and, sometimes, a one-room school.

LIFE IN GEORGIA'S TOWNS

Life in Georgia's towns was quite different from life on the frontier. The *Augusta Herald* and Savannah's *Gazette of the State of Georgia* were the two leading newspapers in the state. Newspapers were also published in Louisville, Athens, Sparta, and Milledgeville. Savannah had a theater where citizens could see Shakespeare's plays, and those by newer writers. It was popular to be a member of a debating society, go to concerts, or be a member of a library society. People attended fancy dress balls and informal gatherings such as barbecues and camp meetings. Horse racing drew large crowds in Augusta. Purses, or winnings, were as high as five hundred dollars, a large amount of money in 1785.

Foods served to guests were simple. Beef, pork, and wild game were popular, and seafood, including shrimp, oysters, and fish, was a favorite. Garden vegetables and sweet potatoes were served as side dishes. Many of the recipes used in southern homes today are the same as those enjoyed during the early 1800s.

Communities took care to provide for those with special needs. Orphanages cared for children without parents. A hospital for the mentally insane was opened in Milledgeville, a school for the deaf at Cave Springs, and the Georgia Academy for the Blind in Macon.

Those who could read enjoyed the humor of Augustus Baldwin, who wrote about life on the frontier.

Bottom: Horse racing offered town-dwellers a relaxing alternative to the usual work week and was one of the popular social activities of the period. *Below:* A town-dweller's pantry might contain meats, seafood and vegetables, as well as a variety of wild game.

RELIGION

After the war, many ministers loyal to England had gone there to live. Still, southern churches grew, both in size and in importance to their communities. In addition to the established Quakers and Baptists, Methodist circuit riders began churches in the frontier region. Sometimes these ministers could have only one service a month for each church. However, they stayed in touch with the members and visited them as often as possible.

In 1787, the Springfield Baptist Church was founded by free blacks. It is still located on the original site. The First African Baptist Church in Savannah was founded in 1788 under the leadership of Andrew Bryan. Church and social activities provided members of the black community with opportunities to share news and openly discuss problems and concerns.

A Jewish Synagogue in Savannah had a small, but committed, membership. Georgia's first Roman Catholic Church was established in 1796 in Wilkes County. A second congregation was formed in 1801 in Savannah.

During the first ten years of the 1800s, towns such as Athens, Monroe, Monticello, Jefferson, Madison, and Milledgeville came into being. As in Savannah and Augusta on the coast, churches were part of town life. They had Sunday and weekday worship services, and their buildings were often used for town meetings and social events.

Above: Rainy weather had little effect on Methodist preachers who traveled a circuit, or territory, which could easily cover 500 miles. ***Right:*** *The First African Baptist Church in Savannah, founded in 1788, is thought to be the first African-American church in the United States. Its present structure, pictured here, was completed in 1859.*

EDUCATION

Educational growth was slow during the post-revolutionary war period. Governor Lyman Hall recommended that the state set aside land for schools, but few were built. Some people received only a few years of elementary education. Often even the best farmers knew little, if anything, about reading or mathematics. Most of Georgia's citizens had not been to school at all.

Even though the building of schools was slow, people believed in the value of education. In 1784, the government set aside twenty thousand acres of land and named trustees to establish a state college for Georgia. The University of Georgia was chartered as a land grant university (a school for which the federal government gave public land) in 1785, and is the oldest school of its kind in the nation. The university, which was to oversee all public schools in

Founded in 1783 in Augusta, the Richmond Academy was Georgia's first public school. When President George Washington spent a week visiting Georgia in 1791, he was so impressed with the welcoming speeches made by students from Richmond Academy that he sent every child a book after he had returned to the nation's capital.

Above: Schoolrooms in 1830 were a far cry from today. Students of all ages were taught together in one room with limited materials.
Below: The University of Georgia was chartered in 1785 as the nation's first land grant university.
Opposite page: The Stewart County Academy, built in 1832, is typical of county schools of the period. It has been reconstructed at Westville.

the state, did not open for classes until 1801. Franklin College was the first building for the all-male, all-white student body. For many years, the University of Georgia was most often called Franklin College.

In 1786, the Georgia legislature passed a law requiring each county to open **academies,** or schools. However, they did not set aside money to build them. In 1820, there were only forty academies in the state. In 1822, some members of the legislature tried to get money for public schools, but failed. However, money was placed in a special "state fund" to pay for the education of poor children.

In the early schools, such as the Academy of Richmond County founded in 1783, male students studied Greek, Latin, grammar, and mathematics. Females were taught the arts and music. The Georgia Female College, later known as Wesleyan College, opened in Macon in 1836. The girls there had classes in French, literature and science education. Tuition was $50.00 a year, unless a student also wanted to study piano, art or foreign languages. Piano lessons cost $17.00 a quarter, art lessons $3.00 a year, and foreign languages, such as Greek, Latin, Spanish or Italian, $5.00 each. Room and board was $15.00 a quarter, and there were extra charges for washing and candles.

The cost does not seem great by today's standards, but only the wealthier merchants and large land owners had enough money to send their daughters to Wesleyan. Many Georgia citizens saw no value in teaching females academic subjects, no matter what it cost. Instead, many young girls were taught sewing, cooking, child care, and music.

TWO GEORGIAS

There were two Georgias during this period: the settled life of growing towns and the adventurous life of the frontier. It was a period of social growth. Organized churches increased, and there was more opportunity for formal education. The University of Georgia was chartered in 1785.

For Georgians, the period from 1782 to 1820 ended in much the same way it had begun: in a search for more land. After the War of 1812, Indians were pushed out of the northern and southwestern

A GEORGIAN DISCOVERS ETHER

A scientific discovery made in Georgia on Wednesday, March 10, 1842, changed medicine forever. Dr. Crawford W. Long, a physician in Jefferson, Georgia, used ether as anesthesia for the first time during surgery to remove tumors from a patient.

Before the use of ether, patients who needed surgery had two main choices. They could die from not having the operation or they could drink large amounts of alcohol to try to numb their senses. Many times, the alcohol was more dangerous than the surgery. Sometimes, doctors knocked their patients unconscious to do surgery. Word spread quickly that Dr. Long could offer his patients surgery without pain.

Crawford W. Long did not publish his discovery. Four years later, Dr. William Morton of Boston also began using ether on his patients. He published the results in medical journals, and is called the inventor of surgical anesthesia. That does not change the fact that Georgia is the state where ether was used as anesthesia for the first time.

Above: Born in Danielsville, Georgia in 1815, Dr. Crawford Williamson Long studied medicine in Philadelphia and New York.
Right: After conducting experiments with sulfuric ether, Dr. Long began using the mixture during surgery at his office in Jefferson, Georgia. The resulting "painless operations" revolutionized medicine.

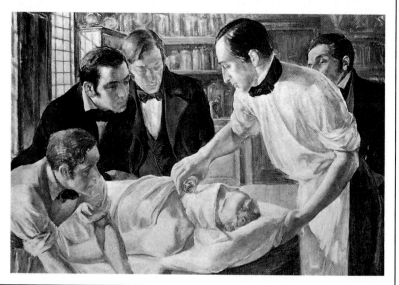

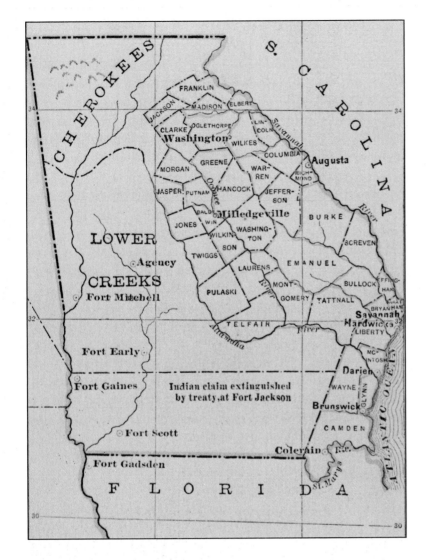

This map of Georgia in 1820 shows the "two Georgias:" the blending of settled towns and communities as they merged with the frontier lands occupied by Georgia's earliest residents, the Indians.

territories. That left those parts of the United States open for expansion. After the Yazoo Land Fraud, the state looked north for expansion into lands which belonged to the Creek and Cherokee Indians.

Do You Remember?
1. Name two social pastimes favored in Georgia's towns.
2. Where was the First African Baptist Church founded?
3. When did the University of Georgia open to male students?
4. What were the "two Georgias" after the revolution?

CHAPTER REVIEW

Summary

From 1782 to 1820, thirteen colonies united to form one strong nation under a central government as outlined in the United States Constitution. The new country extended her frontiers westward because of the Louisiana Purchase and the War of 1812.

Georgia was the fourth colony to ratify the new national constitution. She adopted a state constitution using the same bicameral form of government used for the United States. During this period, the main interest of Georgians was getting land.

Citizens in the towns and on the frontier took part in land lotteries and the "Headright" system to get property. The Yazoo Land Fraud in 1795, ended with the loss of all Georgia lands west of the Chattahoochee River.

The invention of the cotton gin gave major economic help to the state, whose main industry was the growing of cotton and tobacco. As the need for slave labor grew in the South, slavery became a political and social issue. In 1619, Virginia became the first state to have slaves. Georgians began to use African slaves on a limited basis in 1752.

Slavery became a political issue in 1820. The Missouri Compromise was an effort in the United States Congress to keep a balance between slave and free states. Maine came into the Union as a free state and Missouri as a slave state. A dividing line was also established. This line was the westward extension of Missouri's southern boundary across the entire Louisiana Purchase. In the future, all states north of the line would be free states and states south of the line would allow slavery.

A need to move cotton and tobacco to northeastern markets led to the building of highways and railroads. Improved transportation meant ships could unload at coastal seaports and have their freight shipped to other parts of the country. Both the inland agricultural areas and the coastal seaports prospered as the railroads grew.

People, Places, and Terms

Identify, define or state the importance of the following.

1. Governor Lyman Hall
2. amendments
3. Yazoo Land Fraud
4. Cyrus McCormick
5. separation of powers
6. University of Georgia
7. Eli Whitney
8. Denmark Vesey

The Main Idea

Write a short paragraph to answer each of the following questions.

1. Why did Georgia have such a hard time after the American Revolution? Give at least four examples.
2. List the three compromises dealing with slavery that were reached at the Constitutional Convention. Explain why you think that these compromises would be important in 1860 when the Civil War began.
3. Why was the invention of the cotton gin and the grain reaper important to Georgia's economy?
4. Describe the differences between the lives of Georgians living on the frontier and those living in towns, such as Augusta and Savannah.
5. What is a land grant college?

Extend Your Thinking

1. How would the practice of medicine be different today without the discovery of ether by Dr. Crawford W. Long or Dr. William Morton?

Looking Ahead

Georgians continued to want more land for farming, gold mining and the settling of new towns. Much of the unsettled land in Georgia, however, belonged to the Creek and the Cherokee Indians who had lived in the state for thousands of years. In the next chapter, you will learn:

➤ how a man named Sequoyah changed the Cherokee Indian nation.

➤ why the Creek Indians left Georgia.

➤ what life was like among the Indians.

➤ how the "Trail of Tears" got its name.

DID YOU KNOW . . .

. . . Most trains in the 1830s traveled about fifteen miles per hour?

. . . George Washington almost refused to attend the Constitutional Convention in Philadelphia because he suffered from rheumatism and also felt he needed to remain at Mount Vernon to run his plantation?

. . . During the time the Constitution was being written and adopted, ice cream was sold commercially for the first time in New York City, and Swiss watchmakers invented a watch that could be worn on the wrist like a bracelet?

. . . The Constitutional Convention was so secret that a full accounting of what went on during the meeting was not made public until almost sixty years later?

. . . In 1786, the Georgia Legislature passed a law setting up a permanent relief organization for the poor, widows, and orphans?

. . . Women were not admitted to the University of Georgia until 1918, 117 years after the college was opened to men?

. . . In 1836, Wesleyan College (below) in Macon became the first college in the world chartered to grant degrees to women?

This engraving showing Indians at Towaliga Falls in Butts County presents an idealized view of Georgia before the coming of the white man. By 1838 most Indians had been forcibly removed from Georgia.

CHAPTER SIX

A CONQUERED PEOPLE
THE INDIAN REMOVAL
1783 - 1838

The choice now is before you. May the Great Spirit teach you how to choose. The fate of your women and children, the fate of your people to the remotest generation, depend upon the issue. Deceive yourselves no longer: Do not cherish the belief that you can ever resume your former political situation, while you continue in your present residence. As certain as the sun shines to guide you in your path, so certain is it that you cannot drive back the laws of Georgia from among you. Every year will increase your difficulties.

— Andrew Jackson, Washington, March 16, 1835

DURING THE LATE 1700s and early 1800s, white Georgians were working on a state government which would put them in good standing in the Union. They wanted to improve the state's economy and add more land to what they already owned. However, there were thousands of Indians who had hunted in Georgia's forests and fished her streams and rivers for 10,000 years. The fifty-five years from 1783 to 1838 was one of the darkest periods in their history.

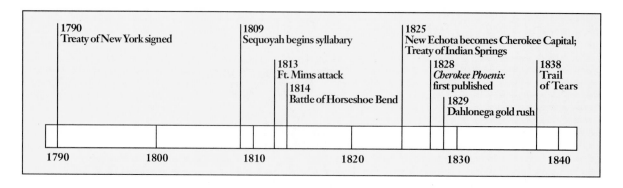

1790 Treaty of New York signed	1809 Sequoyah begins syllabary		1825 New Echota becomes Cherokee Capital; Treaty of Indian Springs	
		1813 Ft. Mims attack	1828 *Cherokee Phoenix* first published	1838 Trail of Tears
		1814 Battle of Horseshoe Bend	1829 Dahlonega gold rush	

| 1790 | 1800 | 1810 | 1820 | 1830 | 1840 |

Opposite page: Yoholo-Micco, who was born about 1788 and died in 1838, was the chieftan of an Upper Creek village located on the Tallapoosa River in what is now Alabama. He was a White Stick, fighting with the United States Army against the British and the Red Sticks. He later served as the Speaker of the Creek Nation.

THE INDIANS AND THEIR LAND

There were small bands of Shawnees and Chickasaws in Georgia, but the two largest Indian tribes were the Cherokees and Creeks. Fourteen tribes with names such as Yamacraw, Yamasee, Ocmulgee, Oconee, Chiaha, and Apalachiee made up the Creek **confederacy,** or nation. Even though the tribes had different names, their language and way of living was much the same. The true name for the Creeks was Muscogee, and they were known for being brave and for carrying on the ways of their fathers.

During the early days of exploration, Europeans discovered a tribe living on the banks of the Ocheese Creek, known today as the Ocmulgee River. The explorers did not know the Indians' tribal name, so they called them Creeks.

There were two main groups of Creeks: the Upper Creeks and the Lower Creeks. The Upper Creeks lived along the Coosa, Tallapoosa, and Alabama Rivers. The Lower Creeks in Georgia made their homes along the banks of the Flint and Chattahoochee Rivers.

One of the largest of the Lower Creek towns was Coweta, which was a "war town." It was across the Chattahoochee River from the present-day city of Columbus. Cusseta, the "peace town," stood on the land where Fort Benning is now.

The Cherokees were the other large tribe in Georgia. They lived in the northwestern mountain region of the state. There were about 22,000 Cherokees in the southeastern United States, and they were all loyal to each other. They called themselves "Awi-yum-wija," which meant "real people" or "principal people." The Cherokees learned more from the life and government of settlers than did any other group of Indians.

Do You Remember?
1. How many tribes were in the Creek Nation?
2. Why were they called Creeks?
3. Where was the Creek "peace town" located?
4. What was the Cherokees' name for themselves?

INDIAN CULTURE

The term "culture" is a word for the beliefs, traditions, music, art, and social institutions of a group of people. Even though there were differences in each tribe's way of life, much of the culture of the Creeks and Cherokees was alike. Most built their villages on high banks or hills along rivers and streams. This gave them rich soil, enough water, fish for food, and a good place from which to defend themselves. The way they built their houses, carried out religious ceremonies, and played was much the same. Since Cherokees still live in the Southeast, they will be used to describe Indian life during the late 1700s and early 1800s.

LIFE AMONG THE CHEROKEES

Cherokee Homes

The Cherokees lived in permanent houses made of wood. They built the early ones by standing large posts two or three feet apart

This lithograph of an early Cherokee village shows the change from a migratory lifestyle to established, permanent settlements.

Above: *The stately three-story brick home located three miles west of Chatsworth was built by Cherokee Indian leader James Vann in 1804. It remains today as a reminder of the Cherokees' wealth and culture.*
Left: *The brightly painted walls of the Vann House dining room are the same colors that were originally in the home. Today visitors can roam the corridors and visit the rooms that contain some of the personal effects belonging to the Vann family.*

and setting smaller posts between them. They then wove twigs or split cane between the posts, giving the walls a basket-like look. The Indians mixed grass and clay to cover the walls, and made their roofs with tree bark or **thatch.** They dug a fireplace in the center of the house, and left a three-inch hole in the roof to allow smoke to escape. In one end of the house were bed frames made from white oak or ash. These had mattresses of dried grasses or some other soft material. Covers were made of buffalo or beaver skins. The family kept their belongings in the other end of the house.

Some houses had another room in which to store food. Like the Creeks, most Cherokee families had a second home which whites called a "hothouse." The people slept in these during the cold winter months. The Indians built hothouses partly under the ground, and lined them with benches. The fireplace in the center of the house doubled as a place for tribal ceremonies.

During the colonial period, some Cherokees built houses like those of white settlers. A few, like Cherokee leader James Vann, lived in large houses. Vann's 800-acre homestead was located east of Dalton. In addition to the main house, there were forty-two cabins, six barns, five smokehouses, a grist mill, blacksmith shop, **foundry,** trading post, and still.

In sharp contrast to the lifestyle of wealthy Cherokees like James Vann, most members of the tribe practiced a lifestyle learned many years before the arrival of the white man. Here you see Cherokee women winnowing wheat. The wheat was repeatedly thrown into the air allowing the air currents to separate the chaff, or husks, from the grain. The delicate process was passed down from generation to generation.

Food

Cherokees ate foods that grew wild in the forest, including plums, blackberries, greens, nuts, mushrooms, and wild potatoes. Both the Creeks and the Cherokees planted beans, pumpkins, squash, and corn. Sunflowers were grown for oil and meal. They grew tobacco for ceremonial uses, and gourds for serving food. The Cherokees used maple sap or honey for sugar, and gathered salt from salt licks in Kentucky or salt springs in Tennessee.

The Cherokees hunted deer, bear, bison, and other large game with bows and arrows, spears, and traps. Blow guns were used to kill small game such as rabbits, squirrels, and birds. They made hooks from animal bones and tied them to thread spun from animal hair so they could fish the streams of North Georgia. Europeans showed the Cherokees how to grow food such as cabbage, peas, apples, and peaches. The Indians dried many of these foods for use during the winter.

Cherokee Clothing and Fashions

Long before the first white settlers arrived, Cherokees could spin animal hair or strips of tree bark into thread. They could then color the thread and weave it for making clothing. They also used deer skins for shirts, boots, and skirts for summer wear. In cold

As more and more settlers moved west into the frontier areas, the primary Indian food sources, deer and buffalo, became scarce.

weather, they wore beaver, otter, bear, and buffalo skins with the fur turned toward their bodies.

The men wore mantles, or loose fitting cloaks, and the women threw feather-trimmed drapes over their left shoulders. Many of the women had clothes which were yellow or red. They sometimes made skirts of turkey feathers held together with strips of tree bark. Young men and women often dressed in six-foot squares of cloth wrapped around their bodies like Roman togas.

It was easy to recognize warriors because they wore red feathers on their heads. Bands of skin held the feathers in place. They also put skin bands around their arms and legs.

Indians trimmed clothing with beads, feathers, and shells. They made bracelets, rings, and pendants from gold, silver, stone, or bones. They wore earrings made of bones, feathers, or stones long before the settlers began to like them.

Cherokee Government

The Cherokees had a strong national government. They divided it into two groups: a **civil** group, and one for times of war. Each tribe had a local government of the same kind.

The chief was both a religious and civil leader. He had a "Right Hand Man" who, along with six other men, formed a council to help make decisions. The "Speaker" was the second highest ranking assistant to the chief. When asked to do so, he gave messages from the chief to the people.

The tribe chose seven women to take seats of honor on the council. One of their duties was to decide if a prisoner would be put to death or become a member of the tribe.

Since seven was a sacred number, the Cherokees used it all through tribal life. Seven men and seven women made up the Council. There were seven clans in the tribe, including Wild Potato, Wolf, Deer, Blue, Paint, Long Hair and Bird. Seven towns served as the clans' headquarters, and the tribe met in a seven-sided council house. Each of the sides was for seating one of the clans.

Wartime

Cherokees were peace-loving people, but they did have battles with the Creeks and, later, some fights with the settlers. When a fight was about to begin, the war chief took over the tribe's government

This model of a Cherokee brave shows us how the Cherokee appeared in the mid-1500s before the arrival of Europeans. During that time, Indian clothing was made of animal skins. Weapons were fashioned from wood, stone or deer antlers. This brave is carrying a blow gun.

and called the warriors together. The warriors first took part in ceremonies they had learned from older men in the tribe. These included singing, dancing, and raising a war flag. The chief then had the warriors promise that, during the battle, they would not shed the blood of women, children, old men, or those who could not defend themselves. A war priest, his assistant, a medicine man, and at least four spies went with the warriors into battle. Each spy wore a skin from either a raven, wolf, owl, or fox wrapped around his neck. Spies used the sound of the animal whose skin they wore to call to the warriors.

The Cherokees' weapons were both strong and useful. They made shields and helmets from buffalo hides. War clubs had sycamore wood handles with a stone ball bound in rawhide at the end. Battle axes or tomahawks were stone axe heads attached to wooden handles. The Indians carefully shaped bows from sycamore or hickory wood, then dipped them in bear oil and dried them with fire. Arrows were cane shafts with eagle feathers at one end and flint heads at the other. Cherokees also used spears, slings, and knives when they fought.

Cherokee Religion

Religion was important in the daily lives of the Cherokees. They believed in a supreme being called *YOWA*, which was a unity of three beings known as the "Elder Fires Above." According to Indian beliefs, *YOWA* formed the earth, and left the moon and sun to govern the world. The Indians believed that the job of Fire was to take care of all mankind. Smoke was the messenger. They had other **sacred** objects, including quartz crystals, corn, rattlesnakes, eagles, and the feathers of eagles.

Cherokees believed in life after death. Priests carried out religious ceremonies using herbs and sacred objects. The most important objects of worship, including an ark, or box, which held a long quartz crystal, were kept in the council house of the tribe. Indians thought the number "seven" was sacred, and they celebrated seven festivals during the year.

Cherokee Families

In Cherokee families, the **clan** of the mother became the clan of her children. If the mother was a member of the Deer Clan, her children would be too. Children were also close to the clans of

Notice the differences in Indian dress from the 1500s as compared with the picture of the brave shown here in the 1830s. The influence of European settlers was reflected in both dress and lifestyle.

The Cherokee council house was much like the ones built by the Mississippian Indians hundreds of years before. It was in the council house that village problems were discussed, arguments were settled, and religious ceremonies were practiced.

their father and both grandfathers. When young people married, they chose someone who was a member of either grandfather's clan. A person could not marry within his clan because of the close kinship between its members. That offense, along with murder, might be punished by death. There were other crimes taken care of by members of the "wronged" family or clan. The civil government acted as both a legislative and a judicial body, but it did not often deal with matters between the clans.

Leisure Time Activities

Many parts of Cherokee life were centered around music and dancing. They had some musical instruments, such as gourd rattlers, drums, and the flageolet (a wind instrument like a recorder). However, most of their music was songs or chants. Parents taught tribal songs to their children. Some were as short as ten seconds. Most dances were done in a circle or a winding pattern, and were often named for animals.

Games were also important to the Cherokees. They played for fun or to settle differences between people or groups. Sometimes, those who watched bet on who would win. Playing games was one way to learn skills needed for war.

Anetsa was a game like lacrosse. There were goalposts at each end of the field, and players used hickory ball sticks and a small ball made of deer skin. For a team to win, the ball had to go through the goalposts a certain number of times. The game had no set rules except that when one team carried a hurt man off the field, the other team had to give up a player. Play lasted until the number of points agreed upon was scored by a team. Legend has it that, once, tribes who had a difference over the land where Atlanta now stands settled it by playing anetsa.

Another game the Indians liked was "tsung-ay'unvi," or chunkey. They used a six-inch disk made of granite or quartzite like a puck. Two players carrying poles eight to ten feet in length played on a small court. As one player rolled the stone, both ran after it and threw their poles where they thought the stone would stop. The player whose pole landed closest to the stone won a point. Men who played this game learned to be more accurate with spear throwing.

Festivals

The Cherokees had seven important festivals, but the one that meant the most to them was the Green Corn Ceremony. The exact time a tribe held the ceremony depended on when the late corn ripened, but it was sometime between late July and early September. In each tribe, the festival was one of thanksgiving for a good corn crop.

The Green Corn Ceremony lasted about four days. It included feasts, sacred fires, dances, ball games, and meetings to settle differences between any members of the tribe. An important part of the ceremony was making the body pure. This most often included a ceremonial bath, going without food for a time, and cleaning the inside of the body with a bitter drink made from tree bark and roots.

After the Green Corn Ceremony, each tribe was ready to begin a new year in which they would again plant and cultivate the fields of corn.

Oconostota, also called Scar Face, was a prominent Cherokee chief.

Above: The Cherokee Phoenix newspaper became possible after the development of a written alphabet for the Cherokee language. The newspaper was published in both English and Cherokee languages. Publication began in 1828 and continued until Georgia politicians ordered the editor to stop publication in 1835. Opposite page: Sequoyah's invention of the syllabary eventually united all Cherokee tribes with one written language. In 1819, Sequoyah, who spoke no English, developed an alphabet of symbols to represent the 80 sounds of the Cherokees' spoken language.

CONTRIBUTIONS TO THE CHEROKEE CULTURE

Sequoyah

At the turn of the century, most Cherokees made their living by hunting or farming, and some owned large plantations. They were quick to learn from white men. One of their most important advancements came from the work of a man named George Gist.

Gist was born around 1760. His father was a Virginia scout and soldier, and his mother was a Cherokee princess. Gist's Indian name was Sequoyah, which meant "Lonely Lame One." Sequoyah was crippled from a childhood illness or a hunting accident, so could not hunt or farm. Instead, he learned to work with silver and, also, became a blacksmith.

Sequoyah was very interested in the white men's "talking leaves," or pieces of paper with marks on them. He noticed that the papers could be carried many miles and the people who got them could understand what the marks meant. In 1809, Sequoyah began to make a kind of alphabet "syllabary." Instead of having the letters A through Z, a syllabary is a group of symbols that stand for whole syllables. With Sequoyah's syllabary, all the Cherokee language but the sound of "m" could be spoken without closing the lips.

It took twelve years for Sequoyah to decide on the eighty-five symbols. According to legend, one time Sequoyah's wife feared the white government would not like what he was doing, so she burned all his work. It took Sequoyah more than a year to do the syllabary over.

At first, members of the tribal council made fun of Sequoyah's work. However, when he taught his daughter and some young chiefs to write the language within a few days, the council members changed their minds. They sent Sequoyah all over the territory to teach other Cherokees to write the language. In about six months, most of the tribes could write and read the new language. The Cherokees were the first Indians to have their language in written form.

People in the United States and Europe praised Sequoyah for his work. The Cherokees gave him a medal which he wore as long as he lived. He was also rewarded by being given about five hundred dollars a year by the Cherokee Nation for the remaining years of his life. This is the first record of a literary prize in America.

New Echota

New Echota became the permanent Cherokee capital in 1825, symbolizing the willingness of the tribe to utilize the best of the white man's government and life styles. In 1838, General Winfield Scott brought 7,000 men into New Echota and set up the headquarters to direct the roundup and removal of the Cherokees from the state.

CHEROKEE PHOENIX

The First Indian Newspaper

By 1828, another Indian leader named Elias Boudinot became editor of the first Indian newspaper. The name of the paper, *Cherokee Phoenix*, meant "I will rise." The newspaper was printed in both Cherokee and English. There were tribes of the Cherokee Nation in Virginia, North Carolina, Northeast Alabama, and Georgia. The paper made it possible to spread news among all of them.

Cherokee Capital Moves to New Echota

Before this time, the capital of the Cherokee Nation had been wherever the principal chief lived. In 1715, it had been in Stephens County, Georgia. At other times, the capital was in Tennessee or South Carolina. However, by 1825, the Cherokees had a per-

The interior of the restored Phoenix office looks today much as it did in the 1830s when the Cherokees represented one of the nation's most civilized cultures. In addition to publishing the Cherokee newspaper, the Phoenix office published portions of the Bible translated into the Cherokee language, a hymnal, political pamphlets, and copies of laws passed by the tribal elders.

manent capital at New Echota, near the present-day city of Calhoun.

One of the twenty government buildings in New Echota was a shop where the *Cherokee Phoenix* and textbooks for Indian schools were printed. Among the other buildings were a national library and a courthouse.

The Cherokees copied what the United States had done and adopted a constitution. They then elected a principal chief and a second chief. Each October, the bicameral legislature and superior court met in New Echota to deal with tribal matters.

Do You Remember?

1. What was the purpose of the Cherokee "hothouse"?
2. Name at least one item worn by the Cherokee Indians that was later popular with the white settlers.
3. What number did the Indians consider sacred? How did the tribes make use of the sacred number. (Give at least three examples.)
4. What was anetsa?
5. What did Sequoyah invent?
6. Where was the Cherokee capital in 1825?
7. Who was Elias Boudinot?

Top: *New Echota in the 1820s. Echota was the Cherokee word for "town."* ***Above:*** *As the editor of the* Phoenix, *Cherokee Elias Boudinot often angered the government of Georgia with his editorials. He was killed in 1838 by fellow tribesmen for his role in signing the Treaty of New Echota.*

Initially, most Indians in Georgia and other parts of the country believed the promises of treaties with white settlers and continued to give up more and more of their tribal lands. It soon became obvious that the government had no intention of abiding by the treaties. Increasingly, the Indians turned to the use of guns to hold onto their lands and to protect their way of life from the white man.

INDIAN RELATIONSHIPS WITH SETTLERS

To understand why the Creeks and Cherokees were pushed out of Georgia, it is helpful to know what happened before that time.

Indians first met white men in 1540 when Spanish explorer Hernando de Soto and his band of soldiers went through Georgia on their search for gold. Other Europeans followed De Soto. Some of them began religious missions, and a few opened trading posts. Slowly the Indians came to know some of the ways and weapons of white men. There were times when this knowledge led to Indian attacks on settlers in Georgia, Alabama, and South Carolina.

For years, a few white traders had cheated, tricked and made slaves of Indians. At one point, traders said the Indians owed them 100,000 deerskins. This would have been equal to two years of work for every adult male Indian. Finally, in 1715, one group of Indians decided to defend themselves.

THE YAMASEE WAR

The Yamasees, a Creek tribe, killed South Carolina Indian agent Thomas Nairne and some traders. They attacked plantations along the South Carolina coast, and killed traders in Creek or Choctaw towns. There were more Indians than whites, so the Carolina settlers tried to turn the Indians against each other. They made the Cherokees believe it would be better for them not to take part in the attack. Once, when some of the Lower Creeks were to meet with the Cherokees to talk about war plans, the Cherokees ambushed and killed them. This led to trouble between the two tribes, which lasted for years.

After the split between the Creeks and Cherokees, it was easy for the English to defeat them. Some of the Creeks became afraid of what might be ahead, and moved west.

During the years that followed the Yamasee War, life changed little for the Creeks until the ship *Anne* arrived. When James Oglethorpe came in 1733, the Yamacraws, a Creek tribe that lived along the Georgia coast, helped the settlers, and the two groups got along well together. However, when the Creeks fought with England during the American Revolution, Georgians no longer trusted them.

THE OCONEE "WAR"

Bad feelings between the Creeks and the settlers grew during the late 1700s. Pioneers kept pushing into Creek lands along the Oconee River. Tribes led by Chief Alexander McGillivray sent warriors against some of the pioneer settlements. The Indians burned houses, stole horses and cattle, and killed or captured over two hundred settlers. Georgia got some men together and told them to kill on sight any Creeks who were not members of friendly tribes.

Fighting between the settlers and the Creeks went on for several years. In 1790, President Washington called Chief McGillivray to New York. Twenty-three men of his tribe went with him. They talked together and exchanged presents, which may have included money. McGillivray then signed the Treaty with the Creeks (Treaty of New York). It stated that the Creeks would give up all their land east of the Oconee River. They would also honor an earlier treaty in which they gave up lands through the Currahee Mountains to Tugaloo. In return, the United States government promised that no whites would go into land west of the boundary. They also agreed to help the Creeks start farms by giving them tools and farm animals.

When word of the treaty reached Georgians, they were very angry because the federal government had taken the side of the Indians. During the next few years, neither group paid any attention to the Treaty of New York. At one point, Governor Edward Telfair was ready to raise an army of 5,000 men to make war against the Creeks, but President Washington talked him out of it. However, there were bad feelings between the tribes and the whites until both groups accepted other treaties. This "peace" would last from 1797 until 1812.

Bitterly angry over the amount of land being taken from the Indians, including his father's home in Savannah, Alexander McGillivray sent warriors against pioneer settlements.

Right: Four hundred people died when the Red Sticks attacked Ft. Mims in Alabama. Below: As a Major General in the United States Army, Andrew Jackson frequently used Indians in battles against the French, British, or Spanish forces or in fights supporting United States troops against other Indian tribes. When he was elected President in 1828, his debt to the various tribal groups was quickly forgotten.

It was during this time that the Yazoo Land Fraud took place. When the federal government stepped in and had Georgia give up all land west of the Chattahoochee River, it also promised to move the Indians out of the state. The federal government did little to carry out this promise. Then, in 1812, the United States was again at war.

WAR WAGED AGAINST THE CREEKS

During this time, some Indian leaders from other parts of the country tried to get all Indians to fight for their right to the land. After the leaders talked with tribes in the Southeast, the Indians became divided into two groups. Those who wanted war were called Red Sticks, and those who wanted peace were known as White Sticks.

During the War of 1812, when British and American troops fought for a second time, many of the Red Stick Creeks fought with the British. The war ended with no real winner, but something happened in 1813 that changed the future of the Creek Nation.

On August 30th, 1,000 Red Sticks attacked Fort Mims in Alabama. During the battle, which lasted for hours, settlers, including women and children, White Stick Creeks, and United States Army officers, were killed. About four hundred people died at the hands of the Red Sticks, and the nation was alarmed. Cries of "Remember Fort Mims" were heard all over the country.

Troops from Mississippi, Georgia and Tennessee began attacks in Creek territory.

Many battles were fought during the next year, but the Creeks were no match for the United States Army. The last battle of the Creek Indian War began on March 27, 1814, at Horseshoe Bend in Alabama. Over one thousand Red Sticks met two thousand members of the infantry, led by General Andrew Jackson. With the help of two cannon, seven hundred cavalrymen, and six hundred White Stick Cherokees, the Creek Indians were defeated. In the following months, they surrendered to Jackson, and gave most of their lands to the United States government. The treaty pleased Georgians because, with it, the Indians owned no more land in southern Georgia.

Because of land **cessions**, Creek tribes became separated from each other. There was little chance for them to talk together or trade with each other. The strong Creek confederacy, which had united the tribes before the arrival of the settlers, was no more. Groups of Creeks would sometimes sign treaties without asking the tribes to agree. This led to the death of one well-known Creek leader.

Murder of Chief William McIntosh
By February 12, 1825, Creek Chief William McIntosh and his first cousin, Georgia Governor George Troup, had worked out the

On March 27, 1814, Andrew Jackson led his troops to Horseshoe Bend on the Tallapoosa River in Alabama against the remaining 1,200 Creek Red Sticks who had been part of the attack on Fort Mims. Within hours, 700 Creeks had been killed. Shortly thereafter, Jackson forced the Creeks to give up twenty-million acres of land.

Below: The Creek General Chief of the Cowetas, William McIntosh, was called Tustunugee Hutkee by fellow tribesmen, meaning "White Warrior." A war hero during the War of 1812, McIntosh achieved the rank of Brigadier General in the U.S. Army. *Right:* Chief McIntosh's signing of the Indian Springs Treaty giving up the last Creek Indian lands in Georgia was seen as a betrayal that led to his murder by fellow tribesmen.

terms of the Treaty of Indian Springs. The United States paid McIntosh and a large group of lower chiefs $200,000 to cede the last of Creek lands in Georgia to the federal government. The government, in turn, gave the use of that land to Georgia.

Groups of Creeks who disagreed with the treaty held secret meetings in east central Alabama to decide how to punish McIntosh. They agreed that he should die. Historians say that between 170 and 400 Indians marched single file from Alabama to McIntosh's home in Butts County, Georgia. After two days, they were a mile from McIntosh's house. Many reports say the Indians got close enough to hear McIntosh and his son-in-law, Samuel Hawkins, talking, but McIntosh did not know the Indians were there.

At daybreak, the Creeks set fire to the McIntosh home. The Indians allowed the women and children to leave before they exchanged gunfire with the chief they had come to kill. Smoke and his wounds stopped McIntosh from fighting. Indians dragged him from the house and stabbed him in the chest. McIntosh's scalp was taken back to Alabama to warn others who might want to give Creek land to white men.

Do You Recall?
1. What was the Yamasee War?
2. Why did the Creeks and Cherokees become enemies?
3. Who was Alexander McGillivray?

THE INDIAN REMOVAL

REMOVAL OF THE CREEKS

In 1829, Andrew Jackson became President of the United States. Jackson had been friendly to the Cherokees when he needed their help to fight the Red Sticks. However, he was wise enough politically to know that white voters wanted the Indians removed from the southern states.

Not long after Jackson became President, a bill in Congress called for the Indians to be moved to the western territories. There were strong feelings on both sides, and the bill passed by only fourteen votes. When Jackson signed the bill into law, there was no question about what would happen to Indians in the Southeast.

The Choctaws, who lived in Alabama and Mississippi, were the first to be moved. The Creeks heard that hundreds of Choctaws died during the march to the west, so they refused to leave the lands of their fathers. When they did this, Alabama took away all Indian legal rights. The Creeks could not defend themselves against whites who moved in and took their lands.

Creeks in Georgia, who no longer had hunting lands, were hungry. Some reports say they stood in the streets of Columbus and begged for food. To add to their hardships, smallpox broke out among the tribes in 1831, and many Indians died. Not long after that, the Treaty of Washington was signed. With this treaty, the Creeks ceded the five million acres of land they still owned to the United States. In return, the government agreed to set aside two million acres on which the Creeks would live and farm. There were some terms in the treaty for both the Creeks and the United States government. 1) Creeks would own a plot of land only after living on it for five years. 2) Creeks could choose to sell the land and move west. 3) The government would protect Creek life and property from whites. 4) The decision to stay on reserved land or to move to the western territory was up to each person.

Once signed, the treaty was broken almost at once. Creek homes were burned, items were stolen from their farms, and Indians were killed. By 1835, some Creeks gave up and began the trip west. However, in 1836, bands of Lower Creeks attacked whites between Tuskegee, Alabama and Columbus, Georgia. The army was afraid of another Indian war, so they captured over 1,000 Creeks

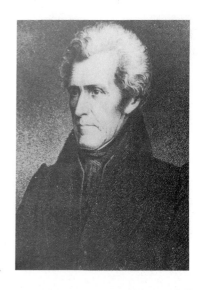

Although most historians give Andrew Jackson high marks as the seventh President of the United States, he did nothing to stop the removal of the Creeks and Cherokees from their native territory.

Top: The governor of Georgia from 1829-1831 and again from 1837-1839, George Gilmer strongly backed the proposal to force the Cherokees from north Georgia. Above: Wilson Lumpkin served as Georgia's governor from 1834-1835. Like Governor Gilmer, Lumpkin made the removal of the Cherokee Indians from Georgia a top priority of his administration.

and took them to the Indian territory. During the next two years, a few Creeks escaped and a few were made slaves, but the federal government forced thousands of them to move west.

Toward the end of the Creek removal in Georgia and Alabama, the United States got into another Indian war in Florida. They asked 700 Creeks to help them fight the Seminoles. After winning the war, the Creeks returned to their families, who had been gathered in camps. Then, the whole group was moved to the west.

REMOVAL OF THE CHEROKEES

While the Creeks were being moved, Georgia was also working to get rid of the Cherokees. Georgians wanted both to homestead the land and to mine the gold which was on Cherokee land.

Gold in Dahlonega

Gold was discovered in Dahlonega in the summer of 1829. In a matter of months, gold fever swept through the north Georgia mountain region. Although the Cherokees knew there was gold in the hills, the person given credit for the discovery was a farmer named Benjamin Parks. Parks found the valuable yellow metal while deer hunting in what was then Habersham (now White) County. Auraria, in nearby Lumpkin County, became the first gold mining center in the United States. Over 10,000 miners with gold pans, picks, and shovels moved to Cherokee land.

The Georgia legislature passed a law which placed part of Cherokee land under state control. They said Cherokee laws were null and void, and would not let Indians speak against white men in a court of law. This meant any white person could hurt, or even kill, a Cherokee without much fear of punishment. A second law, passed on December 19, 1829, refused Indians any right to gold mined in the Dahlonega area. While the miners searched the mountains and streams for "a spot that showed good color," the Cherokees were losing their homes, lands, and legal rights.

The Indians' Last Hope

Most Georgians did not care what happened to the Indians, but a group of white **missionaries** did. To get rid of the missionaries, the Georgia legislature passed a law on December 22, 1830. That law said a white person could not live on Indian land without

taking an oath of allegiance to the governor. Eleven people, including the Reverend Samuel Worchester, postmaster at New Echota, refused to sign the oath and were put in jail in March 1831. They were set free, then arrested again in July of that year. This time they were chained and made to walk from the North Georgia mountains to Lawrenceville. At their trial in September, the jury took only fifteen minutes to return a verdict of guilty. Judge Augustin Clayton sentenced the group to four years at the state penitentiary in Milledgeville. Governor George Gilmer agreed to

Left: The discovery of gold in Dahlonega ended any hope of the Cherokees retaining their lands. Once news spread that gold had been discovered, thousands swarmed into the small town seeking their fortune. Top: Chief Justice John Marshall wrote a Supreme Court opinion supporting the rights of the Cherokee Indians. Above: Chief John Ross tried to obtain help for the Cherokees from the U.S. Congress.

pardon anyone who would take an oath of loyalty to the state, and all but two agreed. Missionaries Worchester and Elizur Butler took their cases to the United States Supreme Court. Chief Justice John Marshall ruled that what the Lawrenceville court decided could not stand because Cherokee territory was not under state law.

The Cherokees thought the ruling meant they might be able to keep their land and government. Chief Justice Marshall ordered Butler and Worchester set free, but the Gwinnett County judge refused. Georgia's newly elected governor, Wilson Lumpkin, would not take a stand against the Gwinnett County judge. Even President Andrew Jackson did not honor the Supreme Court order. He thought state governments should be in charge of Indian territories. He reportedly said, "John Marshall has rendered his 'decision'; now let him enforce it."

Cherokee lands were divided into lots of 40 and 160 acres. In 1832, the government held a state lottery to give Indian lands to white men. Even then, the Cherokees refused to leave their home.

On January 9, 1833, Worchester and Butler gave up and told Governor Lumpkin that they would "abandon **litigation**" and leave the question of their prison sentence to the "**magnanimity** of the State". The governor pardoned them, then said the two missionaries must leave the state and never return.

Cherokee leader, Chief John Ross, made several trips to Washington to ask Congress for help. He wanted the Indians protected and the terms of past treaties honored. No help was given. More

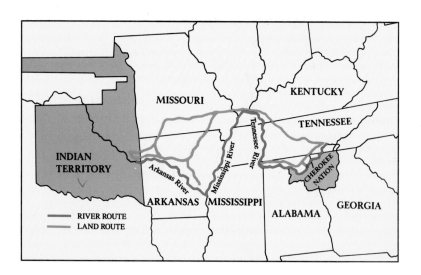

Right: The Trail of Tears followed several routes. *Above:* After moving to Oklahoma on the Trail of Tears, Major Ridge and his son were killed in 1839 for their role in bringing about the Cherokee's removal from Georgia.

and more, the Indians were run off their lands, whipped, and even killed. Time was running out for the Cherokee Nation.

In December 1835, the Cherokees were told to come to their capital, New Echota. There they were to sign a treaty giving up all the Cherokee land that remained in the Southeast. It would be thought that any member of the tribe who did not come agreed with the treaty. Three to five hundred Cherokees out of about seventeen thousand were at the meeting.

A Cherokee trader, Major Ridge, and a small number of Indians agreed to sign the government's treaty. The treaty said the Indians would move west, and Georgia would give them a little money, and food for the trip.

By May of 1838, about 2,000 Cherokees had gone. They left behind about 15,000 others who refused to leave their homes.

Today we can only imagine the heartsick feelings of thousands of Cherokees as they were forced to leave their home, possessions and lands behind and walk from Georgia to Oklahoma. Because of the great suffering and many deaths caused by disease, the cold weather, and deprivation on the forced march, the journey is called the Trail of Tears.

THE TRAIL OF TEARS

Even after the treaty was signed, national leaders like Henry Clay, Daniel Webster and Davy Crockett tried to get the United States government to give the Cherokees the rights due them. No

Top: Famous frontiersman Davy Crockett tried to help the Cherokees retain their lands by talking with members of the United States Congress on their behalf. Above: A well-known and highly-respected U.S. statesman, Kentuckian Henry Clay, publicly spoke out against the Indian removal but his pleas fell on deaf ears. The fate of the Cherokee nation had been sealed.

one listened, and General Winfield Scott was ordered to remove the 15,000 or more Cherokees who were still in Georgia.

In May 1838, Scott and nearly 7,000 troops arrived in New Echota. The troops first built stockades to house the Cherokees. Then they went into homes and community buildings to bring the Cherokees to the stockades. Hundreds of men, women, and children died of cholera, dysentery, and fever while in the stockades. During the summer of 1838, the army loaded several thousand Cherokees onto crowded boats and sent them on the Tennessee, Mississippi, and Arkansas rivers to their new homes. The boats were dirty, and the food the government gave them was often not fit to eat. By the time these Indians arrived in Oklahoma, nearly one-third of the group had died.

A few Cherokees escaped and hid in the North Carolina mountains. The rest began a 700 to 800 mile walk to Oklahoma. It took some people six months to make the trip. Others were there in less time. However, winter winds, snow, and too little food led to the deaths of thousands of Cherokees. Historians do not know the exact number of Indians who were moved, but about 4,000 of this group died while they were in prison before they left or during the march to Oklahoma. They were not the only casualties of the treaty which removed the Cherokees from their land. Major Ridge, his son, and *Cherokee Pheonix* editor Elias Boudinot were killed by Indians for breaking a tribal law forbidding individual Cherokees from signing away land rights without the permission of the entire tribe.

President Van Buren, in his December 1838 address to Congress, said, "the measures of the Removal have had the happiest effect . . . the Cherokees have **emigrated** without apparent reluctance." Today, we can only imagine the fear, despair and hurt felt by those who had to leave the land of the "principal people." The Cherokees called the move to Oklahoma "Nuna-da-ut- sun'y," which means "the trail where they cried."

Do You Remember?
1. What were Andrew Jackson's feelings about Indians?
2. What happened in Dahlonega in 1829?
3. Who was Augustin Clayton and why was he important?
4. What Cherokee trader signed the Treaty at New Echota?

INDIAN PLACE NAMES

PLACE	LOCATION	ORIGIN	ORIGINAL WORD	MEANING
Alaroochee	Irwin County	Creek	Ahalah Uchi	"little river potato"
Amicalola	Dawson County	Cherokee	Anna Kalola	"tumbling water"
Chattooga	Walker and Chattooga Counties	Cherokee	T satu' gi	"He drank river and by sips or He has crossed the stream and come out on the other side"
Chiaha	Floyd County	Creek	Chiaha	"Where the others live"
Chicamauga River	Catoosa, Walker, and Whitfield counties	Muskogean	Tchiskamaga	"sluggish or dead water"
Cohutta	Whitfield County	Cherokee	Cohutta	"frog"
Dahlonega	Lumpkin County	Cherokee	Atela - dalaniger	"yellow money"
Hiawassee	Towns County	Cherokee	A-yu-ua-si	"pretty farm"
Hichiti	Chattahoochee County	Creek	Archilchita	"to look up the stream"
Nahunta	Brantley County	Tuscarora	Nahunta	"tall trees"
Nantahala Mountains	Towns County	Cherokee	Nan-tah-ee-yah-heh-lik	"Sun in the middle noon"
Ocmulgee River	Source at Lake Jackson	Hitchiti	Oki mulgia	"water boiling or bubbling"
Okefenokee Swamp	Southeast Georgia	Seminole	E-cum-fi-nop-can	"trembling earth"
Toccoa	Stephens County	Cherokee	Tagwahi	"where the Catawbas lived"
Wahoo	Lumpkin	Creek	Uhawhu	"cork or winged elm"

Source: Krakow, Kenneth K., *Georgia Place Names*, Winship Press, Macon, Georgia, 1975.

CHAPTER REVIEW

Summary

Georgia was home to two major Indian tribes. The Cherokees, who called themselves the "principal people," lived in the north Georgia mountain region. The largest group of Indians was the Creeks. There were fourteen tribes in the Lower Creek Nation.

Indians had lived in Georgia for thousands of years. By the time early white settlers arrived, both the Creeks and the Cherokees had permanent villages. Some of their homes were wooden and shaped like a rectangle. Others looked like an upside down basket. For food, they grew crops, hunted and fished. They made colorful clothing from woven material, animal skins, or furs. The Indians often wore jewelry and feathers.

The Indians were religious, and believed in gods and life after death. They divided their government into a group for times of war and a group for times of peace.

When Indians were not getting food or working out differences between tribes, they enjoyed music, dancing and games. They had several festivals, but none was more important than the Green Corn Ceremony. This was a time of thanksgiving for a good corn crop.

The Indians copied much of the white man's culture, including some foods and weapons. The Cherokees were also good at starting new ideas. The work of Sequoyah gave the Cherokees a syllabary with which to write their language. The Cherokees established a capital at New Echota where they built schools, started a superior court and printed a newspaper.

Except for the time of exploration and the Yamassee War, Indians and whites were friends.

Bad feelings grew after the Revolution. Indians sided with the British during the American Revolution and the War of 1812. The Creek Indian War of 1813 led to the death of many whites. Settlers in the Southeast wanted lands occupied by the Indians.

Andrew Jackson became President in 1829. He did nothing to stop the removal of the Creeks and Cherokees to a new Indian Territory in the west.

United States treaties with the Indians were broken almost as soon as they were made. The Creeks were forced to move west, and the Cherokees were gathered together and sent on their tragic Trail of Tears.

People, Places, and Terms

Identify, define and/or state the importance of the following.

1. Sequoyah
2. Green Corn Ceremony
3. cession
4. New Echota
5. Dahlonega
6. culture
7. Muscogee
8. syllabary
9. Thomas Nairne
10. confederacy
11. Alexander McGillivray
12. William McIntosh
13. Ft. Mims
14. Red Sticks
15. White Sticks
16. Andrew Jackson
17. Horseshoe Bend
18. The Yamasee War
19. The Oconee War

The Main Idea

Write a short paragraph to answer each of the following questions.

1. In what ways did Sequoyah's work change the lives of the Cherokees?
2. How was the Cherokee government like the United States government?
3. What did the Indians do as leisure time activities?
4. What led to the removal of the Creeks and Cherokees from Georgia?

Extend Your Thinking

Share your own opinion by answering the following questions:

1. Could the settlers and Indians have lived together peacefully? Why or why not?
2. Why is the Trail of Tears referred to by so many writers as "one of the darkest periods in Georgia's history"?
3. In your opinion, was the removal of the Indians right or wrong? Explain your answer.

Map Skills

1. Using an outline map of Georgia, locate 10 counties, rivers, towns or places with Indian names.
2. Using the map on page 178 in your textbook that outlines the Trail of Tears, list the states in the order the Cherokees traveled through them.

Looking Ahead

Once the Indians were removed from the state, Georgians, both black and white, found themselves involved in events that would ultimately lead the country into civil war. This period is known as the "antebellum" period, and means "before war."

As you study Chapter Seven, you will find the answers to questions such as:

➤ did most Georgians have slaves?
➤ in what way did "zero-milepost" become important?
➤ how was Joseph E. Brown important to education?
➤ what did William Lloyd Garrison do to try to abolish slavery?

DID YOU KNOW . . .

. . . The name Cherokee may come from the word "Chilokkita" meaning people of a different language?

. . . The sport of lacrosse originated with the North American Indians?

. . . The Creeks and Cherokees were two of the tribes of Indians known as the "five civilized tribes"? The other tribes were the Choctaws, Chickasaws and Seminoles.

. . . The Indian word maize (corn), meant "our life"?

. . . In the 1820s, nearly one-third of what is now Georgia still belonged to the Creeks and Cherokees?

. . . The Indians referred to Georgia as "E-Cun-Nau-Nux-Udgee" meaning "people greedily grasping after the lands of the red men?"

. . . The giant redwood trees found in California are named in honor of Sequoyah?

. . . Twenty-eight of the fifty states in the United States have names with Indian origins?

. . . By 1851, only 321 Cherokees were found in Georgia?

. . . In the Cherokee syllabary there was no sound for B, J, R, CH or Z?

. . . In some ball games, several hundred Indians would play on the field at the same time?

Slave market auctions were a time of fearful uncertainty and indignation for the slaves.

A NATION DIVIDED

1840-1870

A house divided against itself cannot stand. I believe this government cannot endure, permanently, half slave and half free. I do not expect the Union to be dissolved; I do not expect the house to fall; but I do expect it will cease to be divided. It will become all one thing, or all the other. Either the opponents of slavery will arrest the further spread of it and place it where the public mind shall rest in the belief that it is in the course of ultimate extinction, or its advocates will push it forward till it shall become alike lawful in all the states, old as well as new. North as well as South.

— Abraham Lincoln, June 16, 1858, Acceptance Speech for the Republican Nomination to the U.S. Senate

THE UNITED STATES had been one nation since 1789. However, society, politics, economics, and culture were different in each major section of the country. This was, perhaps, most true between the northern and the southern states. From the early 1800s until the middle 1800s, people talked about these differences at **socials** and church meetings. Newspaper men wrote about them, and politicians made them the subject of speeches. This period is called "antebellum," which means "before war."

Differences between the North and South led to a four-year civil war between 1861 and 1865. The time period following that war is called "Reconstruction," which means "to build again." Reconstruction lasted from 1865 to 1872. This unit examines each of those three periods—the antebellum period, the Civil War, and Reconstruction.

CHAPTER SEVEN

ANTEBELLUM DAYS

1840-1860

We are a peculiar people, sir! You don't understand us . . . because we are known to you only by northern writers and northern papers. . . . We are an agricultural people; we are a primitive but a civilized people. We have no cities—we don't want them. . . . We have no commercial navy—no navy—we don't want them. . . . We want no manufactures; we desire no trading, no mechanical or manufacturing classes. As long as we have our rice, our sugar, our tobacco, and our cotton, we can command wealth to produce all we want from those nations with which we are in amity, and to lay up money besides.

— Texas Senator Lewis T. Wigfall,
who had strong feelings about states' rights.

I N 1850, when the last **decade** of the antebellum period began, the population of the United States was 23,191,876. California became the thirty-first state, and Vice President Millard Fillmore became the thirteenth President following the death of President Zachary Taylor. Americans were reading Nathaniel Hawthorne's novel, *The Scarlet Letter,* and Levi Strauss began making canvas pants called "Levis" for gold miners. Industry was growing in the North, and agriculture was profitable in the South. Bad feelings between North and South were spreading.

There were many issues that divided the United States, but most of them can be grouped under six headings: 1) sectionalism; 2) slavery; 3) solvency; 4) styles; 5) structure; and 6) **secession**.

The stately home of United States Senator Robert Toombs in Washington, Georgia represented much of what the South wanted to save or perpetuate. The plantation classes lived a life of comfort and ease at the hands of others.

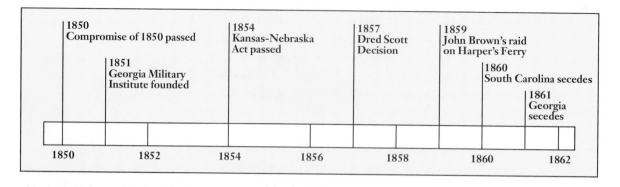

1850 Compromise of 1850 passed	1854 Kansas–Nebraska Act passed	1857 Dred Scott Decision	1859 John Brown's raid on Harper's Ferry	
1851 Georgia Military Institute founded			1860 South Carolina secedes	
			1861 Georgia secedes	

1850   1852   1854   1856   1858   1860   1862

SECTIONALISM

Sectionalism means that people in any given area think their ideas and interests are correct, and more important than those of people in any other region. For example, in the 1850s, most Northerners thought the federal government could pass laws for all the nation's citizens. They felt, if a law was bad, only the United States Supreme Court could have it removed. However, most Southerners believed in "states' rights." They thought powers not given to the federal government in the Constitution belonged to each state. To them, it meant states could ignore federal laws that took away their rights.

The North and South could not agree on issues ranging from how to handle federal money to slavery in western territories. Congress made three important decisions to try to stop growing sectional problems.

THE COMPROMISE OF 1850

In 1848, gold was discovered at Sutter's Mill in California. People from all over the nation moved west to find gold. By late 1849, the population of California was over 100,000, enough to ask for statehood. In 1850, there were fifteen slave states and fifteen free states. California's constitution did not allow slavery. If she became a state, the slave-free balance in the Senate would change. For eight months, what was later called "The Great Debate" went on as Congress tried to agree on what to do about California.

Finally, Congress passed five laws, later called the Compromise of 1850. They offered something to please both North and South. For the North, 1) California came into the Union as a free state; 2) slave trading was stopped in the District of Columbia; and 3) Texas gave up the idea of taking in New Mexico so it could be part of a slave state. For the South, 1) the territories of New Mexico and Utah would decide if they wanted to be slave or free; 2) District of Columbia residents could keep the slaves they had; and 3) Congress would pass a law stating that slaves who ran away to free states would be returned to their owners.

KANSAS-NEBRASKA ACT

The Kansas-Nebraska Act, written in part by Stephen Douglas of Illinois, became law in 1854. This act created two new territories which had "popular sovereignty." This meant, when a territory asked to become a state, the people of a territory could vote to decide if they wanted to be a free or slave state. Northerners were angry because this law changed the Compromise of 1820, which did not permit slavery north of Missouri's southern boundary.

Most people in the new territories belonged to one of two groups: pro-slavery or free soilers. Free soilers were against slavery and also wanted land given to western settlers for farming. After Congress passed the Kansas-Nebraska Act, fights broke out between pro-slave and free soil groups. There were almost two hundred settlers killed. Kansas became known as "BleedingKansas."

DRED SCOTT DECISION

In 1834, Dred Scott, a slave, was taken by his owner from the slave state of Missouri to the free state of Illinois. Later they went to Wisconsin, another free state. Scott returned to Missouri and filed a lawsuit saying he was free since he had lived in a free state. **Abolitionists** from the North raised enough money to take the case to the United States Supreme Court. In March 1857, the Supreme Court ruled on the case. The justices said Scott could not sue because he was a slave, and slaves were not citizens. The Court also said Congress had no right to stop slavery in territories. The Dred Scott decision further divided the North and South, and pushed them closer to war.

Historians know little about Dred Scott. Although he could neither read nor write, he persevered in presenting his case all the way to the U.S. Supreme Court where the Dred Scott decision became a vital part of our nation's history.

Do You Remember?
1. What is the definition of "states' rights"?
2. What is sectionalism?
3. Why was the Dred Scott decision important?

SLAVERY

Slavery was another area of difference between North and South. By 1860, there were over 4,000,000 slaves in the United States. Of that number, 465,000, or 11.6 per cent, lived in Georgia.

DAILY LIFE FOR SLAVES

Life was not easy for slaves, no matter where they worked. They usually ate fat back, molasses, and corn bread. On some plantations, slaves could grow a vegetable garden and fish in streams and ponds. Sometimes, plantation owners gave the slaves rabbits, opossum, squirrels, or other small game they had killed.

Slaves had clothing made from materials which would last a long time. On large plantations, owners bought large amounts of wide-brimmed hats, heavy duty shoes, socks or stockings, and underwear. The clothes did not always fit and, sometimes, slaves worked in the fields barefoot. Plantation families often gave house slaves clothes they no longer wore. These were nicer than clothes given to field workers.

Most slaves lived in one-room huts with fireplaces for heating and cooking. They had little furniture: maybe a table, some chairs, and pallets to sleep on.

Many children started working when they were five years old.

Opposite page: House servants worked from sun-up to long past sun-down but they were usually spared the physical hardships of the field hands. **Below:** Slave children had an all too brief childhood for by age six they generally joined their parents in the field. **Bottom:** Slave quarters offered only the most basic shelter and furnishings.

This idealized version of a Sunday on the plantation was rarely true. On the great majority of plantations, slaves did not have the opportunity to have someone read to them.

They worked until they were either too old or too sick to be of any use in the fields or the "big house."

Field hands worked in the cotton, tobacco, or rice fields six days a week. They started before the sun came up and stayed until sundown. When crops were gathered, both adults and children had a set amount to bring in each day. If a slave did not harvest enough, the owner or overseer might whip him or punish him in some other way. Owners and overseers always watched slaves to make sure they stayed busy.

THE OVERSEER

Overseers on large farms or plantations were paid from $200 to $1,000 a year. Income was based on the size of the farm and the number of slaves. An owner usually gave his overseer the use of a house and a small piece of land.

Many overseers carried whips or other weapons to remind slaves to work. However, they had to know just how much to use such weapons. A "prime field hand" was sometimes worth as much as $1,800. Owners would dismiss an overseer who was so cruel to a slave that he was not able to work.

Overseers used drivers to help them. A driver was often an older slave who was loyal to the owner and could manage the other slaves.

EDUCATION AND RELIGION FOR SLAVES

It was against the law for a slave owner to teach any slave to read or write. However, some owners used the Bible and taught the slaves anyway.

There was a church on most large plantations. Both slaves and the plantation family attended services on Sunday mornings. Sometimes, owners let slaves have church meetings of their own. They kept close watch over these meetings so slaves could not plan to escape.

Spirituals were an important part of slave life. They sang spirituals at church, home, and work. The words gave them comfort, and spoke of faith in God and belief in freedom.

GEORGIAN'S FEELINGS TOWARD SLAVERY

Less than forty percent of white Georgians owned any slaves during antebellum days, but the worth of Georgia slaves ran into millions of dollars. There were a few whites in Georgia who spoke out against slavery. However, most of them simply accepted it as a way of life. Some thought that, through slavery, they were helping to care for blacks. Others said slavery allowed whites to teach blacks about Christianity.

ABOLITIONISTS

Many northern whites and free blacks, called abolitionists, worked to get rid of slavery. They made speeches, wrote books and articles, and offered their homes as "safe houses" for runaway slaves. William Lloyd Garrison published a newspaper called *The Liberator*. Harriet Beecher Stowe wrote about slaves as individuals, rather than as a group, in *Uncle Tom's Cabin*. Although Stowe, who grew up in Connecticut, had seen slaves only once when visiting in Kentucky, her book described some of the worst things about slavery and the Fugitive Slave Law. Three hundred thousand

Born a slave in Maryland, Harriet Tubman escaped to the North in 1849 and became the renowned organizer of the Underground Railroad. Her determination to guide more than 300 slaves to freedom earned her a "Most Wanted" status with plantation owners. $40,000 was offered for her capture, dead or alive. However, that was not to be and she lived until 1913.

copies of the book were sold in a year, and the information in it caused Northerners to like slavery less and abolition more.

Freed slave Sojourner Truth was famous for her speeches, which asked for freedom for all blacks. Others, like Harriet Tubman, helped slaves escape from the South to free northern states. Tubman was a leader in the Underground Railroad. She personally led over 300 slaves to freedom. The Underground Railroad was a chain of homes, farms and churches where runaway slaves could rest, and hide from slave catchers. One person or small groups moved from place to place at night until they reached a free state or Canada. Tubman, and others like her, helped up to 50,000 slaves escape through the Underground Railroad between 1830 and 1860.

JOHN BROWN'S RAID

White abolitionist John Brown, hated slavery. In 1859, he decided to try to help slaves in the South become free of their owners. To do this, Brown needed guns and **ammunition**.

Brown took twenty-one white and black men to raid the federal **arsenal** at Harper's Ferry, Virginia (now in West Virginia). They killed the mayor, and made prisoners of forty citizens. Then Brown and his men hid in a building at the railroad station. Within twenty-four hours, Marines led by Colonel Robert E. Lee captured Brown. Two months later, the state of Virginia tried Brown for treason, and sentenced him to be hanged. Not long before he died, Brown wrote to his family and said he was as content ". . . to die for God's eternal truth on the scaffold as in any other way."

Southerners thought John Brown was a murderer, and they were afraid others would try to lead slaves to rise up against owners. Many Northerners were against the killing Brown did, but they saw him as a hero. Henry Wadsworth Longfellow wrote, "This will be a great day in our history, the date of a new revolution.... As I write, they are leading old John Brown to execution.... This is sowing the wind to reap the whirlwind which will come soon."

*Top: For forty years Sojourner Truth spoke out against slavery and for women's rights. **Above:** Radical abolitionist John Brown.*

Do You Remember?
1. Who was Harriet Tubman?
2. What was a driver?
3. Who wrote *Uncle Tom's Cabin*?
4. What percent of Georgians owned slaves?

SOLVENCY

The third "S" that led to the war between the North and South was solvency. A person who is solvent can pay his debts. People in the North and South stayed solvent in very different ways.

AGRICULTURE VS. INDUSTRY

The economy of the North was based on industry. A cold climate and short growing season in the New England states meant there was little profit in farming. Northerners worked in factories, mines, banks, stores, and on railroads to take care of their families. The railroad system carried industrial products to other parts of the country.

The South depended on agriculture to remain solvent. Cotton and tobacco were the two main crops, but there were also rice plantations on the Georgia and South Carolina coast. Even though cotton was "king" in the South, Southerners shipped most

Although cotton was the most profitable crop in antebellum Georgia, the cultivation of rice was important along the coastal area. Here you see a picture of a rice plantation on the Altamaha River near Darien owned by the Butler family. How do you think life on a cotton plantation might have differed from life on a rice plantation?

of it to northern states where mills made thread and cloth. In 1850, there were 564 mills in New England. These mills used 61,893 workers and had a value of over $58,000,000. This compared with 166 mills in the South, which had 10,043 workers and a value of $7,250,000. In fact, the antebellum South manufactured only ten percent of the nation's goods. Few farmers and planters were interested in factories.

TARIFFS

Tariffs were important to solvency. Northern states wanted foreign countries who shipped goods to the United States to pay high tariffs. This would mean items made in the North would cost less than imported ones. For example, a suit made and sold in Boston might cost $50.00. One like it made in England and sold in Boston might cost $70.00: $50.00 for the suit and $20.00 for the import tax.

Southern states, however, bought many manufactured goods from foreign countries. They didn't want the prices they paid made higher by tariffs on imported goods.

In 1832, South Carolina threatened to secede from the Union because a new tariff was not low enough. South Carolinians began to arm themselves and hold practice drills. President Andrew Jackson asked Congress to allow him to take an army into South Carolina and force acceptance of the tariff. Instead, Congress passed a compromise tariff law, written by Henry Clay. The bill reduced the tariff over a ten-year period. This pleased South

The cultivation of cotton brought a great deal of money to Georgia's planters but it also increased the need for slavery because so many laborers were needed to plant, raise, pick and process the cotton.

Carolina, and they dropped their protest.

The differences over tariffs became worse when a depression, known as the Panic of 1857, hit the country. Before that time, many northern industrialists built their factories with borrowed money. Nearly 5,000 of them went bankrupt during the depression. Owners of factories asked Congress to pass higher tariffs to stop the British from shipping goods to the United States. The depression did not hurt Southerners badly because there were so few factories in the South. Therefore, their representatives would not vote for higher tariffs. This argument further damaged feelings between the North and South. This was not the first time the question of tariffs separated North and South.

This engraving shows cotton bales tumbling down a cotton slide onto a waiting river boat. Most southern cotton was shipped to mills in the North to be turned into cloth.

Do You Remember?

1. What is the meaning of "solvency"?
2. Why did Southerners not want higher tariffs?
3. What percent of the nation's industrial goods were manufactured in the South?

STYLES

A difference in the way people lived, or their "life style" was another reason the North and South did not understand each other. There were several large cities in the North, such as New York, Philadelphia, Washington, Boston, and Chicago. People who lived there could visit museums, or attend operas, lectures, **minstrel shows**, and the theater. They might spend evenings at large dinner parties, receptions, and dances. Horse racing, already known in the South, and baseball became popular sports.

In the South, the rural life style affected most things done for pleasure. There were few chances to attend lectures, concerts, or the theater except in towns such as Athens, Savannah and Augusta. Planters' lives were not much like what movies show. They had

Wearing the latest in fashion was only a part of the Northern lifestyle in the 1860s. Culture, education, and entertainment were also important parts of the lifestyle of the area, and they all differed from the customs of the South.

During the days before the Civil War, social life in the South was at a much slower pace than that of the North. Many social activities centered around farm life. Southerners used events like corn shucking to catch up on news and socialize while helping neighbors with the harvest.

little time for parties and dances. Both whites and blacks had fewer duties on holidays. However, during the rest of the year, they spent the small amount of time away from work attending revivals, quilting bees, and hunting and horse racing parties. The life style stayed much the same, so when a group of traveling minstrels or actors came to an area, it was very exciting.

STRUCTURE

Structure, when it refers to groups of people, means the position one group has in relation to others. In the antebellum South, social classes were important. A small but influential group of planters were at the top of the social ladder. Following them was the largest antebellum group, the middle class. This included yeoman farmers who owned less than 500 acres of land each, doctors, ministers, lawyers, and artisans. Next came poor whites who either owned very small farms, were seasonal laborers for planters or yeoman farmers, or worked at low-paying, **menial** jobs. Blacks and whites alike called a sub-class of this group "poor white trash." These were drifters who could not read and write and who often lived on what other people gave them.

Much of the Northern labor market worked in factories while Southern laborers generally worked in agricultural jobs. Work opportunities in factories, and in the industries they represented, allowed much more movement from one social class to another than was possible in the South.

Blacks were at the bottom of the South's class system, and there were social differences among them too. Slaves admired free blacks and wanted to be like them. Some free blacks owned farms and slaves, but most lived and worked in larger cities.

In the slave population, there was a difference between blacks who were house servants and those who worked in the fields. House servants often had better food, clothes, and working conditions than field hands.

Most of the social structure of the South was based on land and slaves. It was hard to move from one social class to another.

In the North, class structure was more often tied to wealth. This made it easier to move from one class to another. Many of the people worked in industry. Each of them had about the same chance to go to school, travel, and take part in cultural activities. Where there were separate classes, they seemed to be based on money more than on the group into which a person was born.

By 1860, most people in the North did not understand or like the southern social system. However, Southerners were not ready to change their life style.

SECESSION

Secession is the last "S" that separated the North and South. As differences grew, many Southerners felt that the only way they could live as they wished was to secede from, or leave, the Union. They began to think about forming their own nation. After South Carolina's threat to secede in 1832 led to a lower tariff, secession was seen as an effective way to deal with conflict between the states and the federal government. Northerners, on the other hand, wanted to keep the Union together at any cost.

Do You Remember?
1. What were two things people in the North did for pleasure before the Civil War? What were two different things done in the South?
2. What was the largest social group in the antebellum South?
3. What separated social classes in the South during the mid 1800s?
4. How were the North and the South different in their feelings about secession?

ANTEBELLUM GEORGIA

During the early part of the antebellum period, Georgians worked hard to get the Indians removed from the state. After that was done, the state turned its full attention to other interests.

GEORGIA'S ECONOMY

The backbone of Georgia's economy was agriculture. By 1860, there were 68,000 farms in the state, and cotton was the main crop. They produced 700,000 bales of cotton in 1860. This was an increase from 326,000 bales in 1839. Most of Georgia's farmers, about 31,000, had less than 100 acres of land. Only 3,500 farms had 500 acres or more, and could be called plantations. Since land did not cost much, a plantation owner's worth was largely measured by

The South's plantation owners lived in large, impressive homes which served as the center for most of their social activities. This is Stately Oaks near Jonesboro.

Opposite page: *Westville, near Lumpkin, recreates a Georgia town of the 1850s.* **Top:** *A prosperous merchant's home.* **Above:** *A doctor's office.* **Left:** *A living history demonstration of bootmaking.*

In the 1830s, a civil engineer named Stephen Long named the terminal point of the Georgia Railroad "Terminus," which means "end." By 1842, the tracks had been laid from terminus to Marietta. However, there was one problem— there was no engine to pull the train. The closest engine was in Madison. Named the Florida, *the engine was boarded on a huge wagon built especially to carry it. Sixteen mules were hitched to the wagon to pull the* Florida *and two coach cars through miles of woods and over rough trails to the tiny town of Terminus which we now call Atlanta.*

the number of slaves he owned. Only 236 Georgians owned more than 100 slaves and 60 percent of antebellum Georgians had no slaves at all.

In 1845, a prime field hand cost $600 but, by 1860, the price had risen to $1,800. A planter had to sell 16,500 pounds of processed cotton to buy such a slave, and he bought the slave to increase his cotton production. Just before the Civil War, half of Georgia's total wealth, or $400,000,000, was in slaves.

Most manufacturing in Georgia grew out of agriculture. The state had about forty cotton mills in the area where cotton was grown. There were also a few tanneries, shoe factories, iron foundries, grist mills, and brick and pottery factories. Even though it was not many when compared with the North, Georgia had 1,890 factories by 1860. The value of this small industrial base was about $11,000,000.

TRANSPORTATION

The building of railroads in Georgia began in the 1830s. By 1833, a line ran from Charleston, South Carolina to Augusta. A

second line, completed in 1843, went from Savannah to Macon. A few years later, the Western and Atlantic connected the Chattahoochee River to Chattanooga, Tennessee. A settlement called Terminus grew up around the southern end of that railroad line at zero mile post, which marked the end of the Western and Atlantic Railroad. Later, its name was changed to Atlanta.

By 1860, there were 1,226 miles of railroad tracks in the state. Railroads were often poorly built and repaired. Still, they were necessary to the state's economy because growers shipped cotton by train to seacoast ports or mills in the North.

In the 1830s, a few canals were built as the beginning of a system of water transportation. However, little was done about them after railroad building began.

EDUCATION

Education did not get much attention in antebellum Georgia. Some sons of wealthy planters had teachers in their homes or went to private academies. However, most Georgians had little education.

"Old field schools," built on fields which were no longer used, dotted the state. Members of a community built a school, hired the teacher, and bought a few books and supplies. Most students in old field schools attended only two or three years, and learned basic reading, writing, and arithmetic.

In 1850, about twenty percent of Georgia's whites could not read or write. About half of Georgia's children were black and did not go to school at all. In 1858, the state legislature, using income from the state-owned Western and Atlantic Railroad, set aside $100,000 to begin free schools. Before plans were finished, the war started and education was laid aside.

There was some small growth in the field of education during the 1850s. In 1851, Georgia Military Institute was founded in Marietta. It was also during that year that the Georgia Academy for the Blind was begun in Macon. Joseph Lumpkin and Thomas Cobb founded Georgia's first law school in Athens in 1859.

RELIGION

During the 1850s, church membership grew in Georgia and, by 1860, there were 2,393 churches in the state. This made Georgia second only to Virginia in the number of churches. Methodists and

Climax Church, originally in Lumpkin, was built in 1850. Churches like this were the center of religious, civic and social activity during antebellum days in the South. The church has been reconstructed at Westville.

Baptists continued to have more members than any other group. The Episcopal, Catholic, and Presbyterian churches also grew. People of the Jewish faith, one of Georgia's religious groups during settlement days, were small in number, but added to the state's religious diversity. There were a few **segregated** churches, but slaves usually attended the same churches as their masters.

Slavery caused denominations to divide. Methodists in the South pulled out of their national organization and formed the Methodist Episcopal Church. In 1845, Southern Baptists met in Augusta to begin the Southern Baptist Convention. Baptists in the South had left the American Baptist Union when its foreign mission board would not accept slave owners as missionaries.

Religious revivals, especially among Methodists, were often in the form of camp meetings. Sometimes people came from miles away and camped to attend a two or three-day meeting. These meetings sometimes lasted for a week or longer.

GEORGIA POLITICS

It was hard to keep up with political changes in Georgia during the twenty years before the state left the Union. In the 1840s, the two major political parties were Democrats and Whigs.

Robert Toombs and Alexander H. Stephens led the Whigs. Whigs were mostly members of the upper social classes. They favored a moderate protective tariff and federal help for the South.

Democratic leaders were Speaker of the House of Representatives Howell Cobb, Herschel V. Johnson, and Joseph E. Brown. They were for states' rights, and took a strong stand for slavery.

There was little real difference in what the two parties believed, but each wanted to govern the state. During the 1840s, most governors were Democrats, and the Whigs had more members in the legislature. In larger Georgia towns, there were two newspapers: one for Democrats and one for Whigs.

The 1850s brought about a change for both parties. Many Georgians did not like the Compromise of 1850. However, United States Congressmen Cobb, Stephens, and Toombs asked the state to accept it. A convention, held in Milledgeville, adopted the "Georgia Platform" supporting the Compromise. Even Georgians who did not approve knew this was necessary if they were to stay in the Union.

*Above: Robert Augustus Toombs was an ardent secessionist. He served as a United States Representative and Senator. **Opposite page:** As governor of Georgia from 1851-1853, Howell Cobb approved the leasing of the state-owned Western and Atlantic Railroad and worked for increased state funding for education. In 1857, he became secretary of the treasury under President Buchanan but he resigned in 1860. Shortly thereafter, he became president of the Provisional Congress of the Confederacy.*

As the only Georgia governor to serve four successive terms, Joseph Emerson Brown was a strong pro-slavery and states' rights proponent. Like many other Georgia politicians of the period, Brown favored secession and used his terms as governor to prepare the state for war.

Not long after the Georgia Platform was adopted, some Georgians formed the Constitutional Union party. Howell Cobb, an Athens lawyer who had been a Democrat, joined the new party with former Whigs Stephens and Toombs. Cobb was elected governor in 1851. While he was in office, Cobb encouraged the growth of Georgia's railroad system, and state support for schools.

At this same time, Joseph E. Brown, Herschel V. Johnson, and C. B. Strong gathered some Georgians who did not agree with accepting the Compromise of 1850. This group formed the States' Rights party. The party did not want to leave the Union, but they felt southern states should not accept the Compromise until Congress agreed to protect slavery and states' rights.

The Constitutional Union party broke up in August of 1852. It had done what it set out to do: get Georgians to accept the Compromise of 1850. Toombs and Stephens returned to the Democrats, while other Whigs joined the Know-Nothing party. The Know-Nothing party did not want **immigrants** to become citizens, or anyone not born in the United States to hold political office. It was a secret group whose members answered questions with, "I don't know"—thus the name Know-Nothing.

After all the changes, the Democrats became the leading party. In 1856, James Buchanan, the Democratic presidential candidate, carried Georgia with no trouble. The next year, Democrat Joseph E. Brown became governor. Brown believed in states' rights and was also a good manager. He brought about railroad reforms, and used money from state-owned railroads to begin a Common School Fund for public education. Brown was re-elected in 1859, and served two more terms during the Civil War.

Do You Remember?

1. What percent of Georgians owned slaves?
2. How much money did Georgia slave owners have invested in slaves by 1860?
3. What name was later given to Terminus?
4. What were the two main church denominations in Georgia during this period?
5. Who was elected governor of Georgia in 1857?
6. What political party rose to power in the state during the 1850s?

NATIONAL EVENTS FURTHER DIVIDE THE NORTH AND SOUTH

National events added to the sectional problems between the North and South.

LINCOLN ELECTED PRESIDENT

When the Democrats met in Charleston, South Carolina for the national convention in 1860, they decided to campaign on the issue of popular sovereignty. Southern Democrats did not agree, and felt slaves should be allowed in all the territories. The two groups split over the issue. Northern Democrats **nominated** Stephen Douglas for President. Southern Democrats nominated Vice President John Breckenridge.

At the same time, the Republicans met in Chicago, where they nominated Illinois' "favorite son," Abraham Lincoln. The Repub-

During 1858, Illinois residents Stephen A. Douglas and Abraham Lincoln criss-crossed the state debating with each other in an attempt to win the U.S. Senate seat. Lincoln, a tall, six-foot, six-inch, gangly man with a high-pitched voice was an interesting contrast to the deep-voiced, medium height Douglas who was known for his ruffled shirts and embroidered vests. He spoke at a rapid clip compared with the slow-paced speech of Lincoln. Although Douglas won the election to the Senate, the debates threw Lincoln into the national spotlight and led to his election as President two years later.

licans promised they would not try to end slavery in the slave states.

The Know-Nothing party set up a Constitutional Union party and nominated John Bell of Tennessee as its presidential candidate. Their party platform said nothing about slavery. Instead, it asked that people support the Constitution and save the Union. On November 6, Abraham Lincoln was elected President of the United States. Lincoln won without receiving a single electoral vote from states in the South.

SOUTH CAROLINA SECEDES

Southerners knew that, with the election of Lincoln, Congress would not allow slavery in the territories. In December 1860, South Carolina held a state convention to talk about seceding, or pulling out of the Union, and forming a separate government. Many Southerners, including Georgia's Alexander Stephens, said secession was foolish and would hurt the South's politics and economy. However, on December 20, a little more than a month after Lincoln's election, South Carolina left the Union. Radicals in every other southern state wanted to follow South Carolina's lead.

Most Georgians agreed with South Carolina's action. On January 16, 1861, a special convention was held in Milledgeville at

Above: Fifty-two-year-old Jefferson Davis was unanimously elected President of the Confederate States of America on February 9, 1861.

Right: Born in Wilkes County in 1812, Alexander Stephens served as both a state senator and representative. In addition, he represented Georgia as a congressman. Many Southerners opposed Alexander Stephens' selection as the Confederate vice president for he had openly spoken against secession from the Union in the days prior to the outbreak of the Civil War.

the request of Governor Brown. When Eugenius Nisbet proposed a secession **ordinance** to the 297 delegates, 208 voted in favor. On January 19, Georgia was declared an independent republic.

By February 1, 1861, Florida, Alabama, Mississippi, Louisiana, and Texas had also voted to secede from the Union. On February 4, delegates from each of those states met in Montgomery, Alabama and formed themselves into a nation. They named it the Confederate States of America. Mississippian Jefferson Davis became President, Alexander Stephens from Georgia, Vice President, and his fellow Georgian, Robert Toombs, secretary of state. War was only two months away.

GRACE BEDELL

As the story goes, in 1860, eleven-year-old Grace Bedell from Westfield, New York saw a campaign poster of a beardless Abraham Lincoln. Grace thought Lincoln looked far too "homely" to win the election. She sat down and wrote him the following letter:

I hope you won't think me bold to write to such a great man as you are, but want you should be President of the United States very much . . . I have got 4 brothers and part of them will vote for you any way, and if you will let your whiskers grow I will try to get the rest of them to vote for you [period omitted in original] You would look a great deal better for your face is so thin. All the ladies like whiskers and they would tease their husbands to vote for you and then you would be President.

It thrilled Grace when she received a hand-written note from Lincoln. He replied, "As to the whiskers, having never worn any, do you not think people would call it a silly piece of affec[ta]tion if I were to begin it now?" Shortly after Lincoln won the election, he began to grow a beard.

As Lincoln traveled from Illinois to Washington for his inauguration, he stopped the train in Grace's hometown, where he received a warm welcome. It pleased the townspeople when Lincoln mentioned the letter Grace had written him and asked to meet her. A young man in the crowd pointed to an embarrassed Grace Bedell. Lincoln walked over and gave the child "several hearty kisses."

The next time you see a picture of bearded Abraham Lincoln, remember that an eleven-year-old girl influenced history.

Lincoln's gaunt features caused many jokes and cartoons before he grew a beard.

Do You Remember?
1. When was Abraham Lincoln elected President?
2. Which state seceded from the Union first?
3. Why were Southerners against Lincoln's election to the presidency?
4. What was the name the seceding states gave their nation?

CHAPTER REVIEW

Summary

As the antebellum period drew to a close, the differences between the North and South intensified. These conflicts included:

	North	South
Sectionalism	Decisions for good of nation	States' Rights
Slavery	Against	In favor of
Solvency	Industrial Base	Agrarian base primarily as cotton
Styles	Urban/City lifestyle	Rural lifestyle
Structure	Upwardly mobile system	Rigid social class
Secession	Preserve the Union	Establish a separate nation

In the decade right before the Civil War, Georgia had an economy based on farming, and on the institution of slavery. Railroads became the main way to move people and goods. There was little education, but reforms were planned. Church membership grew and Baptists and Methodists were the two largest dominations. In politics, after many changes, the Democrats were in control and Joseph E. Brown was elected governor following the term of Howell Cobb. A combination of national events brought the North and South closer to Civil War. They included: (1) the Compromise of 1850 which limited slavery; (2) the publication of Harriett Beecher Stowe's *Uncle Tom's Cabin*, which increased the influence of abolitionists; (3) the Kansas-Nebraska Act providing for popular sovereignty in deciding if new states would be slave or free; (4) the Dred Scott Decision upholding rights of slave owners; (5) John Brown's raid, which was an example of growing feelings against slavery; (6) the election of Abraham Lincoln in 1860, which caused the southern states to think about leaving the Union; and, (7) the secession of South Carolina, followed by other southern states, and the formation of the Confederate States of America.

People, Places, and Terms

Identify, define and/or state the importance of the following.
1. Joseph E. Brown
2. Kansas-Nebraska Act
3. "Bleeding Kansas"
4. John Brown
5. Robert Toombs
6. Western and Atlantic Railroad
7. Dred Scott
8. "Old Field Schools"
9. secession
10. abolitionist

The Main Idea

Write a short paragraph to answer each question.
1. Describe the life of slaves during the antebellum period.
2. Why was the Compromise of 1850 so important?
3. Why did the election of Abraham Lincoln lead to the South's decision to secede from the Union?

4. List the "six S's" that represented the differences between the North and South and describe each "S."
5. Refer to "Looking Ahead" in Chapter 6. Answer the four questions listed.

Extend Your Thinking

Share your opinion by writing a paragraph or two for each question.

1. Could the Civil War have been avoided? Explain why or why not.
2. Why was slavery called a "peculiar institution"?
3. Read "Did You Know." Which fact interests you the most and why?
4. Re-read Texas Senator Lewis T. Wigfall's comments at the beginning of the chapter. To whom do you think Wigfall was directing his comments? Which of the six issues which divided North and South did he address in his remarks? Give an example of how a particular part of his comments addressed each issue.

Looking Ahead

After seven states had seceded from or left the Union to form their own country, it was only a matter of time until the two sections would be at war. As you study the next chapter, you will discover:

➤ which side—the North or the South—fired the first shot;
➤ how much money a confederate soldier earned each month;
➤ what General Sherman said after marching through Georgia;
➤ when the first black troops were organized;
➤ which battle caused 18,000 men to receive wounds and 4,000 to die.

DID YOU KNOW . . .

. . . Although Abraham Lincoln was the 16th American President, he was the first to wear a beard?

. . . The reference to the South as "Dixie" was used long before the Civil War? Although some say the term came about because of the Mason-Dixon line (the surveyors' boundary between Pennsylvania and Maryland), it is more likely that the term came from New Orleans banks. The "Dix" was a ten dollar bill. Boatmen and tradesmen referred to it as a "Dixie." Since it was a popular money exchange in New Orleans, the lower South became known as Dixieland.

. . . The reason Levis used to have small metal rivets around the pockets dates back to gold mining days? Miners, who put gold nuggets in the pockets, wore out the stitching. A California tailor, Jake Davis, took some pants that needed sewing to a local blacksmith, who put rivets in the pocket corners. The idea worked, and Davis took it to Levis' manufacturer, Levis Strauss. They formed a partnership and continued using the copper rivets until 1937. The company began stitching pockets again because teachers complained that the rivets scratched schoolroom furniture.

. . . Potato chips were the result of a complaint in 1853? A guest at a hotel in Saratoga Springs, New York did not like the thick french fries. To please the diner, the chef sliced the potatoes paper thin and fried them.

. . . In 1860, at Tony's Delight in Chicago, a shave was six cents, haircuts were twelve cents, curling was twenty cents, and a shampoo was twenty-five cents?

. . .The School for the Deaf located in Cave Springs became a state school in 1847?

CHAPTER EIGHT

THE CIVIL WAR
1861-1865

I have no purpose . . . to interfere with the institution of slavery in the States where it exists. I believe I have no lawful right to do so, and I have no inclination to do so. This country, with its institutions, belongs to the people who inhabit it. Whenever they shall have grown weary of the existing government, they can exercise their constitutional right of amending it, or their revolutionary right to dismember or overthrow it. . . . We are not enemies but friends. We must not be enemies. . . . Though passion may have strained, it must not break our bonds of affection. . . . The mystic cords of memory . . . will yet swell the chorus of the Union, when again touched, as they surely will be, by the better angels of our nature.

— Abraham Lincoln, Inaugural Address, March 4, 1861

SEVEN DAYS AFTER Abraham Lincoln spoke the above words, the Congress of the Confederate States of America met in Montgomery, Alabama. Before the day was over, representatives from the seven member states adopted a constitution written in part by Thomas R. Cobb of Georgia. Among other items, the document declared the sovereignty of the states and forbade passage of any laws which would do away with slavery. The stage was set for war.

This memorial to Confederate dead in front of the Bartow County Courthouse in Cartersville was also dedicated to Brigadier General Francis Bartow of Chatham County. Bartow was the first Confederate general to die in battle in the Civil War. Before he lost his life at the Battle of Manassas, it was reported that he suggested the color grey be used for the Confederate uniforms.

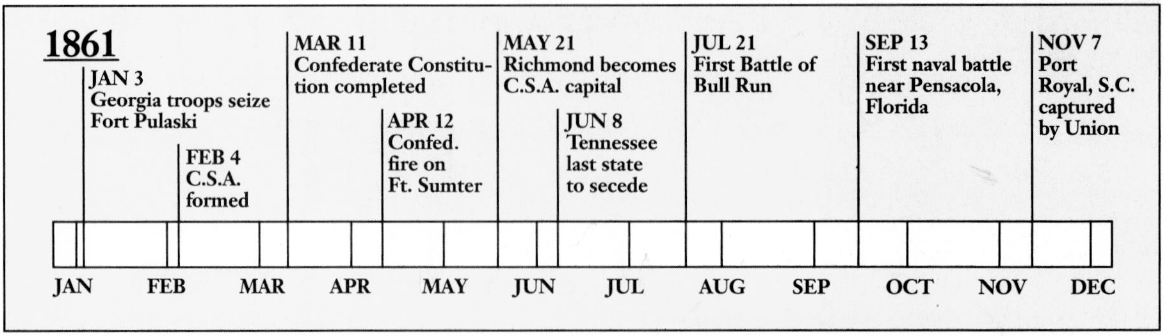

CHAPTER OUTLINE

1. Shots Fired—The Beginning of Civil War

2. The War—Year One

3. The War—Year Two

4. The War—Year Three

5. The War—Year Four

6. The War During the Final Year

SHOTS FIRED — THE BEGINNING OF THE CIVIL WAR

On April 10, 1861, the Confederate government directed Brigadier General Pierre G.T. Beauregard to order the surrender of Fort Sumter, South Carolina by the United States Army **garrison** stationed there. The fort, located in Charleston harbor, was low on supplies. Major Robert Anderson, who felt it was his duty to defend the fort, thought help was on the way, so refused to obey the order.

At 4:30 a.m. on April 12, Confederate troops opened fire on Fort Sumter. When no help arrived, Major Anderson surrendered the fort on April 13, and left it the following day.

Before the fall of Fort Sumter, Confederate forces had captured other federal garrisons in the South. These included Fort Pulaski at Savannah, which fell to Confederate troops on January 3, 1861. However, there were two differences between the other captured garrisons and Fort Sumter. One was that South Carolina had seceded from the Union, and the second was that troops of the North and South exchanged gunfire.

The war, in which seven future United States Presidents fought, which would end slavery, and cause the death of over 618,000 persons, had begun.

PREPARATION FOR WAR

After the firing on Fort Sumter, both North and South stepped up preparation for war. They began training troops and gathering clothing, equipment, and supplies the soldiers would need. Arkansas, Tennessee, North Carolina and Virginia joined the Confederate states, and the capital was moved from Montgomery to Richmond, Virginia.

Conditions in the North and South were very different. The population of the South was about 9,000,000. This included three and a half million slaves, who did not serve as soldiers. The South did not have a strong navy, a trained army, or enough factories to make guns and ammunition. Railroads in the South had been built to move cotton, and the aging railroad system could not easily transport both troops and heavy equipment.

The North's population, on the other hand, was 22,000,000. They had a strong, well-trained army and navy which had protected the country for many years. Northern economy was based on industry, so they could make needed weapons, ammunition, and supplies. Railroads had been built to carry heavy industrial machinery. It was not hard for the Union to gear up for war.

Pro-Union meetings like the one shown here in New York City were commonplace before and after the war began as people demonstrated their support for the Union position.

This review of the troops in Pulaski Square, Savannah, in the first year of the war, was more of a social gathering than a military necessity.

Many citizens on both sides shared one idea. Each thought the war would be short, and each thought his side would win.

During the four years of the Civil War, there were 2,261 battles or engagements. The War Years timelines lists only the major ones. There were often two names for a battle. Most battles were fought in the South, and federal troops did not know the region. They depended on field maps, and usually named battles for nearby streams marked on those maps. The Confederate forces, however, used the names of nearby towns. For example:

Federal	Confederate
Bull Run	Manassas
Antietam	Sharpsburg
Elkshorn Tavern	Pea Ridge
Stone's River	Murfreesboro
Shiloh	Pittsburg Landing

THE WAR — YEAR ONE

On July 21, 1861, three months after the fall of Fort Sumter, the Battle of Bull Run (Manassas) took place. It was the first major battle of the Civil War. Confederate forces won, but no one knows if it was because they fought well or because there was a lot of confusion. Battle flags and uniforms for both sides were very much alike. While the battle was going on, soldiers often could not tell the difference between friends and enemies.

Confederate generals P.G.T. Beauregard and "Stonewall" Jackson and Union General Irwin McDowell had not carried large numbers of men into battle before, so mistakes were common. However, both sides learned something important. Confederate leaders learned that their poorly-trained army could fight. Union leaders began to understand the war would last longer and be harder to win than they had first thought.

When the battle ended, 4,500 soldiers were dead, wounded, or missing. Manassas is near Washington, D.C. Historians will probably always wonder why, after their victory, the Confederate

The first Battle of Bull Run took place next to a creek with the same name. Close to Washington, D.C., the battle drew spectators with picnic baskets who gathered where they could see the battle and cheer for the Union forces. They were very disappointed when the Confederate troops won the first major battle of the war. Notice the array of uniforms shown in the picture.

army did not try to capture the Union capital. One possible explanation is that the newly-formed Confederate forces did not have enough experience in war to take advantage of the situation.

GEORGIA DURING YEAR ONE

At the first Battle of Bull Run, Georgia's 21st Regiment lost 184 of its 242 men, almost 76 percent of its troops. While this was happening, life at home was much as it had been before the war. Georgians Alexander Stephens and Robert Toombs were still major leaders in the Confederate movement. Farmers harvested food crops. They picked cotton and got it ready to ship. Businesses stayed open. Many young men **volunteered** to fight, and soon there were more soldiers than guns. Some troops who went to fight in Virginia were not allowed to take guns out of Georgia because it was thought the guns would be needed to defend the state.

THE CIVIL WAR SOLDIER

Historians have written about big battles and great generals. However, the life of common soldiers gives a truer picture of war. They did not speak exactly the same, and they fought for different governments, but "Johnny Reb" and "Billy Yank" were a lot alike.

Troops had only a few weeks or months to prepare for battle. Farmers, doctors, teachers and merchants suddenly found themselves drilling with weapons they were unaccustomed to using.

Most soldiers were under the age of twenty-three, and some were as young as thirteen. The largest numbers came from the lower economic groups, and knew nothing about war until the fighting started.

Daily Food Ration

Union records from 1864 give the basic daily ration, or portion of food, in ounces for Union soldiers. They received "20-beef, 18-flour, 2.56 dried beans, 1.6 green coffee, 2.4 sugar, .64 salt," and smaller amounts of pepper, yeast powder, soap, candles, and vinegar.

The same kind of records from the Army of Northern Virginia in 1863 list rations for 100 Confederate soldiers over a 30-day period. Each day they had to share "1/4 pound of bacon, 18 oz. of flour, 10 lbs. of rice, and a small amount of peas and dried fruits when they could be obtained."

Both sides depended on food found in the woods or taken from farms. Confederate soldiers may have had more trouble getting what they needed. There were times when they fought for several days with very little to eat. By the end of the war, many of them were starving.

Clothing

At the beginning of the war, Confederate soldiers dressed in double-breasted, hip-length coats and gray pants. These coats were later replaced by short-waisted, single breasted jackets. There was different trim on the uniforms for each branch of the army. Red stood for the artillery, blue for the infantry, and yellow for the cavalry. Officers' uniforms had buttons which showed their branch of service. The uniforms of Union soldiers were blue, but the trim was much the same as the Confederates. Caps and hats had branch insignia in appropriate colors.

Regular foot soldiers on both sides dressed with less care. Early in the war, they did not often wear ties. As the war went on, Confederate soldiers wore clothing made at home and sent by friends and relatives. Soldiers had knapsacks in which to carry writing paper, pictures, books, and toilet articles. However, soldiers found the knapsacks hard to keep up with, and soon lost them. They wrapped personal items in a blanket and carried them in a tent

Under the leadership of twenty-nine-year old John Gordon, a group of mountaineer miners suddenly found themselves Confederate soldiers. They were called the "Racoon Roughs" because the only thing they shared in common as a uniform was their coonskin caps.

In addition to inadequate uniforms, limited food, and the sharp contradiction of bloody days of battle followed by limitless hours of boredom, the soldiers also had to face winter nights with no protection from the cold weather. The lucky ones had larger tents or log huts.

canvas. Soldiers also carried a musket and a leather box for ammunition. On their belts they fastened a cap box, a bayonet in its **sheath**, a sewing kit, and mess equipment. These eating tools consisted of a knife, fork, spoon, cup and, sometimes, a light cooking skillet. All these items together weighed about forty or fifty pounds. The longer a soldier stayed in the army, the more likely he was to leave everything he could do without in camp or along the roadside.

Shelter

During warm months, soldiers slept in two-man tents on the ground. Officers often had A-shaped tents with several chairs, a bed, and a stove inside them. In winter, soldiers sometimes had log huts or larger tents, which offered more protection.

Camp Life

During the first part of the war, camp life for Union and Confederate troops was about the same. **Reveille** sounded at dawn. Men dressed quickly, lined up for roll call and drill, and then ate breakfast. Even though inspections and drills took up most of the day, there was some free time. Soldiers wrote letters, cleaned their rifles, played games, or rested.

After the fighting started, camp life changed. The men spent nights taking care of the wounded, or talking over the day's battle. Between battles, they played cards or checkers, or rolled dice. Sometimes they had foot races, boxed, played leap frog, or wrestled. In winter it was common for companies or regiments to have snowball fights. One such fight is said to have occurred near Dalton in March 1864. Several thousand men representing Georgia and Tennessee took time out from drills to play in the snow.

There are many stories about music around campfires at night. Soldiers who had instruments played while the others sang. Some of their favorite songs were "Tenting on the Old Camp Ground," "Auld Lang Syne," "Rock of Ages," "On Jordan's Stormy Banks I Stand," and "Lorena." The ballad sung most often by men on both sides was "Home Sweet Home."

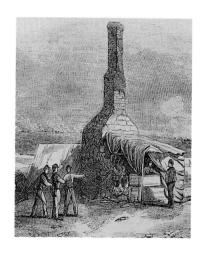

Unlike the well-planned, hot cooked meals provided for combat soldiers today, Confederate and Union troops during the Civil War had to eat whatever was available. Frequently this meant eating spoiled food cooked just enough to make it digestible.

Discipline

As the war continued, behavior was a growing problem. Some soldiers stole, drank, and did not obey their officers. It became common for men to desert the army. About 100,000 Confederate and 200,000 Union troops left without leave.

Soldiers whose wrong behavior was mostly mischief might be shut up in the guard house, or made to drag a cannon ball by a chain fastened around the ankle. Sometimes soldiers were punished by having to wear signs around their necks. Written on the signs were words like "Coward," "Thief," or "I stole a skillet." At other times, someone who did wrong had to wear a barrel, called a wooden overcoat, on which was written what he had done.

For a more serious **offense**, branding was used. The letter describing the offense was stamped on the face, hand or hip. "D" stood for deserter. "C" was for cowardice. "W" represented worthlessness. Some men were killed by a firing squad as punishment for murder, spying, or desertion. Sleeping on duty was considered a capital offense, but there is no record of an execution for such behavior.

Do You Remember?

1. What were the major differences between the North and South in ability to prepare for war?
2. Which Georgia regiment lost 184 men at the first Battle of Bull Run?
3. What was another name for the Battle of Bull Run?
4. What military item was Georgia short of in 1861?
5. What were nicknames for Confederate and Union soldiers?

During 1862, the war escalated quickly. Thirty-seven battles were fought in the second year of the war. They had names like Pea Ridge in Arkansas, Shiloh in Tennessee, and the second Battle of Bull Run in Virginia. These and other battles, including Antietam in Maryland, and Fredericksburg in Virginia, led to heavy losses on both sides. Many records kept by the Confederacy were lost or destroyed. Historians have had to guess the number of Confederate casualties. Estimates of losses from dead, wounded or missing soldiers during these battles number well over 137,742 for Union forces and over 164,177 in the Confederate ranks.

More than 100,000 men took part in the Battle of Shiloh on April 6 and 7. Fresh Union troops arrived on the second day of the battle, and the Union won. However, the number of men hurt or killed made it clear that the war would be costly.

In June, General Robert E. Lee, a West Point graduate and former federal officer, became commander of the Confederate troops in Virginia.

BATTLE OF ANTIETAM

The bloodiest one-day battle of the war was fought in 1862 at Antietam Creek near Sharpsburg, Maryland. Lee lost over 2,000 men and more than 9,000 were wounded. Union forces under General McClellan also had large losses. When the South re-

Known as the bloodiest one-day battle of the war, Antietam near Sharpsburg, Maryland, may have been the result of a careless mistake. It is reported that a Confederate officer wrote down information about the impending battle and wrapped the paper around three cigars. The paper, which he then discarded, was later picked up by a federal soldier and the information on it led General McClellan to attack Lee's divided army. Although historians are unsure which stories about Antietam are true, they do illustrate the tremendous confusion during the ill-planned conflict.

1862	FEB 8 Roanoke Is., N.C. captured by Union	APR 6-7 Battle of Shiloh	JUN 1 Robert E. Lee named commander of Confederate forces	AUG 9 Battle of Cedar Mountain, Virginia	SEP 7 Battle of Antietam
	MAR 6-7 Battle of Pea Ridge				SEP 22 Emancipation Proclamation Issued

JAN	FEB	MAR	APR	MAY	JUN	JUL	AUG	SEP	OCT	NOV	DEC

treated, McClellan did not follow Lee's army and capture the remaining troops. If he had, some historians think the war might have ended then. Because McClellan's army did not take advantage of Lee's retreat, President Lincoln removed him from command.

THE EMANCIPATION PROCLAMATION

On September 22, 1862, five days after the Battle of Antietam, Abraham Lincoln issued the Emancipation Proclamation. He wanted the Confederate states to end the war and return to the Union. In this now famous document, Lincoln stated that unless the South surrendered by January 1, 1863, "all slaves in states or districts in rebellion against the United States on January 1, 1863, will be thenceforth and forever free."

For the next three months and nine days, the Confederacy had a choice. If they surrendered, slavery would continue in the South. If they did not, the institution of slavery would end.

GEORGIA DURING THE SECOND YEAR OF THE WAR

While Confederate forces were fighting in Virginia, two places on the Georgia coast were getting their first major attacks. They were Tybee Island and Fort Pulaski, both located about fifteen miles east of Savannah.

It took eighteen years and over a million dollars to build the brick fort named for revolutionary war hero Count Casimir Pulaski. That was a lot of money in the 1800s, when the whole federal budget was only twenty to thirty million dollars a year. United States troops first occupied the fort in 1847.

Confederate troops took Fort Pulaski on January 3, 1861. They dug trenches and put down heavy pieces of wood to support the

After hundreds of Union troops had fled the battle field at the first Battle of Bull Run on July 21, 1861, an embarrassed President Lincoln appointed General George B. Mc-Clellan as commander of the Union forces. Research the life of McClellan and find out what he thought of Abraham Lincoln.

The heavily armed federal Fort Pulaski, originally built to protect the city of Savannah, was taken over by Confederate forces in the early days of the war. On April 10, 1862, Union troops began a day and a half of steady bombardment and the fort began to fall.

cannon. General Lee visited the fort and thought it safe from Union fire.

Union forces took Tybee Island in early April 1862. They asked Fort Pulaski's 25-year old commander and his 385 men to surrender the fort, which was a mile across the Savannah River. Colonel Olmstead refused, and Union troops started firing on the fort at 8:00 on the morning of April 10. A day and a half later, ammunition from Union guns began breaking down the fort's walls, and Olmstead surrendered.

In a letter to his wife, Olmstead wrote, "I feel that I have done my duty, my whole duty, that I have been forced to yield only to [the] superior might of metal. Guns such as have never before been brought to bear against any fortification have overpowered me, but I trust to history to keep my name untarnished."

After the capture of Fort Pulaski, there were no more forts built of brick.

Union troops moved into the fort and repaired it. They smoothed the grass-covered parade ground where it had been hit by gun shells. Soldiers could then use the grounds for troop drills and baseball games.

In other parts of Georgia, the second year of the war brought the beginning of hardships. It was harder to get clothes, farm tools and food. Governor Brown increased state taxes to try to support the government. At least one reason for the lack of goods was the North's use of **blockades**.

Top: *Today as you walk among the ruins of Fort Pulaski, you can almost hear the roar of the cannon or the pitiful shouts of the injured.*
Left: *After the surrender of Fort Pulaski, Union General Hunter stated that "the result of this bombardment must cause . . . a change in the construction of fortifications. No works of stone or brick can resist the impact of rifled artillery of heavy caliber. . . ."*

A Union ship spots a Confederate blockade runner. Blockade runners risked daily danger and possible death to bring in clothes, medicine, tools and war materiel to ports in the South desperate for these items. In turn, the blockade runners took bales of cotton to European markets. As Union forces sealed these ports, thousands of bales of cotton lay rotting on the docks and the South went without the equipment and supplies needed to sustain the conflict.

BLOCKADES

President Lincoln and Union commanders knew they could hurt the South by closing ports along the 4,000-mile coastline. Confederate ships would then be unable to take out cotton and tobacco or bring in guns and supplies.

There were blockades even before Virginia and North Carolina seceded from the Union. Early in the war, twenty-six Union ships steamed up and down the coast to keep boats from going in or out of the ports. The Union spent millions of dollars to build more vessels. Seventy-four of these ships were iron-clad. They were no match for the Confederate navy or the private ships which tried to steal past the port blockades. There were over 650 private "blockade runners." During 1861, nine out of every ten of them ran past the federal ships and sailed into open waters.

Blockade running was a profitable business. Captains were paid $5,000 for each trip, and pilots earned $3,500. Many ship owners and **speculators** made millions of dollars during the war. For example, the price of cotton was only three cents a pound in the South, but ten cents to a dollar a pound in England. The profit on 1,000 bales of cotton sold in England was about $250,000.

Later in the war, it was not as easy for blockade runners to get past federal ships. By 1863, one out of every four was captured before reaching the open sea. By 1865, only half of them outran federal ships.

By the time Fort Pulaski fell in 1862, the Union had closed most Confederate ports. The economy of the antebellum South was based on farming rather than industry. Always before, they could export what they grew and import items they needed. Now, they could not get enough clothes, medicine, guns, and ammunition. Some Southern leaders wondered if the Confederacy could even hope for victory unless they found a way to bring in supplies.

BLACKS IN THE ARMED FORCES

There were 178,985 **enlisted** men and 7,122 officers in black regiments during the Civil War. About 3,500 of them were from Georgia. The question of large scale use of black troops was a central issue all through the war.

When the war began, the Union refused to allow blacks to serve in the army. Since blacks had fought in the American Revolution

After General David Hunter organized the first black troops in 1862, it was over a year before a black regiment saw active military duty. This picture shows black Union troops fighting in Georgia.

Port Hudson was a Confederate fort on the Mississippi River. On July 8, 1863, after a six-week siege, Confederate General Gardner and his force of 5,500 men surrendered to Union General Banks. Members of the First and Third Louisiana Native Guard, black Union regiments, received commendations for "Meritorious Service" as a result of bravery shown at Port Hudson.

and the War of 1812, leaders like Frederick Douglass thought they should be allowed to fight in this war.

General David Hunter first organized black troops in 1862. When the war department would not back him Hunter disbanded all but one company. General James Lane from Kansas organized black troops who took part in several western battles. Slowly, public opinion changed and, by 1863, the war department allowed governors of several states to seek black soldiers. By October, there were fifty-eight black regiments in the Union army.

At first, many black troops built defenses, manned garrisons, and kept up the camps. Others acted as nurses, scouts, cooks, and spies. In some regiments, most of the infantrymen were black. During one federal attack on Port Hudson, near Baton Rouge, on May 27, 1863, two of these regiments were praised for "meritorious performance." Other major engagements included Milliken's Bend near Vicksburg in June 1863, and an assault on Fort Wagner near Charleston, South Carolina.

Lewis Douglass, son of abolitionist and orator, Frederick Douglass, fought at Fort Wagner. Describing the battle, Lewis Douglass wrote, "I had my sword blown away. . . [and though] swept down like chaff, still our men went on and on."

By the end of the war, nearly ten percent of the Union army was made up of freed blacks and former slaves. About 37,300 lost their lives while serving in 449 engagements. Seventeen black soldiers and four black sailors were awarded the Congressional Medal of Honor.

This picture shows the quarters for black Union soldiers in the Army of the James. Although both black and white served in the Civil War as they had in earlier American wars, the black soldiers were separated from their white counterparts in most battles, duty assignments, and living quarters. While they fought for the same side, they did not literally fight "side by side."

Confederate leaders, seeing the Union example, began to discuss the use of blacks in their army. There was considerable opposition, since the Confederacy had gone to war to defend a social and political system of slavery. General Howell Cobb summarized the thinking of those opposed to using blacks in the Confederate army when he wrote, "You cannot make soldiers of slaves nor slaves of soldiers . . . The day you make soldiers of them is the beginning of the end of our revolution. If slaves will make good soldiers our whole theory of slavery is wrong."

General Robert E. Lee argued, "We must decide whether slavery shall be extinguished by our enemies and the slave used against us, or use them ourselves at the risk of the effects which may be produced upon our social institutions. . . . We should employ them without delay."

On March 13, 1865, President Jefferson Davis took Lee's advice and signed the Negro Soldier Law which allowed slaves to enlist in the Confederate army. A few blacks enlisted in Richmond, but before a black regiment could be organized, Richmond had fallen to Union forces and the Civil War was drawing to an end.

Do You Remember?

1. Who won the Battle of Antietam?
2. What were the terms of the Emancipation Proclamation?
3. Where is Fort Pulaski located? Why was the battle at Fort Pulaski so short?

JAN	FEB	MAR	APR	MAY	JUN	JUL	AUG	SEP	OCT	NOV	DEC

JAN 1
Emancipation Proclamation
put into effect

MAY 1-4
Battle of Chancellorsville

JUL 1-3
Battle of Gettysburg

JUL 4
Vicksburg Surrenders

SEP 19-20
Battle of
Chickamauga

NOV 25
Battle
of
Chatta-
nooga

THE WAR — YEAR THREE

The halfway point of the Civil War was in 1863. During that year there were 627 battles. Over half of them were in Virginia, Tennessee and Mississippi.

In January, Lincoln enforced the Emancipation Proclamation. Southern states did not stop fighting by the end of 1862, so, on January 1, 1863, both abolitionists and slaves rejoiced. However, the Emancipation Proclamation did not end all slavery on January 1, 1863. There was still slavery in the United States until December 18, 1868, when the Thirteenth Amendment to the Constitution was ratified. However, the Emancipation Proclamation gave hope that all slaves would soon be free.

The war was fairly quiet during the early part of 1863. Major

Above: Abraham Lincoln's first choice for commander of the Union Army was Robert E. Lee. However, Lee decided to return to Virginia to lead the Confederate troops instead.
Right: On July 1, 1863, Union General George Meade met a small force of Confederate troops at Gettysburg, Pennsylvania. For two days artillery blazed until Confederate General George Pickett led 15,000 men against Union forces. The attack failed and Confederate forces were forced to retreat.

fighting did not begin again until the spring and summer. Key Confederate victories included the Battle of Chancellorsville in May, under the direction of Robert E. Lee, and the Battle of Chickamauga in September. There were many more Union victories. The Battle of Gettysburg in July was the last battle on Northern soil. All other battles were in the South.

After the Battle of Vicksburg in Mississippi, 31,277 Southern soldiers were listed as dead, wounded, or missing. This battle gave the Union control of the Mississippi River. The Confederacy was cut in half and any hope for Confederate victory ended.

GEORGIA DURING 1863

While Union forces led by General Grant were taking Vicksburg, General William Rosecrans and his army moved against Chattanooga, Tennessee. Chattanooga was a major railroad center

By the fall of 1862, a 250-mile stretch of the Mississippi River between Vicksburg, Mississippi and Port Hudson, Louisiana, was all that remained in Confederate hands. Union General Ulysses Grant led an attack on Vicksburg against Confederate forces under the command of General John Pemberton, but was repulsed. In May 1863, Grant began a siege of Vicksburg that lasted until July 4 when Pemberton surrendered in the face of mutiny by his demoralized troops.

Top: In addition to the lives lost at the Battle of Chickamauga, the South failed to follow up on a strategic victory. Above: General William Rosencrans, commander of federal forces at Chickamauga.

from which supplies and munitions were sent to Southern troops.

On September 19 and 20, Rosecrans' troops met Confederate General Braxton Bragg seven miles south of Chattanooga at Chickamauga Creek. The Indian meaning of Chickamauga is "River of Death." On September 19 and 20, 17,804 Confederate and 15,851 Union troops were killed, wounded, or missing. The Union made several mistakes, so Bragg and his forces won the battle and forced the Union army back into Chattanooga. Bragg did not follow the Union troops northward into Tennessee and, by November, General U. S. Grant arrived with more soldiers. The Battle of Chattanooga, on November 23, 24, and 25, placed the area in the hands of the Union. Bragg retreated to Dalton.

There were not enough medical supplies anywhere in Georgia, and people were very short of other items normally used daily. Farmers planted less cotton and grew more grains and other foods.

LIFE IN THE SOUTH

In 1863, the South depended on importing "everything from a hair pin to a tooth pick and from a cradle to a coffin." They could not get farm supplies, including seed, horse harnesses, rope, and water tubs. The cost of feed for the animals and salt to cure, or preserve, meat was high. It was almost impossible to get coffee and sugar. Household items such as soap, candles, and matches were hard to find. People often went without oil or gas for lighting and wood or coal for heating.

Bread riots broke out in Richmond. Many southerners used food items they had never tried before. Some ate mule meat and rats. Molasses was used instead of sugar. When they didn't have coffee, people made drinks from chicory, peanuts, okra seed, and sweet potatoes.

Women used curtains or carpets to make clothes. Shoes were made from horsehide, deer or pig skin and, sometimes, book covers. When they could not get the right kind of paper, some publishers used multicolored or patterned wallpaper for newsprint.

Prices in the South shot up and money was worth less. Salt, which had cost a penny a pound before the war, rose to fifty cents a pound. Flour jumped to two hundred dollars a barrel. People began to barter or trade items. According to one report, a woman traded a six hundred dollar hat for five turkeys. Newspaper ads with barter requests were common. This notice appeared in the *Savannah Republican*:

> *I will barter salt from my salt factory for produce on the following terms: salt, 50 pounds per bushel; 4 bushels salt for 5 bushels of corn and peas; 1 bushel salt for 5 pounds of lard or bacon; 2 bushels salt for 7 pounds of sugar; 10 bushels of salt for a barrel of "super" flour; 2 bushels of salt for 1 pr. of shoes.*

There were not enough teachers or books to keep most schools open. Soldiers needed ammunition and horses, so there were few hunts and races. Some communities tried to raise money for the war with talent shows, musicals or, occasionally, road shows. The admission price of one such show in Uniontown, Alabama was $2.00 or "one pair of socks."

Neighbors and friends still visited each other, but these gatherings were no longer carefree parties. Southern women, trying to keep up family farms, did not always look forward to getting mail. They knew any letter might bring news of an injured or dead husband, son, or brother. The spirit of the people was not nearly so high as it had been in 1861.

Confederate General Braxton Bragg, commander of the Army of Tennessee, was the officer in charge of the Battle of Chickamauga. His failure to follow the defeated Rosencrans back into Tennessee and to recapture Chattanooga not only cost him his command but led the way for Sherman's disastrous march through Georgia.

In 1863, the United States Congress passed a conscription, or draft, law to increase the numbers of federal troops. As in the South, federal draftees could pay their way out of military service. Many laborers only made about $300 per year and paying their way out of the draft was not an option. Angry and disillusioned, numbers of men joined together in draft riots during 1863. The worst riots, shown here, took place in New York City during four days in July. Over 1,000 people were killed or wounded before federal troops restored order.

LIFE IN THE NORTH

The North did not escape hardships during the middle of the war. Sick and wounded men filled churches, government buildings, and even halls in the Capitol.

Congress passed conscription, or draft, laws in 1863. When the war began, everyone thought it would be over quickly, so thousands of men joined the service. After two years, it was not so easy to get soldiers. Draft riots broke out in New York and some other cities when the conscription offices opened. The Civil War draft law said that all adult males between the ages of twenty and forty-five had one of three choices: 1) They could enter the service to fight; 2) they could hire someone to fight in their place; or 3) they could pay the federal government three hundred dollars and stay out of the service. Men who could afford it often chose one of the latter two options.

Men too old to fight, women, and children filled the places left by soldiers. They worked on farms or in factories. One song popular during that period said:

Just take your gun and go,
For Ruth can drive the oxen, John,
And I can use the hoe!"

However, even with hardships in the North, life was different, mainly because much of it went on without interruption. Most battles were being fought in the South, so farms and factories could continue their work. This resulted in a Northern economic boom.

Farms in the North and West grew, and there was plenty of corn, oats, and wheat. Farmers produced more hogs, cattle, and sheep. They provided a good supply of food, and wool for making cloth.

Factory owners found new or improved ways to make a profit. The sewing machine, invented ten years before the war, made a great change in the production of clothing and shoes. Using a sewing machine, a worker could make a man's shirt in an hour. It took about fourteen hours to make one by hand. Businessmen built new factories to meet the Union's need for uniforms and shoes.

Ways of canning food were improved. Items, including Gail Borden's canned milk, could be sent where they were needed for children and service men.

Union Army hospitals, like Carver Hospital near Washington, D.C., treated over six-million cases during the war. These wards were in sharp contrast to the primitive field hospitals set up at battle sites.

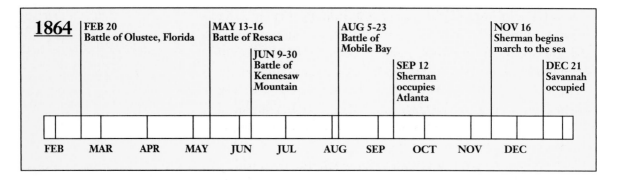

1864	FEB 20 Battle of Olustee, Florida	MAY 13-16 Battle of Resaca		AUG 5-23 Battle of Mobile Bay		NOV 16 Sherman begins march to the sea	
			JUN 9-30 Battle of Kennesaw Mountain		SEP 12 Sherman occupies Atlanta		DEC 21 Savannah occupied

FEB   MAR   APR   MAY   JUN   JUL   AUG   SEP   OCT   NOV   DEC

Ulysses S. Grant, who changed his name from Herman Ulysses Grant to avoid the initials HUG, was a brilliant military tactician. He served as commander of Union forces and later as President of the United States.

Prices for goods rose in the North as well as the South. Many businessmen became very wealthy. Such people as Andrew Carnegie, J.P. Morgan, John D. Rockefeller, Marshall Field, Charles A. Pillsbury, and Gustavus Swift earned most of their money during the war years. Their importance to the economy continued through Reconstruction and into modern times.

Social life in Northern cities did not change much during the war. People still had dinner parties, receptions, and dances. Large crowds attended horse races, the opera, and the theater. In New York, wealthy people had grand picnics in the park. Prize fighting, which was against the law, became a favorite sport of the "less refined." A prize fight between two Irishmen almost drew attention from the Battle of Chancellorsville. A hundred miles from the battle, the two men fought with bare fists for sixty-one rounds while a huge crowd cheered them on.

Another part of Northern social life involved helping others. It was during this time that national charities were begun. Volunteers gave time and money to help those in need. At home, women sewed for men "at the front," and religious groups sent Bibles, pamphlets, and missionaries to the battlefields. Others served as volunteer nurses' aides for the wounded. However, even with the areas which were almost alike before the war, life in the North and South during the Civil War period was quite different.

Do You Remember?

1. Who won the Battle of Chickamauga? What mistake did General Bragg make?
2. What was bartering?
3. What was conscription?

THE WAR — YEAR FOUR

The height of the Civil War was in 1864. There were 779 battles, and most of them were in Virginia, Tennessee, Arkansas, and Georgia.

Confederate General Robert E. Lee won his last major victory at Cold Harbor, Virginia on June 3. Lee's 59,000 troops fought against 108,000 Union men. Confederate forces had already lost many men in battles or to disease and, between May 7 and June 3, they lost 32,000 more. Union losses during this period were 50,000. However, the North could replace its men and the South could not.

Ulysses S. Grant became commander of all the Union forces, and during the next nine months Lee's and Grant's armies met again and again. The Union almost always won.

The fourth year of the war was also an election year. Democrats, who thought the war had gone on too long, nominated General George McClellan for President. Lincoln was again the Republican candidate. Some important Union victories made Lincoln more popular, and he was re-elected on November 8. Andrew Johnson of Tennessee was elected Vice President.

Food, clothing, and medical supplies were needed all over the country. In the South, Confederate money kept dropping in value.

An army wagon train passes through Resaca at night. In mid-May 1864, Confederate General Joseph E. Johnston was able to hold back federal troops at Resaca for a few days, but was finally forced to begin a southerly retreat to Kennesaw Mountain.

The Battle of Kennesaw Mountain

Beginning on June 27, 1864, the Battle of Kennesaw Mountain was a decisive military victory for Confederate General Johnston's troops against Sherman's troops. Although Sherman lost nearly 3,000 men, it did not stop his march toward Atlanta. In addition, Jefferson Davis, dissatisfied with Johnson's constant retreating tactics, replaced the brilliant warrior with General John B. Hood on July 18, to the dismay of the battle-weary Confederate troops.

By the war's end Confederate money was worthless, making the rebuilding of Georgia even more difficult.

A pair of shoes which had cost three dollars before the war now cost over fifty dollars. Quinine, used for fever and infections, cost a hundred dollars an ounce. Toward the end of the year, it took a thousand dollars to buy a barrel of flour.

GEORGIA IN 1864

There were 108 Civil War battles in Georgia, 92 of them in 1864. Most of Georgia's battles were a direct result of the Battle of Chickamauga, when General Bragg allowed Union leader Ulysses S. Grant to take over Chattanooga. When Grant moved his army

From July 28 to August 31, Atlanta was attacked by Union troops on the north and east. The lack of a clear victory forced General Sherman to move his troops south to Jonesboro. The fighting was fierce for the next two days but Hood's outnumbered army was unable to hold out and evacuated Atlanta on September 1.

Top: From September 2 until November 15, federal troops systematically destroyed Atlanta. On November 15, the city was set afire as Sherman left Atlanta on his march to Savannah. The lighted skyline of the blazing city could be seen for miles. Above: To ensure that Confederate troops could no longer transport men or military equipment, Sherman ordered the destruction of the railroad tracks leading in and out of Atlanta.

east to meet Lee, he placed 112,000 men in Chattanooga under the command of General William Tecumseh Sherman. Sherman took his men and started toward Atlanta. Southern General Joseph E. Johnston, who had replaced Bragg because of his military mistakes at Chickamauga, had 60,000 troops to hold back Sherman's army.

During the late spring and early summer of 1864, the two armies fought at Dalton, Resaca, and New Hope. At each of these battles, Johnston had to retreat, but he burned bridges and blocked roads as he went. This slowed Sherman's forward movement to about two miles a day. In June, Sherman attacked Confederate forces at Kennesaw Mountain, and Johnston's army won.

Jefferson Davis, President of the Confederacy, wanted Sherman's army attacked head on. He replaced General Johnston with John Bell Hood. In July, Hood led his men against the Union forces and lost over 11,000 troops in two days. The two armies fought during July and August until Sherman had his forces all the way around Atlanta. Hood left the city on September 1, following the evacuation of Atlanta citizens.

The next day, the Union army moved into Atlanta and took over its railroads and factories. The soldiers stayed until November 15 when, at about three o'clock in the afternoon, they set fire to the city. On November 16, Sherman's army left Atlanta in flames and began their famous "March to the Sea."

Sherman's March to the Sea

Sherman's army moved quickly through the state. Sixty-two thousand soldiers cut a path sixty miles wide on the three-hundred-mile trip from Atlanta to Savannah. Mostly, they lived by killing livestock, and taking food from farms, stores, and homes they burned along the way.

On December 22, 1864, Sherman sent a wire to Abraham Lincoln: "I beg to present you as a Christmas gift the City of Savannah, with one hundred fifty heavy guns, and plenty of ammunition, also about twenty-five thousand bales of cotton." The next day, Union troops took over Savannah. Sherman had finished his plan. The lower South was now cut off from the rest of the Confederacy. Estimates of damage were as high as $100,000,000.

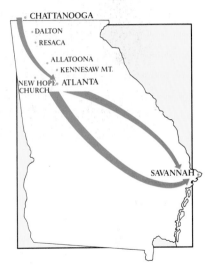

Andersonville Prison

During the fourth year of the war, General Grant stopped exchanging prisoners with the South. This kept the Confederacy from getting back men needed for the army. One of the Confederate prisons for Union men was in Andersonville, Georgia. The prison was dirty, and there was not enough food, water, or medical supplies. Close to thirty percent of the prisoners died. Stories from Andersonville were so bad that the Confederate War Department had a medical team look at the prison. The team suggested moving prisoners to better places. The prison com-

In 1863, the decision was made to build a prison in the deep South. Andersonville, a railroad station twelve miles from Americus, Georgia was chosen as the site. The stockade was built to hold 8,000 to 10,000 men. By May 1864, over 22,000 men were so piled in that each man had a space of 33 square feet. A severe lack of medical supplies and food caused the deaths of more than 13,000 captured Union soldiers, many of whom are buried in Andersonville.

mander at the end of the war, Captain Henry Wirz, was executed in 1865 for "excessive cruelty," although records indicate he did try to improve conditions at the prison. By no means were the horrors of prison camps limited to Andersonville. Over 26,000 Southerners died in Northern camps like Point Lookout, Maryland and Camp Douglas, Illinois.

Neither North nor South had foreseen the large numbers of prisoners or the problem of trying to house and feed them in limited space.

Today, Andersonville, where 13,700 Union dead are buried, is a national cemetery.

Do You Remember?

1. Who led the Union army's march from Atlanta to Savannah?
2. Where was General Lee's last major victory?
3. How many battles were fought in Georgia in 1864?
4. When did Sherman arrive in Savannah?

FEB 7
Columbia, S.C.
set on fire

APR 3
Union troops occupy Richmond

APR 9
Robert E. Lee surrenders at Appomattox Courthouse, Virginia

APR 14
Lincoln
assassinated

MAY 29
President Johnson issues Proclamation
of Amnesty

DEC 18
13th
Amend-
ment
ratified

| FEB | MAR | APR | MAY | JUN | JUL | AUG | SEP | OCT | NOV | DEC |

THE WAR DURING THE FINAL YEAR

Soon after Union troops took Savannah, the war started coming to an end in other parts of the South. On January 15, Fort Fisher, North Carolina was captured. This closed the last Confederate port. A month later, Sherman burned Columbia, South Carolina.

In Virginia, Robert E. Lee kept fighting Grant's army, which was twice the size of the remaining Confederate troops. Lee's men were weary and starving, and so on March 2, he asked for a meeting with Grant to talk about ending the war. President Lincoln refused to allow the meeting unless the South surrendered.

On March 25, Lee tried once again to push federal troops back

On Sunday, April 9, 1865, the Civil War was over. Georgia's Major General John B. Gordon was chosen by General Robert E. Lee to lead his men down the street to the house of Wilmer McLean at Appomattox Court House Village in Virginia. In McLean's home, Lee and Union General Ulysses Grant met. General Grant then carefully wrote out the terms of the Confederate surrender.

from Petersburg, Virginia. He failed and, before he could reach the Confederate army in North Carolina, Union troops cut off the retreat. President Jefferson Davis knew the war was almost over, so he left Richmond and went to Danville, Virginia to avoid capture.

On April 9, 1865, General Lee surrendered to Grant at Appomattox Courthouse in Virginia. There were a few more small battles in North Carolina, but the Civil War was officially over. It was time to make the North and South one nation again.

THE ASSASSINATION OF LINCOLN

On Good Friday, April 14, 1865, five days after Lee's surrender, Abraham Lincoln turned to his wife, Mary Todd, and said, "I never felt so happy in my life." That evening the couple and some friends went to Ford's Theater to see an English play, "Our American Cousin."

The play was nearly over when an actor loyal to the Confederacy entered Lincoln's theater box. At 10:15 p.m., John Wilkes Booth stopped any celebration of Union victory when he shot Abraham Lincoln in the back of the head. Booth broke his leg when he jumped from the box to the stage. As he escaped, he shouted the state motto of Virginia: "Sic semper tyrannis," "Thus ever be to tyrants." President Lincoln was moved to a boarding house next to the theater, where he died at 7:22 the next morning.

Above: John Wilkes Booth, who had been present when John Brown of Harper's Ferry was hanged, allegedly had planned only to kidnap President Lincoln. His decision to assassinate the President had been made on the day of the deed. The reason behind the assassination has never been clear other than the fact that Booth was a Confederate sympathizer. Right: Booth's decision to shoot Lincoln had a dramatic impact on Reconstruction and, perhaps, on the future history of our nation.

O CAPTAIN! MY CAPTAIN!

Walt Whitman

After the death of Lincoln, poet Walt Whitman expressed the
feelings of many in the nation in the following poem.

O Captain! my Captain! our fearful trip is done,
The ship has weather'd every rock, the prize we sought is won,
The port is near, the bells I hear, the people all exulting,
While follow eyes the steady keel, the vessel grim and daring;
     But O heart! heart! heart!
     O the bleeding drops of red,
     Where on the deck my Captain lies,
     Fallen cold and dead.
O Captain! my Captain! rise up and hear the bells;
Rise up - for you the flag is flung - for you the bugle trills,
For you bouquets and ribbon'd wreaths - for you the shores
    a-crowding,
For you they call, the swaying mass, their eager faces turning;
     Here Captain! dear father!
     The arm beneath your head!
     It is some dream that on the deck,
     You've fallen cold and dead.
My Captain does not answer, his lips are pale and still,
My father does not feel my arm, he has no pulse nor will,
The ship is anchor'd safe and sound, its voyage closed and done,
From fearful trip the victor ship comes in with object won;
     Exult O shores, and ring O bells!
     But I with mournful tread,
     Walk the deck my Captain lies,
     Fallen cold and dead.

*Walt Whitman had served as a
volunteer nurse in Washington,
D.C. during the Civil War. His feelings for President Lincoln were eloquently expressed in his famous
poem, "O Captain! My Captain!"*

Extending Your Thinking

After reading Whitman's poem, answer the following questions:
1. How did Whitman feel about the death of Lincoln?
2. Do you think everyone agreed with the sentiments expressed
   by Whitman in the poem? Why or why not?

Historians do not agree on the exact details, but most of them believe John Wilkes Booth went from the theater to a farm in Virginia. He hid there until April 26, when federal troops and secret service agents found him in a barn. Sergeant Boston Corbett, acting against orders, fired into the barn and hit Booth in the neck. The troops moved Booth from the barn, and he died the next day.

Some reports say Corbett was given $1,653.85 for his part in capturing Booth. Later, he tried to kill members of the Kansas legislature and was placed in a hospital for the mentally ill. In the years that followed, as many as twenty men said they were John Wilkes Booth, and there were numbers of stories of his supposed escape.

Today, Chickamauga National Military Park in Catoosa and Walker counties stands as a silent memorial to the ultimate sacrifice of life in war.

GEORGIA IN 1865

The official surrender of the Confederacy was on April 9, 1865, but the war had ended much sooner in Georgia. Historians estimate that as much as $100,000,000 worth of damage was done to the state by federal troops. The main concern of many Georgians was to find food and shelter. Factories, rail lines, mills, plantations, and fields lay around them in ruins as Reconstruction began.

A FINAL NOTE — THE COST OF THE WAR

Missing Confederate records leave us without an accurate picture of Southern strength. However, historians believe that between 750,000 and 1,250,000 soldiers served in the Confederate army. There were 94,000 killed in combat and about 164,000 more who died from diseases, wounds, or while in prison. On both sides, North and South, far more men died from inadequate medical services, poor health, and in prison than were killed on the battlefields.

The cost of the war to the whole nation is estimated to be over $20 billion. By 1910, after benefits were paid to veterans and their widows, the cost of the war increased considerably.

Do You Remember?

1. Where was the last Confederate port taken by Union forces?
2. Where did the surrender of the Confederacy take place?
3. Who shot Abraham Lincoln and what happened to the murderer?

CIVIL WAR "FIRSTS"

The Civil War is called the first "modern" war. There were several inventions connected with it. There were also changes in military methods, and social, political, and economic conduct. Look at the charts below and find Civil War inventions, or "firsts," that are still in use today.

Naval Warfare "Firsts"
- A successful submarine
- A "snorkel" breathing device
- Naval torpedoes (mines)
- Ironclad navy vessels
- Revolving gun turrets
- United States Navy admiral

Weapons "Firsts"
- Flame throwers
- Use of periscope for trench warfare
- Practical machine gun
- Repeating rifles
- Mobile artillery on railroad cars
- Land mine fields
- Telescopic sights for rifles

Medical "Firsts"
- Organized medical and nursing corps
- Hospital ships
- Army Ambulance Corps
- Wide scale use of anesthetics to treat the wounded
- Widespread use of rails for hospital trains

Military "Firsts"
- Organized use of black troops in combat
- Widespread use of railroads to transport men and supplies
- Organized signal service
- Visual signaling by flags and torches during combat
- Military reconnaissance from manned balloons
- Bugle call "Taps"
- Commissioned army chaplains
- Armed services draft system
- Servicemen voting in the fields for a national election
- Black United States Army officer (Major M. R. Delaney)
- Congressional Medal of Honor
- Press correspondents on battlefields
- Organized aerial psychological warfare (Kites were used to drop Lincoln's Amnesty Proclamation behind Southern lines).

Economic "Firsts"
- Income tax
- Tobacco tax
- Union printed fake Confederate bills
- First American breadlines

Other "Firsts"
- Formation of United States Secret Service
- First United States President assassinated
- First photographs taken in battle (by Matthew Brady)
- Extensive use of trenches and wire entanglements

CHAPTER REVIEW

Summary

The Civil War started on April 12, 1861, when the Confederacy fired on Fort Sumter in Charleston Harbor, South Carolina. It ended on April 9, 1865, when Confederate General Robert E. Lee surrendered to Union Commander Ulysses S. Grant at Appomattox Courthouse, Virginia.

There were several reasons for the South's defeat. Among those reasons were: 1) the Union had a larger and more experienced army than the Confederacy; 2) the North had an established navy, and added over 200 ships to it during the war; 3) the South had little industry to provide weapons and supplies for the army; 4) the South's small population made it difficult to replace those wounded, killed, or taken prisoner; 5) the North's blockade of the South's seaports cut off the South from all exports and imports.

The war was fought at great personal cost. Between 618,000 and 700,000 service men died. More men died from diseases, wounds, or while in prison than were killed on the battlefields.

One hundred eight battles were fought in Georgia during the Civil War, and most of them were in 1864. After Chattanooga fell in 1864, General William Tecumseh Sherman's army moved through north Georgia to Atlanta, the state's major city and railroad center. On September 1, 1864, Southern General J. B. Hood left Atlanta, and the city fell to Union forces. General Sherman burned Atlanta on November 15, and began his "March to the Sea" the next day. The army cut a 60-mile wide path through the state as they marched the 300 miles to Savannah. Georgia's major port city fell on December 22. This cut the lower South off from the rest of the Confederacy and ended major Georgia battles.

Even though blacks had fought in the Revolution and the War of 1812, black regiments were organized for the first time during the Civil War. Black regiments fought in 449 battles.

The Civil War caused many social, political, and economic changes that will be discussed in the next chapter. Some lasting outcomes of the war include a change in ship design, and the use of submarines. The war produced organized military medical groups and a broad use of anesthesia. This was the first war in which servicemen voted in the fields during a national election. It also saw the first black United States Army officer and the first awarding of the Congressional Medal of Honor. The United States Secret Service was formed during the Civil War, and Matthew Brady took the first photographs made in battle.

When the war was over, the South lay in ruins. Farms, plantations, cities, railroad lines, bridges, roads, and fields had been destroyed. A farm economy had supported Southerners before the war. It could not be rebuilt until people found food and shelter and could take back their land.

People, Places, and Terms

Identify, define or state the importance of the following.
1. Thomas R. Cobb
2. Fort Pulaski
3. Fort Sumter, South Carolina
4. Battle of Bull Run
5. Robert E. Lee
6. Major General David Hunter
7. "Johnny Reb"
8. blockade runners
9. Ulysses S. Grant

The Main Idea

Write a short paragraph to answer each of the following questions.

1. The Emancipation Proclamation was issued on one date and went into effect on another. Describe each event and tell how it affected slaves.
2. Describe General Sherman's "March to the Sea."
3. Compare and contrast life in the North and South during the middle of the war.
4. Describe the role of blacks in the military during the Civil War.
5. Compare and contrast how the North and South were prepared for war.
6. In summary, describe life in Georgia during the Civil War.

Extend Your Thinking

Give and support your opinion by answering the following questions.

1. Was General Sherman a "bad" commander?
2. Should students study the Civil War period?
3. Was the South fighting for a "lost cause" in the Civil War?
4. Did Abraham Lincoln want the country to become involved in a civil war?

Using Mathematics

1. During the period from May 7 to June 3, 1864, what percent of the men in the Confederate forces died?
2. What were the approximate combined North and South costs of the war in money, excluding benefits?

Looking Ahead

The nation was torn apart during the Civil War. The seven-year period that followed it was called "Reconstruction." During this period, the North and South officially became one nation again. Efforts were made to rebuild Southern economy and politics. Some groups helped former slaves who needed to learn to live in freedom.

As you read Chapter Nine, "Reconstruction: The Rebuilding Years," you will find the answers to the following questions:

➤ who were "carpetbaggers" and "scalawags"?
➤ what did the Freedmen's Bureau do to assist freed slaves?
➤ what well-known black schools still in existence today were established during the Reconstruction period?
➤ how did Reconstruction contribute to the formation of the KKK?
➤ which well-known Georgia writer gained national recognition during Reconstruction?
➤ did Reconstruction hurt the freed slaves?

DID YOU KNOW . . .

. . . Firing during battles was so inaccurate that historians think it took 240 pounds of gun powder and 900 pounds of lead for each Confederate soldier shot?

. . . Although 4,000 died at the Battle of Chickamauga, only one soldier, Private John Ingraham of the Georgia Volunteers, is buried in the battlefield? Ingraham was an orphan, and friends buried him where he fell.

. . . In 1864, Confederate pay for a private was $18.00 a month?

. . . Four of Abraham Lincoln's brothers-in-law were Confederates?

. . . Georgia's poet, Sidney Lanier, spent four months in a federal prison during the war? While imprisoned, he became ill with tuberculosis, which caused his death sixteen years later.

CHAPTER NINE

THE REBUILDING YEARS

RECONSTRUCTION 1865 - 1870

...If the South is ever to be made a safe republic let her lands be cultivated by the last of the owners on the free labor of intelligent citizens. This must be done though it drive her nobility into exile. If they go, all the better."
— Radical Republican Thaddeus Stevens' Views on Reconstruction

PLANS FOR RECONSTRUCTION

THE WORD "RECONSTRUCTION" means "the act or result of rebuilding." During Reconstruction in the United States, former Confederate states reorganized their governments, and the states again became part of the Union.

After the Civil War, many leaders, including President Lincoln and Vice President Andrew Johnson, wanted the South back in the Union as soon as possible. Others, known as Radical Reconstructionists, thought former Confederates should be punished for forcing the nation into war. The ways in which these different ideas were carried out affected rebuilding in Southern states.

In addition to rebuilding as a direct result of Sherman's devastation, Georgia also had to replace railroad tracks and factories, like this rolling mill outside Atlanta, that the Confederate troops had destroyed in order to keep Sherman's men from using them.

1865		1867	1868	1869	1870
Freedmen's Bureau created		Atlanta U. chartered	Georgia adopts new Constitution	Georgia Act passed	Georgia readmitted to the Union
Ku Klux Klan organized in Pulaski, Tennessee		Morehouse Coll. founded			
		Clark College opened	*Atlanta Constitution* founded		

| 1865 | 1866 | 1867 | 1868 | 1869 | 1870 | 1871 |

CHAPTER OUTLINE

1. Plans for Reconstruction

2. Reconstruction Brings New Groups to the South

3. Political Reconstruction in Georgia

4. Economic Reconstruction

5. Reconstruction: Social and Cultural Change

GEORGIA AT THE END OF THE CIVIL WAR

When Georgia's war weary Confederate soldiers returned home, the state was not as they had left it. Fields lay in ruins. Most houses were badly run down or had been destroyed. Owners of many factories, railroads, and stores had stopped doing business. Some quit because of war-time danger. Others did not have enough money to stay open. There was not enough food, and many people were starving. Confederate paper money was worth nothing, and numbers of banks had closed their doors. Georgia had a war debt of $20,000,000.

There were many black freedmen who had no education or training. They went from place to place looking for food, shelter, and work. Most whites were not much better off than the newly freed blacks. Those who had land sold much of it. They used the money to buy supplies to rebuild smaller farms. During Sherman's March to the Sea, soldiers burned whole communities of houses. Many people had to live in make-shift housing or tents. For most Georgians, there were new struggles each day. These grew worse as Reconstruction began.

LINCOLN'S PLAN FOR RECONSTRUCTION

During the closing days of the war, President Lincoln outlined a plan to reunite the country quickly and with little pain. Except for Confederate civil and military leaders, Lincoln wanted to pardon all Southerners who took an oath of allegiance to the United States. The oath stated, in part, "I do solemnly swear, or affirm, in the presence of Almighty God, that I will henceforth faithfully Support, Protect, and Defend the Constitution of the United States and the union of the states thereunder, and that I will, in like manner, abide by and faithfully support all laws and proclamations which have been made during the existing rebellion with reference to the emancipation of slaves so help me God."

After ten percent of those in each state who had voted in the 1860 election took the oath, Lincoln planned for them to form new state governments. They could then ratify the Thirteenth Amendment, which ended slavery, and repeal the Ordinance of Secession. When that was done, the states could return representatives to the United States Congress. The government would forgive each state's war debt.

Lincoln was assassinated before his plan for Reconstruction went into effect. Vice President Andrew Johnson became the nation's seventeenth President. Johnson continued with Lincoln's plan for a short while. Then, a group of radical Republicans gained control of Congress. One of the concerns of this group of Republicans was that blacks would be **disenfranchised**. They thought Lincoln's plan did not punish the South enough. They quickly outlined a program of Reconstruction which would be harder for the South to meet. One of the first changes made was to give the Freedmen's Bureau more power.

THE FREEDMEN'S BUREAU

Congress organized the Freedmen's Bureau in March 1865. Its first commissioner was Union General Oliver O. Howard, who later founded Howard University in Washington D.C. The

Above: Andrew Johnson, the former governor of Tennessee, was as stunned as the rest of the nation over the assassination of President Lincoln. He quickly decided to carry out Lincoln's moderate plan of Reconstruction but the radical Republicans had other ideas. **Left:** Former slaves found themselves without homes, jobs, or education in the uncertain Reconstruction times.

Freedmen's Bureau was established to teach blacks to use their right to vote. A year later, over President Johnson's veto, an act was passed which allowed the Bureau to help freed slaves in all areas of need. The Bureau provided food, clothes, and medical supplies. They helped freedmen find houses and jobs. The Bureau also began and kept up schools for blacks all over the South. The Bureau tried, but was unable, to help blacks acquire land and thus economic freedom. The Freedmen's Bureau watched closely to be sure blacks were not denied their civil rights.

Do You Remember?

1. What was Georgia's war debt after the Civil War?
2. Which Congressional group wanted the South punished during Reconstruction?
3. Who was the first commissioner of the Freedmen's Bureau?
4. What was the Thirteenth Amendment?
5. What were Lincoln's conditions for Southern reconstruction?

*Top: The Freedmen's Bureau was created to assist former slaves who suddenly found themselves without homes, jobs or direction. **Above:** General Oliver Otis Howard.*

RECONSTRUCTION BRINGS
NEW GROUPS TO THE SOUTH

The streets of the South filled with Union soldiers who carried out the plans of the radical Republicans. Other groups were also formed and tried to manage the economic, political, and social life of the South.

CARPETBAGGERS AND SCALAWAGS

In Georgia and the rest of the South, some people used the hardships of others to make money or get influence for themselves. One group moved in from the North. They bought land cheaply, then resold it at higher prices. Some of the land these businessmen bought had been taken by the government for overdue taxes. They also opened stores and sold needed goods at high prices. Some of them took the money they made and paid high-

This Reconstruction period cartoon shows a carpetbagger riding in a bag that rests on the back of the South. Notice the Union soldiers with chains leading to the figure of the solid South. What is the meaning of the cartoon? Examine the background carefully and list the significance of the various images.

ranking officials for positions in the Reconstruction government.

Many of these Northern businessmen came South with their belongings in a suitcase made of carpet. Southerners called them "carpetbaggers." There were numbers of jokes and unkind remarks made about carpetbaggers. However, it was the scalawags that most Southerners intensely disliked. "Scalawag" means "rascal." It was the name given to people from the South who worked with Northerners.

Southerners who did not agree with Radical Reconstructionists thought scalawags acted against their own neighbors. Some scalawags helped carpetbaggers find land to buy. Others tried to gain political power by paying freedmen and poor whites to vote for them. Some scalawags may have been ready to give freedmen all the rights of citizenship. However, whether scalawags were good or bad, most Southerners did not trust them.

KU KLUX KLAN

A third group, the Ku Klux Klan, became powerful during early Reconstruction. "Ku Klux" comes from a Greek word that means "a circle." "Klan" was added to the name because of the Scotch-Irish population of the area. It was one of several secret organizations which tried to keep blacks from using their newly-granted civil rights.

Above: For freed men, the rise of the Ku Klux Klan was another terrifying experience as the Klan worked to prevent former slaves from using their newly won freedom and rights. Right: Initially a social club formed by Confederate war veterans, the Ku Klux Klan quickly became a symbol of terrorism, hatred and lawlessness.

Begging for one's life had little effect on the hardened Klansmen embittered over the South's defeat in the war and the economic hardships of Reconstruction.

The Ku Klux Klan began in Pulaski, Tennessee in 1865, as a social club for returned soldiers. However, it very quickly changed into a force of terror. Members dressed in white robes and hoods so no one would know them. They moved at night and frightened black leaders with whippings and murders.

By 1868, the Ku Klux Klan was active in Georgia. It tried to keep black citizens from voting or taking any part in government. The Klan became so powerful in the South that Congress passed laws, including the Force Act of 1870, to end its activities. The military enforced the laws and, by 1871, most of the terrorism of the Klan seemed over.

Do You Remember?

1. Who were the carpetbaggers?
2. Who were the scalawags?
3. When was the Ku Klux Klan formed and why? What did it become?

Top: Appointed by President Andrew Johnson, James Johnson served as Georgia's provisional governor from June to December, 1865. Above: Assuming the role of governor in December 1865, Charles Jenkins' primary achievement was rebuilding the depleted state treasury and repairing Georgia's destroyed railroads.

POLITICAL RECONSTRUCTION IN GEORGIA

It was often hard to tell who was in charge of Georgia politics during the mid to late 1860s. The state worked through three separate phases of political reconstruction during the five years before Congress readmitted her to the Union.

POLITICAL RECONSTRUCTION — PHASE I

Federal troops occupied both Savannah and Macon before the state knew the Civil War was over. Governor Brown and other well-known Georgia Confederates were no longer in power. President Johnson appointed former Congressman James Johnson as **provisional** governor.

The President directed Governor Johnson to hold a constitutional convention in Milledgeville six months after Lee surrendered at Appomattox. The convention repealed the Ordinance of Secession, and voted to do away with slavery. It wrote a new constitution which was like the Constitution of 1861. In November, the state elected Charles Jenkins, its only candidate, as governor. It also elected representatives to the United States Congress. After the election, the legislature met and formally ratified the Thirteenth Amendment to the Constitution, which **abolished** slavery. By December 1865, President Johnson had removed the provisional governor, and the state inaugurated Jenkins.

The Georgia General Assembly met again in January 1866, and elected two United States senators: Alexander Stephens and Herschel Johnson. The general assembly also voted to give civil rights to freed blacks. However, like other Southern states, Georgia limited those rights with "black codes." These were laws to keep blacks from voting, speaking against whites in court, or marrying outside their race. Even with the codes, Georgia had done what President Johnson's plan required, and was ready to re-enter the Union.

POLITICAL RECONSTRUCTION — PHASE II

When the radical Republicans took control of Congress, they decided Southern states were not "adequately reconstructed." Radicals added requirements for re-entering the Union. They said Southern states must ratify the Fourteenth Amendment. This amendment gave blacks full citizenship and equal protection under the law. In November 1866, Georgia joined all other Southern states except Tennessee, and refused to ratify the amendment. Five months later, in April of 1867, Georgia was again under military rule. Congress divided the states still out of the Union into five military districts. An army general was appointed to govern each of them, and had federal troops to keep order. Georgia, Alabama, and Florida were in the third military district governed by General John Pope.

Georgians saw many changes from March 1867 through July 1868. The military government registered blacks to vote and made lists of all eligible voters.

Constitutional Convention

During the fall of 1867, an election was held to decide if there should be a constitutional convention and to elect delegates to it. This election marked the first time blacks could run for and hold public office in Georgia. The voters decided to hold a constitutional convention, which began in Atlanta on December 9. The convention worked three months to draw up a new constitution. Most of the 169 delegates were scalawags. There were twelve conservative whites and nine carpetbaggers. Thirty-seven delegates were black. Some of them had moved to the South after the war. They had varied backgrounds. Some could not read and write, and had no experience in government. Others were educated professionals, such as ministers, lawyers, teachers, and government employees.

Three of the better known black delegates were Tunis G. Campbell, Henry McNeal Turner, and Aaron A. Bradley. Campbell was a native of New Jersey, and a Freedmen's Bureau agent. He is remembered for introducing **legislation** that kept people from going to prison because they could not pay their debts. Henry Turner was born free in South Carolina and worked with the Freedmen's Bureau immediately after the war. Turner was the first black chaplain in the United States Army. He later served as a minister in Macon, Georgia. Turner was an advocate of civil rights and public education.

Aaron Bradley had been a slave in Georgia until he escaped to New York twenty-six years before the Civil War. After the war, he

*Top: As a leader in the state convention while James Johnson was governor, Herschel Vespasian Johnson was elected as one of Georgia's two U.S. Senators in January, 1866. **Above:** Commander of the Third Military District, John Pope was directed to provide voter registration for blacks and a few whites who met voter qualifications.*

Top: A New Yorker, Rufus Bullock had served in the Confederacy during the war. Although elected governor of Georgia in 1868 by popular vote, his administration was marked with scandals of embezzlement and corruption. After resigning as governor and fleeing the state, he was arrested but later acquitted of illegally using public funds. Above: Benjamin Conley became governor when Bullock suddenly resigned. He is most well known for being the state's last Republican governor.

settled in Savannah. Bradley was outspoken and had an angry, quick temper. After several outbursts, the convention **expelled** him by a unanimous vote. However, he was popular with blacks, and was elected to the Georgia Senate in 1868.

Even though they had heated debates during the convention, the delegates were pleased with the new constitution. It gave civil rights to all the state's citizens. It also made Georgia the first state to allow married women to control their own property. The constitution approved free public education for all children.

Delegates to the constitutional convention enjoyed their stay in Atlanta. Milledgeville hotels would not house black legislators, and those in Atlanta would. These facts may have influenced the 1868 legislature to move the state capital to Atlanta.

Georgians Approve New Constitution and Elect Bullock

In April of 1868, Georgia voters approved the new constitution. They also elected Republican Rufus Bullock as governor by a 7,000 vote majority. Bullock, a native of New York, had been in Georgia for only nine years. He defeated John B. Gordon, a well-known Confederate commander said to be a leader in the Ku Klux Klan. In July, the general assembly ratified the Fourteenth Amendment to the United States Constitution, and Bullock was inaugurated. Georgia had, for a second time, met the requirements to be readmitted to the Union.

POLITICAL RECONSTRUCTION — PHASE III

Once again, Congress would not let Georgia re-enter the Union. When the legislature met in September, the conservative group who had opposed Bullock was in control. Over Governor Bullock's strong objections, they expelled twenty-eight of the thirty-two black legislators. The conservatives said the right to vote did not carry with it the right to hold public office.

Georgia Under Military Rule Again

There was evidence that increased Ku Klux Klan activity kept blacks from voting in the 1868 Presidential election. Congress responded by passing the Georgia Act in December 1869. This act placed Georgia under military rule for the third time. It also stated that Georgia would have to ratify the Fifteenth Amendment to the

United States Constitution before the state could reenter the Union. This amendment states, "The right of citizens of the United States to vote shall not be denied . . . on account of race, color, or previous condition of servitude." General Alfred Terry became Georgia's new military commander and Bullock became provisional governor.

Georgia Supreme Court Rules Blacks Can Hold Office

The Georgia Supreme Court ruled that blacks were eligible to hold office. When the general assembly met in January 1870, it reseated the expelled representatives. The legislature again approved the Fourteenth Amendment, and ratified the Fifteenth Amendment. Georgia was readmitted to the Union in July of 1870. Senators Joshua Hill and H.V.M. Miller, elected in 1868, were seated in Congress. Reconstruction was officially over in Georgia.

Democrats Regain Control of State Politics

There was one final political note to the end of Reconstruction. The Democrats regained control of both houses of the Georgia General Assembly in the December 1870 election. Governor Bullock, a Republican, knew the general assembly would impeach him when they met in November 1871. Rather than face impeachment, Bullock resigned. He secretly swore in a friend, Benjamin Conley, who had been president of the senate during the last legislative session. Conley served as governor only two months before the general assembly ordered a special election. In December, Democrat James M. Smith, former speaker of the house of representatives and a lawyer from Columbus, ran unopposed for the office of governor.

Smith was inaugurated on January 12, 1872. From his election in December 1871, through the 1990 election 119 years later, Georgia's governors have been members of the Democratic party.

Do You Remember?

1. How many years did Reconstruction last in Georgia?
2. What legislation did Tunis G. Campbell introduce?
3. What were the three Constitutional amendments Georgia had to ratify to be readmitted to the Union? What are the rights provided by each amendment?
4. Why was Georgia refused readmission to the Union in 1866?

Top: Joshua Hill, who had opposed Georgia's secession, served as one of the state's two representatives to the U.S. Senate from 1872 to 1873 after the state was re-admitted to the Union. Above: James Smith, a Democrat from Twiggs County, followed Benjamin Conley as governor and served from 1872 to 1877.

ECONOMIC RECONSTRUCTION

It was necessary for Georgia to rebuild economically as well as politically. Banks had failed all over the South. Confederate money was worth nothing, and at least two-thirds of the railroads could not be used. Southern states owed millions of dollars in war debts. Former slaves, who had lived and worked on large farms and plantations, now had no jobs. Most whites who owned farms needed laborers, but could not pay them. Reconstructionists had promised freed blacks "forty acres and a mule," but that promise was never kept. As a result, land owners and workers agreed on two new ways to farm.

SHARECROPPING AND TENANT FARMING

Workers who had nothing but their labor to offer often became "sharecroppers." Under this system, the land owner provided land, a house, farming tools and animals, seed, and fertilizer. The worker agreed to give the owner a share of the harvest. Until a worker sold his crop, an owner often let him have food, medicine, clothing, and other supplies at high prices on credit. Cotton was a major crop in Georgia. If a sharecropper made 500 bales of cotton and had agreed to give the landowner half, each would get 250 bales. After selling his cotton and paying his bills, the typical sharecropper had little, if any, cash left. Year after year, sharecroppers were in debt. There was little hope they could ever save enough to buy their own land and equipment.

"Tenant farming" was similar to sharecropping. The main difference was that tenants usually owned agricultural equipment, and farm animals, such as mules. They also bought their own seed and fertilizer. Tenants worked the owner's land using their own equipment and supplies. At the end of the year, they either paid the land owners a set amount of cash, or gave them an agreed-on share of the crop.

Tenant farmers owned more than sharecroppers, and usually made a small profit for working the land. However, the lives of both groups were very hard. The tenant and sharecropper systems allowed land owners to keep their farms in operation without having to spend money for labor.

On the surface, it appears that land owners who used tenants and

For many freed slaves, work during Reconstruction continued much as it had before the war. Seen here are sharecroppers laboring to eke out a living on someone else's land for a share of the harvest.

sharecroppers made a profit while taking few risks. However, many owners financed their farms with crop liens. If an owner did not have enough money to buy the seed, fertilizer, and tools needed by sharecroppers, he would mortgage crops before they were planted. Interest on such loans was often more than the crops were worth. Bankers expected farmers to grow cotton or tobacco in the same place year after year. This ruined much of the soil. The crop lien system caused many land owners in the South, like the sharecroppers and tenants who worked their land, to become poorer each year.

At the end of Reconstruction, cotton was again the most important crop in many parts of Georgia. In 1870, the state produced 726,406 bales of cotton. There were 700,000 bales grown the year before the Civil War. The coastal region, however, never regained its prewar position in either cotton or rice production.

A living history demonstration at Tifton's Agrirama. Tenant farmers, like the sharecroppers, worked long days in an attempt to make ends meet. The primary difference between the two was that the tenant farmers owned their own horses or mules, farm equipment and seeds so even though they worked other people's land, they could hope to make a small profit from the shared harvest.

*Above: Slowly, cotton became an important means of revitalizing Georgia's postwar economy and cotton-laden riverboats were once again seen moving along the Savannah River. **Opposite page, below:** An aerial view of Atlanta in 1871. **Opposite page, above:** Downtown Atlanta began a slow but steady rebuilding process following the destruction caused by Sherman's burning of the city as he began his infamous "March to the Sea."*

INDUSTRY, RAILROADS, BUSINESS AND SHIPPING

Increasing cotton production brought industry to some parts of Georgia. Northern investors put money into building textile mills. Slowly, banks began to reopen and were able to loan money to merchants and businessmen.

By the late 1860s, dry goods stores, shops, and hotels were again in business. Atlanta, almost completely destroyed during the war, grew rapidly after it became the state capital.

Railroads, necessary to the success of Georgia's economy, expanded during this time. At the end of the Civil War, only the state-owned Western and Atlantic Railroad was still in operation. Union soldiers had kept it up to transport troops and equipment. In the eight years immediately following the war, rail companies laid 840 miles of track in Georgia. Rail lines began to compete with each other.

Shipping companies also took on new life. Savannah again became the major port for exporting cotton, and Brunswick was a close second. Even with the growth of banks, rail lines, and shipping companies, economic reconstruction was slow. However, as Georgians worked together, they made steady progress.

Do You Remember?

1. What was the difference between a sharecropper and a tenant farmer? How were they alike?
2. What is the definition of crop lien?
3. How much cotton did Georgia produce in 1870? How did this compare to production the year before the war?
4. Which Georgia railroad was in operation at the end of the Civil War? Why was this railroad intact?
5. What were Georgia's two major seaports after the war?

SOCIAL AND CULTURAL DEVELOPMENTS DURING RECONSTRUCTION

Above: The Hebrew Benevolent Society provided a permanent home for Atlanta's Jewish population in 1875 when the first synagogue was built in the city. **Opposite page:** *After serving one term in the Georgia legislature from 1868 to 1870, Henry McNeal Turner became actively involved in the A.M.E. Church. A fiery orator and writer, Turner later actually favored African colonization. Why do you think Henry Turner advocated blacks migrating to Africa?*

RELIGION

At the end of the Civil War, churches also had to rebuild. There were not enough ministers, and many buildings had been burned. However, church membership grew rapidly, and people began to replace their houses of worship.

Most major Christian denominations divided over slavery before the war. Episcopalians from former Confederate states met in Augusta soon after Reconstruction and chose to reunite their churches with those in the North. Methodists made a like decision in 1939. However, Georgia Baptists and some Presbyterians are still part of mostly Southern denominations. Jews had been among the first colonists in Georgia. In 1875, the Hebrew Benevolent Congregation built its first synagogue in Atlanta.

Black churches grew in number and influence. A few blacks continued to attend white churches, but most went to churches begun by blacks. These churches were centers of social and religious life. It was during this time that Henry Turner, a representative to the Georgia General Assembly, established the African Methodist Episcopal, or A.M.E., Church. Black ministers quickly became leaders in religious, community, and civil rights matters.

EDUCATION

The Freedmen's Bureau started over 4,000 primary schools, 64 industrial schools, and 74 teacher training institutions for black young people in the South. Northern individuals and missionary societies helped by sending both money and teachers. In 1867, the American Missionary Association sponsored the chartering of Georgia's Atlanta University. That same year, the American Baptist Home Mission Society organized Morehouse College in Augusta. The Augusta school, which moved to Atlanta in 1870, is still in operation today. A third Georgia Reconstruction school was Clark College in Atlanta. It first opened as a school for children and, by 1877, had become a college.

The public school system in Georgia, as we know it today, did not grow greatly until the early 1900s. The Georgia Education Association was formed in 1869 and Gustavus J. Orr became its

chairman. Educational gains during Reconstruction came about mainly because of his work.

In a meeting of about twenty-five Georgia educators, Orr spoke on the state of public education. The 1868 Constitution provided for schools "free to all children of the state," but did not fund them. The 1870 general assembly, following the state constitution, passed an act to "establish a system of public education." The legislation divided the state into local school districts. It also provided for a state school commissioner and a state board of education.

The 1870 school law provided for separate but "equal" schools for black and white children. Two years later, a new law read, "equal as far as practicable." In many towns, the school "year" was four months. The four-month school "year" was largely due to the need for farmer's children to help in the fields during the time of planting and harvesting. In 1871, there were only 49,578 pupils in Georgia schools. Today, over a million young people attend school daily.

General J. R. Lewis was the first state school commissioner. Orr replaced him in 1872, and is called the father of public education in Georgia. Cities such as Savannah, Atlanta, and Columbus did not wait for the state. They began their own school systems. It was 1873 before common (public) schools received any state support.

LITERATURE

There were several popular works of American literature published during the post war period. These included *Hans Brinker, or The Silver Skates*, *The Story of a Bad Boy* by Thomas Aldrich, and Mark Twain's *Innocents Abroad*. No story was more popular with girls than *Little Women*, written by Louisa Mae Alcott. Over 2,000,000 copies of the book have been sold, and it continues to be a lasting work of American literature.

A well-known Georgia author during this period was Charles H. Smith, who used the pen name Bill Arp. His books included *Bill Arp, So-Called, A Side Show of the Southern Side of the War*, published in 1866, and *Bill Arp's Letters*, published in 1868. Both books used humor to describe the woes of the defeated South.

Southern Cultivator, the only Georgia magazine that did not stop publication during the war, continued to give farming information. Magazines, such as *The Atlantic Monthly* and *The Saturday Press*, had readers all over the country. The latter magazine, published in New York, played a major part in bringing fame to Samuel Langhorne Clemens. Clemens, better known as Mark Twain, wrote a tall tale called "Jim Smiley and His Jumping Frog," and *The Saturday Press* printed it in 1865. Major newspapers in the country reprinted the story. We know the work as "The Celebrated Jumping Frog of Calaveras County."

After the war-time paper shortage was over, newspapers grew in numbers and began to look more like the ones we see today. They again reported state and local events. The *Atlanta Constitution*, started in 1868, soon became the "Voice of the South."

THE END OF RECONSTRUCTION

Reconstruction was officially over in 1870. Even though there were federal troops in the South until 1876, Georgia began its slow climb toward full economic and social recovery.

Do You Remember?
1. How did black churches change during Reconstruction?
2. Who was Gustavus Orr?
3. What Georgia newspaper was begun in 1868?
4. When was the Georgia Education Association formed?
5. Who was Charles H. Smith?

Top: Another writer to use a pseudonym was Samuel Clemens, better known by his pen name, Mark Twain. Above: Carey W. Styles, a former colonel in the Civil War, founded the Atlanta Constitution *on June 16, 1868.*

CHAPTER REVIEW

Summary

Reconstruction was a difficult period for Georgia and the South. Much of the region lay in ruins following the war. Both Presidents Lincoln and Johnson wanted the South readmitted to the Union as quickly and painlessly as possible. Their plan of Reconstruction required the Confederates to swear allegiance to the Union, ratify the Thirteenth Amendment abolishing slavery, and repeal the Ordinance of Secession. They did not want to punish the Southern states.

However, a group called Radical Reconstructionists gained political control of Congress. They passed a series of reconstruction acts which made re-entry into the Union much more difficult. States gaining admission had to adopt the Thirteenth, Fourteenth, and Fifteenth amendments to the Constitution.

During Reconstruction, the Freedmen's Bureau helped freed slaves find jobs and housing. The Bureau led efforts to begin schools and register blacks to vote. Other groups in the South during Reconstruction were scalawags and carpetbaggers. Scalawags were Southerners who agreed with Northern policies. Carpetbaggers were Northerners who came to make quick money in the South's weakened economy. Many Northerners, including organized missionary groups, came south to help rebuild and expand the region's schools and churches.

Former Confederate soldiers organized the Ku Klux Klan. Its members frightened black citizens to keep them from voting or using any other civil right. Congress passed laws to stop Klan activities.

Georgia went through three phases of political reconstruction before she was readmitted to the union. The state was under military rule for five years. Georgia had five different governors during Reconstruction. Some were elected and the others were appointed by the federal government.

Blacks were elected to the state's general assembly for the first time. They were expelled, and then reseated before Georgia was readmitted to the Union in 1870. It was during Reconstruction that the legislature moved the state capital from Milledgeville to Atlanta.

Georgia's farms operated with little money for labor during Reconstruction by using two systems known as tenant farming and sharecropping. Owners divided farms into fifteen to twenty acre plots. Workers lived on these plots and worked the land for a share of the year's production. Cotton remained the major crop of the state. A banking loan program known as "crop liens" allowed many owners to keep their land during this period. However neither the owners, the tenant farmers, nor the sharecroppers made much profit.

Black churches established during Reconstruction included the African Methodist Episcopal Church. Several major black schools were founded, including Atlanta University, Morehouse College and Clark College. The general assembly took the first steps toward starting a statewide public school system.

People, Places and Things

Identify, define or state the importance of the following.

1. James Smith
2. Henry McNeal Turner
3. *Southern Cultivator*
4. Atlanta University

5. Tunis Campbell
6. Charles Jenkins
7. Rufus Bullock
8. Ku Klux Klan
9. Freedmen's Bureau
10. Gustavus Orr

The Main Idea

Write a short paragraph to answer each of the following questions.

1. If Lincoln had lived, would Reconstruction in the South have been different? Explain your answer.
2. Name each of the leaders involved in Phase I of Georgia's Reconstruction and define their roles.
3. Compare and contrast scalawags and carpetbaggers.
4. In what ways were the three phases of Georgia's Reconstruction similar? How were they different?

Extend Your Thinking

Write a short paragraph(s) to answer each of the following.

1. Take on the role of Gustavus Orr in 1870 and write a speech urging the formation of free schools for all Georgia children.
2. Some historians have said that one of the biggest mistakes of Reconstruction was the federal government's decision not to give land grants to blacks. Argue either for or against such land grants.

Looking Ahead

As Reconstruction ended in Georgia, the state directed all of its energies and resources toward redeveloping the state economically and socially. During this time, Georgia exemplified the "New South" spirit of progress. As you read the next chapter, you will be able to:

➤ identify the contributions of Henry W. Grady to the development of the "New South";
➤ identify the three men who made up the Bourbon Triumvirate;
➤ identify Dr. William H. Felton and Rebecca Felton;
➤ explain how farmers organized and became a political force;
➤ identify Georgia's best-known populist and his contributions.

DID YOU KNOW . . .

. . . In 1866, Georgia became the first state to grant full property rights to married women?

. . . Cycling became popular during Reconstruction?

. . . The familiar phrase in typing books, "Now is the time for all good men to come to the aid of their party," was first used in 1867 to test the first practical typewriter?

. . . Corruption in politics was so undisputed during Reconstruction that one governor in Louisiana made $8,000 a year for four years in office, but retired with half a million dollars?

. . . The purchase of Alaska was called "Seward's Folly" because Seward was foolish enough to buy what was considered to be "worthless property"?

. . . By 1880, some Georgia sharecroppers made as little as $130.00 a year?

. . . Many historians indicate that Georgia entered Reconstruction after losing over seventy-five percent of its material wealth during the Civil War?

. . . Philanthropist George Peabody established a million dollar fund in 1867 to help begin schools in the South?

A NEW SPIRIT
THE NEW SOUTH
1873-1899

I see a South, a home of fifty millions of people, who rise up every day to call her blessed; her cities, vast hives of industry and thrift; her country sides with treasures from which their resources are drawn, her streams vocal with whirring spindles; her valleys tranquil in the white and gold of the harvest; her mountains showering down the music bells, as her slow-moving flocks and herds go forth from their folds; her rulers honest and her people loving, and her homes happy and their hearthstones bright, and their waters still, and their pastures green, and her conscience clear; her wealth diffused and poorhouses empty, her churches earnest and all creeds lost in the gospel. . . her two races walking together in peace and contentment; sunshine everywhere and all the time.

— Henry Grady, in a speech on October 26, 1887

*Above: Henry Grady was the unofficial spokesman for the New South. His writings reflected the spirit of the area following the dark days of Reconstruction. **Opposite page:** Located in the middle of downtown Atlanta, the memorial statue to Georgia's New South spokesman, Henry W. Grady, was dedicated in 1891, two years after his death. It is a monument surrounded by the city which Grady helped to rebuild following the Civil War.*

THE FORTY-SEVEN YEARS between 1873 and 1920 are referred to as the "New South" era (1873-1899) and the "Progressive Period" (1900-1920). Important and far reaching changes took place during both periods. The nation took part in a World War. Industry, technology, and science made progress. Georgia and the rest of the nation were working with the economics of rebuilding and expanding businesses and factories.

There was racial and civil unrest during the late 1800s and early 1900s. This unrest drew attention to the need to make the rights of all citizens equal.

Political scandals during the New South era tested the patience of the American public. However, even with the changes, there was hope for a better future.

CHAPTER TEN

THE NEW SOUTH
THE REDEMPTION ERA —
GEORGIA POLITICS
1871 - 1899

The New South is enamored of her work. Her soul is stirred with the breath of a new life.... She is thrilling with the consciousness of growing power and prosperity ...
— Henry W. Grady in a speech delivered to the New England Club in New York City in 1886

THE NEW SOUTH DEFINED

ATHENS-BORN HENRY W. GRADY was a journalist and speaker. He also was the first to use "New South" to describe southern progress in the late 1800s. It is reported that the term appeared in 1874 in an *Atlanta Daily Herald* editorial. In the article, Grady described the need for Georgia and the rest of the South to become more like the industrialized North.

In 1880, Grady became managing editor of the *Atlanta Constitution*. During his brief but brilliant career, Grady made many speeches in Georgia and across the country. He also published numbers of articles which described a South that could compete economically with its northern neighbors. Shortly before his death, Grady spoke in Boston of the need for industry in Georgia:

I attended a funeral in a Georgia county. It was a poor one-gallused fellow. They buried him in the midst of a marble quarry; they cut through solid

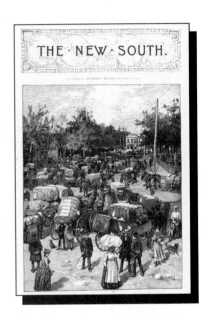

THE · NEW · SOUTH.

Opposite page: Henry Grady in his study. Above: The prosperity of the New South was still based on agriculture in Georgia although attempts to direct its energies toward industrial development were noted in national magazines including the Harper's Weekly shown here.

1873
John Gordon elected to U.S. Senate

1874
H. Grady defines New South

1876
Alfred Colquitt
elected Governor

1880
Joseph E. Brown appointed to U.S. Senate

1883
Colquitt elected
to U.S. Senate

1886
Gordon elected
Governor

1890
Watson elected
to U.S. House

1891
Gordon
back to
Senate

1872   1876   1880   1884   1888   1892

CHAPTER OUTLINE

1. New South Defined by Grady

2. National Events During New South Era

3. The Men of the Bourbon Triumvirate

4. The Farmers Unite

marble to make his grave; yet the little tombstone they put above him was from Vermont. They buried him in the midst of a pine forest, but his pine coffin was imported from Cincinnati. They buried him within touch of an iron mine, but the nails in his coffin and the iron in the shovel that dug his grave were from Pittsburgh. They buried him near the best sheep-grazing country in the world, yet the wool in the coffin bands was brought from the North. They buried him in a New York coat, a Boston pair of shoes, a pair of breeches from Chicago, and a shirt from Cincinnati. Georgia furnished only the corpse and a hole in the ground.

Ten days later, on December 23, 1889, Grady died of pneumonia. Over 7,000 mourners attended his funeral to pay tribute to a man who saw a new South:

a home of fifty millions of people, who rise up every day to call her blessed . . . her cities, vast hives of industry . . . her rulers honest and her people loving . . . her two races walking together in peace and contentment.

Historians can only guess at the changes that might have taken place in Georgia if Henry W. Grady had lived past the age of thirty-nine.

Do You Remember?

1. Henry W. Grady was the managing editor of what newspaper?
2. To what does "New South" refer? Where and when was the phrase first used?
3. What was the topic of Henry Grady's Boston speech?
4. What kind of South did Grady describe in his articles?
5. How old was Grady when he died?

NATIONAL EVENTS DURING THE NEW SOUTH ERA

Terror filled the city of Chicago from October 8 to 11 in 1871 when fire raged through three and one-half square miles of the city.

By 1871, Georgians were free of Reconstruction law and federal troops. Except for South Carolina and Louisiana, who were under federal rule until 1877, the South began rebuilding. Southerners also turned their attention to national events in the exciting 1870s.

The Chicago fire of 1871 was a topic of conversation all over the nation. The fire started in the barn of a laborer named Patrick O'Leary, and raged through the city for four days. When it was over, 17,500 buildings had been destroyed, about 250 people killed, and 98,500 others left homeless. The fire did over $200 million worth of damage.

Even though Ulysses S. Grant's administration had been filled with scandals, he was re-elected President of the United States in 1872. Grant was an honest man, but many of his advisors were not. One scandal involved the Credit Mobilier. Congress had given a great deal of money to the Union Pacific and Central Pacific railroads during the Civil War. These two companies were building a transcontinental railroad. The Union Pacific formed a new company, the Credit Mobilier, to do the work of building. The Credit Mobilier charged more than the work cost, and kept the extra money. Shares of stock in the new company were given to members of Congress. When the scandal was discovered, many Congressmen were forced to resign, and Vice President Schuyler Colfax quickly retired from office.

An even bigger scandal involved "Boss Tweed," who headed New York's Democratic organization called Tammany Hall. Tweed was found guilty of robbing the city of over $100,000,000. These scandals, and the economic panic of 1869, which wiped out hundreds of businesses, all reflected on President Grant's leadership.

In other areas, roller skating was popular in 1872. It was also in that year that Susan B. Anthony tested the constitutionality of the Fifteenth Amendment. She led a group of women who cast ballots in the presidential election. Anthony was arrested, found guilty, and fined $100, which she refused to pay.

In 1873, penny postcards were issued for the first time, and Memorial Day became a legal holiday in New York. In 1875, a Civil Rights Act was passed guaranteeing blacks "equal rights in public places and prohibiting blacks from being excluded from jury duty."

In 1876, General George Custer and 265 troops were killed by Sitting Bull's war party of Sioux Indians at the Battle of Little Big Horn in Montana. Colorado became the thirty-eighth state.

HAYES WINS DISPUTED ELECTION FOR PRESIDENT

In 1877, one of the most disputed national elections of all time was settled between Republican Rutherford B. Hayes and Democrat Samuel Tilden. Tilden won the popular vote. However, the Republicans would not concede the election because of disputed returns from Florida, Louisiana, South Carolina, and Oregon. A single disputed vote from Oregon was settled for Hayes. The other three states had both Democratic and Republican election boards. Each of these boards declared its party's **candidate** the winner of its state's electoral votes. Congress appointed fifteen men to an electoral commission to decide who would become President. There were five members each from the

William "Boss" Tweed provided newspaper readers with stories of outlandish instances of corruption and embezzlement. He was able to steal over $100,000,000 from New York City through control of the city government and state legislators.

Senate, House of Representatives, and Supreme Court: eight Republicans and seven Democrats.

Tilden had 184 electoral votes and needed only one more to become President. The commission voted along party lines, and the disputed votes went to Hayes. This gave him 185 electoral votes and the presidency.

After his election, in an effort to bring the states together, Hayes ended carpetbag rule. He removed all federal troops from Louisiana and South Carolina. Reconstruction was over and the New South era fully began.

A large crowd turned out to hear Rutherford B. Hayes when he gave a speech from the balcony of Atlanta's Markham House.

Do You Remember?
1. In whose barn did the Chicago Fire of 1871 start?
2. What was the Credit Mobilier affair?
3. Who was "Boss Tweed"?
4. Who was elected President in 1877? How does this year differ from all other presidential election dates?

THE MEN OF THE BOURBON TRIUMVIRATE

The period right after Reconstruction is known as the "Redemption Era." The purpose of the time was to "redeem" the state from the hardships which followed the Civil War years. The job of redemption fell mainly to three Democrats: John B. Gordon, Alfred H. Colquitt, and Joseph E. Brown. Like Grady, these men wanted stronger economic bonds with the **industrial** North. Unlike Grady, they wanted to keep many old Southern traditions and, particularly, white supremacy. Brown, Colquitt, and Gordon were active in Georgia politics from 1872 to 1890. Their influence carried over into the twentieth century.

The three Georgia leaders were called the "Bourbon Triumvirate." "Bourbon" was the name of a castle and state in France, and of a line of French kings who ruled for 231 years. "Triumvirate" means a ruling body of three. Each man was different from the others in background. However, politics and power drew them together.

JOSEPH E. BROWN

Joseph E. Brown, the oldest member of the Triumvirate, was born on April 15, 1821, near Pickens, South Carolina. During his youth, his family moved to Union County in the North Georgia mountains. There he worked as a day laborer to repay money borrowed for a year of tuition at a school in South Carolina. Brown, who was a bright student, attended a rural school in Georgia, and became a teacher. At night, he "read the law," preparing to attend Yale Law School. After graduating from Yale in 1846, Brown opened a law office in Canton, Georgia. He was elected to the state senate in 1849, and served there until 1855. Brown then became a judge for the Blue Ridge Judicial Circuit. During the time he served as a judge, he also raised wheat on his North Georgia farm.

In 1857, the state Democratic Convention had trouble selecting a candidate for governor. After twenty ballots, and without his consent, Brown was suggested as a compromise candidate. The shy, serious judge and farmer shocked the rival American Party by narrowly defeating well-known politician, Benjamin Hill. Brown became a popular "States Rights" governor, and was re-elected to

Opposite page: After serving a term as one of Georgia's U.S. Senators in 1880, Joseph E. Brown, one of the members of the Bourbon Triumvirate, retired from active politics and turned his attention to educational interests. Above: Benjamin Hill, a sparkling orator, was shocked at his defeat for the governorship by Joseph E. Brown.

a second term. He knew the Civil War was coming, so he **appropriated** a million dollars to equip the Georgia State Militia. He was re-elected for an unprecedented third term, even though he did not seek the post.

Governor Brown guided the state through the difficult war years and was re-elected to a fourth term in office. When Reconstruction began, Brown lost much of his popularity by asking Georgians to go along with radical reconstruction policies. He believed this would shorten Reconstruction. Brown remained in office until June 1865, when federal officials took over. Reconstruction Governor Rufus Bullock appointed Brown chief justice of the Georgia Supreme Court. He served there two years before resigning to head a company that leased the Western And Atlantic Railroad.

Brown was a talented businessman and made a large fortune. In 1880, he entered politics again. When John Gordon resigned from the United States Senate, Governor Colquitt appointed Brown to Gordon's Senate seat. Brown stayed in the Senate until 1891.

During his retirement years, Brown continued his public service in education. He was a trustee of the University of Georgia for thirty-two years, and president of the Atlanta Board of Education.

Brown, born into poverty, died a millionaire on November 30, 1894. Fifteen years later, his son, "Little Joe," became governor of Georgia. Brown's tombstone in Atlanta's Oakland Cemetery reads: "His history is written in the **annals** of Georgia."

ALFRED H. COLQUITT

Colquitt was born April 20, 1824 in Walton County. He was the son of United States Senator Walter Colquitt, for whom Colquitt County is named.

Alfred Colquitt graduated from Princeton University with a law degree, then fought in the Mexican War from 1846 to 1848. He was twenty-five when he entered Georgia politics. Colquitt joined Joseph E. Brown in the state senate in 1849. The two developed a political bond that lasted for the next forty- four years. Before the Civil War, Colquitt also served in Congress and at Georgia's Secession Convention. During the war years, he was an able military leader and rose to the rank of major general.

Colquitt became a wealthy farmer and businessman during

Opposite page: As the second member of the Bourbon Triumvirate, Alfred Holt Colquitt served as Georgia's governor from 1877-1882. While governor, Colquitt provided leadership for a new state constitution which lasted until 1945.
Above: Virginia-born Walter Colquitt was the father of Governor Alfred H. Colquitt. A Methodist minister, Walter Colquitt served Georgia as an attorney, judge, and United States Senator. Colquitt County is named for him.

Reconstruction. He re-entered politics and was elected governor in 1876. Several thousand friends asked for about thirty open government jobs. Those who did not get one of the jobs tried to turn voters against Colquitt. There were rumors that Colquitt had been involved in illegal dealings with the Northeastern Railroad. Colquitt himself called for an investigation, hoping to end the scandal.

A legislative committee found Colquitt innocent. However, other members of the executive branch of Georgia's government were found guilty of illegal dealing. Colquitt was re-elected, and served as governor until 1882. During his administration, he reduced the state's debt and a new state constitution was approved. This constitution was not re-written until 1945.

Colquitt was elected to the United States Senate in 1883 and 1888. He died in March 1894, three months after the death of his political **ally,** Joseph E. Brown.

JOHN B. GORDON

John B. Gordon, the third member of the "Bourbon Triumvirate," was the son of a minister. He was born in 1832 in Upson County, and attended the University of Georgia. Gordon left the university to study law with Logan Bleckley, an attorney who became a Georgia chief justice.

Gordon decided against being a lawyer. He worked for a while as a newspaper correspondent, then as manager of a coal mine in Dade County. When the Civil War broke out, Gordon was twenty-nine years old. He had no military experience or definite career plans.

During the war, Gordon proved an able leader. He fought in many major battles, and became one of three Georgia officers who reached the rank of lieutenant general. Gordon's wife often traveled with him and occasionally followed him into battle.

After the war, Gordon wrote a book called *Reminiscences*, and became a popular speaker across the nation. It has been said, but never proved, that he was head of Georgia's Ku Klux Klan during Reconstruction.

In 1872, Gordon defeated Alexander Stephens to become a United States Senator. In 1880, he resigned from the Senate and accepted a position with one of the railroads.

The former vice president of the Confederacy, Alexander H. Stephens' last period of public service came in November, 1882, when he was elected as governor. Ill health prevented him from serving more than four months and he died on March 4, 1883.

As the third member of the Bourbon Triumvirate, Gordon was a United States Senator from 1873-1880 and governor of the state from 1886-1890. It is alleged that he was head of the Georgia Ku Klux Klan during Reconstruction. It is interesting to note that none of the three members of the Bourbon Triumvirate had a Georgia county named for him.

Right: Former Governor John B. Gordon is the only statue figure on horseback on the grounds of the state capitol. Below: As the New South era emerged as a period of growth and futuristic thinking, the days of influence from men like Robert Toombs were numbered. Following the war, Toombs refused to sign the Oath of Allegiance to the Union and never regained his U.S. citizenship.

In 1886, John Gordon began one of two terms as governor of Georgia in the new state capitol building. While governor, Gordon reduced the state's debt, and brought new industry into the area.

Gordon returned to the United States Senate in 1891, and served until 1897. He died on January 4, 1904, while visiting the family farm in Miami, Florida. On the day his body was returned to Atlanta for a hero's burial, one newspaper headline read "Hat's Off! Gordon Comes Home Today."

Gordon College in Barnesville is named for John Brown Gordon. His is the only statue of a man on horseback on the state capitol grounds.

THE DECLINE OF THE BOURBON TRIUMVIRATE

Brown, Colquitt and Gordon helped carry Georgia through economic reconstruction. Under their leadership, taxes in the state were lowered, the state's war debts were reduced, and business and industry expanded. Those who did not like the "Triumvirate" said they did little to improve the lives of the poor, especially tenant farmers. In addition, education suffered when funds were cut. There was little support for reforms in prisons and mental hospitals, and working conditions in factories were not improved.

A CHALLENGE TO THE BOURBONS

After Reconstruction, the Republican party was just about wiped out in Georgia. They did not select a gubernatorial candidate in 1872. However, not all Georgians agreed with the beliefs or practices of the Democrats who controlled state politics.

In 1874, Bourbons like Robert Toombs and the Triumvirate faced a new type of Democrat: the Independent Democrat. The change began in north Georgia in the Seventh Congressional District. A group of Independents, led by William H. Felton of Cartersville, began to seek offices in local elections. Dr. Felton was both the leading spokesman for this group and their candidate for Congress.

The Feltons Seek Change

William Felton was a doctor, farmer, Methodist preacher, and convincing public speaker. He and his wife, Rebecca Latimer Felton, traveled around the Seventh District speaking against the Bourbons. Felton argued that the regular Democratic party was not concerned with the poor and lower middle income farmers. Instead, they supported a "planter aristocracy" and new businesses. Mrs. Felton continued the attack in the family-owned newspaper, The *Cartersville Courant*. She wrote often about the evils of the Bourbons. One of her special concerns was the Georgia convict lease system, which Brown and Gordon used.

The Convict Lease System

One of the most serious problems facing Georgia during the New South era was the treatment of prisoners. Many prisons were destroyed during the Civil War. After the war, lack of jobs led to an increase in the number of people who committed crimes, particularly those who stole to feed their families. The state had to decide what to do with the added prison population. One solution was to lease prisoners to people who provided them with housing and food in exchange for labor.

When the convict lease system began in 1866, convicts were used to complete public works projects, such as rebuilding roads destroyed during the war. However, by 1879, most of the prisoners were leased to one of three large companies. Each of the companies agreed to pay the state $25,000 a year, no matter how many

Rebecca Latimer Felton and her husband William H. Felton were reformers who helped end the influence of the Bourbon Triumvirate.

ALEXANDER H. STEPHENS

Alexander Stephens State Park
The home of Alexander Stephens, called Liberty Hall, is located in Crawfordville and is now a state park. Stephens, despite ill health much of his life, served Georgia in the state assembly, as governor, and in the U.S. Senate, and was vice-president of the Confederacy.

Leased convict labor provided Georgia companies, especially railroads, with workers who had no choice other than to work long hours of back-breaking labor and to face imprisonment at the end of the workday. The state gained little economic profits from leasing the convict labor and the workers gained none. Only the companies who received the cheap labor profited from the system.

convicts they used. Two of these companies were owned by Bourbons Joseph E. Brown and John B. Gordon. The third was a railroad construction company. Leases were increased from the original five year period to twenty years. Work ranged from clearing land and farming to mining coal and building railroads.

Companies who leased convicts agreed to provide medical care, allow prisoners to rest on Sundays, and see that housing and clothing were adequate. However, these rules were widely ignored.

Prisoners were not the only ones to suffer from the lease system. Paid laborers were not given jobs convicts could do. Instead, they had to compete for limited numbers of jobs with very low wages. This increased the large number of poor and unemployed.

In 1880, a special legislative committee was formed to look into the handling of leased prisoners, but few changes were made. William and Rebecca Felton continued to demand reforms. It was not until 1897 that the lease law was changed.

A commission was appointed to buy a prison farm so youthful offenders and old or sick inmates could be separated from other prisoners.

Dr. Felton Elected to Congress

Dr. Felton was elected to Congress for three terms, serving from 1874 to 1880. In 1880, he became a member of the Georgia General Assembly. While in the legislature, Felton pushed for improvements in education, prison reform, and limits on alcohol traffic in the state. Because of the work of the Feltons, the roots of the Populist Movement were planted in the state.

Rebecca Latimer Felton — A Final Note

Rebecca Latimer Felton was involved with, and spoke about many causes. She was already publicly active before the early 1900s, when women began to push for equal rights.

In 1889, Hoke Smith, publisher of the *Atlanta Journal*, asked Mrs. Felton to be a columnist. She was a popular writer, and worked with the newspaper until her death in 1930.

Mrs. Felton wanted the state to fund public education adequately. Vocational training for poor white girls was of particular interest to her. In 1915, with Mrs. Russell Sage of New York, Felton began the Georgia Training School for Girls in Atlanta.

At age 87, Rebecca Felton became the first female to serve in the United States Senate. Although her appointment was an honorary one and she served only ten days until the election of Walter F. George, it was a tribute to her diligence and efforts supporting causes like prison reform, women's rights and education.

Rebecca Ann Latimer Felton, feminist crusader, journalist, and political activist, died on January 24, 1930 in Atlanta at age 94. Some say had she lived in a more enlightened time, her contributions to society would have been far greater. After reading about Mrs. Felton, what do you think she would support in reform causes today?

Mrs. Felton worked to get the University of Georgia, where her husband graduated, to accept women students. She was also a leader in the **suffrage** and **temperance** movements.

On October 4, 1922, Senator Tom Watson died. Governor Thomas Hardwick named Rebecca Felton a Junior United States Senator until someone could be elected to Watson's seat. In a black dress and bonnet, the eighty-seven year old lady was sworn in as the first female Senator in the nation's history. Ten days later, the Georgia legislature elected Walter F. George as the new Senator. Mrs. Felton died in 1930, active to the end trying to right social injustices.

Do You Remember?

1. In what profession did all three members of the Bourbon Triumvirate work?
2. What are at least two things that all three politicians supported during the Redemption period?
3. In what way or ways did each of the Bourbon leaders help Georgia?
4. What were some of the public accomplishments of Rebecca Latimer Felton?
5. How long did Mrs. Felton serve as a United States Senator? Who succeeded her?

THE FARMERS UNITE

When the United States was formed, farm families made up most of the population. As the country grew, so did the need for farm products. To produce needed crops, farmers had to be willing to work hard and take risks. Weather, insects, plant diseases, bank loan interest, shipping costs, and market prices were all beyond the farmers' control.

THE GRANGE IS FORMED

In 1866, a clerk in the Bureau of Agriculture toured the South and found farmers discouraged, tired, and often without enough money. The next year he formed the "Patrons of Husbandry," which soon became known as the Grange. Grange is a word which means a farm and its buildings.

Market day in Newnan. During the New South Era as industry became the focus of future development, farming remained the fundamental economic model of the present. Market day offered area citizens the chance not only to sell their cotton at highly competitive prices but also an opportunity for residents to exchange news and socialize.

Right: *The Grange, initially a social gathering for farmers to discuss their common problems, had become a major political force by 1875.* **Opposite page:** *Examine the Grange poster extolling the virtues of farming life. Choose three of the pictures and list what each represents as it relates to farm life in the New South.*

At first, Grange meetings were mostly social. Farmers gathered and talked about common problems. Sometimes there were dances or other social activities, or speakers who talked about farming improvements.

After the early 1870s, farm prices began to drop. A bushel of wheat which sold for $1.21 in 1873 dropped to $.49 by 1885. In 1873, a pound of cotton sold for $.21 but, by 1893, the price was only $.05. During this same time, banks were not lending farmers as much money as before. Many were forced into bankruptcy. In the 1880s, after paying the land owner, a small Georgia sharecropper might not make more than $130 for his cotton crop.

THE GRANGE BECOMES A POLITICAL FORCE

Because of such economic conditions, the Grange became more political. In 1872, Granges began organizing and meeting in Georgia. By 1875, there were 18,000 members of Georgia's Grange chapter, and about 750,000 members in the nation. Georgia's Grange put enough pressure on the state legislature to force the formation of a state department of agriculture in 1874. Georgia was the first state in the nation to have a government agency concerned entirely with farming. Some midwestern groups elected legislators who favored farm supports. They were also able to get laws passed to regulate railroad freight rates. However, in the rest of the country, the Grange did not become a major political power.

FORMATION OF THE FARMERS' ALLIANCE

During the late 1870s and early 1880s, the Farmers' Alliance was formed. There was one large group in the Northwest and another in the South. Like the Grange, the alliances began as social organizations. However, many of the local alliances formed cooperative buying stores, or co-ops. The co-ops purchased goods and equipment directly from producers. This allowed farmers to buy seed, fertilizer, and farm tools at wholesale prices.

Farmers' Alliance leaders worked against high railroad freight rates and high interest rates charged by banks for farm loans.

THE ALLIANCE AND LABOR JOIN FORCES TO FORM "PEOPLE'S PARTY"

The Alliance's political influence grew along with its membership and, in 1890, forty-five "Alliancemen" were elected to Congress. The alliances backed men who became governors in several southern states. Encouraged, the Alliance began talking about selecting the President of the United States in the 1892 election.

Members of labor organizations joined with the Alliance to form a new political party in 1891. They named it "People's party," but it

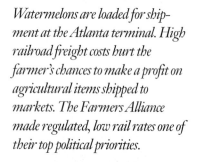

Watermelons are loaded for shipment at the Atlanta terminal. High railroad freight costs hurt the farmer's chances to make a profit on agricultural items shipped to markets. The Farmers Alliance made regulated, low rail rates one of their top political priorities.

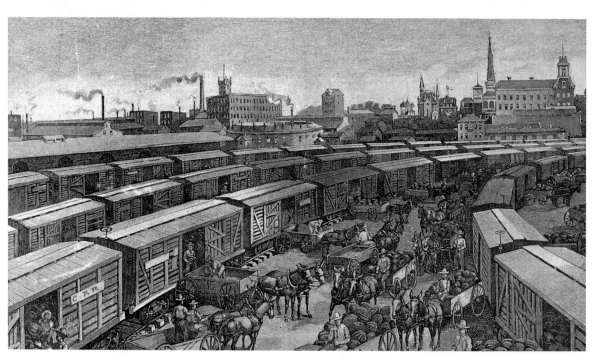

Below: Grover Cleveland, the nation's 22nd and 24th president, served from 1885 to 1889 and 1893 to 1897. Georgia's Hoke Smith served as Cleveland's Secretary of the Interior from 1893 to 1896. Left: Atlanta crowds welcome President Grover Cleveland to the city for the Piedmont Exposition in 1887.

was usually called the Populist party. The first business of the Populist party was protest. Surpluses of cereal crops, cotton, and silver lowered market prices. This forced both farmers and miners into poverty or "suffering amidst plenty." The first Populist party nominating convention met in Omaha, Nebraska in July of 1892. Their platform contained many "futuristic reforms." Among them were: 1) an eight-hour work day; 2) government ownership of railroads, and telephone and telegraph services; 3) a graduated federal income tax; 4) "free" or unlimited coinage of silver into dollars; 5) the direct election of Senators; 6) restrictions on immigration; 7) use of the "Australian" **ballot** [a ballot printed by the government rather than by a political party, distributed and collected at **polling** places so votes would be secret]; 8) a program of government loans to farmers who would store crops in government warehouses as security for the loans.

In the 1892 election, the Populist candidate for President was James B. Weaver. Democrat Grover Cleveland won the election, but Weaver received over a million popular votes and twenty-two electoral votes. This was a large number for a third party candidate. By openly asking for black votes, the Populist party lost much of its popularity and support in the South. However, its platform of reform had opened the way for future changes.

GEORGIA'S BEST-KNOWN POPULIST

A colorful national leader of the Populist party was Georgian Tom Watson. Born near Thomson in 1856, Thomas Edward Watson became one of the state's most controversial politicians.

As a youth, the slim, red-haired Watson was an excellent student. By the age of fourteen, he had written a series of essays, poems, and speeches. He had to drop out of Mercer University when his father went bankrupt during the economic panic of 1873. Watson taught school and "read the law" until he passed the state bar exam in 1877, at the age of twenty-one.

Watson was a criminal lawyer known for his "down to earth" style of defense. Even though he became wealthy, Watson was concerned because poor and struggling farmers in Georgia needed help. He accepted the goals of the Farmers' Alliance and, with their backing, was elected to Congress. Watson, a Democrat, represented the Tenth Congressional District, which stretched from Augusta west across the state.

A year later, Watson switched political sides and spoke for the causes of the Populist party. In one of his many congressional speeches for farmers, the firebrand Watson declared, "Before I give up this fight, I will stay here till the ants tote me out of the keyhole."

Watson Introduces Rural Free Delivery Bill

Watson represented Georgia in the House of Representatives only two years. However, he gained a place in congressional history by introducing the Rural Free Delivery (RFD) Bill. The RFD Bill required the United States postmaster general to spend $10,000 to find a way to deliver mail to homes free of charge. It took several years to put the system into action in rural areas. However, Watson's bill resulted in farm families no longer having to go to the nearest post office for their mail. The first official Rural Free Delivery route in Georgia was in Warren County.

Watson was known all over the country because of the RFD bill and his support of farmers. In 1892, the Democrat turned Populist became a candidate for re-election from the Tenth District. However, the state's Democratic party wanted Watson out of Georgia politics. Since he had no organized support, Watson tried to get black farmers to join white ones and return him to Congress. By

Above: Born in 1856 near Thomson, Georgia, the young Tom Watson was viewed as a hero to the struggling Georgia farmers whom he wanted to represent. **Opposite page:** Elected to Congress in 1890, Thomas Watson's greatest accomplishment was getting the Rural Free Delivery Bill passed in Congress. The RFD Bill enabled farmers, and others living in rural areas, to receive free mail delivery at their homes.

Today a statue of Thomas Watson stands at the main entrance to the state capitol building in Atlanta.

election day, there were reports of vote buying, physical attacks, and attempts to frighten people. Watson supporters claimed that the Tenth District's black voters were denied credit at stores if they supported Watson. They said murders had been committed to keep black farmers from backing Watson. When the **polls** closed and the votes were counted, Watson had lost his bid for re-election. He ran for Congress again in 1894, and was again defeated. Watson returned to his home, Hickory Hill, near Thomson, to influence politics through the power of the press. He began two magazines: *The Weekly Jeffersonian* and the monthly *Watson's Jeffersonian*. He also wrote a ten-volume *Story of France*, and biographies of Andrew Jackson and Thomas Jefferson.

Watson Is Nominee for Vice-President

In 1896, Watson was the Populist party's nominee for Vice President. He ran with Democrat and "free silver advocate" William Jennings Bryan. The election ended in another defeat, and Watson returned to writing.

In 1904, the dying Populist party nominated Watson for President and, once again, he lost. The next year, Watson returned to the Democratic Party and successfully backed Hoke Smith for governor of Georgia. However, his stand on civil rights had changed. Fifteen years earlier, Watson had asked for black votes. Now, his opposition to minority rights included those for blacks, Catholics, and Jews. In 1920, Watson ran against Hoke Smith and won the United States Senate race. Two years later, he died in Washington, D.C.

A statue of Watson stands by the main entrance to the state capitol. On it are the following words:

> *Democratic institutions exist by reason of their virtue. If ever they perish it will be when you have forgotten the past, become indifferent to the present, and utterly reckless as to the future.*

Do You Remember?

1. Why was the Farmers' Alliance formed?
2. Why was the People's Party formed?
3. What major bill did Tom Watson get passed during his one term in the United States House of Representatives?

A SPLENDID LITTLE WAR

American interests in Latin American countries increased after the Civil War. Cuba was of particular interest to the United States. The large, rich island lay ninety miles south of Florida. It was owned by Spain, but many Americans wanted it to be part of the United States. They felt it would be good for trade. It would also provide military protection for our interests in the southern part of the hemisphere. Groups of Cubans wanted to be free from Spain. Some of them came to the United States to get money and arms for a revolution. American aid allowed Cubans to rebel against Spanish control. There were rebellions from 1868 to 1878, and again in 1895.

On April 11, 1898, President McKinley sent a message to Congress asking for "forcible intervention" to establish peace in Cuba.

On February 15, 1898, one of America's newest battleships, the Maine, *was blown up in Havana harbor. Two hundred sixty men died in the explosion. No one ever knew who sank the* Maine *but American newspapers reported that it was the work of a Spanish submarine and Americans demanded retaliation. "Remember the* Maine*" became a popular slogan.*

Congress responded with a resolution stating that Cuba was independent and the President could use force to make Spain leave the island. The stage was set for the Spanish-American War, called by diplomat John Hay "a splendid little war."

Dewey Destroys Spanish Fleet In Manila

The first part of the war began thousands of miles away from Cuba in Manila in the Philippines. Commodore George Dewey was sent to wreck the Spanish fleet harbored there. The Spanish were not prepared, and their fleet was destroyed with heavy casualties. The six-ship American fleet was hardly touched.

American Troops To Cuba

The United States Army and Marines were more eager for war than ready. On June 14, 17,000 troops left Tampa. Many of the troops became ill from yellow fever, typhoid, or bad food. However, they quickly defeated the Spanish Army. In December 1898, representatives of both governments met in Paris to sign a formal treaty ending the Spanish-American War.

Georgians Enlist

About 3,000 Georgians enlisted to fight in Cuba. Georgians who saw action in the war included Thomas Brumby of Marietta, who was Admiral Dewey's flag officer at the Battle of Manila Bay, and Confederate hero and former Congressman Joseph Wheeler.

The Importance Of The Spanish-American War

The Spanish-American War was important to the United States for several reasons. Among them:

1. During peace negotiations, Spain gave up control of Cuba and ceded the Philippine Islands, Puerto Rico and Guam to the United States for $20,000,000. The Philippines gave the United States far reaching control and vital military bases in Asian waters.
2. The war brought up the question of annexing the Hawaiian territory. By 1900, Hawaii was given territorial status. This led to a strong United States military base on the islands.
3. The United States was seen by other nations as an "emerging world power."

Above: *During the early morning hours of April 30, Commodore George Dewey gave the command to fire. By noon of that day, the Spanish Fleet at Manila Bay was destroyed.* **Far left:** *Theodore "Teddy" Roosevelt established himself as a popular military hero while leading the "Rough Riders."* **Left:** *The charge of Roosevelt's Rough Riders up San Juan Hill.*

CHAPTER REVIEW

Summary

As Georgia recovered from the years of strife and economic hardship following the Civil War, the state entered a period of growth and development called the New South era. Atlanta journalist, Henry W. Grady, coined the phrase "New South" to describe visions of the future of Georgia's business, industry, and technology.

The Redemption Period, the first phase of the New South era was a time of economic growth during which Georgia was controlled by three powerful politicians known as the Bourbon Triumvirate—Joseph E. Brown, Alfred H. Colquitt and John B. Gordon. All three men served the state both as governors and as Congressmen. The three leaders carried Georgia through an economic renewal after the Civil War.

The decline of the Bourbon Triumvirate came because social reforms and educational progress were limited during their rule.

The groundwork for social reforms was laid, in part, by Georgians William H. Felton and his wife, Rebecca Latimer Felton. They believed the traditional Democratic party was ignoring the interests of the poor and the lower middle class. With supporters, they formed an Independent party to campaign for social reforms. Dr. Felton served the state both as a Congressman and as governor. Mrs. Felton, a noted journalist, was honored by being named the first woman to serve in the United States Senate. Her appointment was an interim term lasting only ten days until the election of Walter F. George.

During the late 1800s, two national political movements spread to the farms of rural Georgia. The Grange and the Farmers' Alliance both turned to political activity to help farmers. Seeking a stronger voice in politics, the Farmers' Alliance joined forces with members of labor unions to form a new political party. The new party, the People's party, soon became known as the Populist party.

The Populist party campaigned for massive reforms favoring farmers and factory laborers. Georgia's best-known Populist was Thomas Watson, a politician and journalist who introduced the Rural Free Delivery Bill in Congress.

People, Places, and Terms

Identify the following people or events.
1. Joseph E. Brown
2. Commodore George Dewey
3. suffrage
4. Bourbon Triumvirate
5. John B. Gordon
6. redemption
7. Rebecca Felton
8. Thomas E. Watson
9. Henry W. Grady
10. Alfred H. Colquitt
11. Susan B. Anthony
12. Robert Toombs

The Main Idea

1. Outline the public offices held by each member of the Bourbon Triumvirate along with the dates.
2. Explain how the beliefs of the Bourbon Triumvirate differed from those of Henry W. Grady.
3. When the Populist party's nominating convention met in Omaha in 1892, they urged passage of many reforms. Which reforms called for at that time are in effect today?

True or False

Decide which of the following statements are true and which are false. If the answer is false, rewrite the statement to make it a true statement.

1. Tom Watson was Georgia's most well-known Republican.
2. Henry W. Grady wanted a New South based on a strong agricultural economy.
3. Rebecca Latimer Felton wrote for the *Atlanta Journal*.

Looking Ahead

You have been studying the political scene during the New South era. In the next chapter you will learn about other activities during the New South era. You will learn:

➤ about Sidney Lanier
➤ about Joel Chandler Harris
➤ how a headache led to Coca-Cola
➤ how Rich's department stores got started
➤ how Atlanta rose from the ashes of Sherman's burning
➤ how science and technology improved people's lives
➤ about education in the New South era
➤ how textiles changed life in Georgia

DID YOU KNOW . . .

. . . Comic drawings first appeared in newspapers in 1896? The first comic strip was the "Yellow Kid." The following year, the second comic strip, "The Katzenjammer Kids" began.

. . . "Yellow Journalism," a sensational approach to news stories, was named after the comic strip "Yellow Kid" in Joseph Pulitzer's *World*?

. . . Brass mortars captured at Santiago, Cuba during the Spanish-American War are on display at Georgia's state capitol?

. . . During the Chicago Fire of 1871 (above), the original draft of Abraham Lincoln's Emancipation Proclamation was destroyed?

. . . After the Battle of Manila Bay an American chewing gum manufacturer produced a popular gum named "Dewey's Chewies" in honor of Spanish-American War hero George Dewey?

. . . Joseph E. Brown was the only Georgia Governor to serve four terms?

. . . In 1898, Nome, Alaska was founded as a result of a gold strike? Nome was named as a result of a misspelling of a nearby cape. On maps, the cape was referred to as "no name" cape.

. . . There is a statue of Joseph E. Brown and his wife on the lawn of the State Capitol?

. . . Under Presidents McKinley and Roosevelt, Judson Lyons of Augusta was register of the United States Treasury, the highest appointive federal office held by a black person during that era? Georgia led the South in the number of blacks holding federal jobs.

CHAPTER ELEVEN

THE NEW SOUTH ERA
SOCIETY, CULTURE AND TECHNOLOGY
1871-1899

The very spice and essence of all literature ... is in its localism.... All fiction is historical in the sense that it deals with a definite period of time, and with the ways of life that are characteristic of it.
— Joel Chandler Harris, 1879
From an essay on the literature of the South

THE ARTS DURING THE NEW SOUTH ERA

DURING THE LATE nineteenth and early twentieth centuries, artists, musicians, and writers reflected the events and culture of the period. Winslow Homer painted anything that interested him, but was best known for his pictures of the sea and of ordinary people. Frederick Remington worked as a cowboy and panned for gold to get ideas for his paintings of the American West. John Singer Sargent was famous for his portraits.

Blues and ragtime were popular in the New South. Musicians like Scott Joplin, W.C. Handy, and "Jelly Roll" Morton wrote songs still heard today. The marches of John Philip Sousa, and

Joel Chandler Harris did much of his writing at his home, "Wren's Nest," located on Snap Bean Farm in the west end of Atlanta. "Wren's Nest" got its name from a family of wrens which set up housekeeping on Harris' mailbox.

Frederick Remington (1861-1909) was a well-known and respected artist of the period. In this painting, he captured the drama of Custer's Last Charge at the Little Big Horn in 1876.

"America the Beautiful" by Katherine Lee Bates stirred patriotic feelings.

Architects Frank Lloyd Wright and Louis Sullivan were known around the world for their new looks in building. Their ideas are still being used.

Writers like Mark Twain, Stephen Crane, Sarah Jewett, Zane Grey, Ida Tarbell, Booth Tarkington and Sinclair Lewis told about both good and bad America during the New South and Progressive periods. Adventure stories, mysteries, and tales for children became more popular. The poems of Henry Wadsworth Longfellow, Emily Dickinson, Edwin Arlington Robinson, Amy Lowell, and Carl Sandburg were read all over the world. Paul Laurence Dunbar, who wrote his first poem at the age of six, published his first book of poems, *Oak and Ivy*. These works spoke of the past glories and future hopes of the nation. Georgia was the birthplace of two widely-read authors of the period: Sidney Lanier and Joel Chandler Harris.

Left: Sidney Lanier was born on February 3, 1842, in this house in Macon. ***Below:*** *Sidney Lanier graduated from Oglethorpe University, a Presbyterian school at Midway near Milledgeville, in 1860, and became a tutor.*

SIDNEY LANIER AND JOEL CHANDLER HARRIS — A STUDY IN CONTRASTS

Sidney Lanier was born in Macon in 1842. His family was musical and, even as a young child Lanier could play the flute, violin, organ, piano, and guitar. Lanier entered Oglethorpe University in Midway at the age of fourteen. He graduated in 1860, and became a tutor. In 1861, Lanier and his brother, Cliff, enlisted as privates in the Confederate Army. The brothers turned down promotions so they could stay together. They became army scouts and later joined the Signal Service.

Union troops captured Sidney Lanier while he was blockade running off the coast of Wilmington, North Carolina. He was in prison for five months at Point Lookout, Maryland. During that time, he became ill with tuberculosis. Lanier hid a flute in his sleeve when he went to prison. He still had it when he was released. Lanier and a friend walked most of the way back to Macon. He reached home on November 15, 1865, and spent the next few months trying to get back his strength.

Lanier wrote his first novel *Tiger Lilies*, while working in a store in Montgomery, Alabama. Because the book did not sell, Lanier was not sure about his writing. In 1867 he opened a school in Prattville, Alabama, and married Mary Day from Macon.

Lanier and his wife returned to Macon because of his poor health. There he worked as an assistant in his father's law office. In December 1872, he moved to Texas, but the dry heat was not good for him. While in Texas Lanier felt he had little time to live. He wanted to spend that time with the books and music he loved. In

THE SONG OF THE CHATTAHOOCHEE

Sidney Lanier

Out of the hills of Habersham,
  Down the valleys of Hall,
I hurry amain to reach the plain,
Run the rapid and leap the fall,
Split at the rock and together again,
Accept my bed, or narrow or wide,
And flee from folly on every side,
With a lover's pain to attain the plain,
  Far from the hills of Habersham,
  Far from the valleys of Hall.

All down the hills of Habersham,
  All down through the valleys of Hall,
The rushes cried, Abide, Abide,
The wilful waterweeds held me thrall,
The laving laurel turned my tide.
The ferns and the fondling grass said Stay,
The dewberry dipped for to work delay,
And the little reeds sighed, Abide, Abide,
  Here in the Hills of Habersham,
  Here in the valleys of Hall.

High o'er the hills of Habersham,
  Veiling the valleys of Hall,
The hickory told me manifold
Fair tales of shade, the poplar tall
Wrought me her shadowy self to hold,
The chestnut, the oak, the walnut, the pine,

Overleaning, with flickering meaning and sign,
Said, Pass not, so cold, these manifold
  Deep shades of the hills of Habersham
  These glades in the valleys of Hall.

And oft in the hills of Habersham,
  And oft in the valleys of Hall,
The white quartz shone, and the smooth
  brookstone
Did bar me of passage with friendly brawl,
And many a luminous jewel lone —
Crystals clear or a-cloud with mist,
Ruby, garnet, amethyst —
Made lures with the lights of streaming stone
  In the clefts of the hills of Habersham,
  In the beds of the valleys of Hall.

But oh, not the hills of Habersham,
  And oh, not the valleys of Hall
Avail: I am fain for to water the plain.
Downward the voices of duty call —
Downward, to toil and be mixed with the main,
The dry fields burn, and the mills are to turn,
And a myriad flowers mortally yearn,
And the lordly main from beyond the plain
  Calls o'er the hills of Habersham,
  Calls through the valleys of Hall.

Pictured here at age 37, Sidney Lanier died in Lynn, North Carolina two years later in 1881. His last verse started, "I was the earliest bird awake, It was a while before dawn, I believe, But somehow I saw around the world, And the eastern mountaintop did not hinder me. I knew the dawn by my heart, not by mine eyes."

1873 the family moved to Baltimore where he played first flute in the Peabody Symphony.

It was in Baltimore that Lanier had his first success as a writer. His first poems, published in 1875, were well received. Lanier was asked to write words for a **cantata** to celebrate America's 100th birthday. The music was sung at the Centennial Exposition in Philadelphia. One of his better known works, "Evening Song," was written during 1876.

Lanier went to other states looking for a climate in which he could feel well. However, he returned to Baltimore to play with the symphony and give private lectures on Elizabethan verse. On his birthday in 1879, he was asked to teach at Johns Hopkins University. This job provided his first steady income since his marriage.

Lanier published "The Song of the Chattahoochee," and "The Marshes of Glynn." He also began a group of poems, "Hymns of the Marshes," which was never finished. One of those poems, "Sunrise," is perhaps his most famous.

Lanier's health grew worse and, on the advice of his doctors, the family moved to the crisp, clean air near Asheville, North Carolina to live in a tent. His final move was to Lynn, North Carolina.

JOEL CHANDLER HARRIS

Joel Chandler Harris was born in Eatonton in 1848. Because his father left the family before Joel's birth, Mary Harris had to raise her son alone. Harris joked with friends but was shy with strangers. He went to school in Eatonton until he was twelve. At that time Joseph Addison Turner of Turnwold Plantation, nine miles from Eatonton, asked Harris to live with him. Turner owned the only newspaper ever published on a plantation. Harris became an apprentice for that paper, *The Countryman*. Some days, after he finished his work, the thirteen year old read books borrowed from Turner's library. On others, he walked around the plantation and listened to tales told by the workers. Harris learned to speak the workers' dialect very well. With Turner's approval, Harris began writing both serious and funny stories for the paper.

Shortly before Sherman's march through Georgia, Harris became a printer for the *Macon Telegraph*. He stuttered and, when invited to lecture at Vanderbilt University, said, "I could not deliver a lecture in public for a million dollars."

After a short time Harris moved to New Orleans and worked six months as secretary to a newspaper publisher. His next move was to Forsyth, Georgia, where he wrote humorous articles for the *Monroe Advertiser*. The *Savannah Morning News* named him as an associate editor and, while living there, Harris married Esther La-Rose.

In 1876, yellow fever swept through Savannah. The twenty-eight-year-old Harris, his wife, two children, and their nurse, fled to Atlanta. He met with *Constitution* editor Henry Grady, and accepted a position on that paper. Harris helped Grady make the *Atlanta Constitution* a New South paper.

Harris' most popular and lasting contributions to Southern literature were the legends and folk tales which were told to him by former slaves. *Uncle Remus, His Songs and His Sayings*, written in

Wren's Nest was such a safe haven for the shy writer Joel Chandler Harris that he rarely left home even to go to the Atlanta Constitution *offices to write his editorials. When President Cleveland visited Atlanta and wanted to meet Harris, editor Henry Grady had to send another reporter to be sure the writer would leave his home for the meeting.*

The shy and retiring Joel Chandler Harris had among his many friends, industrialist Andrew Carnegie. Atlantans owe Carnegie a special thanks. In 1889 the wealthy Carnegie gave $100,000—an enormous amount of money during that time—to Atlanta to build a library.

1880 when Harris was 32, began as a column in the *Atlanta Constitution*. During the next 26 years, he wrote *Uncle Remus and His Friends*, *Told by Uncle Remus*, and *Uncle Remus and Br'er Rabbit*.

Harris did much of his writing at his Atlanta home, "Wren's Nest." It is said that Harris gave his home its name after a family of wrens built a nest on the mailbox. Today, Wren's Nest, located in Atlanta's West End, is a museum.

Joel Chandler Harris kept his childhood shyness. It is told that in 1905 President Teddy Roosevelt visited Atlanta and wanted to meet the popular writer. The *Atlanta Constitution's* publisher had three reporters take Harris to the President's train, and "see that he's there if you have to hog-tie him."

Harris died on July 3, 1908, at the age of fifty-nine. He wrote the words carved in stone over his grave in Atlanta's Westview Cemetery:

I seem to see before me the smiling faces of thousands of children—some young and fresh—and some wearing the friendly marks of age, but all children at heart, and not an unfriendly face among them. And while I am trying hard to speak the right word, I seem to hear a voice lifted above the rest, saying, 'You have made some of us happy,' and so I feel my heart fluttering and my lips trembling and I have to bow silently and turn away and hurry into the obscurity that fits me best.

Do You Remember?

1. What happened to Sidney Lanier while he was in prison at Point Lookout, Maryland? How old was he at the time?
2. What was the name of Lanier's first novel?
3. What musical instruments did Lanier play?
4. Who wrote "America The Beautiful"?
5. What was the title of Paul Dunbar's book of poems?
6. What is the name of one of Joel Chandler Harris' books?
7. For which newspaper did Joel Chandler Harris write a column for twenty-six years?
8. For what type of art was American painter Fredrick Remington known?
9. What are two poems written by Sidney Lanier?
10. What is the name of Joel Chandler Harris' home? Where is it located?

EDUCATION IN THE NEW SOUTH

Education in Georgia in the late 1800s and early 1900s was quite different from education in the state today. "An Act to Establish A System of Public Instruction" was passed in 1870.

The legislation also established a state board chief executive officer to supervise public schools. The annual salary for this officer was set at $2,500. The first state school commissioner was J.R. Lewis, who kept the job a year.

Each county in the state was to have a single school district, except those where Atlanta, Macon, Augusta, Savannah, and Columbus were located. These cities already had school systems paid for with local taxes. In such cases, both county and city systems were allowed.

In 1871, Girl's High in Atlanta was established and opened with 153 female students. List some differences you can observe between the class of 1875 shown here and the graduating classes of today.

TESTS FOR TEACHERS

In 1870, local school commissioners made up tests for people who wanted to teach. In most cases, a passing grade was seventy. Tests for teachers covered such subjects as orthography (spelling), reading, writing, English grammar, and geography. Sometimes, when a county needed teachers, there would be a "spur of the moment" question and answer session with applicants. It was as important for a teacher to show good moral character as to be able to teach. Very few teachers had been to college. Most finished common school, then took the teacher's test. An 1872 job description for teachers included the following:

The responsibilities assigned to teachers in the 1870s were far different from today's job descriptions. Name some of these early duties that teachers do not have today.

1. Teachers each day will fill lamps, clean chimneys;
2. Each teacher will bring a bucket of water and a scuttle of coal for the day's session;
3. Make your pens carefully. You may whittle nubs to the individual taste of the pupils;
4. Men teachers may take one evening each week for courting purposes, or two evenings a week if they go to church regularly;
5. After ten hours in school, the teachers may spend the remaining time reading the Bible or other good books;
6. Women teachers who marry or engage in unseemly conduct will be dismissed;
7. Every teacher should lay aside from each day's pay a goodly sum of his earnings for his benefit during his declining years so that he will not become a burden on society;
8. Any teacher who smokes, uses liquor in any form, frequents pool or public halls, or gets shaved in a barber shop will give good reason to suspect his worth, intention, integrity and honesty; and,
9. The teacher who performs his labor faithfully and without fault for five years will be given an increase of twenty-five cents per week in his pay providing the Board of Education approves.

STATE FUNDS SCHOOLS

In 1871, the first year Georgia had state funded schools, 49,570 students enrolled. The state agreed to spend $175,000 for the three-month school term. Only thirteen percent of the pupils were black. Because there was not enough money, many teachers were not paid during the first year.

DR. GUSTAVUS ORR — "FATHER OF GEORGIA PUBLIC SCHOOLS"

Dr. Gustavus James Orr, who began the Georgia Teachers Association, was appointed state school commissioner in 1872. Two of his goals were to improve funding, and provide equal treatment for black students. Orr said, "I am in favor of affording them [black students] a fair field for self-development, that they may have the opportunity of exhibiting to the world. . .what they can accomplish." Orr worked with Atlanta University to train black teachers. In 1874, the Georgia General Assembly agreed to give the university $8,000 a year. In return, Atlanta University would admit, free of tuition, as many black students as there were members in the Georgia House of Representatives.

Orr also believed in vocational education. He thought it would help students learn skills to fill the needs of a growing labor market. However, even with "all Orr's work," lack of money kept many communities from having schools.

In the 1877 Georgia Constitution, public education was still limited to elementary school. People could teach if they had basic subject knowledge. In 1870, Georgia tried to start a normal school (school to train teachers). The legislature said it would pay $6,000 a year if Peabody Normal School would move from Nashville to Georgia. The proposal was rejected by Peabody, and it was 1882 before there was any formal teacher education in the state.

In 1882, the legislature set aside funds to send 252 teachers (154 white and 98 black) to a one-month training institute in either Americus, Milledgeville, or Toccoa. There were 6,128 teachers instructing 243,000 Georgia school children at that time. These institutes were the state's first efforts to improve the skills of teachers.

Gustavus James Orr, known as the "Father of the Common School System" in Georgia, worked from 1872, when he was named state school commissioner, until his death in 1887, to improve education in Georgia.

THE THREE-MONTH SCHOOL "YEAR"

The three-month school term was held at different times in different counties. Because of this, it was possible for teachers to teach in more than one county. College students, ministers, and doctors sometimes served as teachers.

Each local district decided where school would be held. In one rural county, the citizens used a building "good enough to winter a cow." In another, forty or fifty children crowded into a poor build-

Right: The Normal and Industrial College at Milledgeville was established as a teacher training school for female students in 1889. Below: Gustavus Glenn became Georgia's school commissioner in 1894. He made the improvement of teacher licensing one of his top priorities.

ing with sawmill slabs for seats. Restrooms were outdoors, and drinking water was in buckets. Some schools had a hand bell. In others, teachers hit the door with a stick to call children to class.

MORE MONEY FOR SCHOOLS

In 1887, Commissioner Orr, known as the "Father of the Common School System in Georgia," died. He was replaced by Sandersville attorney James S. Hook. Hook worked, as Orr had, for a state normal school. One was established in 1895. Monies raised from school taxation also increased, so that by 1893, $699,650 was spent on public schools. Still, teachers made little more than farm laborers. Most schools had about forty-five students, and an average attendance of thirty. This meant most teachers were paid about a dollar a month for each student.

Gustavus Glenn, a former physics professor at Macon's Wesleyan College, became the new education commissioner in December 1894. Grades required on teacher exams were increased to 100 for a three-year license and 70 for a one-year license. Teachers who had taught many years, and who managed their classrooms well, were given permanent licenses. Glenn said, "We adopt books for five years; why not adopt teachers for five years?"

By 1895, due largely to efforts of local newspapers such as the *Atlanta Constitution* and the *Augusta Chronicle*, $100,000 a year was raised for school buildings. Most of the money came from local communities. Landscaping of school grounds was done because of an 1890 law which required students to observe Arbor Day on the first Friday in December.

TEACHER SALARIES

Each county set salaries for those who taught in its schools. In 1900, the average salary of a black male teacher was $25 a month. A white male might be paid as much as $65. Sixteen counties paid teachers the same amount, no matter what their race or sex. One county, Oconee, paid black teachers more than white ones because black teachers were harder to find.

DISCIPLINE IN THE SCHOOLS

Teachers were expected to teach basic subjects and see that students behaved. An 1871 set of rules had to be learned in rhyme:

For study each pupil is furnished a seat; he must keep it in order and perfectly neat; his books and his desk, with what appertains, he must notice and care for; with similar pains; and the floor close about him must also be kept . . . as free from all litter as when it was swept. Suspension or even expulsion from school . . . may follow persistent breaches of rule. . . disobedience stubborn, repeatedly shown . . . . disorderly conduct or quarrel alone . . . or truancy, too, or indolent waste . . . profanity's words or language unchaste. . . .

If a student did not behave, he was usually whipped. There were two popular ways to do this. The first was called "the horse and rider." The child to be punished was placed on the back of another student so the hickory rod was closer to the target. The second was called the "circus wag." A group of students who had misbehaved or who had done their lessons poorly were marched clockwise in a circle and hit with a hickory stick as they passed by.

Do You Remember?
1. Who was known as the "father of the common school system in Georgia," and why?
2. How much did most teachers earn in 1893?
3. How long was the elementary school year?
4. What were two rules for teachers that show the morals of the period?

Education during the New South Era was a serious undertaking for students and teachers alike. There was little time for play or "extra" activities. Students who did not behave appropriately were severely chastised.

COMMUNICATIONS

Thomas Edison invented the mimeograph in 1876. That same year, Alexander Graham Bell received the first United States patent for the telephone. On March 10 of that year, Bell was working on his invention when he spilled acid on his clothes. He shouted to his assistant, "Mr. Watson, come here. I want you." Watson was working in the next room and heard Bell's voice over the telephone. By 1883, there was telephone service between New York and Chicago. In 1900, 1,335,991 telephones were in use across America.

In 1884, Lewis Waterman patented the fountain pen. It replaced quills dipped in ink for writing. Newspapers were able to print late news faster because Ottmar Mergenthaler improved the Linotype in 1885. In 1886, *The New York Tribune* put the automatic typesetting machine into use.

TRANSPORTATION

It was announced in 1893 that Henry Ford had constructed a gasoline engine. Even though French and German inventors had proved the worth of gasoline-powered automobiles, many Americans laughed at Ford's "contraption."

Above: Ottmar Mergenthaler invented the Linotype machine in 1884. His invention enabled typesetters to set type a line at a time instead of a letter at a time. The first major newspaper to use the revolutionary machine was The New York Tribune *in 1886. **Right:** This photograph, taken in 1946, shows Henry Ford in the first Ford automobile, built in 1896. The other man is his grandson.*

At two o'clock on the morning of June 4, 1896, the first Ford automobile was completed. The car was built in a brick shed in Detroit. No one noticed that it was wider than the shed door. Before the car could be taken outside to drive, workers took an ax and knocked out the bricks which framed the door.

AGRICULTURE

In 1872, black **horticulturist** Luther Burbank developed a strand of potato plants which produced seed balls. From the seeds, Burbank produced hearty plants which were later called the "burbank potato."

During the next few years, Burbank's research produced many new types of fruits, vegetables, and grains. In 1873, Illinois-born Joseph Glidden invented barbed wire. Ranchers used it to fence land on which they raised cattle. The use of fences made it possible for ranchers and farmers to live in peace on their land. Fences also meant fewer cowboys were needed to keep the cattle where they belonged.

Daniel Halladay invented the Halladay windmill in 1854. Use of the windmill grew in the 1870s and 1880s. The mill could pump enough well water to supply the needs of farms and ranches.

MEDICINE

In 1880, French biologist Louis Pasteur discovered a vaccine for chicken cholera. He also developed a successful vaccine against rabies in 1885. Within a few years rabies, one of the most dreaded diseases of the times, could be controlled. A major advancement in surgery took place in 1890 at Baltimore's Johns Hopkins Hospital. For the first time, rubber gloves were used during operations. This cut down on the number of post-operative infections.

In 1893, a milestone was reached in Chicago. Black surgeon Daniel Hale Williams performed the first open heart surgery in history.

In 1895, German Wilhelm Roentgen discovered rays that could pass through solids. He called them X-rays because he did not completely understand them. Today, doctors and dentists use them to take pictures of broken bones or cavities in the teeth.

In 1898, during the Spanish-American War, Dr. Walter Reed learned that mosquitoes carried yellow fever. Later, when the

Known as the "plant wizard," Massachusetts-born Luther Burbank was famous throughout the world for his improvement of plants through cross-breeding. From 1875 when he opened a nursery in Santa Rosa, California, until his death in 1926, he developed numerous varieties of plums, berries, roses, and daisies. Research the work of Luther Burbank and determine which foods you eat are a result of his efforts.

Panama Canal was built, this discovery saved hundreds of lives. Doctors were able to end the spread of malaria and yellow fever by killing the mosquito population.

INDUSTRY

In 1873, nitroglycerin was used to build a 4.75 mile railroad tunnel in Massachusetts. In 1886, Charles Hall invented an economical way to take aluminum from ore. The process was so successful that the price of aluminum dropped from five dollars a pound in 1888 to eighteen cents in 1914.

Celluloid, a hard plastic, was produced commercially for the first time in 1872. It had been invented during the Civil War, but did not come into general use until later.

In 1883, black inventor Jan Matzeliger revolutionized the shoe industry. The machine he made attached soles to shoes and sewed the leather together. Before Matzeliger's invention, a cobbler could make six to eight pairs of shoes a day. With the new machine, about a thousand pairs could be made in a day.

Technology Affects Home Life

In 1877, Thomas Edison presented the phonograph. The first words recorded on it were "Mary had a little lamb." Two years later, he improved the **incandescent** lamp by carbonizing a filament of cotton that would last forty hours. The invention began to replace oil lamps. Edison also supervised the building of the first central electrical power plant in the world. By 1881, the New York plant was in operation.

Photography became popular when George Eastman introduced the Kodak camera. The Kodak camera was a square box which used a film roll. In the beginning, the camera, with the used roll of film, was sent to the factory. The film was developed, the camera was reloaded with new film, and both were returned to the owner.

The Singer Manufacturing Company in Elizabethport, New Jersey made and sold the first sewing machines. They were welcomed by homemakers and the sewing industry.

In 1891, Thomas Edison received a patent for the first motion picture camera. Silent films did not become common until the early 1900s. However, Edison's invention was the beginning of the movie industry.

In 1888, George Eastman of Rochester, New York, perfected the box camera and roll film. The manufacturing of the "Kodak" provided Americans with a new hobby. This self-portrait is a test-exposure with Eastman's notes written across it.

Above left: A poster advertising the phonograph, invented by Thomas Edison in 1877. *Above:* Thomas Edison, pictured here in his lab at Menlo Park, New Jersey, had only four years of formal schooling but was considered to be a genius. In what ways do you think his invention of the electric light revolutionized America's economy and society?

Do You Remember?

1. What were two advancements made in medicine during the late 1800s?
2. In what year was the first Ford automobile made?
3. Why was the invention of barbed wire important?
4. When was the telephone invented? By whom?
5. What did Luther Burbank accomplish?
6. What invention popularized photography?
7. Which inventor revolutionized the shoe industry?
8. Who received a patent for the first motion picture camera?

THE RISE OF ATLANTA

A SLOW START

In 1839, Terminus was the southeastern end of the Western and Atlantic Railroad. That year, John Thrasher opened the first store in the crossroads location. That store failed because most people stopped to buy supplies in nearby Decatur. By 1842, the railroad had grown, and the population had increased to almost thirty residents. The most impressive building in Terminus was a two-story house used by railroad officials. During 1842, Willie Carlisle opened a store on Marietta Street. In 1843, Terminus was renamed Marthasville in honor of Governor Lumpkin's daughter.

Above: In 1843, Terminus was renamed Marthasville and the small settlement began to grow. **Opposite page:** In 1845, Marthasville was renamed Atlanta, for the Western and Atlantic Railroads. The paintings on these and the next two pages are by Georgia artist Wilbur G. Kurtz, who did many paintings depicting the early history of Atlanta.

By 1860, Atlanta had a population of 9,500 and was Georgia's fourth largest city, after Savannah, Augusta, and Columbus.

In the next few years, the growing community added a sawmill, a general store, a bonnet and hat shop, and several small grocery stores. The town also had a real estate office and a small hotel. On December 29, 1845, Marthasville was incorporated as a city and called Atlanta. The name is the feminine version of Atlantic. Thus, the city was named for the Western and Atlantic Railroad.

Soon, Atlanta had its first book store, about thirty other stores, a second hotel, two newspapers, and two schools. An 1847 visitor reported that 187 buildings were built during an eight-month period. Its population was 2,500. By 1860, the once sleepy town was Georgia's fourth largest city, with over 9,500 people. Only Savannah, Augusta, and Columbus were larger.

Left: This painting shows Atlanta in 1864, before Sherman's occupation. After Sherman left on his march to the sea, the city lay in wood cinders and chunks of brick. However, the spirit of Atlanta had not burned, and rebuilding began at once. In 1866, the population was 20,000, and there were 250 stores in a 3-mile downtown area. Street lamps and gas lights were back in place.

GRAND STAND

MAIN BUILDING

ATLANTA HOSTS THREE NATIONAL EXHIBITIONS

Three **exhibitions** in Atlanta during the 1880s and 1890s drew the nation's attention to Georgia. They had been the dream of Henry Grady, who wanted the nation to know about progress in the South. In 1881, the International Cotton Exposition had over a thousand displays from many states and several foreign countries. In 1887, the Piedmont Exposition brought over 200,000 visitors, including President Cleveland, to Georgia. The largest and most publicized exhibition was in 1895, when 800,000 visitors came to Atlanta during the three-month-long Cotton States and International Exposition. There, they saw new machinery, and

Opposite page top: *Three expositions were held in Atlanta between 1881 and 1895. The Piedmont Exposition was held in 1887.* **Opposite page bottom:** *Georgia's Governor Colquitt opened the International Cotton Exposition of 1881.* **Left:** *This special newspaper supplement celebrates President Cleveland's visit to the Piedmont Exposition.*

At the suggestion of Macon industrialist John Hanson, State Representative Nathaniel Harris proposed a bill in the General Assembly to establish a state technical school. The result of that bill was that the Georgia School of Technology (Georgia Tech) opened its doors in 1888 with two buildings. Today it is known throughout the country as one of the nation's leading colleges of engineering.

how cotton was made into marketable products.

Visitors also enjoyed Buffalo Bill's Wild West Show, and tapped their feet to the lively patriotic music of John Philip Sousa. Booker T. Washington became nationally known when he dedicated an exhibit building which highlighted black contributions to Southern economy.

GEORGIA TECH OPENS

Georgia School of Technology, or Georgia Tech, opened in 1888. This was a sign that the state wanted Georgia's role in the nation's industrial economy to grow. Georgia Tech, located in Atlanta, attracted those interested in using technology to improve industry.

Do You Remember?
1. Why was Terminus renamed Marthasville?
2. What was the population of Atlanta in 1842? 1847? 1866?
3. What year did Georgia Tech open?

THE DEVELOPMENT OF MANUFACTURING

Much of the state's attention was centered on farming. However, Henry Grady's dream of a New South based on business and industry was, in part, coming to pass.

TEXTILES IMPORTANT TO GEORGIA

One of the state's first industries was **textiles**. Textile mills used raw materials, including cotton and wool, to produce woven material for clothing, bed sheets, blankets, and carpets. Before the Civil War, the center of the textile industry was in New England. In the late 1800s, mills began to spring up in Georgia. Today, over 176,000 Georgians are employed in the textile industry.

Once begun, Georgia's textile industry experienced steady growth. The main manufacturing centers were located along the

The Eagle and Phenix Mill in Columbus was one of the state's first textile mills. Destroyed during the Civil War, the mill was quickly rebuilt. Before Georgia's early mills opened production, the cotton grown in the state was exported to other countries or shipped to northern industrial centers to be used in the manufacture of finished goods.

Below: Living in a mill village was almost as difficult as working in the loud, dirty, and cotton-fiber filled mills themselves. Living quarters like the ones shown here, built in Roswell in 1839, were barely adequate and frequently unsanitary.
Bottom: Built in 1900, the Scottsdale Cotton Mill in Decatur was named for its founder, Colonel George W. Scott. Surrounding the mill were tiny one- and two-room houses for the mill workers.

fall line in Augusta, Columbus, and Macon. There, major rivers provided water power. However, there were also mills in smaller towns. By 1890, Georgia's textile industry produced over $12,500,000 worth of goods.

Life in a Mill Village

In order to house textile workers, mill owners built villages. The small houses were usually all alike. Mill houses were often not in good repair and without indoor bathrooms or running water. Sometimes, families with five or six children lived in houses about the right size for one person.

Mill pay was small, often only a few cents an hour. Parents and children sometimes worked up to seventy hours a week. Mill workers usually bought food, clothes, and supplies from company-owned stores. Most families had to charge purchases, and many owed the company stores more than they could make in a year. Because of this, workers were locked into jobs with the company. In many mill villages, the churches were owned by the mills. Sermons were about the values of hard work, loyalty to employers, and the evils of unions. There was enough medical care to keep the work force healthy so women and children, especially, would not miss work. Often, workers suffered with lung illnesses from breathing cotton lint. However, even with the hardships, many second and third generation families kept working in the mills.

INDUSTRIAL EXPANSION

As railroad lines expanded, and support for industry continued, other manufacturing and mining corporations began to develop. Many acres of timberland offered millions of dollars worth of material for building, furniture manufacturing, and naval stores (turpentine, rosin, tar, and pitch). These products were called naval stores because they were used in shipbuilding.

Kaolin, gold, coal, and iron mining grew. The worth of Georgia's products jumped from seven million dollars before the Civil War to over eighty million by 1900.

Naval stores, like those seen here on one of the Savannah docks, represented one of Georgia's leading industies during the New South era.

Do You Remember?

1. What are three industries besides textiles which grew during this period?
2. Where did mill workers usually buy their food and clothing?
3. What type of transportation played a major role in Georgia's industrial expansion?

MORRIS RICH, A PORTRAIT OF A NEW SOUTH BUSINESSMAN

Morris Reichs was born in Hungary in 1847. His family moved to America and settled in Cleveland, Ohio. The young immigrant, now called Morris Rich, set out with his brothers to make a living. He moved to Georgia and traveled the state selling items such as needles, thread, cooking pots, and other household goods. He also managed stores in Albany and Chattanooga. In 1867, Rich decided to settle in Atlanta.

Above: Hungarian immigrant Morris Rich was typical of the entrepreneurs who, through diligent and hard work, built prosperous businesses in Atlanta. Right: The small Rich's store of 1867 rapidly grew into one of Atlanta's shopping institutions. During the early to mid-1900s, it was a social highlight for Atlantans to don hats and gloves, shop for a while and eat lunch in the store tearoom. In 1991, due to the increased popularity of suburban malls, the downtown Rich's closed its doors after 67 years.

Rich borrowed $500 from his older brother, William, who was an Atlanta merchant. He bought a small wooden building near the railroad tracks. One of his first services to customers was to cover a mud hole in front of the store with planks. Rich stocked many items, but the best selling goods were corsets, which cost fifty cents, and calfskin boots. When customers did not have cash to pay with, Rich was willing to exchange goods for chickens, eggs, or vegetables.

In 1881, Morris Rich and two of his brothers bought a new and larger store on Whitehall Street. The inside of the building was decorated in black and gold, and it had Atlanta's first plate glass store windows.

For sixty-one years, until his death in 1928, Morris Rich was an example of the best of the rising merchant class. In 1924, his store moved to the corner of Broad and Alabama streets in the heart of downtown Atlanta. The downtown store closed in the summer of 1991, but there are Rich's in other areas of Atlanta and across the Southeast.

Morris Rich — A Final Note

Most Georgians know Rich's because of the annual "Lighting of the Great Tree" each Thanksgiving night to begin the Christmas and Hanukkah holidays. Atlanta teachers remember another gift of the Rich family. During the 1930 Depression, Atlanta had no money for teachers' salaries, so it paid them in scrip (paper money which is not legal currency). Rich's accepted the scrip at face value in payment for goods bought in their stores. It is not known if the business got full value for the scrip after the Depression. However, the help they gave teachers was long remembered. In 1931, Rich's accepted up to 5,000 bales of cotton from Georgia farmers in exchange for merchandise.

For many years, many Georgians made yearly trips to Atlanta to shop at Rich's. In the early 1960s, shopping malls became popular and large department stores opened mall branches. The advertising department at Rich's ran newspaper ads to let shoppers know the downtown Atlanta store would stay as it was. However, the ads also said, "You don't have to wear a hat and gloves to shop at Rich's! You can always shop at the new suburban mall Rich's at Lenox Square."

From 1948 until the closing of the downtown Rich's store in 1991, the lighting of the "great tree" on Thanksgiving night atop the Rich's "crystal bridge" meant the beginning of the holiday season for Georgians and thousands of out-of-state visitors.

FROM $2300 TO BILLIONS OF DOLLARS A YEAR — ALL BECAUSE OF A HEADACHE

Coca-Cola began in the backyard of Atlanta Druggist John Styth Pemberton. Pemberton was a successful wholesale pharmacist in Columbus before the Civil War. He served in the Confederate Cavalry, then moved to Atlanta. There, he mixed and sold medicines such as Globe of Flower Cough Syrup and Triplex Liver Pills. The most popular of "Doc" Pemberton's mixtures was a tonic called French Wine Coca. This was a syrup which included alcohol and coca. The coca came from the South American coca plant, the same leaf that produces cocaine. There is no record of the amount of coca in the tonic, but there was a good bit of alcohol. To keep up with the demand for his "Delightful Nerve Tonic and Stimulant That Never Intoxicates," Pemberton built a small chemical plant for $160.

The Temperance Movement Forces a Change

In 1885, citizens of Fulton County voted their county "dry." The ruling would take effect on July 1, 1886. Pemberton began looking for a way to take the alcohol from his tonic. He put a three-legged, thirty-gallon brass stirring kettle over a fire and started work on a new recipe. Instead of alcohol, Pemberton used an extract of the African kola nut, a stimulant brought to the South during antebellum days. After months of measuring and mixing,

Above: After the Civil War, pharmacist John S. Pemberton, better known as "Doc," settled in Atlanta and began distributing his popular nerve tonic, "French Wine Coca."
Right: In the backyard of "Doc" Pemberton's home was a three-legged iron pot used to mix his newest concoction, Coca-Cola.

Left: A 1910 Coca-Cola fountain tray. Today, Coke memorabilia is almost an industry within itself.
Above: Asa G. Candler traveled to Atlanta from Villa Rica with a dollar and some change in his pocket. After selling patent medicines for a few years, the wholesale druggist managed to purchase Pemberton's business and the Coca-Cola secret mixture for $2,300.

Pemberton developed a new syrup that was both a stimulant and pleasant tasting. This new "Brain Tonic" was named Coca after the coca plant and Cola after the kola nut. It was put into pint beer bottles and called the "Intellectual Beverage and Temperance Drink." Several Atlanta drug stores sold it for twenty-five cents. According to Coca-Cola Company historians, a chance, but important, event changed the course of the beverage industry. Willis Venable was the soda fountain man at Jacob's Drug Store. One day a customer came in with a severe headache. He bought Coca-Cola syrup, and asked Venable to mix some with water so he could take it immediately. The tap water faucet was at the other end of the counter, so Venable suggested soda water instead of plain water.

The customer agreed and, when he drank the mixture, said it was much better than with plain water. Within weeks, several other drug stores began mixing the medicine with soda rather than tap water. By the time the "dry" law went into effect, syrup sales had jumped. Within a year, they grew from 25 to 1,049 gallons.

New Ownership

In July 1887, Pemberton's health began to fail. He needed money, so he sold Venable a two-thirds interest in his company. Equipment, supplies, and advertising items were moved from Pemberton's home to the basement of Jacob's Pharmacy. Among them were the brass stirring kettle, 500 street car signs, 4 Coca-Cola cards, oils of nutmeg, spice, lemon, lime, and vanilla. Other ingredients included extract of coca leaves, citric acid, orange elixir, oil of neroli, and caffeine. The total value was $283.24.

Pemberton died penniless in August 1888. Before Pemberton's death, Villa Rica native and druggist Asa Candler bought all the Coca-Cola stock. Candler paid $2,300.

By 1892, the drink had become so popular that Candler sold his drug store and formed the Coca-Cola Company. Candler grew wealthy, and gave money to establish Emory University and Hospital. He served without pay for several years as mayor of Atlanta.

The use of coca leaves in the drink was stopped in 1903. In February 1919, Candler's wife Lizzie died, and he went into a deep depression. The following September, Candler's son quietly sold the company to Atlanta businessman Ernest Woodruff for $25,000,000. At that time, it was the largest business deal ever made in the South.

Under the new ownership, Coca-Cola continued to grow. However, by 1920, the company had financial trouble. In 1923, Ernest Woodruff's son Robert, became president. Robert Woodruff was only three years old when Pemberton mixed the formula for Coca-Cola but, as an adult, he led the company into a multibillion dollar, international business. Woodruff built bottling plants in Europe during World War II. This gave American soldiers a little touch of home, and Europeans began enjoying the American "pause that refreshes."

Like Asa Candler, Robert Woodruff gave money to worthy causes. His gifts included $105,000,000 worth of Coca-Cola stock

The early straight-sided bottle on the left was replaced by the familiar curved bottle on the right in 1916.

to Emory University. This remains the largest single gift in American history.

Today Coca-Cola products are enjoyed around the world by over 470,000,000 people each day. What was begun by "Doc" Pemberton, soda fountain man Willis Venable, and the customer with a headache was, in 1990, worth $444,000,000 retail dollars for each percentage point of sales.

Do You Remember?

1. How old was Morris Rich when he opened his first Atlanta department store?
2. What did Rich sometimes accept for goods in place of money?
3. Why did Pemberton change his original tonic formula?
4. How many gallons of Coca-Cola were sold the first year?
5. Who was Willis Venable?
6. Who purchased Coca-Cola from John Pemberton and Willis Venable?
7. Who was Ernest Woodruff?

Above right: After World War I, millionaire Asa Candler sold Coca-Cola to a group of investors headed by banker Ernest Woodruff. His son, Robert Woodruff, pictured here, took over the company shortly thereafter and ran the global enterprise for almost 50 years. Above left: During World War II, the Coca-Cola Company provided soldiers with a taste of home.

CHAPTER REVIEW

Summary

Atlanta journalist Henry W. Grady coined the phrase "New South" to describe visions of Georgia's future in business, industry, and technology which would rival the economic growth and independence of the New England states.

The arts flourished as did business, industry, and technology in the "New South" era. Two famous Georgia authors, Sidney Lanier and Joel Chandler Harris, are representative of this period.

A state public school system was begun during the latter part of the New South period. Under the leadership of the state's first education commissioners, J.R. Lewis, Gustavus Orr, James S. Hook, and Gustavus Glenn, a free public school system of elementary education was implemented. Although funds for schools were limited, both white and black children gained access to the three-month school terms each year.

While teaching conditions were very rugged and salaries were low, progress was also made in the training and licensing of teachers during the late nineteenth and early twentieth centuries.

The present capital of the state, Atlanta, grew rapidly as a center of business and commerce during this period. From a sleepy railroad terminus for the Western and Atlantic railroad, Atlanta became the fourth largest city in the state behind Savannah, Augusta and Columbus.

Throughout the New South period, Georgia's base of business and industry continued to prosper. The textile manufacturing industry was among the leaders, and Georgia hosted three national and international expositions: The International Cotton Exposition of 1881, the Piedmont Exposition of 1887, and the Cotton States and International Exposition of 1895. During this period of industrial expansion, the Georgia School of Technology (later known as Georgia Tech) was founded.

Two of the leading businesses of Georgia were begun in Atlanta during the New South Period—Rich's Department Store chain and Coca-Cola.

Georgia's economic development was supported by an efficient railroad transportation system, a cheap labor supply willing to work for low wages, ample water power for factories, and an attitude of anti-unionism. Numerous mill towns and villages sprang up throughout the state as manufacturing increased.

As Georgia and the rest of America entered the twentieth century, attention could again be turned to expanding business, industry and technology. America was gaining a reputation as an emerging world power and Henry W. Grady's visions of a New South were becoming a reality.

People, Places, and Terms

Identify, define, or state the importance of each of the following.

1. Morris Rich
2. kaolin
3. Joseph Pemberton
4. Joel Chandler Harris
5. Sidney Lanier
6. Robert Woodruff
7. Asa Candler
8. textiles
9. scrip
10. Terminus

The Main Idea

1. What was Henry Grady's "dream"?
2. Why did a school term last only three months?

3. What two major companies were founded in Atlanta during the New South Era?
4. What two Georgia writers gained fame during this era?
5. What were the four largest cities in the state in 1860?
6. Examine the topics dealt with in the section on education. Which are still of concern today?

True or False

Decide which of the following statements are true and which are false. If the answer is False, rewrite the statement to make it a true statement.
1. Coca-Cola was once owned by the Rich family.
2. Sidney Lanier was a famous Georgia poet.
3. Atlanta was named for the Atlantic Ocean.
4. Textiles were one of the state's first industries.
5. Joel Harris was best known for his humorous articles in newspapers.
6. Sidney Lanier played the flute.
7. Dr. Gustavus Glenn was known as the "Father of the University of Georgia."

Extend Your Thinking

Re-read Joel Chandler Harris' epitaph and answer the following questions:
1. To whom is Harris referring when he said "and some wearing the friendly marks of age, but all children at heart"?
2. Why did he say "and hurry into the obscurity that fits me best"?
3. Why did he think "you have made some of us happy"?

Looking Ahead

The New South and the Progressive Period were bridged by the Black Civil Rights movement. You will explore the progress of this movement and identify black Georgians who contributed to its increasing momentum. You will also study the beginning of Jim Crow laws and examine racial problems that were of concern to blacks and whites alike.

As you read the Chapter, you will find the answer to questions such as:
➤ who wrote *The Souls of Black Folks*?
➤ how did Alonzo Herndon become a millionaire?
➤ where did the term "Jim Crow" originate?
➤ how did Booker T. Washington and W.E.B. DuBois differ?
➤ why was *Plessy v. Ferguson* important?
➤ who were John Hope and Lucy Laney?
➤ who were the first black graduates of West Point Military Academy?

DID YOU KNOW . . .

. . . The Atlanta Cyclorama, which depicts the Battle of Atlanta, was painted by a group of eight German, Austrian and Polish artists in 1886?

. . . According to many reports, only three Coca-Cola employees know the entire formula for Coke? Reportedly, in order to protect the secret formula, the three are never allowed to fly or travel in the same car together.

. . . In 1895, Athenian Samuel Harris became the first black student to attend the University of Georgia? Although never officially on roll, Harris attended classes for five years, completing his own studies and tutoring hundreds of white students who were officially enrolled. Harris was later awarded his degree by Morris Brown College and taught school for $270.00 per year. After his teaching career, Harris supervised all of the black schools in Athens. Today, one of Clarke County's public schools in Athens is named in Harris' honor, Burney-Harris-Lyons Middle School.

CHAPTER TWELVE

A NEW ERA IN CIVIL RIGHTS

1871-1920

I am as good as anybody else. God had no different dirt to make me out of than that used in making the first lady of the land.
— Lucy C. Laney,
Founder of Augusta school for black children

CIVIL RIGHTS ARE rights which belong to a person because that person is a citizen or a member of a civil society. The Thirteenth Amendment to the United States Constitution, put in force December 18, 1865, did away with slavery. In July 1868, the Fourteenth Amendment declared all persons born or naturalized in the United States to be citizens. The Fifteenth Amendment, put in force March 30, 1870, said the right to vote could not be denied because of "race, color, or previous condition of servitude."

Congress passed a Civil Rights Act in 1875. It ensured that black citizens would be able to serve on juries. It also stated:

All persons within the jurisdiction of the United States shall be entitled to the full and equal enjoyment of the accommodations, advantages, facilities, and privileges of inns, public conveyances on land or water, theaters, and other places of public amusement; subject only to the conditions and limitations established by law and applicable alike to citizens of every race and color, regardless of any previous condition of servitude.

Opposite page: *The ninth of ten children, Macon-born Lucy Craft Laney graduated from the original Atlanta University in 1873. One of four teachers in the graduating class that year, Laney went on to become a leading Georgia educator.* ***Above:*** *This cartoon took the position that nothing would be wrong with race relations in the South if it were not for interference from the North, in the person of President Harrison.*

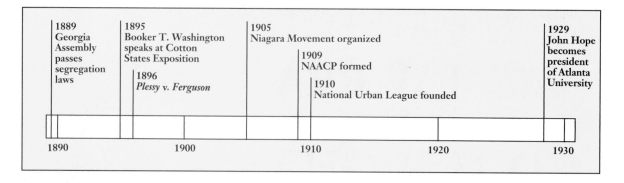

1889 Georgia Assembly passes segregation laws	1895 Booker T. Washington speaks at Cotton States Exposition	1905 Niagara Movement organized	1929 John Hope becomes president of Atlanta University
	1896 *Plessy v. Ferguson*	1909 NAACP formed	
		1910 National Urban League founded	

1890   1900   1910   1920   1930

A STRUGGLE FOR CIVIL RIGHTS

Getting a law passed does not always mean it will be carried out. There was a strong belief in "white supremacy" all over the western world. During Reconstruction and the New South era, most whites and many blacks accepted racial **segregation** as a way of life. The Georgia Constitution of 1877 allowed only blacks who had paid taxes to vote. Georgia's public schools, which had opened in 1871, were totally segregated by 1877. Federal laws, and the judges who reviewed them, had little, if any, impact on customs and traditions. Sociologist William Sumner said, "Stateways cannot change folkways."

JIM CROW LAWS

In 1881, Tennessee became the first Southern state to pass a bill to **segregate** railroad cars. Every other Southern state followed. These were known as "Jim Crow" laws. Blacks protested these laws in public meetings from Maine to Florida. Georgia's Henry McNeal Turner, an African Methodist Episcopal bishop, called the new civil rights laws, and the segregation that followed, "barbarous."

Segregation in rail cars led to other Jim Crow laws. In 1889, the Georgia General Assembly passed laws which segregated theaters, convict prison camps, water fountains, restrooms, restaurants, park benches, and other public facilities. In much of the South, signs appeared which read "WHITES ONLY."

Who Was Jim Crow?

Use of the term "Jim Crow" dates back to 1828. It probably became popular because of an entertainer named Thomas Rice.

He is supposed to have met a black handyman named James Crow in Louisville, Kentucky. Rice wrote a song about Crow.

Step first upon yo' head
An 'den upon yo' toe,
An 'ebry time you turn around
You jump Jim Crow.

Next fall upon yo' knees
Then, jump up and bow low,
An 'ebry time you turn around
You jump Jim Crow."

In 1832, "Daddy Rice," in "blackface" makeup, sang the song in New York's Bowery Theater. It became an instant hit.

By 1838, "Jim Crow" was often used in place of "Negro." There was even an anti-slavery book written in 1839 called *The History of Jim Crow.*

PLESSY v. FERGUSON

Homer Plessy was a light skinned man who was part white and part black. Plessey boarded a train in New Orleans, planning to travel to Covington, Louisiana. He sat in a car for "Whites Only," and, when asked, would not move to a car for "Coloreds." The police were called, and Plessy was removed from the train, arrested, tried, and convicted. His fine was $25.00. Plessy sued the railroad, claiming that, under the Fourteenth Amendment, segregation was illegal. The case moved through the court system, and each court agreed with the railroad company. Finally, in 1896, Plessy appealed to the Supreme Court.

After hearing the case, the Supreme Court ruled that the Civil Rights Act of 1875 stated only that all citizens had the right to public accommodations. It made no mention of segregation. If the facilities provided were equal, segregation was valid. The Court said "separate but equal" was all that was required by the law.

The decision in *Plessy v. Ferguson* opened the door for more Jim Crow laws. Soon sports, hospitals, orphanages, funeral homes, and cemeteries were added to the list of "separate but equal" provisions. It made segregation the law of the land until 1954.

In the 1870s and early 1880s, black and white Georgians sat together on streetcars, shopped in integrated business districts, shared public parks and playgrounds and, sometimes, lived in the same neighborhoods. With the birth of "separate but equal," integration became part of the past.

The Atlanta of the 1870s and 1880s before Plessy v. Ferguson *was, to a limited degree, integrated. However, the social actuality was far different from the picture seen here. Notice the stereotyped depiction of blacks and whites. What messages does the picture give?*

During the New South and Progressive eras, African-Americans had few economic options and were often either teachers, ministers, servants, like those pictured above, laborers, sharecroppers, or farm hands.

BLACKS IN GEORGIA

By 1900, close to twelve percent of the blacks in the nation lived in Georgia. These one million black citizens were forty-nine percent of the state's population. Most of them lived in the farming centers of middle and southwest Georgia. However, a number moved to the cities and built social, business, religious, and educational centers. Nearly one-third of Georgia's cities had black majorities and half of this population lived in Atlanta, Savannah and Augusta. It was in these cities that people protested most against Jim Crow laws. However, protests were not the same as votes.

Blacks could vote in general elections, but Georgia law allowed only white males to vote in primary elections. More and more, blacks felt pushed aside and without power.

Northern states practiced segregation in neighborhoods, schools, and jobs. Black protests continued, but so did segregation. Black leaders began to speak out against segregation.

Do You Remember?
1. What did the Supreme Court rule in *Plessy* v. *Ferguson*?
2. In what year did Jim Crow laws first appear?
3. Who was Thomas Rice?

Booker T. Washington worked his entire adult life to build Tuskegee Institute in Alabama into an institution known throughout the world. His death in 1915 at the young age of 59 was mourned by educators and citizens alike.

BOOKER T. WASHINGTON AND THE ATLANTA COTTON EXPOSITION

One leader who stood out was Booker Taliaferro. Born into a slave family in Virginia, Taliaferro was nine years old when the Civil War ended. His family moved to Malden, West Virginia, and Booker was put to work in a salt furnace. When the town got a school teacher, Booker first had to work during the day and be taught at night. Later, he was allowed to work before and after day classes. When asked for his name at school, he called himself "Washington" because, as he later explained, "it made me feel equal to the situation." When he was sixteen, Booker Taliaferro Washington entered Hampton Institute, a vocational school for blacks in Virginia. He graduated in 1875 as a brick mason. Four years later, he became a night instructor at Hampton.

Students at Tuskegee studied and worked from the wake-up bell at 5:00 in the morning until retirement at 9:30 at night. Students learned skills ranging from the harness making shown here to many other trade skills including carpentry, cabinet making, printing, farming, shoemaking, and others.

Washington Addresses The National Education Association

A year after the civil rights decision of 1875, Booker T. Washington addressed the National Education Association at their meeting in Wisconsin.

> *Brains, property, and character for the Negro will settle the question of civil rights. The best course to pursue in regards to the civil rights bill in the South is to let it alone; let it alone and it will settle itself. Good school teachers and plenty of money to pay them will be more potent in settling the race question than many civil rights and investigating committees.*

Washington's belief in the power of education became well known. In 1881, two men from Tuskegee, Alabama wrote to Samuel Armstrong, who had founded Hampton Institute. They were looking for an educator to establish an industrial and professional school for black students. Armstrong suggested Washington. Since Washington believed economic independence for blacks would lead to social and political equality, he agreed to take the job. The school began in a church and a run-down house. During the next thirty-four years, Washington worked beside teachers and students as they built Tuskegee Institute's buildings.

Students received a "hands on" approach to education as they shaped bricks, poured foundations for buildings, built walls, and made furniture. In addition to his work at Tuskegee, Washington traveled in the United States and Europe, speaking and asking for money to expand the new school.

Washington Speaks Out At The Atlanta Cotton States Exposition

On September 18, 1895, in Atlanta, Georgia, Washington made one of his most famous speeches. Visitors from all over the nation were in Atlanta for the opening of the Cotton States Exposition. A racially integrated crowd heard the opening day speeches in Exposition Hall.

After several remarks by industrialists and politicians, Professor Booker T. Washington was introduced. What he said that day shaped race relations and strongly influenced black leadership for the next twenty years. Washington, a tall, muscular man with a strong, clear voice, began to speak:

During the Atlanta Cotton States Exposition, Booker T. Washington electrified the crowd with his "Cast down your bucket" speech. His influence was extended during the administrations of Presidents Theodore Roosevelt and William Howard Taft as both men consulted with the Tuskegee Institute founder. Washington urged southern blacks to remain in the South and rebuild the region rather than migrating to northern cities to seek prosperity from factory jobs.

A ship lost at sea for many days suddenly sighted a friendly vessel. From the mast of the unfortunate vessel was seen a signal, "Water, water; we die of thirst!" The answer from the friendly vessel at once came back, "Cast down your bucket where you are." A second time the signal" Water, water; send us water!" ran up from the distressed vessel, and was answered, "Cast down your bucket where you are!" A third and fourth signal for water was answered, "Cast down your bucket where you are."

The captain of the distressed vessel, at last heeding the injunction, cast down his bucket and it came up full of fresh, sparkling water from the mouth of the Amazon River. To those of my race who depend on bettering their condition in a foreign land or who underestimate the importance of cultivating friendly relations with the southern white man, who is their next door neighbor, I would say: "Cast down your bucket where you are...."

To whites, Washington offered the same advice:

Only thirteen years after Thomas Edison first distributed electricity in New York City, the 1895 Cotton States Exposition at night was an impressive sight to the many visitors.

Cast down your bucket . . . among the eight millions of Negroes . . . who have, without strikes and labor wars, tilled your fields, cleared your forests, builded your railroads and cities . . . the most patient, faithful, law-abiding, and unresentful people that the world has seen.

Suddenly, Washington flung his hand up, the fingers held apart.

In all things that are purely social, we can be as separate as the fingers, yet [he balled the fingers into a fist] *one as the hand in all things essential to mutual progress.*

The crowd in Exposition Hall went wild. People cheered and waved handkerchiefs. Loud applause interrupted Washington's speech. After the shouts finally died down, Washington addressed the problems of social equality:

The wisest among my race understand that the agitation of questions of social equality is the extremist folly, and that progress in the enjoyment of all the privileges that will come to us must be the result of severe and constant struggle rather than of artificial forcing. . . .

No race that has anything to contribute to the markets of the world is long in any degree ostracized. It is important and right that all privileges of the law be ours, but it is vastly more important that we be prepared for the exercise of those privileges. The opportunity to earn a dollar in a factory just now is worth infinitely more than the opportunity to spend a dollar in an opera house.

When Washington made his comments on social equality, he believed in them from a practical and realistic point of view that reflected the time.

Booker T. Washington's speech became known as the "Atlanta Compromise," because it proposed that blacks and whites should agree to benefit from each other.

Do You Remember?

1. Why did Booker Taliaferro call himself Washington?
2. What school did Booker T. Washington begin?
3. In your own words, what was the "Atlanta Compromise"?

W.E.B. DuBois
And The Niagara Movement

William Edward Burghardt DuBois (pronounced Du Boyce) was one who did not agree with Booker T. Washington. DuBois was born in Great Barrington, Massachusetts on February 12, 1868, the year Congress passed the Fourteenth Amendment. His **ancestry** was French, Dutch, and African.

Will, as he was called, was left penniless at sixteen when his mother died. He worked as a timekeeper in a textile mill, and became the first black student to graduate from Barrington High School. DuBois received a scholarship to Fisk University in Nash-

The originator of the "Talented Tenth" philosophy, Dr. W.E.B. Du-Bois, had a far different view of black progress than did Booker T. Washington. After reading the opinions of both men, what is your view of their philosophies?

ville, Tennessee. After he graduated from Fisk, he earned a master's degree from Harvard University. DuBois then studied at the University of Berlin in Germany before returning to Harvard. He was the first African-American to receive the doctor of philosophy degree from Harvard. DuBois taught in colleges in Ohio and Pennsylvania before coming to Atlanta University in 1897.

In Atlanta, Dr. DuBois taught economics and political science. At first, he thought truth and knowledge would help blacks and whites understand and accept each other. DuBois wanted social and political integration, and higher education for ten percent, a "Talented Tenth," of the black population. He believed this group could become leaders for all other blacks.

However, the late 1800s were a time of extreme racial unrest. Between 1884 and 1918, there were over 2,500 reported lynchings of blacks in the United States. DuBois described each death as "a scar upon my soul." He decided knowledge and truth alone were not enough. There must also be action if blacks and whites were to understand and accept each other.

After Booker T. Washington made his famous "Cast down your buckets" speech at the Cotton Exposition, a difference in ideas caused disagreement between Washington and DuBois. DuBois did not like what he called the "Tuskegee Machine." This meant he thought Washington made social, political, and economic decisions which affected all blacks. DuBois also disagreed with Washington's idea that blacks who were economically successful and waited long enough would see race relations improve. In his book, *The Souls of Black Folk*, DuBois wrote:

> *. . . Manly self-respect is worth more than land and houses, and . . . a people who voluntarily surrender such respect, or cease striving for it, are not worth criticizing.*

DuBois concluded,

> *So far as Mr. Washington preaches Thrift, Patience, and Industrial Training for the masses, we must hold up his hands and strive with him. . . . But, as far as Mr. Washington apologizes for injustices, North or South, does not rightly value the privilege and duty of voting, belittles the emasculating effects of caste distinctions, and opposes the higher training and ambition of*

William Monroe Trotter, born in 1872 near Chillicothe, Ohio, graduated from Harvard College. After several years in the real estate business, Trotter was frustrated by the Jim Crow system and began publishing a newspaper called the Guardian. *An overnight success, the* Guardian *publicly opposed the philosophy of Booker T. Washington and the "Tuskegee Machine" in support of DuBois' position.*

our brighter minds,—as far as he, the South or the Nation, does this—we must unceasingly and firmly oppose them."

In order to work for what he believed, DuBois, with the help of William Trotter, drew together some black educators and professional men. They met secretly near Niagara Falls, New York in 1905, and drew up a list of demands that included the abolition of **discrimination** based on race or color. The following year, the group held its first national convention at the site of John Brown's raid in Harper's Ferry, Virginia. At this meeting, the Niagara Movement published its purpose and goals:

We will not be satisfied with less than our full manhood rights. We claim for ourselves every right that belongs to a free-born American—political, civil and social—and until we get these rights, we will never cease to protest and assail the ears of America with the story of its shameful deeds towards us. We want full manhood suffrage and we want it now, henceforth and forever.

When Georgia's blacks learned about the Niagara Movement, a number of them came together to protest injustices. Augusta educator and political leader William White led several hundred teachers, farmers, ministers, and other professionals who met in Macon in February 1906. There were speeches against the convict lease system and the fact that blacks were not allowed to serve on juries. Some speakers discussed the fact that white and black schools did not get the same amount of money. Others spoke against paying low wages to blacks for hard labor. William White told the audience that, to improve their condition, they must:

. . . buy lands and homes. We must encourage Negro businessmen . . . we must agitate, complain, protest, and keep protesting against the invasion of our manhood rights. . . . And above all, organize these million brothers of ours into one great fist which shall never cease to pound at the gates of opportunity until they shall fly open.

During the year the Niagara Movement held its first national meeting, and the Macon convention met, Atlanta had one of the worst race riots in the nation's history. Some thought the riots

Considering the uneasy racial times in the first decade of the 1900s, the formation of the Niagara Movement to protest racial injustices was a brave and daring step. The movement called for five improvements: full manhood suffrage immediately; discrimination in public accommodations to cease; freedom to talk; the enforcement of laws against rich as well as poor, white as well as black; and, illiteracy to be eliminated and black children educated.

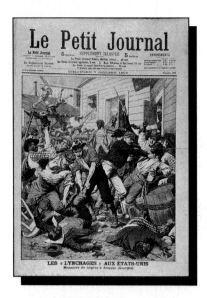

Le Petit Journal

LES « LYNCHAGES » AUX ÉTATS-UNIS
Massacre de nègres à Atlanta (Géorgie)

Atlanta gained international news coverage as a result of the 1906 race riot. During the ten-year period prior to the Atlanta riot, there had been instances of racial violence in Danville, Virginia; Carrollton, Mississippi; New Orleans, Louisiana; Wilmington, North Carolina; and Brownsville, Texas. In each instance there had been multiple injuries, deaths, or both. But the new reports of these instances did little to prepare Atlantans, both black and white, for the two days and nights of rioting. It would take years to heal the emotional damage that resulted from the riot.

came about because men like Tom Watson spread racial fears. Others felt gubernatorial candidate Hoke Smith had used racial fears to gain votes. Still others blamed Atlanta newspapers, which printed stories of black on white racial violence. Local newspaper headlines on the afternoon of Saturday, September 22, 1906, carried false reports of black assaults. By nine o'clock, there was an integrated crowd of over 5,000 on Decatur Street. Some accounts reported that thousands of whites bought guns and began to roam the downtown area. Fear grew, and attacks became real. The riots lasted two days. Eighteen to twenty-five blacks and one to three whites were killed, and hundreds of people were injured. Martial law was declared before the city became calm.

BLACKS ORGANIZE

THE NAACP IS FORMED

Following the Atlanta riots, there were periods of racial unrest in numbers of cities across the country. From August 14 to 19, 1908, black homes and businesses in Springfield, Illinois were burned, and some blacks were killed. Abraham Lincoln had lived in Springfield, and some historians think this is why riots there drew the attention of liberal whites. Oswald Garrison Villard, grandson of William Lloyd Garrison, asked white liberals to join with the Niagara Movement and form a new organization. This group became the National Association for the Advancement of Colored People, or NAACP.

The goal of the NAACP was to work for the rights of black Americans. W.E.B. DuBois left Atlanta University to live in New York and edit *The Crisis*, a monthly NAACP publication. In his column, "As The Crow Flies," DuBois used humor and wit to support black protest. NAACP chapters were organized all over the country. It became strong in Georgia during World War I.

THE BACK TO AFRICA MOVEMENT

Some Georgia blacks did not agree with either Booker T. Washington or W.E.B. DuBois. Instead they were influenced by Marcus Garvey and A.M.E. Bishop Henry Turner. These men favored a "back to Africa" movement. Popular in the 1890's, the movement promised cheap transportation to Liberia for the pur-

The NAACP magazine edited by W.E.B. DuBois enabled branches of the newly formed NAACP throughout the country to keep up with political events affecting the black community. Examine the pictures of influential African-Americans seen on the cover. Research the contributions of each man to the Black Renaissance, or rebirth.

pose of establishing colonies. Small groups did go to Liberia, but tales of hardships, starvation, and death from fever discouraged future settlements. By 1900, the movement had ended.

THE NATIONAL URBAN LEAGUE

A third organization, the National Urban League, was begun in 1910. It was an interracial group that worked with social problems facing blacks who lived in the cities.

1. Who became a professor at Atlanta University in 1897, and later edited The *Crisis?*
2. What are four examples of Jim Crow laws?
3. What incident led to the formation of the NAACP?
4. What did DuBois mean by the "Talented Tenth"?
5. What were two purposes of the Niagara Movement?

GEORGIA LEADER, JOHN HOPE

John Hope was a Progressive Era leader who earned national respect. He was born in Augusta, Georgia, on June 2, 1868, to a white father and a black mother. During early childhood, Hope was treated as the son of a plantation owner. However, his father died when John was eight, and he had little money or social acceptance.

As a teacher, college and university president, and political activist, John Hope made significant contributions in education and in raising the collective consciousness of both blacks and whites. Dr. Hope was buried in a grave below what had been his office on the Atlanta University campus.

Hope attended Augusta public schools and, in 1886, went to Worchester Academy in Massachusetts. He could have passed as a white person, but was proud to be black. Hope graduated from Brown University and taught at Roger Williams University in Nashville from 1894 to 1898. He then joined the faculty of Atlanta Baptist College, which became Morehouse in 1913. Hope became the school's first black president in 1906. In 1929, he was selected as president of the new Atlanta University.

Hope worked for social equality all his adult life. He heard Booker T. Washington's Atlanta Compromise speech in 1895, but did not share his views. Speaking to a debating society in 1896, Hope said:

If we are not striving for equality, in heaven's name, for what are we living?... Now catch your breath, for I am going to use an adjective. I am going to say we demand social equality!

Hope believed in a type of education different from Washington's vocational training.

The Negro must enter the higher fields of learning. He must be prepared for advanced and original investigation.... More honesty, more wealth will not give us rank among the other peoples of the civilized world; and,

what is more, we ourselves will never be possessed of conscious self-respect until we can point to men in our own ranks who are easily the equal of any race."

W.E.B. DuBois, on the faculty at Atlanta University, and John Hope, at Atlanta Baptist College, became close friends. Hope attended the Niagara Movement meeting with DuBois. He was the only college president at the 1909 protest meeting in New York which resulted in the founding of the NAACP. During the Atlanta race riot, Hope was an active civic leader, working to restore calm to his city.

John Hope was president of the National Association of Teachers of Colored Schools, and a leader in the Association for the Study of Negro Life and History. He gained international recognition for his work with the YMCA. Under Hope's leadership, Morehouse, Spelman, Morris Brown and Clark colleges,

Improving life in the black community and increasing cultural understanding between blacks and whites was a family affair for John Hope and his wife Lugenia, and their sons, Edward and John, Jr. Lugenia, a former social worker, began volunteer work in 1898 which resulted in the founding of the Neighborhood Union ten years later.

An Atlanta University chemistry lab. Under Dr. Hope's leadership, Atlanta University continued to grow into a school respected throughout the nation.

Gannon Theological Seminary, and Atlanta University formed the Atlanta University Center. These six schools, all located on adjoining campuses in Atlanta's west end, form the largest complex of predominantly black educational institutions in the world.

John Hope's wife, Lugenia, was also a well-known civic leader. She organized the Neighborhood Union which offered vocational classes for children, a health center, and clubs for boys and girls. As a community action organization, the Union Center provided financial aid for needy families. It also put pressure on city leaders to improve roads, lighting, and sanitation in the black neighborhoods of Atlanta.

MOST BLACK GEORGIANS DENIED THE RIGHT TO VOTE

While Washington, DuBois, White and Hope worked in their own ways for racial equality, blacks continued to have problems. This time, laws were passed to keep them from voting.

In 1908 Georgia followed other Southern states and adopted a "grandfather clause." It stated that if a man's grandfather or father had been eligible to vote in 1867, then the man was eligible to vote in 1908. Few blacks could vote in 1867, so the grandfather clause kept almost all Georgia's blacks from voting. People not covered under the clause had to pass a literacy test, own property, and pay a poll tax six months before an election in order to vote.

There is a story about a black teacher with a degree from Harvard who tried to register to vote in a Southern state after 1908. The voting registrar had the teacher read parts of the United States Constitution and pages from several books. The registrar then had the teacher read in Latin, French, German, and Spanish, which he did successfully. Finally, the frustrated registrar held up a page of Chinese characters and asked, "What does this mean?"

"It means," responded the teacher, "that you do not want me to vote."

No one knows if the story is really true. However, it does show how hard it was for blacks to register to vote.

Do You Remember?

1. What were the two universities John Hope served as president? What were two other accomplishments of Hope?
2. What is meant by "grandfather clause"? What was its purpose?

BLACK GEORGIA IN THE NEW SOUTH AND THE PROGRESSIVE ERAS

A LEGACY OF CONTRIBUTIONS

Lucy Laney

Many black Georgians worked to improve life for their race. To some, Lucy Laney was as well known as John Hope. She was the ninth of ten children born to carpenter David Laney and his wife Louisa. Lucy could read by the time she was four. In 1873, she was a member of the first graduating class of Atlanta University. After graduation, Laney taught in Savannah for ten years. She then moved to Augusta and opened a school in the basement of Christ Presbyterian Church. There were only 5 pupils the first year, but 234 by the end of the second.

In 1886, Francine Haines, a white Presbyterian churchwoman from the North, offered help and financial support. With her backing, Laney opened the Haines Normal and Industrial Institute in Augusta. For sixty years, the school was known for excellent instruction and teacher training. Mary McLeod Bethune, founder of Bethune-Cookman College in Florida, did her first teaching at Haines.

Laney also began Augusta's first black kindergarten and a nursing training program. When she died in 1933, the *Augusta Chronicle* wrote, "Lucy Laney was great because she loved people." Laney's portrait was hung in the Georgia Capitol in 1974.

William Finch

William Finch, was known as the "Father of Black Public Schools" in Atlanta. In 1870, Finch, a successful tailor, was elected to Atlanta's city council. At that time, only two Atlanta public schools were open to black students. While on the city council and after returning to private life, Finch worked successfully for more schools for Atlanta's black youth.

Richard Robert Wright, Sr.

Richard Robert Wright, Sr. was born in 1855 in Dalton. He graduated from Atlanta University with Lucy Laney. Wright became principal of an elementary school in Cuthbert. While in

Top: Lucy Craft Laney was an inspiration to all who knew and worked with her. One of her most notable students was John Hope. Above: A multi-talented man, Richard Wright, Sr., was an educator, politician, editor, and banker. Here he is wearing the uniform of the army paymaster, during the Spanish-American War.

Cuthbert, he organized farming cooperatives and conducted the state's first black agricultural county fair. Wright is credited with organizing the Georgia State Teachers' Association. In 1900, he started, in Augusta, the state's first public high school for blacks.

President McKinley appointed Wright, an active Republican, as army paymaster during the Spanish-American War. He was given the rank of major, the highest military rank held by a black man at that time. After the war, Wright became president of the State College of Industry for Colored, now known as Savannah State College.

After thirty years with the college, Wright joined his son and daughter in Philadelphia. There he founded the Citizens and Southern Bank and Trust Company, the first black-owned trust company in the United States. He was asked to be the United States ambassador to Liberia, but did not accept because of his family and business.

Alonzo Franklin Herndon

Alonzo Franklin Herndon may be one of the best known black business leaders of the Progressive era. Herndon was born in 1858 as a slave on a Walton County plantation, and grew up in Social Circle. He worked for his former master for a while after the Civil War for a salary of $25.00 a year.

Herndon learned to be a barber, and moved to Jonesboro to open his own barber shop. He thought he could have a good business in Atlanta, so he went there and worked in a barber shop. Within six months, he owned a half interest in the business. By the early 1900s, he had opened three new shops for white customers. Herndon began buying property, and soon owned a block of office buildings on Auburn Avenue, and a hundred rental houses.

In 1905, Herndon purchased a small insurance company for $140.00. He knew little about insurance, so he hired black college graduates to run the Atlanta Mutual Insurance Company.

Along with W.E.B. DuBois and John Hope, Herndon was present at the first meeting of the Niagara Movement in New York. He gave freely of his wealth to civil rights causes. Herndon was still president of his insurance company when he died in 1927. That company is now the Atlanta Life Insurance Company. It is one of the largest black-owned businesses in the United States, and

Alonzo Franklin Herndon was one of the most astute businessmen of his time. Through hard work, Herndon built a business empire worth millions of dollars. Visitors can walk through his palatial 1910 mansion in Atlanta. Read the section carefully to find his secret to success. What does his statement mean?

has a net worth of over $100,000,000. Perhaps the secret of Herndon's success in business was best explained when he said, "Some of us sit and wait for opportunity when it is always with us".

Henry O. Flipper

Henry O. Flipper was born in Thomasville in 1856. His slave father was a skilled workman who bought his family's freedom. After the Civil War, Flipper attended Freedman's Bureau American Missionary Association schools. He next went to Atlanta University and, in 1873, was appointed to West Point Military Academy.

Second Lieutenant Flipper was the first black to graduate from West Point. He was assigned to the all-black Tenth Cavalry. During the next four years, he served on five army posts in Texas. At Fort Davis, Flipper's commanding officer accused him of "embezzling funds and conduct unbecoming an officer and gentleman." The officer said Flipper failed to turn in $4,000 in **commissary** funds. At a general court martial, Flipper was found innocent of taking the money, but guilty of "bad conduct." On June 30, 1882, he was discharged from the Army.

Flipper remained in the west and became a successful engineer and special agent for the United States Department of Justice. When the Spanish-American War broke out, he offered his services to the army. Bills were introduced in both houses of Congress to have Flipper's army rank restored. Both bills were defeated.

Senator Albert Fall brought Flipper to Washington as a congressional subcommittee translator and interpreter. Flipper later went to Venezuela and worked for an oil company. In 1930, he returned to Atlanta and lived with his brother Joseph, an A.M.E. Church bishop. From 1882 until his death in 1940, Flipper said he was innocent of the army's charges. While at Fort Davis, he had gone horseback riding with one of the few white women in the territory. He thought this was one reason for his discharge. In 1973, Flipper was cleared of all charges.

The following year, a bust of Flipper was unveiled at West Point. At the ceremony, the superintendent of the Academy said Flipper had "become one of the most honored citizens of the nation, a credit to all of its people and its rich diversity."

"I hardly know how I endured it all so long." These were the sentiments of Henry O. Flipper describing his years as the first black graduate of West Point Military Academy. But endure he did and went on to attain success despite an unfair army discharge that was not rectified until 91 years later when his name and army record were cleared.

RELIGIOUS LEADERS

Henry Hugh Proctor, born in Tennessee in 1868, became pastor of the First Congregational Church in Atlanta in 1894. From the time he moved to Georgia, Proctor began to establish missionary work among the city's poor and in Atlanta's jails. He got national attention following the Atlanta riots in 1906. Proctor and white attorney Charles Hopkins formed a committee of forty blacks and whites to work against racial tension in the city.

Under Dr. Proctor's leadership, his church built a gymnasium, opened a library and an employment bureau, and had a counseling program. The church also provided a home for working girls and a kindergarten. It built a model kitchen and serving room to use for teaching, and an auditorium that would seat a thousand people. Many visitors came to Atlanta to see these community action services. Two notable guests were United States Presidents Theodore Roosevelt and William Howard Taft.

During World War I, Dr. Proctor was appointed to a special position to encourage black troops. During 1919, he traveled in Europe, speaking and helping over 100,000 black soldiers.

James Augustine Healy was born in 1830 near Macon. He left Georgia while a young man. Healy was valedictorian of his class at Holy Cross College in Massachusetts. He became a Catholic priest and, in 1875, became the first black Catholic bishop in the United States. Bishop Healy worked in Portland, Maine until his death in 1900.

Father Healy's sister, Eliza, was Mother Superior in a Vermont Convent School. His younger brother, Patrick, also a Catholic priest, became the first black president of Georgetown University in Washington, D.C. Michael, another brother, was an officer in the United States Revenue Cutter Service, the forerunner of the modern Coast Guard.

Adam Daniel Williams was born January 2, 1863. He grew up in Greene County, and entered the ministry. He became pastor of Ebenezer Baptist Church in Atlanta in 1894. At that time, the church had thirteen members. However, under Williams' leadership, the church grew and was active in community and civil rights causes. Williams organized **boycotts** and rallies to demand equal treatment for blacks. He supported W.E.B DuBois, and was a charter member of the Atlanta chapter of the NAACP.

*Top: The First Congregational Church in Atlanta was led into prominence by minister Henry Hugh Proctor. Under his leadership, the church offered social, welfare and cultural programs to the entire black community. **Above:** Henry Hugh Proctor distinguished himself as a minister, community activist, and race relations mediator.*

When Williams died in 1937, his son-in-law, Martin Luther King, Sr., continued his work. King, Sr. was followed by his son, twentieth century civil rights leader Dr. Martin Luther King, Jr.

A HUMANITARIAN — CARRIE STEELE

Carrie Steele was a maid at Atlanta's Union Railroad Station. At the station, she found children left by parents who could not care for them. Steele took the children to her home, fed, clothed, and cared for them. It was not long before there were more children than there was space. Steele sold her house and took money given by people in the community to open the Carrie Steele Orphanage in 1888. Its founder died in 1900, but the orphanage, known today as the Carrie Steele Pitts Home, has cared for over 20,000 children.

AN IMPORTANT COURT CASE

Amanda Dickson was born in Hancock County in 1849, the daughter of David Dickson, a white planter, and a slave named Julia. When Dickson died, he left control of his **estate** to Amanda. Dickson's white relatives filed suit, charging that a white man could not leave property to non-white children. Amanda Dickson fought the suit all the way to the Georgia Supreme Court. In 1887, the court ruled that a person with black and white ancestry could inherit from a white parent. The ruling gave Amanda Dickson an estate worth $300,000. She moved to Augusta and lived in comfort until her death in 1893.

Carrie Steele could not bear to see children suffer from hunger and neglect. She made it her life's work to provide a safe, caring environment for children in need.

Do You Remember?

1. Name one of Lucy Laney's most famous pupils.
2. Who was William Finch?
3. What Georgian was the founder of the largest black-owned life insurance company in the nation?
4. Who opened Haines Normal and Industrial Institute?
5. For what was James Healy known?
6. Who was the grandson of Rev. Adam Daniel Williams?
7. Which black Georgia minister worked to improve black-white relationships after the Atlanta Riot of 1906?
8. Who was Richard Robert Wright, Sr.?
9. Name some famous visitors to the First Congregational Church in Atlanta.

While there were gains made in civil rights for blacks during the Progressive Era, there were also setbacks. This was especially true in 1915. There were many newsworthy events during that year. Booker T. Washington died. The British steamship Lusitania was sunk by a German submarine, killing 114 Americans. Taxicabs were first seen in the country's major cities. A record player, called a Victrola, was introduced. Georgia native Ty Cobb stole ninety-six bases in a season and set a major league record.

THE TRIAL OF LEO FRANK

It was also 1915 when Georgia became the center of national attention because, on August 16, twenty-nine-year-old Leo M. Frank was lynched in Marietta.

Frank was superintendent of the National Pencil Company factory in Atlanta. On April 26, 1913, he was charged with the murder of Mary Phagan, a fourteen year old employee. The trial which followed was one of the most debated in Georgia's history. There was little evidence. Frank was convicted and sentenced to death, largely because of the testimony of Jim Conley, the factory's black janitor. Conley was also a suspect so, normally, his testimony would not have been heard. However, Frank was Jewish, and during that time, many people disliked Jews. Frank's lawyers appealed the case to the Supreme Court. Georgia Governor John Slaton was pressured to pardon Frank. The day before his term of office ended, June 1915, Slaton changed Frank's sentence from death to life imprisonment. Tom Watson used his magazine, *The Weekly Jeffersonian*, to lead a public outcry against Slaton's action.

THE KLAN IS REBORN

In July, amid anti-Semitic, or anti-Jewish feelings and continuing racial discord, the Ku Klux Klan received a charter from the Fulton County Superior Court.

Anger toward Slaton because of the change of Frank's sentence caused him to leave the state. Two months after the sentence change, twenty-five armed men walked into the state penitentiary in Milledgeville and took Frank from his prison cell. They drove to Marietta, the home of Mary Phagan, and hanged Frank from a

Probably the most sensational trial in Georgia's history, the Leo Frank case in 1915, brought reporters from throughout the nation. Governor Slaton commuted Frank's sentence based on what he called "conflicting testimony." The governor received over 100,000 national appeals to grant clemency to Frank. Frank's hanging and the resulting demonstration showed the degree of racial and religious intolerance during the Progressive era.

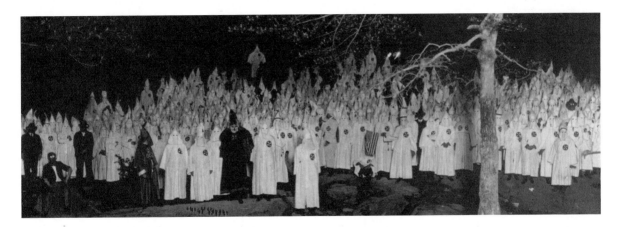

tree. The next day, about 15,000 people filed by Frank's open casket in an Atlanta mortuary. Pictures of Frank's hanging body were sold, and a song, "The Ballad of Mary Phagan," became popular.

On Thanksgiving night, 1915, Atlanta preacher and salesman William Simmons and thirty-four others climbed to the top of Stone Mountain near Atlanta. There, the group lit torches as they circled a burning cross. The Ku Klux Klan was reborn in Georgia.

By 1924, the modern Klan was strong in all Southern states, and in Oklahoma, California, Oregon, Indiana, and Ohio. At its height, the Ku Klux Klan claimed over four million members.

The reorganization of the Ku Klux Klan, depicted here at Stone Mountain in 1921, revived feelings of fear and intolerance that had been buried since Reconstruction days. Between 1920 and 1923, Ku Klux Klan membership nationwide grew from 5,000 to several million members.

THE GREAT MIGRATION

It was also in 1915 that the "Great Migration" began. Southern blacks began moving north to industrial centers, and west to California. They were looking for better jobs and less racial segregation. About 2,000,000 blacks took part in this migration.

Do You Remember?
1. When was the Ku Klux Klan revived in Georgia?
2. What events led to the lynching of Leo Frank?
3. What was the "Great Migration"?

A FINAL NOTE

Seventy-one years after Leo Frank was hanged, Governor Joe Frank Harris issued him a pardon. Frank's family asked for the pardon because the convicted murderer's appeals process had been cut off by the lynching.

CHAPTER REVIEW

Summary

In addition to passage of the Thirteenth, Fourteenth, and Fifteenth amendments, Congress enacted the Civil Rights Act of 1875. This Act provided for equal public accommodations for blacks and whites and said blacks must be allowed to serve on juries. In 1883, the Supreme Court ruled the Civil Rights Act of 1875 unconstitutional. Segregation became legal all over the country as states passed "Jim Crow" laws. In the beginning, the laws applied to separate railroad cars, but they soon spread to other areas of life. In 1889, the Georgia General Assembly segregated theaters, prison camps, water fountains, restrooms, restaurants and other public facilities.

It was during this period that Tuskegee Institute President, Booker T. Washington, spoke at the Atlanta Cotton Exposition. His speech, referred to as the "Atlanta Compromise," urged blacks and whites to benefit from the strengths of the other. He encouraged blacks to achieve social equality by gaining economic power. W.E.B. DuBois was Washington's most outspoken opponent. Dr. DuBois believed in the education of a "talented tenth," who could lead the remainder of the black population.

In 1896, in the case of *Plessy* v. *Ferguson*, the United States Supreme Court said it was acceptable to have separate accommodations so long as they were equal. In an attempt to end the discrimination laws, the Niagara Movement, led by W.E.B. DuBois, was formed in 1905. Inspired by the efforts of the Niagara Movement, a group of black Georgians led by William White met in Macon to denounce discriminatory practices in Georgia including the convict lease system, the exclusion of blacks from juries, the unequal allocation of state educational funds, and the low wages paid to black workers. In that same year, 1906, Atlanta experienced a race riot.

Two years later, national attention focused on riots in Springfield, Illinois. As a result of the increasing violence, the Niagara Movement and a group of white liberals joined together to form the National Association for the Advancement of Colored People. A few years later, in 1910, the biracial National Urban League was formed to deal with problems facing blacks living in cities.

Throughout the New South and Progressive eras, many black Georgians were working hard to bring about positive changes. One of the most influential was John Hope, who became President of Morehouse College and later served in the same capacity for Atlanta University. A leading educator and civic leader in Atlanta, Hope, and his wife Lugenia worked to improve services to black neighborhoods. They organized a variety of community action groups.

During this period, many blacks began to move from Georgia and other Southern states to seek job opportunities in the northern industrial states and in California. This movement became known as the "Great Migration".

People, Places, and Terms

Identify, define, and/or state the importance of each.

1. The Atlanta Compromise
2. Niagara Movement
3. Carrie Steele
4. NAACP
5. Adam Daniel Williams

6. *Plessy v. Ferguson*
7. Lugenia Hope
8. Henry O. Flipper
9. anti-Semitic
10. migration

The Main Idea

1. Compare and contrast the opposing philosophies of Booker T. Washington and W.E.B. DuBois.
2. Compare and contrast the purposes and goals of the Niagara Movement, the NAACP, and the National Urban League.
3. What were Jim Crow laws?
4. Describe some of the requirements for voting in elections which were designed to limit black voting power.

Extend Your Thinking

1. Which event or person was of most interest to you in this period of Georgia's history? Explain why that individual or incident interested you.
2. Choose one thing you learned while studying the chapter that you did not know beforehand. How did this new information affect you?

Looking Ahead

Chapter Thirteen continues the New South period and early Civil Rights era by examining reforms of the Progressive Era, the scientific and technological advancements, and Georgia's involvement in World War I.

As you study the chapter, you will learn:
➤ who the infamous "muckrakers" were.
➤ who the President was during World War I.
➤ where the Girl Scouts of America were organized.
➤ what a "hatchetation" was in 1900.
➤ when Georgia adopted prohibition.
➤ when Carrie Nation carried an ax in one hand and a Bible in the other.
➤ how the Triangle Shirtwaist Company Fire led to building code reforms.
➤ how Georgians felt about World War I.

Sharpen Your Graphing Skills

Using information in the text, design a graph to illustrate Georgia's black population numbers and locations in 1900. (You may use any type of graph such as circle, bar, line, etc.)

DID YOU KNOW . . .

. . . During this period, George Washington Carver developed over 300 products from peanuts including milk, cheese, face power, shampoo, printer's ink, vinegar, coffee, soaps, and wood stains? He also created 118 products from the sweet potato including rubber glue for postage stamps.

. . . The first recorded transportation boycott occurred in Louisville, Kentucky in 1871? Blacks refused to use the city's trolley cars until they were allowed to ride with whites.

. . . In the late 1870s and early 1880s, there were towns with all-black populations in Kansas and Oklahoma?

. . . In 1924 Booker T. Washington High School opened in Atlanta. For years it was the largest black high school in Georgia with over 4,000 students. The school's alumni include, Dr. Martin Luther King, Jr., Secretary of Health, Education, and Welfare Dr. Louis Sullivan, comedian Julius "Nipsey" Russell, National Basketball Association star Walt Frazier, and civil rights leader Vernon Jordan.

CHAPTER THIRTEEN

A TIME OF REFORM
THE PROGRESSIVE ERA
1900 - 1920

We see in many things that life is very great ... but the evil has come with the good.... Our duty is to cleanse, to reconsider, to restore, to correct the evil without impairing the good.
— From President Woodrow Wilson's First Inaugural Address in 1913

THE TERM "PROGRESSIVE" comes from the word progress which means to improve or move forward. People who worked for progress were called "reformers."

Political reformers wanted honest, well-managed government which protected its citizens. They also wished to give the people more power in decision making. Some political reformers worked to gain the right to vote for women. Social reformers wanted changes in society. Their interests included better working conditions for laborers and help for the poor, especially those in inner city neighborhoods. They wanted better education for children and improved prison systems. Supporters of the temperance movement were social reformers, as were those who worked for the civil rights of all citizens.

Most students in the graduating class of 1917 at Georgia Tech in Atlanta did not have the opportunity to begin a career. It was war time and many of the graduates had already been given their army assignments. Generally, graduation is a time for joy and excitement, but for these students it was a day filled with apprehension.

1900		1906		1911	1914	1917	
Carrie Nation attacks saloons in Kansas		Hoke Smith elected governor		Hoke Smith appointed to U.S. Senate	World War I begins	U.S. enters World War I	
	1901 Berry Schools founded		1908 "Little" Joe Brown elected governor		Equal Suffrage Party formed in Georgia		1918 World War I ends

1900   **1905**   **1910**   **1915**   **1920**

CHAPTER OUTLINE

Alexander Graham Bell invented the telephone in 1876.

THE REFORM MOVEMENTS

The reform movements were largely due to changes in industry and agriculture. Many people left farms to work in city manufacturing plants. Such moves did not always improve financial or housing conditions. Newspapers, magazines, and books printed stories about dishonesty in business, corruption in government and politics, and the horrors of being poor. Theodore Roosevelt said these writers raked filth for their reports. From then on, writers who wrote about the problems of American life in the early twentieth century were called muckrakers.

One of the most famous muckrakers was Upton Sinclair. His book, *The Jungle*, was published in 1906. The novel described horrible working conditions at Chicago's meat packing plants. It told how meat was produced in dirty conditions. As a result of this book, President Roosevelt pushed for a congressional bill that same year. The Meat Inspection Bill required sanitary conditions in packing plants. It also allowed federal inspection of plants which shipped meats to other states.

Another cause of the reform movements in the Progressive Era was the influence of the Populist Party. This party made voters more aware of problems facing the nation in the 1890s. Populists had little political power by 1900 but, because of them, Americans understood the need for governmental and social reform.

Reforms in the Progressive Era were made more possible because of inventions in the late 1800s. The typewriter, invented in 1868, was followed by the telephone in 1876. The wireless telegraph was invented in 1895. All of these combined to spread both good and bad news quickly across the country.

During the early 1900s, attempts to design programs to rehabilitate prisoners were unheard of. The Georgia chain gang shown here was considered the just punishment for criminals. In your opinion, would the threat of being placed on a chain gang be a deterrent to crime today? Why or why not?

PRISON REFORM

In 1880, a special legislative committee was formed to look into the handling of leased prisoners, but few changes were made. It was not until 1897 that the lease law was changed.

A commission was appointed to buy a prison farm so youthful offenders and old or sick inmates could be separated from other prisoners. On the farm, prisoners grew their own food and built and kept up their living quarters. The farm, located near Milledgeville, was built in 1900. A year later, a large federal penitentiary was built in nearby Atlanta.

Chain Gangs Replace Prisoner Lease System

In 1908, the lease system was eliminated completely. It was replaced with another method of dealing with prisoners: county work camps, or "chain gangs." Prisoners in work camps wore black-and-white-striped uniforms, and were chained by their wrists and ankles so they could not escape. The work they did was hard, and whippings were common. No efforts were made to get them ready for life after their prison sentences were done. Housing, sanitary conditions, and the quality of food were often poor.

Georgia's ways of dealing with criminals did not improve greatly until the early 1940s. Then, modern equipment replaced chain-gang workers. However, one positive change was made during the Progressive Era. In 1915, at the urging of social reformers, the

Georgia General Assembly created the juvenile court system. For the first time, young offenders were tried and punished differently from adults.

LABOR REFORMS

In 1900, unskilled workers were earning ten cents an hour during twelve hour days in factories and manufacturing plants. Many of these workers were children. Across the nation, weekly pay was less than $10.00. A man's shirt cost fifty cents, and meat was ten cents a pound. Workers could hardly provide for their families and had little hope of things getting better.

The American Federation of Labor Union is Formed

Factories were often unsafe, and job-related accidents and deaths were common in both factories and mines. People who tried to form labor unions were often punished or fired. However, one organization, the American Federation of Labor, or AFL, was successful. It was begun in 1886 with Samuel Gompers as president. AFL members worked to bring about collective bargaining, higher wages, shorter working hours, and better working conditions.

During the Progressive era, Georgians, like most other Southerners, did not push for unions. In many cases, industries were locally owned and workers lived in the community. They attended church, social activities, and ball games with the factory, mill, or mine owners. In Georgia's mill towns, the homes of many workers and many of the town stores belonged to mill owners. Most workers thought, if they caused trouble or took part in unions, they would lose their jobs and the houses in which they lived.

A Strike Fails at the Columbus Textile Mill

In 1898, Prince W. Greene organized workers at the Columbus Textile Mill and led them in a strike against the company. This strike, and efforts by workers in Atlanta and Augusta to promote membership in the National Union of Textile Workers, part of the AFL, was not successful. By the early 1900s, attempts to form unions ended in Georgia. However, in other places in the nation, unions were gaining influence.

A cigarmaker by trade, English-born immigrant Samuel Gompers worked tirelessly for labor reforms that would provide men and women with a life without poverty and despair. He helped found the Federation of Organized Trade and Labor Union in 1881. When the union reorganized in 1886 into the American Federation of Labor, Gompers became its president.

Fire At Triangle Shirtwaist Company in New York

The Triangle Shirtwaist Company in New York made women's blouses. On Saturday, March 25, 1911, just before closing time, a fire broke out. Eight hundred fifty employees, most of them young women, were in the building, which was thought to be fireproof. Burning fabric spread fire through the building. The one fire escape was blocked, and screaming employees jumped out windows. One hundred forty-six workers were killed in the thirty-minute fire. As a result, local building codes and labor laws were changed to make work places safer. There was also an increase in the membership of the International Ladies Garment Workers Union, which had been formed in 1900.

Child Labor Laws Passed

Reform was slow in the area of child labor. In 1900, over 1,000,000 children under the age of 16 worked 13 or more hours a day in northern clothing factories known as "sweatshops," or in southern cotton fields and textile plants. Most made only a few cents an hour. Slowly, state legislatures, including Georgia's, passed laws to set minimum wages for children. School attendance was required, and children could no longer work in dangerous places, such as around fast-moving machines or in some types of mining. However, it was the 1930s before there was enough legal protection for child workers.

Photographer Lewis Hine, famous for his pictures showing the hardships of the downtrodden, captured this young girl working at a textile mill in Macon before child labor laws were passed. In his notes he stated, "She was so small, she had to climb up on the spinning frame to mend the broken thread." How do you think photographs like this one helped ensure the passage of child labor reforms in Congress?

The six-foot-tall Carrie Nation was both an impressive and intimidating sight. Armed with her Bible and hatchet, she took messages of temperance to anyone who would listen and even to many who wouldn't. Much of her fervor stemmed from the death of her first husband from alcohol abuse. On one occasion, a policeman tried to arrest Carrie Nation for defacing property. Mrs. Nation drew herself up to her full height and screamed at the officer, "I am defacing nothing, I am destroying!"

THE TEMPERANCE MOVEMENT

The Women's Christian Temperance Union

One of the most successful organized attempts at reform during the Progressive Period was the temperance movement. Since Colonial days, groups had tried to end the production and use of alcoholic beverages. In 1873, women in Hillsboro, Ohio heard a lecture by a health authority, then began a crusade to close the town saloons. The campaign spread to other communities and, within two months, twenty states had become "dry" without any laws being passed.

In November, 1874, women from seventeen states gathered in Cleveland, Ohio to form a permanent organization. It was called the Women's Christian Temperance Union, or WCTU. Led by Frances Willard, the WCTU grew rapidly. In 1893, a second group, the Anti-Saloon League, was formed to force saloons to close.

A Hatchet in One Hand and a Bible in the Other

One of the most colorful persons of the period was Carrie Nation. The six-foot-tall, one hundred seventy-five pound woman entered Dobson's Saloon in Kiowa, Kansas on June 7, 1900. Armed with rocks, she took careful aim at the bottles behind the bar.

Within minutes, the floor was covered with broken glass. Looking at the speechless bar owner, Nation is reported to have said, "Now, Mr. Dobson, I have finished! God be with you." She walked out of the bar and, taking a buggy load of rocks, went down the street, and wrecked two other bars. Mrs. Nation demanded that the sheriff arrest her, but the shocked lawman just asked her to leave town quickly. As president of the local WCTU, Nation started a series of raids on saloons in Topeka and Wichita. For those, she carried a hatchet in one hand and a Bible in the other. Her "hatchetations" continued in other parts of Kansas and in such cities as New York, Washington, D.C., and San Francisco. Conservative prohibitionists disagreed with Nation's tactics, but other women followed her example. Mrs. Nation was arrested more than thirty times. She raised money to pay her fines by making speeches and selling tiny silver hatchets as souvenirs.

Georgia Women Speak Out Against Demon Rum

During this same time, Georgia's reformer, Mary Harris Armor, was also speaking against demon rum. She was a skillful speaker, and raised money for the temperance movement. Armor spoke to conventions in Boston, London, Glasgow, and Toronto. During World War I, President Wilson asked her to be the official United States representative to the World Congress on Alcoholism in Milan, Italy.

Rebecca Latimer Felton also joined hundreds of Georgia women in the WCTU These women did not have the right to vote, but had a great deal of political influence. As the movement grew stronger, temperance leaders got the Georgia General Assembly to outlaw the sale of liquor in areas near schools and churches. This was followed with laws which allowed each county to decide if it wanted to be wet or dry.

Georgia Acts Against the Use of Alcohol

By 1881, forty-eight Georgia counties had banned the sale of alcohol. There was a state temperance conference in Atlanta in July 1881. The group who met committed themselves to making the entire state dry. By 1884, **prohibition** was one of the main topics of conversation in churches, political meetings, and at many dinner tables. Ninety counties had voted to go dry. Atlanta and Fulton County joined them in 1885. Businesses which depended on the sale of alcohol formed a group and, in 1887, temperance forces in Fulton County lost. By the end of 1888, twenty-six other counties were again wet.

Prohibition **activists** tried to get rid of **distilleries** but, in 1900, there were 135 of them in the state. Making liquor raised tax money for counties where the distilleries were located, and provided $150,000 for education in the state.

In 1907, with the support of Governor Hoke Smith, the legislature passed a law prohibiting alcohol. Joseph M. Brown, son of a former Bourbon Triumvirate leader, became governor in 1909. He thought the state should go back to earlier laws which allowed counties to decide if prohibition was best for them.

The 1907 law was hard to enforce. Saloons selling near-beer began to open. Soon, they were selling liquor with little attention from officers of the law. Individuals could buy liquor outside the

This cartoon, published in 1908, shows "Carrie Nation cadets" marching through Georgia. Had you lived during the days of the temperance movement, would you have supported "hatchetations"? Why or why not?

state and bring it into Georgia. It was not long until railroad station unloading platforms were filled with small boxes of liquor.

In 1913, the United States Congress passed the Webb-Kenyon Bill, making it illegal for railroads to carry alcohol into dry states. However, the near-beer saloons and clubs which kept liquor for members grew in number.

In 1914, Georgians elected Nathaniel E. Harris as governor. Harris called a special legislative session and pushed through a bill to close the near-beer saloons and private clubs. By 1919, it was illegal for a Georgian to even have beverage alcohol.

The Eighteenth Amendment

That same year, the last of the nation's then forty-eight states voted to ratify the Eighteenth Amendment to the Constitution. This amendment prohibited the manufacture, sale, and transportation of "intoxicating beverages." For the next fourteen years, the nation was legally dry. Carrie Nation could put away her hatchet.

THE FIGHT FOR SUFFRAGE

The fight for suffrage began long before the Progressive Era. In the late 1700s and early 1800s, there was little difference between the roles of men and women. Women who moved west with their families were equal pioneers with their husbands. In the industrialized North, factory jobs and teaching positions were filled by both men and women. However, by 1830, "a woman's place was in the home." Married women had few chances to earn money, and what they had was controlled by their husbands.

Women Organize for the Right to Vote

There was little hope that a woman could be a political or business leader. Those who wanted freedom for slaves began to speak out for the rights of women also. In July 1848, Lucretia Mott, Elizabeth Cady Stanton, and three other women met at the Stanton Home in Seneca Falls, New York. They decided to get others involved in the cause of women's rights. On July 19th, more than 300 people, including black publisher Frederick Douglass, gathered in the Senaca Falls Methodist Church. The group talked about subjects that included property rights, divorce laws, and voting rights.

Attorney Nat Harris, Georgia's governor from 1915 to 1917, was the last Confederate veteran to serve as the head of state. His effectiveness as governor was sorely tested by the state's division over the issue of alcohol sales. Read about Harris' actions and discuss what you would have done in his place.

As word of the convention spread, thousands of women joined to demand the right of women and blacks to vote. A few years later, Susan B. Anthony and Elizabeth Stanton met, became friends, and went all over the country to share their beliefs.

The Fifteenth Amendment, passed in 1870, gave black men the right to vote, but did nothing for women. "Suffragettes" felt they were getting somewhere when, in 1869, the territory of Wyoming gave women the right to vote. When the territory applied for statehood, some Congressmen asked them to change the suffrage law. Wyoming leaders wired their answer: "We will remain out of the Union 100 years rather than come in without the women." In 1890, they became the first "women's suffrage state." By 1900, women could also vote in Utah, Colorado, and Idaho.

The Georgia suffragettes cared little that they were the recipients of cat-calls and jokes as they paraded in downtown Atlanta. In most parades, they were put at the end of the pro-cession behind the cleanup carts.

Georgia Women Form Equal Suffrage Party

Augusta Howard organized Georgia women to work for suffrage. Their first meeting was in Columbus in July 1890. Several years later, the National Association Suffrage Convention met in Atlanta.

The Equal Suffrage Party was formed in 1914 by Georgia women, including W.G. Raoul, Mary Raoul, and Emily Mac-Dougald. They wanted to get support for passage of the Nineteenth Amendment, which would give women the right to vote. Within a year, the party has 2,000 members. In November 1915, some of them marched in Atlanta's annual Harvest Festival Parade. The place assigned to them was at the end of the parade, behind the city trash carts. Thirty-five states had ratified the Nineteenth Amendment by the summer of 1920. One more was needed to make it law. On Wednesday, August 18, the Tennessee legislature met to consider the amendment. Legislators in favor of it wore yellow roses in their lapels. Those against it wore red roses. Harry Burn, a young legislator who had promised his support, had on a red rose. Suffragists, or "Suffs," in the visitors' gallery watched. The first vote ended in a tie. On the second vote, Burn changed his "no" to "aye," and the Nineteenth Amendment became the law of the land.

Georgia was one of five states who did not ratify the Nineteenth Amendment. Suffragette Rebecca Felton said, "It is embarrassing to apologize for the ignorance and stupidity of the state legislature."

Rebecca Felton supported many progressive causes and reforms. She assisted her Independent Democrat husband, Reverend William Felton, in his successful political campaigns in the 1870s and early 1880s. Their shared political campaigns led to this popular political jingle: "Some parsons hide behind their coat, To save their precious life; But Parson Felton beats them all, He hides behind his wife."

Do You Remember?

1. What was the "Progressive Era"?
2. What were two causes of reform in the Progressive Era?
3. What prison method replaced the convict lease system?
4. How much did most laborers make for an average work day in 1900?
5. What is the AFL? What is its purpose?
6. What labor laws were passed during the Progressive period to affect children?
7. What do the initials WCTU stand for?
8. What are the names of two Georgia temperance leaders?
9. In terms of alcohol, what are the meanings of "wet" and "dry"?
10. Which amendment to the Constitution enacted prohibition?
11. What is the definition of the term "suffrage"?
12. Who were two Georgia women who fought for suffrage?

LIFE IN THE REFORM ERA

THE "GILDED AGE"

During the Progressive Era, a new group of people came into being. They made a great deal of money buying and selling land and taking financial risks in business. These people were called the "nouveau riche," or new rich. They spent money so freely that the late 1880s through the early 1900s became known as the "Gilded Age."

The "Nouveau Riche"

Houses of the new rich were showy. They usually had richly woven rugs, heavy furniture, carved staircases, and many original paintings.

Bigger was better, and many people like Jay Cooke, William Vanderbilt, and Jay Gould built giant stone mansions with fifty to seventy rooms. Steel baron Andrew Carnegie built beautiful railroad cars with living and office space. In New York, he had a huge house complete with gold plumbing fixtures. On Nob Hill in San Francisco, mining tycoon James Flood built a forty-two-room house surrounded by a block-long bronze fence. It took a full-time employee just to keep the fence polished.

Georgia's Jekyll Island became a retreat for such wealthy families as the Astors, Vanderbilts, and Rockefellers. Their winter "cottages," were, in reality, large estates. Jekyll Island was a playground for the rich and famous from 1888 to the early 1940s.

Many wealthy people in the Gilded Age built their large houses outside the cities where there was enough land for them. This was part of a cycle, with middle income families moving to the outer circles of the cities, and poorer families staying near the center.

A few Americans, like industrialist Andrew Carnegie, could afford a life of untold luxuries. However, the Scottish-born immigrant first worked as a bobbin boy in a cotton mill for $1.25 a week, a telegrapher, and a railroad superintendent before becoming a wealthy steel industrialist. He gave away enough money to open 2,800 public libraries across the country, including a number in Georgia.

LIFE FOR MOST AMERICANS

Life for the middle class and poor was quite different from that of the very rich. The work week, which had been fifty to sixty hours in 1890, dropped to forty-eight hours by 1920. Baseball became more popular, and people both played in their neighborhoods and attended professional games. Dr. James Naismith of the Young Men's Christian Association College in Springfield, Massachusetts, introduced basketball, the only major sport that

After the first game of basketball was played in 1891, the sport quickly grew in popularity. Here you see a game between Atlanta's Boys' High and Tech High in 1919. In earlier games, a peach basket was used as the goal. After each basket, a member of the team had to climb up on a ladder to retrieve the ball.

originated in the United States. Within a few years, people of all ages were enjoying the new game. College football, an American form of the English game of Rugby, caught on slowly. Often, the players were also the cheering section.

Bicycling was the primary means of transportation. Some larger cities had street cars. Automobiles were not widely used until after World War I. Other favorite pastimes included going to **vaudeville, burlesque,** and musical comedy shows. The first moving pictures in America were shown in 1905 at a Pittsburgh movie theater. Movies spread quickly across the country. It usually cost a nickel to see one, and people called the theaters "nickelodeons." Popular books of the era included Rudyard Kipling's *Captains Courageous*, L. Frank Baum's *The Wonderful Wizard of Oz*,

Left: Mail order businesses like Sears Roebuck allowed people living in small towns and on farms to choose the latest in fashions, furniture, farm equipment or household appliances and have them delivered. *Above:* The bicycle remained a favorite means of transportation until the arrival of the automobile.

Mrs. Wiggs of the Cabbage Patch by Alice Rice, and the stories of Jack London including *White Fang, The Call of the Wild,* and *The Sea Wolf.* Newspapers and magazines were widely read, and most Americans became better informed about events affecting their lives. A big change during this era involved mail-order shopping. Before, people had no way to shop except in community general stores or specialty stores in the cities. When Montgomery Ward and Sears, Roebuck and Company went into the catalog sales busi-

Right: Another popular sport of the period was football. This 1911 Georgia Tech team was coached by John W. Heisman. In honor of his contributions to the sport, the annual award to the top college player is called the Heisman Trophy. Below: Methodist evangelist Samuel Jones traveled throughout the state preaching against many of the "new-fangled" ideas and leisure time activities of the early 1900s.

ness, it was possible to shop by mail. Catalogs offered almost any needed item at a price working people could afford. In one early catalog, a fancy ladies' hat was less than $3.00, and a fine brass bed was $32.95.

RELIGION DURING THE PROGRESSIVE ERA

During the Progressive Era, many social and political events centered around religion. Baptists and Methodists remained the major protestant denominations in Georgia. Churches tried to help their members who were in need, and had programs for young people.

Revivals and Evangelism

After the major work of planting was done, and before time to harvest, most churches had summer revivals. People came from miles around to hear famous preachers who spoke each night for one or two weeks. Georgia enjoyed the preaching of Cartersville resident Samuel Porter Jones. Jones was a Methodist circuit rider who preached against drinking, gambling, card playing, baseball, bicycling, novel reading, and dancing. Sin and the devil were the main targets of loud, foot-stomping sermons.

Billy Sunday Comes to Atlanta

There was a spirit of religious revival all over the nation in the early twentieth century. Former professional baseball player and YMCA worker, William Ashley Billy Sunday, was one of the most popular preachers of the day. Sunday came to Atlanta in 1917. When he arrived, he said, I expect Atlanta to come to the plate and line them out so fast that the Devil will have his tongue hanging out and . . . the score will be one of which Atlanta will be proud. During his seven-week revival, thousands came to a huge tent in the city to hear the fiery evangelist speak out on the evils of alcohol, in particular, and sin, in general.

THE BERRY SCHOOLS

Martha McChesney Berry was born into a wealthy family near Rome on October 7, 1866. She attended a private school in Boston, then traveled in Europe. After she returned to Oak Hill, the

*Above: A well-known religious leader of the period was Billy Sunday. In 1908, the former professional baseball player was ordained a Presbyterian minister. He traveled across the country electrifying the crowds with his flamboyant actions and intense services. **Left:** When she was not horseback riding or strolling the 300-acre grounds of her comfortable home, Martha Berry could often be found working in her study.*

Top: Martha Berry's dream of helping others by providing educational opportunities is still carried on today at Berry College. Above: Martha Berry's home, Oak Hill.

family plantation, Martha often rode horseback with her father to give food and clothing to the poor.

Martha Berry's "Gate of Opportunity"

Martha's study, where she liked to write, was a log cabin on the plantation. One Sunday afternoon, three boys in ragged overalls were playing outside the study. Martha asked them to come in, gave them apples, and told them Bible stories.

The next Sunday, the boys brought their brothers and sisters. Soon, parents came for Martha's weekly "Sunday School." The group outgrew the cabin, so they moved to an old church building at Possum Trot. When there were too many people to get in that building, Berry began other Sunday Schools in nearby communities. The people of the area called Martha Berry the "Sunday Lady of Possum Trot." In addition to sharing Bible stories, Martha taught reading, singing, and good health practices.

Berry School Opens

In 1901, Berry used $1,000 of her own money and eighty-three acres of land to establish a school. With the help of her students, she built a small school house across the road from her home. The next year, Miss Berry, her sister, and Elizabeth Brewster added a dormitory so students could live at the school. There was no tuition, but each student worked. They grew vegetables, raised cattle, and helped to build roads and classroom buildings as needed. Berry called the entrance to the school the Gate of Opportunity. Here, poor young boys of the mountain area learned to read, write, and cipher (do arithmetic). They also got job training which would help them find work when school days were over.

Like the Sunday classes, the school quickly became over-crowded. Berry asked for and got help from two of America's wealthiest businessmen, Andrew Carnegie and Henry Ford. In 1909, she started a girl's division of the school and renamed it The Berry Schools. After World War I, when more students were entering high school, Berry knew she needed additional teachers. In 1926, she opened Berry Junior College to train them and, by 1932, the small college had become a four-year institution. Martha Berry died in 1942. The school she started now covers 30,000 acres and has modern buildings and courses. Her goal was to free the children of the mountain forests; to give them to America, strong of heart, mind and soul.

GIRL SCOUTS ORGANIZED

Another Georgia woman, Juliette Gordon Low, also rose to fame working with young people. Daisy, as she was called, was the daughter of a wealthy Confederate Army captain. She met her husband, Willy Low, while traveling in England after the Civil War. Daisy knew people like King Edward VII, Winston Churchill, and Rudyard Kipling. She introduced her English friends to southern foods, such as grits, sweet potatoes, and cucumber pickles.

After her husband died, Mrs Low met Sir Robert Baden-Powell, the founder of the Boy Scouts. His sister had organized a group for girls called Girl Guides. The brother and sister got Daisy to start Girl Guides in Scotland. She then began two more groups in London. Mrs. Low thought American girls would enjoy scouting activities. She returned to her native Savannah and, with the help

A multi-talented woman, Juliette Gordon Low, who founded the Girl Scouts of America in Savannah, Georgia, was an artist, sculptor, world traveler, and wealthy socialite. Her talents also extended to writing the Girl Scout Handbook.

Shown here is a picture of "Daisy" Low presenting a scout with the Golden Eaglet, then the highest Girl Scouting award. Although Mrs. Juliette Gordon Low did not have any children of her own, she has influenced millions of young girls through the scouting program which she began in 1912.

of her family, started a Girl's Guide group with fifteen members. The girls wore uniforms of dark blue skirts, middy blouses, black cotton stockings, and black hair ribbons.

The group was immediately successful and, in 1915, a national headquarters was established in Washington, D.C. under the name of Girl Scouts of America. Until her death in 1927, Low worked to promote Girl Scouts. Today there are over three million Girls Scouts who enjoy the fun of scouting Mrs. Low brought to the United States from England.

Do You Remember?

1. What name was given to the late 1800s and early 1900s when the wealthy lived so extravagantly?
2. When did the average work week become 48 hours?
3. What did Dr. James Naismith invent?
4. Who wrote the novel *Sea Wolf?*
5. Who was Billy Sunday?
6. What were the two main Protestant denominations in Georgia during the Progressive period?
7. When were revivals usually held?
8. Who encouraged Juliette Gordon Low to organize her first group of Girl Guides?
9. What nickname was given to educator Martha Berry? How did the name originate?
10. When and where were the Girl Scouts of America organized?

CHANGES IN THE WIND

In 1906, an earthquake rocked San Francisco, California. Fires burned around the city for three days. When the smoke cleared, 452 people were dead and 225,000 were homeless. 1906 was also the year when President "Teddy" Roosevelt became the first American to receive the Nobel Peace Prize.

GEORGIA POLITICS

The year 1906 was an election year in Georgia. Two newspaper men ran against each other for the office of governor. Clarke Howell, publisher of the *Atlanta Constitution*, ran for the state's highest office as a conservative Democrat. His opponent was attorney Hoke Smith, owner of the *Atlanta Evening Journal*, known today as the *Atlanta Journal*. Smith was a reform candidate. He promised that corporations and private railroad companies would no longer have any power in state government.

Hoke Smith Elected Governor

Populist Tom Watson agreed to support Smith's campaign if Smith would support a law to disenfranchise blacks. Each of the candidates ran as a conservative white supremist. A statement in the black-owned *Savannah Tribune* read: "God help the civilization and future of the Democratic white man if Hoke Smith represents his ideas." Smith won by a landslide. His election was seen as a victory for both the state's reformers and farmers. Smith gained farm support by promising to take political power away from the cities and return it to the rural areas. After Smith's election, rural Georgia remained the principal power base of state politics for the next fifty-six years.

"Little Joe" Brown Elected Governor

"Little Joe" Brown defeated Hoke Smith in the 1908 election. Brown used the problems caused by a 1907 economic depression to blame Smith for Georgia's difficulty. One of Brown's slogans was: "Hoke And Hunger; Brown And Bread." Another cause for Smith's defeat was that Tom Watson changed his support to Brown. Watson's friend Arthur Glover was convicted of murdering a woman in Augusta and sentenced to be hanged. Watson

The publisher of the Atlanta Constitution, *Clarke Howell, was unsuccessful in his 1906 bid for governor against rival* Atlanta Journal *owner, Hoke Smith.*

asked Governor Smith to change the sentence to life in prison. Smith refused, and Watson withdrew his support.

Smith Re-elected

Smith was re-elected in 1910. He still believed in white supremacy and supported Jim Crow Laws. Under his leadership, the Georgia General Assembly passed a constitutional amendment which said a person had to read and own property to be able to vote. Because of this, most blacks and many poor whites were removed from the voter rolls.

There were also positive changes during Smith's two terms in office. The Railroad Commission became responsible for the regulation of gas lines, electric power companies, and street railroads (trolley cars). Public schools received better funding, and child labor laws changed. Smith worked with the legislature to regulate lobbying groups and to place limits on campaign contributions.

Smith Appointed to Senate

In 1911, the Georgia General Assembly named Hoke Smith to succeed Joseph M. Terrell in the United States Senate, where he served until 1921. While in the Senate, Smith was responsible for two major pieces of legislation: the Smith-Lever Act and the

The county unit system gave rural areas, such as Baldwin County (county seat, Milledgeville), considerable political power when united with other rural areas. They could influence the outcome of state elections. Smaller counties of the state received two unit votes. Rural Georgia dominated state politics and decision making until 1962.

Smith-Hughes Act. The 1914 Smith-Lever Act created the Agricultural Extension Service. It gave matching federal funds to states who spent money to teach young people better farming methods. The Smith-Hughes Act helped establish vocational programs in public schools across the nation. The Act also set up a federal board for vocational education to help states plan and carry out vocational training goals. By the 1920s, young people were being trained in trades, agriculture, and home economics as a result of Smith's legislation.

The County Unit System

The 1917 Neill Primary Act established a county unit system for political primaries. At that time, the Democratic Party was the only active political party in the state. This meant the outcome of primary elections and general elections were usually the same. Because that was true, the county unit system, in fact, affected both elections. The Neill Primary Act provided:

1) All primary elections for major offices, such as governor, U.S. senators, justices of the Supreme Court, Court of Appeals judges, and statehouse offices would be held on the second Wednesday in September in the years of general elections;

2) Candidates who received the largest popular vote in a county would "carry that county" and receive all of the county's unit votes;

3) County unit votes would be determined by the number of lower house representatives in the general assembly, with counties receiving two unit votes per representative;
4) In the event of a tie between two candidates in a county's primary election, the unit votes for that county would be split;
5) A majority of the county unit votes would be required to nominate a candidate for governor or for the United States Senate. If there was a tie, the candidate who received the most popular votes would be nominated;
6) For all other offices, a tie would result in a second primary election, allowing the top two county unit winners to run against each other again;
7) A plurality of county unit votes was required to elect an individual in any race except those for governor and the United States Senate.

Larger counties, such as the 254-square-mile Bibb County (county seat, Macon), with a far larger population than small rural areas, received only six county unit votes. The combined unit votes of the majority of Georgia's population were still not sufficient to overcome the unit voting blocks of the small rural counties.

Rural Counties Control Politics Under County Unit System

Under the county unit system, the eight most populated counties had six county unit votes each. The next thirty had four, and the remaining one hundred twenty-one had two. In small counties, a unit vote could represent 879 people. In larger counties, it might represent as many as 91,687 people. The thirty-eight largest counties had two-thirds of Georgia's voters, but the other one hundred twenty-one counties together could decide a state election. Those against the county unit system pointed out that people were elected to office without a majority of the state's popular vote. Those for it said the system allowed small, less populated counties to have the same power and influence as larger ones. The county unit system was in effect until 1962.

Do You Remember?

1. Which politician supported the election of Hoke Smith as governor in 1906, but withdrew his support two years later?
2. What were two of Hoke Smith's campaign promises?
3. What was Georgia's county unit system? How was political power spread throughout the state under that system?
4. What were three accomplishments of Governor Hoke Smith?
5. How did Governor Smith affect the voting rights of blacks while he was governor?

COMMUNICATIONS

On January 25, 1915, Alexander Graham Bell sat with Bell Telephone Company officials in New York. At 4:30 p.m., Bell lifted a telephone receiver and said, Ahoy, Ahoy! Mr. Watson. Are you there? Do you hear me?

In San Francisco, 3,400 miles away, Bell's assistant responded, Yes, Dr. Bell, I hear you perfectly. The first transcontinental telephone call had been completed.

The Telegraph Leads to Radio

Italian Guglielmo Marconi received a British patent for a wireless telegraph in 1897. Using a code of dots and dashes, messages could be sent immediately for long distances. Reginald Fessenden wondered if wireless messages could be sent in waves like sound vibrations. If they could, music and speech could be transmitted. Fessenden's experiments worked. At 8:00 p.m. on Christmas Eve, 1906, shipboard wireless operators off the New England coast heard human voices instead of the usual dots and dashes. A woman sang a Christmas carol; someone played the violin; another person read a passage from the Bible. At the end, Fessenden wished the operators Merry Christmas. The first radio program had been sent. In the years that followed, Fessenden continued to improve radio transmission. The word broadcast took on a new meaning. In 1901, it was defined as the act or process of scattering seeds. By 1927, it meant to scatter or disseminate, specifically, radio messages, speeches, etc. Georgia joined the radio generation in 1922, when WSB radio was established in Atlanta.

TRANSPORTATION

In 1901, France admitted failure of a twenty-year effort to build a canal in Panama to connect the Atlantic and Pacific oceans. With President Theodore Roosevelt's encouragement, the United States took over the project in 1902. Colonel George Goethals was in charge of 30,000 to 40,000 workers. They removed 240,000,000 cubic yards of earth to build over 50 miles of locks. When the canal opened in 1914, it had cost $380,000,000. Ships from all over the world use the canal to shorten travel time.

Top: *This photograph of Alexander Graham Bell was taken in 1915, the year of the first transatlantic phone call.* **Above:** *Italian Guglielmo Marconi shared the Nobel Prize for Physics in 1909 for his pioneering work with the wireless telegraph.*

Henry Ford's First Automobile

After Henry Ford finished his first automobile, he built a factory for making cars. It was ready for operation in 1903. People no longer laughed at the "new-fangled contraption." They bought it. In 1900, 4,000 cars were made. In 1910, 187,000 rolled out of factories. At that time, an average three-bedroom house cost $2,650, and a new Ford cost $780.

The Wright Brothers' First Flight

Another major transportation step was taken on December 17, 1903. It was a cold and windy Thursday. In Kitty Hawk, North Carolina, Wilbur and Orville Wright and five helpers dragged a 605 pound machine along the beach to the base of Kill Devil Hill. The machine, which looked like a giant box kite, was named "Flyer." Its forty-foot wings were covered with thin muslin cloth. Flyer was pulled up the hill and placed on a sixty-foot creased launching track. At 10:30 a.m., the final adjustments were made,

During the last days of construction of the Panama Canal, tourists visited the world-famous, 51-mile long canal. The locks' great chambers, shown here, could be raised to 85 feet so ships could pass through the canal. The United States was in charge of construction for the last ten years the canal was being built. The canal took a total of 33 years to build, but it provided a route linking the Caribbean Sea with the Pacific Ocean.

As early as the late 1400s when Italian Renaissance artist Leonardo da Vinci first tried to fly with wings attached to his back, man had long dreamed of joining the birds in flight. In 1903, two brothers, Orville and Wilbur Wright, came a step closer to realizing this dream at Kitty Hawk, North Carolina.

and the engine was started to turn the two propellers. Orville lay face down strapped to the lower wing. Slowly, the throttle was pushed, and the four-cylinder, twelve-horsepower aircraft came to life. Five minutes later, Orville released the restraining wire and became a historical figure. The flight lasted only twelve seconds. Flyer went up ten feet and traveled one hundred twenty feet. The Wright brothers made three other flights that day. The longest was 852 feet and lasted 59 seconds. Air travel had begun.

Other Transportation Firsts

In 1904, New York City's subway opened. It became the country's largest underground transportation system. Also in 1904, an engine made by German inventor Rudolf Diesel was shown at the St. Louis Exposition. We know it as the diesel engine.

INDUSTRY

Rayon, a man-made fabric, was introduced in 1902. In 1909, Leo Baekeland invented Bakelite. This product, which could be molded to any shape, was later called plastic. Manufacturers in a number of areas began using the new substance.

Henry Ford's Assembly Line

In 1913, Henry Ford began building cars on an assembly line. Using this method, a car could be put together in ninety-three minutes instead of several hours. The number of cars produced

Shown here is the first Ford automobile assembly line. With this innovation in manufacturing, cars could be made much more quickly and at far less expense. Once the assembly line went into operation, Ford could produce a car in 93 minutes compared with the several hours required to make a car before the line was completed.

rose from 570,000 in 1914 to 1,600,000 in 1919. Ford's assembly line worked so well that, by 1924, the price of a black Model T dropped to $290.

Before Velcro

Whitcomb Judson of Chicago invented the "clasp locker or un-locker for shoes" in 1891. Before this, shoes were fastened with laces or buttons. In 1913, a friend of Judson's, Levis Walker, per-fected what would become the modern zipper. At first, only actors used the fastener for quick clothes' changes between theater acts. In 1917, a tailor began using the fastener on sailors' money belts. The B.F. Goodrich Company used it in 1923 on galoshes or rain shoes. To promote the product, advertisements encouraged people to "Zip 'er up! Zip 'er down!" The name stuck, and zippers became the nickname for galoshes. It was not long before zippers were used for other kinds of footwear and for clothing.

Do You Remember?

1. Who was Reginald Fessenden?
2. What city boasted the largest subway system in the world in the early 1900s?
3. What happened at Kitty Hawk, North Carolina to change modern day transportation?
4. What industrial change did Henry Ford make for the production of his automobiles? How did it affect the price of cars?

THE NATION RETURNS TO WAR — WORLD WAR I

World War I began in 1914. Forty million people lost their lives in a war that included thirty-one countries. There were several causes for World War I. The major ones among the European nations were about trade, naval and military power, and jurisdiction over colonies. Countries began to form alliances. They agreed that friendly nations, or allies, would help any nation in the group if it were attacked. The major alliances included:

Triple Entente	Triple Alliance
Great Britain	Germany
France	Austria-Hungary
Soviet Union	Italy (later changed sides)
United States (1917)	Turkey

Countries within the two major alliances increased trade, made their armies and navies larger, and built weapons. Most larger countries added new territories and colonies to increase their size. Nations did not trust each other. Any dispute might set off a war.

AN ASSASSINATION LEADS TO WAR

On June 28, 1914, Archduke Franz Ferdinand, heir to the throne of Austria-Hungary, was in the Austrian province of Bosnia. He was being driven along the street of Sarajevo when a nineteen-year-old Serbian nationalist stepped out of the crowd and began shooting. The Archduke and his wife were killed instantly. For years, Serbia had spoken against Austria-Hungary. Emperor Franz Joseph used the assassination as his reason and, on July 28, 1914, declared war on Serbia. France and Russia were allies of Serbia, so Austria-Hungary was soon at war with them, too. Germany, Austria-Hungary's ally, declared war on both Russia and France. Germany invaded Belgium in order to cross into France. Great Britain, an ally of France and Belgium, declared war on Germany because of that invasion.

On June 28, 1914, Gavrilo Princip, a high school student and member of the Black Hand, a terrorist group, assassinated the Archduke Ferdinand. Four years later, he died in prison of tuberculosis but not before his impulsive action had triggered World War I.

MODERN WEAPONS TO MAKE IT A SHORT WAR

When the war began, most European military and political leaders thought modern weapons would make it short. They were wrong. For four long years, battles were fought in mud-filled trenches in Europe. The machine gun, first developed in 1882, was a powerful weapon. It could wipe out a whole column of advancing troops. Poison gas choked and blinded thousands. Tanks, and airplanes carrying bombs, were used for the first time.

AMERICA REMAINS NEUTRAL

The United States was not prepared for war. Our army was small, our navy no match for the German one, and we had no air power. Most Americans agreed with President Woodrow Wilson

The automatic machine gun was invented in 1882 by Hiram Maxim and was first used in battle during World War I. The rapid fire weapon could fire over ten shots per second and resulted in the deaths of thousands of soldiers on both sides of the battlefields.

that the United States should remain neutral. Americans went on with life as usual. Business was good, and most Americans were satisfied with Progressive Era social and political reforms.

In Sioux City, Iowa, Eddie Rickenbacker won an automobile race by driving an unheard of seventy-eight miles an hour. The newest best seller was *Tarzan of the Apes*, by Edgar Rice Burroughs. People danced the waltz and the two-step. Congress declared the second Sunday in May as Mother's Day. President Wilson asked citizens to fly the United States flag on that day to express love and reverence for the country's mothers.

German Submarine Attack Changes a Nation's Mood

America was brought closer to war on May 7, 1915, when the British liner *Lusitania* was sunk. A German submarine torpedoed the liner off the coast of Ireland. The big liner sank in 18 minutes, and 1,198 people were drowned, including 63 small children. There were 128 United States citizens lost, and Americans were angry because a non-combat vessel had been destroyed without warning. German submarine warfare continued. Many United States merchant ships carrying food and supplies to Great Britain and France were sunk and American lives were lost. Still, anti-war sentiment in this country was strong. One popular song said, I didn't raise my boy to be a soldier.

In 1916, Wilson was re-elected President. His campaign slogan was, He kept us out of war. In March 1917, British agents intercepted a telegram sent to Mexico by German Foreign Secretary Alfred Zimmermann. In the telegram, Mexico was asked to ally itself with Germany and fight the United States. After victory, Germany would return Texas, New Mexico, and Arizona to Mexico. The Zimmermann note was published in American newspapers, and American citizens became even more angry. On April 2, 1917, President Wilson asked Congress to declare war against Germany. He called on the country to make the world safe for democracy. On April 6, America's newspaper headlines read, U.S. AT WAR.

AMERICAN TROOPS JOIN ALLIES IN FRANCE

Thousands of American military men went to France to help push the Germans back into their own country. The first United

Woodrow Wilson was elected the nation's 28th president in 1912. Wilson believed strongly that the United States should remain neutral in the war raging in Europe. When he was re-elected in 1916, it was largely on a campaign slogan praising him and saying, "He kept us out of war!"

States troops arrived in St. Nazaire, France on June 26. Intense battles were fought in such places as Contigny, St. Mihiel, and Meuse-Argonne. Today, France is dotted with the graves of many of the 53,513 Americans who died there between April 6, 1917 and November 11, 1918.

"First Your Country, Then Your Rights"

The 4,743,829 men and women who served in the armed forces included 370,000 African-Americans. Treatment of blacks in the military was influenced by Jim Crow laws. Blacks were not allowed to join the Marines, and the Navy offered them little hope of promotion. W.E.B. DuBois asked blacks to "close ranks." In July 1918, he wrote, "Let us not hesitate. Let us, while the war lasts, forget our special grievances and close ranks shoulder to shoulder with our white fellow citizens . . . fighting for democracy." To those who did not agree with him, Dubois said, "First your country, then your rights!"

Americans Are Equal To The Task At Home

In the United States, bonds were sold to finance the war. Less gas and rubber were used so they would be available for military vehicles. Women met to make bandages from bed linens and to knit socks for servicemen. To make sure there was enough food for

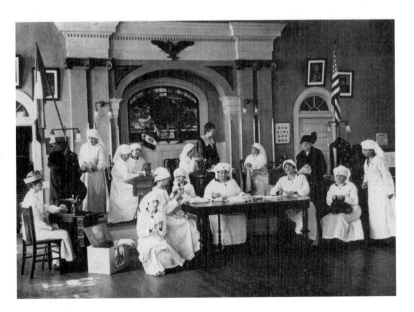

Above: The world's largest steamship, Lusitania, *leaving on its final voyage. On May 7, 1915, off the coast of Ireland, she was struck by two torpedoes. The ship began to list almost immediately, preventing most of the 1,251 passengers and 650 crew members from escaping.*
Left: First organized by nurse Clara Barton in 1881, the American Red Cross has provided food, shelter, medical aid, and comfort to millions during wartime and natural disasters. Here are Atlanta Red Cross volunteers in 1918.

the military, citizens agreed on days when they would not eat meat, sugar, or wheat. Children bought "thrift stamps" at school, and collected peach pits to be used in the filter systems of gas masks.

THE WAR COMES TO AN END

The Soviet Union, one of the nations in the Triple Entente, signed the Treaty of Brest-Titovsk with Germany on March 3, 1918, ending their part in the war. This treaty gave Germany one-third of the Soviet Union's people, nine-tenths of its coal mines, and all of the Caucasian oil fields. However, Germany could not match the military power of Britain, France, and the United States. Germany's allies quit fighting and, on November 7, 1918, revolution broke out in Germany. Kaiser Wilhelm, leader of Germany, fled to Holland, and the Republic of Germany was founded.

Peace — An Armistice is Signed

About noon that day, United Press offices in New York received a cablegram which read, "Urgent, **Armistice** Allies Germans Signed . . . hostilities ceased." However, in the middle of the evening's celebrations, Roy Howard, president of United Press, was handed a coded memo: "Armistice report untrue. War Ministry issues absolute denial and declares enemy (agents of government) to be still on way through lines.. . . Wire details of local hoax

Above: At 11:00 a.m. on November 11, 1918, on a private French railroad car in the Compiegne Forest north of Paris, the war came to an end as French Marshal Ferdinand Foch received the surrender from German spokesmen. Right: Leaders of the Triple Entente met in Paris in 1919 for the Versailles Peace Conference. The four statesmen were (left to right): Vittorio Orlando of Italy, David Lloyd George from Great Britain, Georges Clemenceau of France, and President Woodrow Wilson.

immediately. Howard, who had released the original news, thought his career was over. However, the naval admiral who had given Howard the story took responsibility for the mistake.

Peace was officially declared at 11:00 a.m. on the eleventh day of the eleventh month of 1918. The Armistice was signed in a railroad car in the Compiegne Forest north of Paris.

The final count of lost lives and property was huge. The 31 countries involved had over 61,000,000 people in military service. In many battles, thousands of lives were lost for a few yards of land. More than 10,000,000 military people were killed, and about 13,000,000 civilians died from starvation, diseases, or war injuries. The cost of war, including destroyed property, was more than $350,000,000,000.

The Search For a Lasting Peace

Five separate peace treaties were signed with Germany and her allies. Together they were called the Peace of Paris. President Wilson and a group of close personal advisors represented the United States in Paris. David Lloyd George, the Prime Minister of Great Britain, and George Clemenceau, the Premier of France, rounded out the representation for the Big Three powers. Blame for the war was placed on Germany. She lost a seventh of her land and all overseas territory. Germany could not pay all the money asked of her. Her military powers were cut sharply. She thought the treaty unjust.

President Wilson proposed a fourteen point plan intended to end all future wars. Among the points were:

➤ an end to secret **diplomacy** between nations;
➤ restored freedom of the seas;
➤ adjustment of national boundaries so all people could practice self government;
➤ the establishment of a League of Nations to ensure justice and preserve peace throughout the world.

The United States refused to join the League of Nations. By the late thirties, the League had few members. In 1946, the League of Nations was replaced by the United Nations. This organization offers peaceful ways for countries all over the world to gather and discuss differences.

The signing of the Armistice ending the war was cause for celebration for soldiers who could finally leave the muddy trenches of Europe. It was also a time of remembrance for the ten million lives that had been lost.

Right: *One of the nation's POW (prisoner of war) camps during World War I was located in Fort McPherson in East Point just outside of Atlanta. Here we see a captured German U-boat crew being transported to the fort to wait out the war's end.* **Below:** *These 1917 postcard illustrations of Camp Gordon shows only one of five World War I Georgia training camps. The location of military installations in the state has been a major factor in Georgia's economy. Troops shown below are hearing a lecture on military tactics. Today the army post is located outside of Augusta and is known as Fort Gordon.*

GEORGIA DURING WORLD WAR I

When the United States declared war in 1917, Georgia's citizens were ready to help. Between 85,000 and 100,000 of them joined the armed forces. Soldiers came from other states to be trained at Fort McPherson, Fort Oglethorpe, Camp Benning, Camp Gordon, and Camp Wheeler. Under orders from General John Pershing, Camp Benning was opened in 1917. Located near Columbus, Camp Benning trained infantry troops. Named in honor of Confederate General Henry Benning, it became Fort Benning in 1922. During the war, a German submarine crew was imprisoned at Fort McPherson.

Textile mills made fabric for military uniforms. Railroads carried arms, ammunition, and soldiers to ports where ships waited to sail for Europe. Farmers grew more food crops, tobacco, and livestock. Many town residents planted victory gardens to release other food for the military. Women gave their time to work for the Red Cross, be friendly to soldiers, knit, and help sell bonds. However, the most important thing Georgia gave was its 3,000 young people who died in an effort to "make the world safe for democracy."

The Atlanta Fire

On May 21, 1917, Atlanta's attention was drawn sharply back to a local event. Early that morning, many residents were told to collect water needed for the day because the city's supply would be off for a while. Fire broke out in the west end of town, and firemen had little water to put it out. During the next ten to twelve hours, more than eighty blocks were destroyed.

Dry weather and wooden houses built close together made it easy for the fire to spread. About 1,900 houses and 1,553 other buildings were destroyed. There were between 6,000 and 10,000 people left homeless.

Do You Remember?

1. What event set off World War I?
2. What was the "Zimmermann note"?
3. When did World War I begin? When did the United States enter the war?
4. Name three things Americans did to help in the war effort.
5. What organization did President Wilson help form at the end of World War I?

*Top: After the Atlanta fire in 1917, all that was left of 300 acres were chimneys which were a tragic reminder of the city's loss. **Above:** Atlanta's West End fire left 6,000 residents of the city homeless.*

CHAPTER REVIEW

Summary

The Progressive era ran from 1900 to 1920 and was marked by major social, political, and economic reforms throughout Georgia and much of the nation.

Business and industry expansions during the Progressive Era were rapid. The major business expansion throughout the state was in the textile industry because of Georgia's cheap labor supply, abundant water power, and anti-union spirit. Mill towns and villages sprang up throughout the state. Working conditions in the mills were very difficult. Wages were low and thousands of mill workers were locked into low-paying jobs by debts owed to company stores. In the mill towns, even the workers' homes belonged to the company.

Social reforms of the period included temperance campaigns led by such outspoken feminists as Carrie Nation. The temperance movement in a spirit of religious fervor led to the prohibition of alcohol.

Suffragettes, including Georgian Rebecca Felton, were active in trying to earn the right to vote for women. Although Georgia did not ratify the Nineteenth Amendment to the United States Constitution, the amendment did pass in 1920, allowing women to go to the ballot boxes for the first time.

The Progressive period was also a time of religious fervor as a spirit of evangelism swept Georgia and the nation. The famous revival preacher, Billy Sunday, became one of the most well-known Americans of the era.

Educational progress was made in the state as funds to support the new public schools were appropriated. Leading Georgia educator, Martha Berry, founded the Berry Schools and Berry College during this era to provide educational opportunities for the children and youth of the north Georgia mountain areas.

Major political changes took place in Georgia during the early 1900s although not all could be considered reforms. Under the leadership of Governor Hoke Smith, the Georgia General Assembly imposed literacy and property ownership requirements on voters, effectively removing most blacks from voting rolls. Governor Smith was also instrumental in two significant national pieces of legislation during this period. As a Senator from Georgia, he sponsored the Smith-Lever Act which created the Agricultural Extension Service and the Smith-Hughes Act which created vocational training programs and schools throughout the nation.

The most significant political change in Georgia during the Progressive era was the establishment of the County Unit System. The Neill Primary Act of 1917, created a primary election system which allowed the candidates who received the largest popular vote in a county's primary election to carry all of that county's unit votes in the state election. Unit votes were allocated so that the influence of the expanding cities in the state could be controlled by the rural politicians.

As the Progressive era drew to a close, Georgia and the rest of the nation found themselves again drawn into war. We entered World War I in April 1917, to fight with Great Britain, France and Russia against the Triple Alliance led by Germany. Although the war ended in November 1918, more than 53,500 American lives were lost in battle. World War I stimulated the state's economy as military training bases expanded, particularly Fort Benning, Fort McPherson and

Camp Gordon, which are all major military installations today.

President Wilson's League of Nations was formed at the end of World War I although his own country, the United States, did not join the League. Not until the League of Nations became the United Nations in 1946 did the United States become a member.

People, Places, and Terms

Identify, define, or state the importance of the following.

1. The Wright brothers
2. Mary Harris Armor
3. suffrage
4. progressive
5. muckrakers
6. Hoke Smith
7. temperance
8. Billy Sunday
9. Mary Raoul
10. Smith-Hughes Act
11. Juliette Gordon Low
12. Martha Berry
13. Carrie Nation

The Main Idea

Write a short answer for each of the following questions.

1. Where did the term "zipper" originate?
2. Name one reform that occurred as a result of the Triangle Shirtwaist Company fire.
3. What were some of the major political changes that took place in Georgia during the early 1900s?

Extend Your Thinking

Using your own opinions, answer the following questions and support your responses with information gained from the text:

1. Was Georgia's chain-gang system fairer than convict leasing?
2. Review the inventions of the late 1800s and early 1900s. Select any two inventions and describe the ways in which they affect you today. How would your life be different without these inventions?
3. Why do you think it took so may years before women in America were given the right to vote?
4. How do you feel about the events that led to the passage of child labor laws? Should young people under the age of 16 be allowed to work? Explain your answer based on events of the Progressive period.
5. Name two reforms from the Progressive era that are still intact today.
6. Do you think that the country unit system was in the best interests of the state of Georgia? Defend your answer with facts.

Looking Ahead

As the Progressive period drew to a close, Georgia, along with the rest of the nation, experienced a difficult period. As you study the next chapter, you will be able to:

➤ describe events that led to the Great Depression;
➤ identify the effect of the boll weevil on Georgia's farm economy;
➤ describe the influence of Eugene Talmadge;
➤ describe life in the "roaring twenties";
➤ identify the purpose of the CCC, HOLC, AAA, and WPA;
➤ list events that led to World War II;
➤ describe a "date which will live in infamy";
➤ determine how Georgia's children helped in the war effort.

CHAPTER FOURTEEN

GEORGIA BETWEEN WARS
1921-1945

I hope for a world founded upon four essential freedoms — freedom of speech, freedom of religion, freedom from want, and freedom from fear.
— President Franklin Delano Roosevelt, January 1941, Annual Address to Congress

THE ROARING TWENTIES
A TIME OF PROSPERITY

AFTER WORLD WAR I, most Americans enjoyed a time of prosperity that had begun with production of war goods. By the late 1920s, no one expected the progress to end. With the exception of rural areas, most homes had electricity and modern appliances such as refrigerators. Wages were the highest in the nation's history, and people spent freely for goods and services.

Over 100,000,000 tickets were sold each week for the new talking movies. Live entertainment was also popular. This was particularly true in New York City's Harlem neighborhood. Black artists, writers, and entertainers came by the hundreds to share

Georgia governors from 1911 to 1941 represented a period of change in the state's history. Posing together in 1939 are some of Georgia's most powerful politicians. They had a direct impact on the state for 32 years (left to right, Ed Rivers, Eugene Talmadge, Richard B. Russell, Jr., Clifford Walker, Thomas Hardwick, Hugh Dorsey, John Slaton).

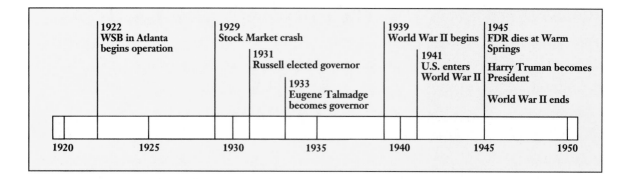

| 1920 | 1925 | 1930 | 1935 | 1940 | 1945 | 1950 |

1922
WSB in Atlanta begins operation

1929
Stock Market crash

1931
Russell elected governor

1933
Eugene Talmadge becomes governor

1939
World War II begins

1941
U.S. enters World War II

1945
FDR dies at Warm Springs

Harry Truman becomes President

World War II ends

CHAPTER OUTLINE

1. The Roaring Twenties

2. The Great Depression

3. Roosevelt's New Deal

4. Political Scenes in Georgia

5. America Enters WW II

6. Georgia During WW II

their talents. Musicians like Bessie Smith, Duke Ellington, and Bill "Bojangles" Robinson entertained huge audiences at places such as The Cotton Club, Barron's, and the famous Apollo Theater. Writers, including Langston Hughes, Claude McKay and James Weldon Johnson, stamped a lasting impression on literature.

It was not unusual for families to have radios. In 1922, WSB in Atlanta began operation as "the voice of the South." By 1924, there were 580 radio stations complete with live bands. More money was spent on education in the United States than in the rest of the world put together. With advanced medical knowledge, the fear of childhood diseases such as typhoid, measles, and diphtheria was ending. Catalog orders from businesses like Sears Roebuck and

*Above: Edward Kennedy "Duke" Ellington, was a leading jazz pianist and composer. **Right:** Langston Hughes visiting an Atlanta school.*

Montgomery Ward were at an all-time high.

The twenties were the age of the "flappers." The dictionary definition of flapper is a young woman "who shows bold freedom from convention in conduct and dress." A dance called the Charleston, and jazz music became popular. Prohibition became law on January 17, 1920, so drinkers went to "speakeasy" night clubs, where alcohol was served in tea cups. Groups headed by such people as Al Capone, Jack "Legs" Diamond, Frank "the Enforcer" Nitti, and George "Bugs" Moran became organized crime "families." They grew wealthy selling illegal liquor to thousands of private "clubs."

In 1927, Charles H. Lindbergh, "Lucky Lindy," became an American hero overnight. In his plane, The Spirit of St. Louis, Lindbergh flew across the Atlantic Ocean from New York to Paris. This was the first recorded nonstop transatlantic flight. Mass-produced automobiles could be bought for about $500. A group of businesses grew up to service the traveling public: gasoline stations, garages, and motor hotels, known as motels.

For many Georgians, however, the twenties were not a time of abundance. A small, grayish, long-snouted beetle was causing trouble.

*Top: Beginning operations in 1922, WSB radio provided millions of hours of entertainment and information long before the advent of television. **Above:** One of Atlanta Penitentiary's most notable inmates was prohibition-era gangster "Scarface" Al Capone. Capone was convicted of tax evasion.*

Above: Regardless of the advertisement promise, there was little Georgia farmers could do to stop the ravages of the small but deadly boll weevil. Above right: By the time the boll weevil and the 1925 drought hit Georgia, there was little farmers could do to stop the devastation. Low cotton prices at the time were the final blow to Georgia's rural economy, so the farm depression arrived in Georgia long before the general depression hit the nation in the 1930s.

THE DESTRUCTION OF KING COTTON

The boll weevil came from Mexico, through Texas, and into the southern states in the 1890s. The beetle hatched in the yellow flower of the cotton plant. As the flower became a boll, the larvae fed on the growing white, fluffy cotton, making it useless. The boll weevil appeared in southwest Georgia in 1918. It quickly spread across the state, destroying thousands of acres of Georgia's number one crop. By 1923, cotton production had dropped from a high of over two million bales in 1918 to slightly more than a half million. The postwar price was only fifteen to seventeen cents a pound. Georgia also had a disastrous drought in 1925. The sunbaked fields slowed down the destruction of the boll weevil, but ruined most of Georgia's other crops while doing so. Over 375,000 farm workers left Georgia between 1920 and 1925. The number of working farms fell from 310,132 to 249,095. Black farmers, in particular, moved to northern industrial cities such as Chicago and Detroit, hoping to find work in factories and assembly plants.

When farms failed, banks who had loaned the farmers money took huge losses. Many farm-related businesses closed. Georgia was in economic depression.

Do You Remember?
1. Who was Charles Lindbergh and why was he famous?
2. What does the word "motel" mean?
3. What two things hurt Georgia's farmers most during the 1920s?

THE GREAT DEPRESSION

In his March 1929 inaugural address, President Herbert Hoover confidently declared that the end of poverty was near. The stock market was unstable, some banks had closed, and factories had to lay off workers. However, few people stopped spending long enough to notice.

THE STOCK MARKET CRASHES

Many banks were in trouble. Farmers were not able to pay off loans, and more and more Americans were borrowing money to buy houses, cars, and household goods. Factories produced too much, then had to cut back on the number of workers until the goods sold. This left workers without money to repay the bank loans which had been so easy to get.

To add to the problem, many Americans had bought stock with borrowed money, hoping the value of the stock would rise and they could sell it to earn more money.

Some people became millionaires by buying stocks at low prices and selling them when the prices went up. The stock market was like a roller coaster. Prices shot up one day, then fell several weeks later. If a buyer waited too long to sell, the original investment was lost. If that investment was borrowed, the buyer could not repay the bank. As a result, banks failed, businesses closed, and many people were out of work. On October 24, 1929, the bubble of prosperity burst when the value of stocks suddenly dropped. Investors tried to sell their stocks at any price. On October 24, 13,000,000 shares of stock changed hands. Thousands of stockholders across the country lost a great deal of money.

A stunned crowd mills around on Wall Street in New York City on October 29, 1929, "Black Tuesday."

"Black Tuesday"

The market continued to fall and, on October 29, "Black Tuesday," over 16,400,030 shares of stock were unloaded. With each day that passed, the nation went deeper into a depression, now called the Great Depression. The values of stocks on the market fell by $40,000,000,000 before the end of 1929. A share of United States Steel which had sold for $262.00 dropped to $22.00. Montgomery Ward stock sank from $138.00 to $4.00 a share, and a share of General Motors plunged from $78.00 to $8.00.

BANKS CLOSE THEIR DOORS

In 1928 and 1929, hundreds of banks shut their doors because of unpaid loans. People who had money in the closed banks could not get it out. All over the country, lines formed at bank doors as people tried to take out their savings. Banks who could not meet the demands for cash failed. Over 650 banks closed their doors during the first year of the depression. Thirteen hundred failed in 1930, and another thousand in 1931.

ONE-FOURTH OF NATION UNEMPLOYED

By 1932, almost thirteen million, or one out of four, able bodied Americans were out of work. Those who couldn't afford rent or house payments could sometimes live with family or friends. Shacks made of cardboard and flattened tin cans became homes for many unemployed. Collections of these shacks were called "Hoovervilles" after President Hoover. Thousands of Americans were very hungry, and families could be seen regularly looking through garbage for food. Churches, community groups, and the federal government opened "soup kitchens" to keep people from starving. Men, women, and children stood in long "bread lines" waiting for the food.

Top: Throughout the country, people lined up at bank doors to withdraw their money. *Above:* A Depression era breadline.

College enrollment went down because most people could not pay tuition. Young adults, without jobs, put off getting married.

Hundreds of thousands of men and boys roamed the countryside. They walked or rode on railroad freight cars, and did whatever work they found in exchange for food. Sometimes groups of these homeless camped together in hobo villages. Thousands of businesses, factories, and furnished houses were for sale, but only the wealthiest Americans could buy them.

GEORGIANS HIT BY DEPRESSIONS

Georgia was already in an economic depression when the stock market fell. Her citizens did not immediately feel the impact of "Black Tuesday," as did those in other states. However, between 1929 and 1932, an average farmer's income dropped from $206 a year to $83, and cotton fell to $.05 a pound. By 1930, over sixty percent of Georgia's farms were worked by tenants.

During the depression, Georgia's health care and highway construction were not funded. Many rural children did not get enough education. For most Georgians, meeting the needs of every day was a challenge.

Do You Remember?
1. What was the "stock market crash" of 1929?
2. Why did many banks close during the depression?
3. What were "Hoovervilles"?

Above: Dust storms and drought in the midwest caused thousands to pack up their families and head for California. Left: Rural education was poorly funded during the Depression and many rural schools were forced to close for lack of funds.

Garnering support during his 1932 campaign, Franklin Delano Roosevelt always felt comfortable in his second home—Georgia. Here he shows his well-known smile as he visits Atlanta in 1932. After his election, President Roosevelt invited the citizens of Warm Springs and patients at the spa to Washington, D.C. for his inauguration.

ROOSEVELT BRINGS NEW DEAL TO NATION

In the fall of 1932, the depression was at its worst. One of the musical hits of the year was, "Brother, Can You Spare A Dime?" It was also an election year. Herbert Hoover was running for a second term on the Republican ticket. His opponent was New York Governor Franklin Delano Roosevelt. At the Democratic Convention in Chicago, Roosevelt easily won his party's nomination on the first ballot.

Just before Roosevelt made his acceptance speech, his chief writer added a final sentence: "I pledge you, I pledge myself, to a new deal for the American People." Roosevelt had been ill with polio in 1921, and wore steel braces on his legs. He walked with two canes and, often, used a wheel chair. However, his spirits were high as he campaigned for the presidency, and he became very popular with the American people. Roosevelt won with an elec-

Above: *Located in Meriweather County, Warm Springs was the location of President Roosevelt's second home, the "Little White House." He first visited the area in 1921 seeking the treatment of the hot springs for his crippling infantile paralysis, or polio.* **Left:** *The economic, political, and social problems left FDR little time to relax alone and contemplate his next step. Shown here at Warm Springs is a stolen moment when the President simply became a man fishing with his dog beside him.*

Top: On May 18, 1933, two months after his inauguration, President Franklin D. Roosevelt signed the Tennessee Valley Act into law. The Act was designed to control the Tennessee River floods and to provide water for rural electrification. Above: Governor E.D. Rivers is shown breaking ground for a new hospital, a Works Progress Administration (WPA) project in Milledgeville.

toral majority of 472 votes to Hoover's 59. In his inaugural address, Roosevelt said:

> *We are stricken by no plague of locusts. Compared with the perils which our forefathers conquered because they believed and were not afraid, we have still much to be thankful for. Nature still offers her bounty and human efforts have multiplied it. Plenty is at our doorstep.... The only thing we have to fear is fear itself.*

His speech and his natural optimism won the people's confidence. They believed Roosevelt would try new ways to end the depression which was, by then, felt all over the world. Roosevelt's summer "White House" was in Warm Springs, Georgia, where he could bathe his crippled legs in the water of the springs. This made it possible for Georgians in the area to know FDR, as he was called, on a personal basis.

ROOSEVELT'S NEW DEAL

When Roosevelt took office on March 4, 1933, he took steps to fulfil his promise of "a new deal for the American people." A four day bank holiday was declared to stop the panic run on banks. This gave customers time to calm down and examiners time to find out which banks were sound. After the holiday, over 5,000 banks were able to reopen.

A SUMMARY OF NEW DEAL PROGRAMS

FDIC To prevent future bank failures, Congress created the Federal Deposit Insurance Corporation. This FDIC insured bank savings up to $5,000.00 per account. The FDIC is still in operation, insuring accounts for up to $100,000.

CWA The Civil Works Administration, employed people for government jobs. Many of these government programs were called "boondoggles" because they involved "made up" work rather than needed services.

AAA The Agricultural Adjustment Act paid farmers not to raise livestock, and to destroy acreage already planted in order to decrease crop production by thirty percent. Cutting down on crop production pushed up prices.

TVA During the first 100 days of Roosevelt's term, Congress passed a bill creating the Tennessee Valley Authority. A government hydroelectric plant and two munitions factories from World War I were located on the Tennessee River at Muscle Shoals, Alabama. Roosevelt put the electric plant back in operation. It made enough electric power to serve parts of seven states, including Georgia. The munitions factories became fertilizer plants. The TVA also worked with flood control, wild life preservation, fisheries, soil improvements, and pest control. The TVA is still active today.

HOLC The Home Owners Loan Corporation was established to loan money to nonfarmers because they couldn't pay their mortgages. Over one million homes were saved from **foreclosure** during this period, and government-backed mortgages for buying homes are still available today.

SOCIAL SECURITY ACT Some provisions of the act were:

➤ gave needy persons over age 65 an "old age pension" of up to $30 a month.
➤ provided old age and survivors' insurance from $10 to $85 a month to workers after their retirement or to their survivors.
➤ established unemployment insurance so that workers who lost their jobs had money to live on while finding other work.
➤ provided small monthly payments to help dependent children and their mothers if they had no way to make a living. Payments were also set up for the blind and disabled.

The Social Security Act is still in force. Over the years, payments have changed to reflect the nation's economy.

FERA The Federal Emergency Relief Administration was designed to give money to states so they could, in turn, provide jobs and financial relief for workers.

REA The Rural Electrification Administration was organized to help supply electricity to farms and other non-urban areas.

WPA The Works Progress Administration was formed in 1935. It gave jobs to over 4,000,000 persons, most of whom were unemployed laborers. Civilian Conservation Corps (CCC), a division of WPA, provided jobs for young men. The Corps built camps to house workers between the ages of eighteen and twenty-five. Workers were paid $30.00 a month, of which $22.00 was sent home to their families. They cleared brush, planted trees, built

Top: More than three million young men were provided with jobs for a dollar a day from the Civilian Conservation Corps, the CCC.
Above: Robert Weaver, a native of Washington, D.C., was confirmed as Secretary of the new Department of Housing and Urban Development. Weaver was the first African-American to hold a cabinet position.

parks, and worked on roads. They also erected small dams and stocked streams with fish. They drained swamps and built fire breaks in the nation's forests. The CCC lasted until 1945 and was one of the most popular of the New Deal programs. The National Youth Administration paid college students to grade papers and do office chores. The NYA also provided an income for needy artists and actors. They painted murals on government buildings, built statues in parks, and worked in plays and benefit performances.

NIRA Some New Deal programs were not successful. For example, the National Industrial Recovery Act was meant to promote private businesses by getting manufacturers to cooperate, instead of compete, with each other. To help workers, minimum wages were set, and workers could freely join unions. By 1935, the program had been declared unconstitutional by the United States Supreme Court.

Most of President Roosevelt's recovery efforts were successful in giving people needed jobs, a sense of self worth and, most importantly, a renewed faith in the economic future of the country.

BLACK AMERICA DURING THE NEW DEAL

Although most African-Americans supported President Roosevelt, the black community as a whole did not make great gains under New Deal reforms. For example, under the AAA, farm rent went to property owners, rather than to the tenant farmers, who were predominantly black.

The Social Security Act was not designed to provide an income for farm and household workers. Therefore, those working at such jobs received no share of the pension and unemployment benefits. When the WPA and other federal relief programs were organized, President Roosevelt ordered state relief officers "not to discriminate . . . because of race or religion or politics." In spite of a lack of support from Governor Eugene Talmadge, those responsible for New Deal programs in Georgia made every effort to equally distribute WPA programs.

Several prominent blacks were instrumental in leading the New Deal programs, including Clark Foreman, a staff member at the office of the secretary of the interior. Foreman brought qualified blacks into government agencies, and checked on complaints about racial discrimination. Another African-American, Robert

Perhaps the most prominent black to serve in the government during the New Deal was Mary McLeod Bethune. In addition to founding Bethune-Cookman College, she became a high-ranking official under Roosevelt. In 1936, Bethune was given charge of the Office of Minority Affairs in the NYA, the National Youth Administration.

Weaver, started his government career during the New Deal and, in the 1960s, became the first head of the Department of Housing and Urban Development. William Hastie, also a leading black figure in the New Deal, later became a federal judge.

A similar organization in Georgia was the Atlanta based Commission on Interracial Cooperation. This group worked to ensure the equal administration of federal relief efforts. By 1944, the commission had become the Southern Regional Council, which played a major role in civil rights programs of the 1960s.

William Henry Hastie, an NAACP attorney during Roosevelt's terms, was the first African-American to be appointed a federal judge in the United States, and the first African-American territorial governor (of the Virgin Islands).

Do You Remember?

1. What were the purposes of the CCC?
2. What does REA stand for and how did it help farmers?
3. What role did Mary McLeod Bethune play in the New Deal?
4. How did the FDIC calm investors' fears during the depression?
5. How did the TVA help Georgia?

A YEAR IN THE LIFE OF YOUR GREAT-GRANDPARENTS

In 1934, the United States was between World Wars and caught up in a depression. Your great-grandparents were in the work force. Your grandparents were likely still in elementary school and not yet planning for the jobs and families that lay ahead, and, of course, your parents had not been born at this time. Take a look at the lifestyles of your great-grandparents during that year.

World news headlines read "Adolf Hitler Proclaims Himself Ruler in Germany."

There were news stories in the United States about droughts in the midwest and the resulting "dust bowl" storms. John Dillinger, number one on the Federal Bureau of Investigation's Most Wanted list, was shot and killed by law enforcement agents during the year. Georgia Congressman Richard B. Russell began the second of thirty-eight years of service in the United States Senate. Georgia's governor was Eugene Talmadge.

Popular songs on the radio during this period included "Stars Fell on Alabama," "Deep Purple," "Winter Wonderland," "Santa Claus is Coming to Town," and "Blue Moon."

The picture voted best movie of the year was "It Happened One Night." The leading actor was Clark Gable and the leading actress was Claudette Colbert. The most popular book titles for 1934

Top: Nazi Germany's dictator, Adolf Hitler. ***Above:*** *Child star Shirley Temple sang and danced her way into the hearts of millions of Americans.* ***Right:*** *The popular Ford automobile helped make the United States a "nation on wheels."*

were *Good-By Mr. Chips* by James Hilton; *Tender Is the Night* by F. Scott Fitzgerald; and, *The Thin Man* by Dashiell Hammett. The St. Louis Cardinals beat the Detroit Tigers in the World Series.

Famous people born in 1934 include actor and singer Pat Boone, baseball legend Hank Aaron, actress Shirley Jones, and consumer rights advocate Ralph Nader.

The average annual income of Americans in 1934 was $1,237. The average three- bedroom house cost $2,925. A new Ford could be bought for $535, and a gallon of gas for that Ford was $.19. Bread was $.08 a loaf and milk $.44 a gallon.

Child star Shirley Temple appeared in "Little Miss Marker" and "Stand Up and Cheer." Popular newspaper comic strips were *Li'l Abner* and *Flash Gordon*. In the world of sports, brothers Dizzy and Daffy Dean pitched for the St. Louis Cardinals, winning forty-five games between them. The New York Giants defeated the Chicago Bears 30-13 for the National Football League championship.

Ask your parents or grandparents to share some of their experiences of things they heard from their parents about the Great Depression and the years before World War II began.

Top: Clark Gable and Claudette Colbert won Academy Awards for their roles in It Happened One Night. *Gable is best remembered for his role as Rhett Butler in* Gone With the Wind. ***Above:*** *Though they had humorous nicknames, brothers Dizzy and Daffy Dean were both great baseball players.*

THE DEPRESSION YEARS, THE NEW DEAL, AND WORLD WAR II

The Depression years brought new leadership to Georgia. Like the nation, Georgians based their hope for a better future in this new leadership.

Richard Russell, Jr. Elected Governor

In 1931, Winder resident Richard Russell, Jr. succeeded Lamartine Hardman as governor. A former member and speaker of the Georgia House of Representatives, Russell used his experience to make some needed changes. One of his first was to reduce the number of state boards from 102 to 18. In an equally daring political move, he combined the boards of trustees of state colleges and universities into one governing group called the University System of Georgia Board of Regents. Some colleges were closed, and others were combined. Russell appointed Hughes Spalding, an Atlanta lawyer, as the first chairman of the board of regents.

Russell tried to run the state like a successful business. This eased some of the problems brought on by the depression. In 1932, Governor Russell was elected to the United States Senate, where he served for the next thirty-eight years. Russell favored national military preparedness and states' rights. He was a respected advisor to six United States Presidents and, as president pro tempore of the Senate, he was third in line for the presidency. Russell died on January 21, 1971.

Eugene Talmadge Becomes Governor

State government changed greatly when Eugene Talmadge became governor in 1933. The Forsyth farmer, lawyer, and saw mill owner was elected commissioner of agriculture in 1926, and served three years in that position. Talmadge was a dramatic politician in the style of Tom Watson. He often compared himself with Watson, especially when trying to get the support of rural voters. He was a conservative white supremist who did not like federal government intervention or government debts. Talmadge especially disliked relief efforts, public **welfare,** and federal assistance programs.

*As governor of Georgia, Richard B. Russell, Jr., son of a Georgia Chief Supreme Court Justice, gained statewide recognition by reorganizing Georgia's government to a more manageable number of bureaus, offices, and departments. As a United States Senator, he served more than half his life in service of his state and nation. **Opposite page:** Known for his red suspenders and "down home" ways, Eugene Talmadge was a powerful figure in Georgia politics.*

E.D. "Ed" Rivers campaigned across the state in support of Roosevelt's New Deal policies during the 1936 governor's race against Charles Redwine.

After becoming governor, Talmadge began trying to rid the state of New Deal programs. He also reduced property taxes and utility rates. Car tags, which had been five or ten dollars, could be bought for three dollars. Federal funds were used to build highways more often than for needed relief.

Talmadge Re-elected in a Landslide

Talmadge was elected to a second term in 1934 by a landslide margin. Because he refused to follow federal New Deal regulations, the federal government took over New Deal programs in Georgia.

Government officials who disagreed with Talmadge were fired and replaced with his supporters. Once, Talmadge ordered the highway commissioner to reduce spending or resign. The commissioner refused to do as asked. Talmadge called in the National Guard, declared martial law, and had the commissioner physically removed from his office. A Talmadge supporter was named as the new commissioner.

In 1934, during the state's worst textile strike, the governor declared martial law again, and used guardsmen to arrest strikers. However, Talmadge's political power plays did not change the fact that Georgia law would not allow him to serve more than two consecutive terms.

Rivers Succeeds Talmadge as Governor

In 1936, Talmadge ran for the United States Senate against Richard Russell and was soundly defeated. His hand-picked successor for governor, Charles Redwine, was beaten by Lanier County resident Eurith "Ed" Rivers.

Governor Rivers, a former newspaperman and speaker of the Georgia house of representatives, supported President Roosevelt's New Deal programs. He also supported, and gained passage of, constitutional amendments granting health services for all Georgians, old age pensions, teacher pay raises, a seven-month school year, homestead exemptions for taxes, and expansion of the state's highway system.

Under Rivers' leadership, electrical services were expanded to rural areas of the state. Georgia moved from the lowest ranked state to the top of the list in the number of Rural Electrification

Associations. The State Bureau of Unemployment Compensation was created, allowing Georgians to receive unemployment benefits.

After Rivers' reelection in 1938, he ran into problems financing many of his improvement programs. The budget was reduced by twenty-five percent. Even so, he was able to influence the legislature to create the Georgia Housing Authority, and obtain federal funds to build public housing. It was during this time that Atlanta's Techwood Homes and University Homes were built. Several other Georgia cities also began public housing programs.

During Rivers' second term, there were political scandals and charges of corruption. Some staff members did not follow proper procedure in awarding highway contracts. Some of them sold prison pardons. Many of Rivers' appointees and staff members were charged with corrupt practices. These charges reflected poorly on the governor.

Governor E.D. "Ed" Rivers gives his first inaugural address. On the right is outgoing governor Eugene Talmadge.

Above: In the 1940 governor's race, Eugene Talmadge softened his attitude toward Roosevelt's New Deal. Here he even went to Washington on an Inaugural Special. Right: Eugene Talmadge's stance, "I may surprise you, but I will never deceive you" led him to the campaign trail for the third time and voters continued to elect Georgia's friend to the farmer.

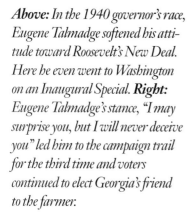

Talmadge Elected Governor Again

Following Rivers' second term Talmadge ran for governor again, and was elected. Talmadge had softened his anti-Roosevelt stand. He began using modified versions of New Deal legislation. The state's economy was growing. Then, a series of events angered the voters and put Georgia in an unfavorable national position.

A Talmadge supporter was an instructor at the University of Georgia. He told the governor that one of the deans at the university and the president of the Teachers College in Statesboro (now known as Georgia Southern University) had plans to integrate the school. Talmadge convinced the board of regents to fire the two individuals. He also managed to get rid of several members of the board of regents who publicly opposed his interference in the university system. There was a great deal of national publicity. The situation so offended the Southern Association of Colleges and Schools that they voted to dismiss white Georgia colleges from the listing of accredited schools. Georgians were upset with both the association and the governor. Talmadge was not re-elected in 1942.

Arnall Becomes Governor

Ellis Gibbs Arnall won the governor's race in 1942. Arnall was a native of Newnan and a lawyer who had served as the state's attorney general. A constitutional amendment passed during Talmadge's third term made Arnall the first Georgia governor to serve a four-year term.

Arnall removed the university system from the influence of the governor's office. Terms of regents were staggered so there would always be experienced members serving the board. Arnall won re-accreditation of Georgia's colleges and universities by the Southern Association of Colleges and Schools.

Arnall removed the prison system from the political influence of the governor's office. He established a board of corrections to oversee state prisons and a pardon and parole board to handle requests for pardons and paroles. Arnall also abolished the poll tax. Under his leadership, a new state constitution was adopted in 1945.

Governor Arnall is probably most well-known for leading Georgia to become the first state in the nation to grant eighteen-year-olds the right to vote. When young men were drafted into the armed forces during World War II, Arnall argued that youths old enough to fight for their country were old enough to vote for their country's leadership.

Ellis Arnall, elected governor in 1942, was the first Georgia governor to serve a four-year term.

Do You Remember?

Which of Georgia's governors, including Richard Russell, Eugene Talmadge, Ed Rivers and Ellis Arnall:

1. lowered license tags to $3.00?
2. had served as attorney general?
3. reduced the number of state boards to eighteen?
4. granted the right to vote to eighteen-year-olds?
5. disliked Roosevelt's New Deal programs?
6. implemented major prison reforms?
7. organized Georgia's public colleges under one governing body?
8. served in the United States Senate for 38 years?
9. used martial law to enforce his orders and directives?
10. extended the school year to seven months?
11. was often compared to Tom Watson?

*Top: "Fuhrer" of more than 70 million people, Hitler is shown here reviewing his troops. **Above:** Benito Mussolini wanted to return Italy to its former glory. He, like Hitler, ruled his people with an iron fist daring anyone to disagree with him.*

AMERICA ENTERS WORLD WAR II

The United States was still recovering from the Great Depression when World War II began. Japan, led by Emperor Hirohito, Germany, led by Nazi Adolf Hitler, and Italy, led by dictator Benito Mussolini, formed a military alliance known as the Axis powers. They went to war to gain control of territories and resources in Europe and the Far East.

AXIS POWERS CONQUER SMALLER NATIONS

One by one, the Axis powers conquered smaller nations. When Poland fell to Germany on September 1, 1939, Great Britain and France declared war on Germany, and World War II began. Russia invaded Poland to protect its own frontier, and was drawn into the war on the side of the Allied powers, Great Britain and France. Germany occupied Denmark and Norway in April 1940, and overran Belgium, the Netherlands, and France within the next two months. British forces were removed, and the Axis powers controlled all of Europe. During this Blitzkrieg, or "lightning war," period, massive air attacks were launched against Great Britain. In 1941, Germany attacked Yugoslavia, Greece, and Russia. Only the Russian capital did not fall to German control, and the "Eastern Front" of the war stalled when the German army was stopped at Stalingrad.

Italian dictator Mussolini, called "Il Duce" (the leader), tried to move his army from Libya into Egypt in a desert war in North Africa. A British victory at El Alamein in Egypt in 1942 started the first retreat by the Axis powers.

JAPAN ATTACKS PEARL HARBOR

The United States supplied arms and materials to back Great Britain. However, the country did not enter the war until after the Japanese attacked Pearl Harbor in Honolulu, Hawaii. Many soldiers and sailors were still asleep on Sunday morning, December 7, 1941, when the Japanese hit. While the bombs fell, Japanese diplomats in Washington were pretending to continue a friendly relationship with our country. Their nation attacked without an

On December 7, 1941, approximately 360 Japanese bombers flew undetected across the Pacific to attack the United States military base at Pearl Harbor, Hawaii. Within two hours, eight United States battleships, 14 smaller boats, and 200 aircraft were destroyed. Twenty-four hundred members of the armed forces were killed.

official declaration of war against the United States. In less than two hours, eighteen warships were sunk or grounded, three warships were badly damaged, and over one hundred seventy-seven planes were destroyed. The United States lost 2,400 servicemen.

The following day, President Roosevelt asked Congress to declare war on Japan. He called the surprise attack without a declaration of war a "date that will live in infamy." War was declared, and the United States entered on the side of the Allied powers: Great Britain, France, Russia, China, Australia, and Canada.

Japanese attacks continued into early 1942. They captured Burma, Hong Kong, Malaya, the Dutch East Indies, Thailand, and the Phillippines. Japan threatened New Guinea and Australia before their assault in the Pacific was stopped.

THE ALLIES FIGHT BACK

Joining the Allies meant the United States had to fight on two fronts. We faced Germany and Italy in Europe and Africa, and Japan in the Pacific. British and American troops invaded North Africa in late 1942, and won control of the area by May of 1943. From Africa, the Allied armies moved into Sicily and Italy. The Italian people overthrew **Fascist** dictator Mussolini, and joined the Allies. Germany and Japan were the remaining Axis powers.

World War II was fought differently from earlier wars. Tanks had become swift and powerful. Rockets and bazookas, or rocket launchers, were used for the first time. They allowed troops to fight each other from a distance rather than hand to hand. Airplanes, used mostly for observation in World War I, now carried bombs and machine guns. Air raids had become a major part of combat. It was also possible to drop paratroopers behind enemy lines, or quickly move troops and heavy equipment great distances.

On the seas, giant aircraft carriers transported planes used to drop bombs on enemy ships and land targets. Radar, radio detection and ranging, and sonar, sound navigation ranging, tracked the movements of enemy aircraft, ships, and submarines.

Called Operation Overlord, *on June 6, 1944 Allied forces invaded the beaches of Normandy, France to push back the German army. Future United States President Dwight Eisenhower led the assault that involved 4,000 ships, 11,000 planes, and 176,000 soldiers.*

D-Day, The Beginning of the End

On June 6, 1944, D-Day, Allied forces landed on Normandy beach in northern France. Involved were 4,000 landing craft, 600 warships, 176,000 soldiers, and 11,000 planes. By early 1945, the troops had pushed the German army out of France and across the Rhine River to Germany. At the same time, the Russian army recaptured four smaller countries which were part of the German alliance: Bulgaria, Finland, Hungary, and Romania.

The "Big Three," Britain's Prime Minister Winston Churchill, United States President Franklin Roosevelt, and Soviet Dictator Joseph Stalin, met on the grounds of Livadio Palace at Yalta in February, 1945. The three tried to agree on plans for the postwar world. Look at the pictures carefully and you'll notice how ill the president looked at that meeting. He died only a few weeks later.

The Yalta Conference

By February 1945, the war was almost over. President Roosevelt, British Prime Minister Winston Churchill, and Russian Dictator Joseph Stalin met at the Russian sea resort in Yalta. During the Yalta conference, the "Big Three" leaders discussed how to end the war in Germany and Japan; ways to reorganize Germany once victory was achieved in Europe; and how the United Nations, a peace keeping organization, should be set up. By the end of the eight-day, top secret meeting, it was agreed that the Soviet Union would be offered territory lost in an earlier war with Japan in exchange for entering the current conflict against that country. She would also be given eastern Poland, and in exchange, Poland would receive part of Germany at the end of the war.

It was also agreed that Germany would be divided into four zones. Britain, Russia, France, and the United States would each occupy and govern a zone. Berlin, the capital of Germany, was in the Russian zone, but each of the four countries would share in administering that city.

Finally, a charter for the establishment of the United Nations was accepted in principle by the three leaders. Europe was freed from Hitler's control in April 1945, when the Russian and American troops came together at the river Elbe in the interior of Germany. Adolph Hitler committed suicide on April 30, and the last German forces surrendered to the Allies in May.

The War In The Pacific Comes To An End

The Japanese advance in the Pacific was ended in 1942, when Japan was defeated by the United States Navy in the battles of the Coral Sea and Midway. In early fall 1942, the Allies began to recapture Pacific islands from the Japanese. The Gilbert, Marshall, Caroline, and Mariana islands were re-taken. Allied planes launched offensive bombing strikes against the Japanese mainland from bases in the Marianas. In the fall of 1944, the United States invaded the Philippines, and Great Britain invaded Burma. Allied forces moved through to China.

During the summer of 1945, successful daily air raids were made on Japan. On July 26, Allied leaders issued the Potsdam Agreement, demanding unconditional surrender. Emperor Hirohito was willing to surrender, but the Japanese foreign minister was not. A week later, on August 6, the Enola Gay, a United States bomber, dropped an atomic bomb on Hiroshima. A fireball 650 feet wide scorched everything in its path. Shock waves destroyed brick buildings a mile from the blast, and wooden ones simply disappeared. A fire storm swept the city, followed by a muddy, chilling rain that poured radioactive materials over a wide area. By mid-afternoon, 80,000 were dead, and 120,000 more were dying. The city lay in ashes.

The Japanese still refused to surrender. A second atomic bomb was dropped on the city of Nagasaki on August 9. Japan surrendered to the Allies on August 15, 1945. The bombings of Hiroshima and Nagasaki are the first and last times to date that atomic warfare has been used to settle differences between nations.

The decision to drop the atomic bomb on Japan's Hiroshima was a painful one for the nation's new President, Harry S. Truman. Military commanders convinced the President that hundreds of thousands of American soldiers' lives would be lost if an invasion of Japan became necessary. On August 6, 1945, the A-Bomb, with the explosive force of 20,000 tons of TNT, was dropped on Hiroshima resulting in the deaths of thousands.

Do You Remember?

1. What new forms of warfare were used in World War II?
2. President Roosevelt spoke of a "date which will live in infamy." What was it?
3. Which country was divided after World War II and "occupied" by Great Britain, the United States, Russia, and France?
4. What bombing raids led to the surrender of Japan?

Four-time President Franklin Delano Roosevelt was taken ill on April 24, 1945 as he posed for this portrait by artist, Elizabeth Shumatoff. With little warning the President, beloved by millions, died at the Little White House in Warm Springs, Georgia. The painting was left unfinished.

GEORGIA DURING WORLD WAR II

GEORGIA LOSES A FRIEND

President Roosevelt visited Georgia regularly, spending time at the "Little White House" in Warm Springs. The President often played with the children who were there, bathed in the springs, or rested in the sunshine. With the help of friends, Roosevelt founded the Warm Springs Foundation so children and adults crippled with polio could receive therapy. His effort led to the March of Dimes.

After the Yalta meeting with Churchill and Stalin in February 1945, the President returned to the Little White House. He planned to rest and work on a speech for the United Nations. On April 24, Roosevelt was sitting for a portrait, surrounded by his model ships. His Scottish terrier, Fala, was nearby. Suddenly, the President put his hand to his head and said, "I have a terrific headache."

At 5:48 p.m., a stunned nation was told that the man who led the country through recovery from the depression, the New Deal, and to the brink of victory in World War II, was dead. A **cerebral hemorrhage** killed him while the artist was painting. Mrs.

Roosevelt, who was in Washington, sent messages to her sons, all of whom were in the military service. She wrote, "He did his job to the end as he would want you to do. Bless you all and all our love. Mother." Vice President Harry S. Truman became President on the death of Roosevelt, and was the nation's commander-in-chief during the final months of World War II.

GEORGIANS JOIN THE MILITARY EFFORT

Following the United States declaration of war, over 320,000 Georgians between the ages of 21 and 35 put on military uniforms. Of that number 7,388 died in battle. Eight Georgians received the Congressional Medal of Honor, the nation's highest military decoration. World War II brought prosperity to Georgia. Because of its climate, and the influence of politicians like Senator Richard Russell, Jr., Senator Walter F. George, and Representative Carl Vinson, the state became the site of several military installations.

Millions of federal dollars poured into the state, strengthening the economy. Major military bases included Fort Benning in Columbus, Camp Gordon in Augusta, Fort Stewart and Hunter Air Field in Savannah, and Warner Robins Air Field near Macon. Airmen from Glynco Naval Air Station, near Brunswick, flew blimps along the southern Atlantic coast in search of German submarines. Several cities, including Americus and Augusta, were the sites of German prisoner of war camps.

As the flag-draped horse-drawn casket carrying Roosevelt made its way down Pennsylvania Avenue, the nation stopped to mourn the man who had led the country through a depression and a world war. The next time you spend a dime, think of Roosevelt. His picture is imprinted on that coin in memory of the March of Dimes polio appeal. About eight years after Roosevelt's death, Dr. Jonas Salk announced the discovery of a polio vaccine.

The Bell Bomber Plant, where World War II B-29s were manufactured, closed after the war. It reopened in the 1950s as Lockheed-Georgia. Today it is a 76-acre factory which produces many of America's foremost military aircraft including the B-47 jet bomber and the C-130 Hercules transport.

Fort McPherson, in the Atlanta area, was a major induction center for newly-drafted soldiers from all over the country. A military hospital, which had been used in World War I, was reopened in Atlanta. In nearby Clayton County, an army storage facility and railroad yard began operation.

GEORGIANS SUPPORT THE WAR EFFORT

In Marietta, 30,000 men and women built B-29 bombers at the Bell Bomber Plant. Thousands of Georgians were also employed in automobile and textile plants which were being used to produce military vehicles and uniforms.

Women moved into the work force, filling jobs formerly held by men. They became welders, and worked on assembly lines, helping to produce weapons, tanks, jeeps, and aircraft.

Georgia farmers planted peanuts for their oil, grew vegetables, and raised cotton and livestock to help feed America and its allies. By 1944, the annual farm income was $454, over three times what it had been in 1940.

Left: Fort Benning, Georgia, near Columbus, covers 181,500 acres and serves as the United States Army Infantry Training School. It is the world's largest infantry camp.

With over 16 million men and women in the World War II armed forces, scores of women left at home were also called on to help. They performed an invaluable service to their country in time of war by keeping the country's factories at full production to provide the needed weapons, equipment and supplies to support the war effort.

Volunteers watched the sky for enemy planes. Some prepared Red Cross kits for service men. They contained such items as soap, toothpaste, and sewing kits. Children helped grow "victory gardens" in their yards. Across the country, such gardens supplied over forty percent of America's fresh vegetables during the war. Children also collected scrap metal to be melted down and reused in factories. Gasoline, and food items such as meat, butter, and sugar were rationed. Women used leg makeup because it was hard to get silk and nylon stockings. Georgia joined the rest of the nation in donating 13,000,000 pints of blood for the war wounded.

During this time, two pieces of national legislation affected all citizens. The first was a tax on income, which was withheld from workers' pay and sent directly to the United States Treasury. The second, passed in 1944, was the Serviceman's Readjustment Act. This "G.I. Bill," as it was called, made low cost loans to veterans who wanted to buy homes or start businesses. It also paid tuition and bought books for those who went back to school. Both programs, the withholding tax and the G.I. Bill, are still in effect today.

The untold tragedies of war could not match the horror of the German concentration camps where six million Jews were murdered. Survivors of Evenste Camp in Austria are shown here. What do the faces tell you? Could the "Holocaust," as the attempted destruction of the Jewish race was called, happen today? Why or why not?

A FINAL NOTE: THE HOLOCAUST

One of the horrors of World War II was Hitler's effort to kill all the Jews in Europe. Before the war ended, 6,000,000 Jewish men, women, and children had been murdered on Hitler's orders. They were rounded up by the thousands, and packed into trains going to **concentration camps** like Auschwitz, Treblinka, Belsen, and Buchenwald. Many died because they could not breathe on the crowded trains. Others died of starvation or disease in the camps. Millions were shot, or gassed in huge building where **canisters** of poisonous gas were released from shower heads. Their bodies were burned in gigantic **crematoriums** as part of Hitler's "final solution to what he called the "Jewish problem," the wiping out of a whole race of people.

Do You Remember?

1. For what reasons did Georgia become a major site for military installations during World War II?
2. Which military installation was located in Columbus?
3. What were two ways that children assisted with the war effort?
4. How did the status of women change during World War II?
5. What two pieces of legislation passed during World War II are still in effect today?

CHAPTER REVIEW

Chapter Summary

The prosperity of the "roaring 20s" in America was short lived as the nation plunged into a great depression in the early 1930s. The depression caused tremendous unemployment and financial hardship. The depression was triggered by the crash of the New York stock market on October 29, 1929.

During this period, many people lost their money as banks and businesses closed. By the end of 1931, more than 12 million Americans were unemployed. President Herbert Hoover was defeated in his bid for re-election by Franklin Delano Roosevelt in 1932.

Massive federal relief programs provided aid to the victims of the depression in a series of legislation known as the "New Deal." New Deal programs put the unemployed back to work, provided insurance and pensions for retirees, and delivered electrical power to the nation's rural areas. Farm relief and subsidies helped the farmers save their farms in the midst of the depression.

As Roosevelt led the nation's recovery from economic depression, the country was again drawn into war by the Japanese attack on Pearl Harbor on December 7, 1941. The United States joined the Allied Powers in the war against Germany, Italy, and Japan. The war in Europe ended with the surrender of Germany in April 1945. The Japanese surrendered in August 1945 after the United States had dropped atomic bombs on Hiroshima and Nagasaki.

Georgia was a reluctant participant in Roosevelt's New Deal. Eugene Talmadge, who was elected governor in 1932, did not favor the relief programs and policies of Roosevelt. Talmadge wanted fewer government controls and services, and lower taxes. He used federal funds to build highways rather than maintain the New Deal programs. Only when Governor Ed Rivers took office was Georgia able to take advantage of the New Deal programs effectively. Rivers is also known for initiating the public housing activities in Georgia as Techwood Homes and University Homes became Georgia's first efforts in public housing.

In 1941, in a third term as governor, Eugene Talmadge softened his stance toward the New Deal. He adopted modified New Deal programs for the citizens of Georgia. During his third term, Talmadge's politics caused the university system to lose its accreditation.

Governor Ellis Arnall, who succeeded Talmadge was effective in removing politics from the university system and restoring the university system's accreditation and reputation.

During World War II, the economy of Georgia prospered as military bases and factories for producing military weapons expanded. Fort Benning, Camp Gordon, Fort Stewart, and Fort McPherson were major military training centers.

As World War II drew to an end, the state entered a new period of economic growth and industrialization. The rural population of Georgia was declining and urban areas were expanding.

People, Places, and Terms

Identify the following people, places, or terms by describing their importance to Georgia or the nation.

1. Eugene Talmadge
2. Richard Russell
3. Hiroshima and Nagasaki

4. Social Security Act
5. Holocaust
6. Pearl Harbor
7. Eurith Rivers
8. TVA
9. Franklin D. Roosevelt
10. Mary McLeod Bethune

The Main Idea

Write a short paragraph to answer each of the questions below.

1. Which of the "New Deal" programs are still in existence today and how do they benefit you?
2. What were the major campaigns, or fronts, in World War II?
3. What was Hitler's "final solution" for the Jewish people?

Extend Your Thinking

Write a short paragraph to answer each of the questions below.

1. Should President Truman have dropped the atomic bomb on Japan in 1945? Why or why not?
2. Explain the meaning of Roosevelt's statement, "a date which will live in infamy."
3. How was the atrocity of the Holocaust possible? Could it happen again to any group of world citizens? Why or why not?
4. Without World War II, America's economy might not have recovered from the Great Depression. How does war affect the economy?

Map Skills

Using a world map, show the location of the following places and identify their importance to World War II.

1. Stalingrad (now called Volgograd)
2. El Alamein
3. Pearl Harbor
4. Normandy
5. Hiroshima and Nagasaki
6. Yalta

Looking Ahead

The period of Modern Georgia was a time of change with new industrialization and population growth. It was also a time that included American involvement in three more wars—Korea, Vietnam, and the Persian Gulf.

Wide sweeping reforms were accomplished in the areas of civil rights in Georgia. Even the courses you now study in school were the result of changes that occurred during this fast moving period.

As you read the next chapter, you will learn:

➤ about the strangest election in Georgia's history;
➤ about the role of Dr. Martin Luther King, Jr. in the struggle for civil rights;
➤ the difference in the "two Georgias";
➤ how the Vietnam conflict affected our nation;
➤ how Georgian Jimmy Carter became President of the United States;
➤ about the "Crisis in the Gulf."

DID YOU KNOW . . .

. . . The "Star Spangled Banner" did not become our national anthem until 1931?

. . . President Hoover cut his own salary by one fifth when the economy collapsed during the Great Depression.

. . . The day Pearl Harbor was bombed, Japanese pilots left their carriers with shouts of "Banzai, Banzai," a battle cry meaning "forever"?

MODERN GEORGIA
1945-Present

No memorial or eulogy could more eloquently honor President Kennedy's memory than the earliest possible passage of the civil rights bill for which he fought. We have talked for one hundred years or more. Yes, its time now to write the next chapter—and to write it in the book of law.
— President Lyndon B. Johnson speaking to Congress, 1964

IN EXAMINING modern Georgia, each decade is remembered by events that affected Georgians and all Americans. The decade of the fifties was marked with racial unrest and the Korean War. In the sixties, the feelings of the nation about the Vietnam conflict were sharply divided. The seventies marked the end of the Vietnam conflict, but political scandal forced President Richard Nixon to resign.

During the 1980s, people were concerned about the stability of the economy. A "war" against drugs and disease was carried out, and there seemed no end to environmental problems.

As the last decade of the century opened, many of the problems of the eighties were still on the minds of the people of our nation. Once again America was at war. The Middle East was the battleground as the United States joined with other nations to push Iraq's troops out of Kuwait.

A grateful mother welcomes her son home from the 1991 Persian Gulf War, the first major, post-nuclear conflict in this century. Combat lasted only forty-three days due to the allies' technologically advanced "smart" weaponry. Georgia provided thousands of men for the war effort and their homecoming was a time of thanksgiving and celebration.

CHAPTER FIFTEEN

GEORGIA TODAY

1945 - Present

All human beings are born free and equal in dignity and rights . . . are endowed with reason and conscience and should act towards one another in a spirit of brotherhood.
> — 1948 United Nations General Assembly Declaration of Human Rights

A NATION GROWING AND CHANGING

THE 12,300,000 MEMBERS of the armed forces returning home in 1945 and 1946 after World War II were welcomed as heroes. In the United States, life was mostly good and progressive. Business was booming. City factories and office buildings were springing up in Georgia and across the nation. People were moving out of larger cities into neighborhoods called "suburbs." As these new residential areas grew, shopping centers, schools, churches, and highways were built to serve them.

JACKIE ROBINSON—FIRST BLACK IN THE MAJOR LEAGUES

In 1947, the world of major league sports changed when Jackie Robinson became the first black player in a major sport. He signed with the Brooklyn Dodgers baseball club. Robinson, born in Cairo, Georgia, was later elected to the Baseball Hall of Fame.

The period covering 1945 to the present day was a time of racial unrest, but also of civil rights progress. Demonstrations, like this one in front of Atlanta City Hall in 1947, became the predominant method of protest.

1946 "Three Governor" episode	1961 Blacks admitted to U. of Georgia	1976 Jimmy Carter elected President	1991 Zell Miller becomes governor
1949 Herman Talmadge elected governor	1963 Pres. Kennedy assassinated	1980 Reagan elected President	U.N. coalition wins Gulf War
1950 Korean War begins	1968 Nixon elected President	1983 Harris becomes governor	

1945   1955   1965   1975   1985   1995

Jackie Robinson, born in Cairo, Georgia, was the first black player in major league baseball.

THE NATION'S "BABY BOOM"

This period was known for its "baby boom," as millions of children were born during the postwar years. These babies, now in their thirties and forties, grew up during a time of excitement and fun. During the 1950s and 60s, rock and roll was the musical fad. Elvis Presley and the Beatles joined hundreds of other rock stars as musical trends were set. In 1958, Berry Gordy, Jr. founded Motown Records in Detroit. Motown quickly made stars of musicians like the Supremes, Smokey Robinson and the Miracles, and Marvin Gaye.

TELEVISION CHANGES FAMILY LIFE

Teenagers in the 1950s grew up with television. At first, television programs ran only six or seven hours a day. Families

gathered around the small black and white sets to watch such popular performers as Jackie Gleason in The "Honeymooners," Lucille Ball in "I Love Lucy," comics Sid Caesar and Milton Berle, and major productions such as the "Ed Sullivan Show." Television viewing began to replace family games and conversation as the evening entertainment of choice. Even food changed. Frozen TV dinners were developed to shorten the time spent in preparing evening meals.

One of the most popular books for young adult readers in this period was J.D. Salinger's *Catcher In The Rye*. A new comic strip, "Peanuts," introduced by Charles Schultz, caught America's fancy.

SALK DEVELOPS POLIO VACCINE

In 1953, Dr. Jonas Salk announced the development of polio vaccine. In 1954, a mass inoculation program began all over the nation. Within a few years, the feared and crippling disease was only a memory to most Americans.

Do You Remember?
1. How did Jackie Robinson change major league baseball?
2. What is meant by "baby boom"?
3. How did television affect family life?
4. Why was Dr. Jonas Salk's work so important?

Top left: The Beatles appeared on the Ed Sullivan Show in 1964. Top: Elvis Presley adapted black rhythm and blues for a white audience, inventing rock 'n roll. Above: One of the most enduringly popular television shows of the 50s was I Love Lucy.

When about 313,000 soldiers and sailors returned to Georgia after the war, they found the Empire State changing rapidly. Many people had moved off farms to work in wartime industries. When man-made fabrics were introduced, the demand for cotton fell. Trees, and row crops such as peanuts, soybeans, and corn, were planted in place of cotton. The use of farm machinery allowed fewer workers to produce higher yields per acre. This sent even more farm employees to cities in search of jobs.

A MAJOR CHANGE IN THE STATE'S AGRICULTURE

Jesse Jewell, a farm feed merchant from Gainesville, was responsible for another major change in the state's agriculture. In 1936, Jewell began selling baby chicks and feed to area farmers, and marketing mature broilers to processing plants. There were over 7,000 commercial poultry farms in the state by 1950, making Georgia second only to Texas in the poultry industry. Today, Georgia is second, just behind Arkansas, in the production of broilers. Over 2,000,000,000 pounds of chicken a year and 15,000,000 eggs a day are produced in Georgia.

Industry continued to move into the state. Georgia's mild climate lured many Northern industries who wanted to escape bitter cold winters, high heating costs, and transportation slow-

Above: Gainesville's Jesse Dixon Jewell was instrumental in developing Georgia's poultry industry. Today chickens and eggs rank as one of the state's most valuable commodities. Right: The University of Georgia Extension Service worked in conjunction with poultry farmers throughout the state in maximizing the poultry potential.

GOV. TALMADGE   SEN. GEORGE   WRIGHT BRYAN

downs caused by snow and ice. By the late 1940s, air conditioning took care of Georgia's only climate drawback: the intense summer heat.

The state also had low business and individual tax rates. In 1949, a typical Georgian paid only $38.00 in state taxes. Most importantly, Georgia was a non-union state. Workers could be hired at lower wages and with fewer labor demands than in states controlled by unions.

EDUCATION CONTINUES TO CHANGE

With more industry, larger cities, and fewer farms, education in Georgia changed. County and city school boards had been responsible for managing and financing elementary and secondary schools. A new state constitution extended schools to include grades one through twelve and, in 1949, the Georgia General Assembly passed "The Georgia Minimum Foundation Program for Education Act." This act lengthened the school year to nine months, and raised standards for buildings, equipment, transportation, and school curricula. A three percent sales tax was passed in 1951 to pay for these changes.

In 1946, Georgia Senator Richard B. Russell sponsored a bill in Congress that affected the entire nation. It was called the National School Lunch Act. The act outlined a program insuring that school children ate nutritious lunches. It also encouraged school

The advent of television in 1948 not only provided entertainment but also impacted the political scene. Politicians such as Governor Herman Talmadge and Senator Walter George, seen here on a WSB interview program, quickly learned that they could reach thousands of voters through the new medium in a matter of minutes as compared with the weeks of travel on the "chicken salad" circuit.

During the 1940s and 1950s cars became more than just a means of transportation. They became status symbols. Compare this advertising photograph for a Buick in the 1950s with a Buick ad today. What are the similarities? What are the differences?

cafeterias to use government surplus food items such as cheese, flour, and peanut butter. Because of his work, Senator Russell is known as the "father of the school lunch program."

OTHER CHANGES IN GEORGIA

The postwar years introduced other changes in Georgia. In 1940, less than half of Georgia's homes were wired for electricity, and only a fourth had refrigerators. After World War II, most Georgia home owners, even in rural areas, could afford indoor plumbing and electric lights. In 1948, the state's first television station, WSB-TV in Atlanta, began operation. The call letters stood for Welcome South Brother. Georgians earned more money in the 1950s and 1960s; purchasing power increased; and former luxuries, such as automatic washers and dryers, dishwashers, and televisions, became commonplace.

Do You Remember?

1. What were two major changes that took place in Georgia following World War II?
2. How much was Georgia's sales tax in the 1950s and what was the tax levied to support?
3. Where was Georgia's poultry industry started?
4. What made Georgia attractive to northern industries who moved into the state?

WHO IS GOVERNOR?

No political change in Georgia during the postwar years got more publicity or caused greater confusion than the "Three Governor Episode."

COUNTY UNIT SYSTEM HELPS EUGENE TALMADGE

The successful terms of Governor Ellis Arnall drew to a close and, because he could not succeed himself, Georgians had to elect a new governor in 1946. The field of candidates included Arnall's arch rival, segregationist Eugene Talmadge, former Governor E.D. Rivers, and James Carmichael, who had headed the Marietta Bell Bomber Plant during the war. In the primary, Carmichael won the popular vote. This was due, in large part, to the fact that,

Above: Little did the Georgia voters realize that when Eugene Talmadge paid his entry fee to run for an unprecedented fourth term as governor, the state would soon be embroiled in the "three governor episode." *Left:* Businessman James Carmichael campaigned hard before the 1946 election. Although he received 7,644 votes more than Talmadge, the county unit vote made "Gene" the Democratic nominee.

Above: Herman Talmadge (center, to right of woman), Eugene's son, just after the state legislature put him in the governor's seat, following the death of his father. He served only 67 days before the Georgia Supreme Court upheld the right of Lt. Governor Melvin Thompson to serve as the rightful head of state.

Right: The dual heads of state, Herman Talmadge (left) and Melvin Thompson (right), could both answer "Yes?" when someone called out "Mr. Governor."

for the first time since Reconstruction, black voters could take part in the primary election. However, Talmadge won the County Unit vote, making him the Democratic candidate.

The Republicans did not run a candidate, so the unopposed Talmadge would win the November general election. Talmadge was sixty-two years old and in poor health. Because his close advisors were afraid he would not live long enough to begin a fourth term, they made a secret plan.

A "Write-In" Campaign

It was decided that a few hundred selected supporters would write the name of Eugene Talmadge's son Herman on the ballot as

Newnan resident and governor from 1943-1947, Ellis Arnall refused to give up his governor's seat to Herman Talmadge. After Talmadge forcibly took over the governor's office, Arnall set up his office at the information booth in the capitol rotunda. Needless to say, this episode was a newsman's dream come true.

After a three-day stay at the information booth, Ellis Arnall officially resigned as Georgia's governor and walked down the capitol steps.

the second gubernatorial choice. When the general election was over, Eugene was elected governor, and Melvin Thompson was elected lieutenant governor. Shortly before Christmas, and before he was sworn in, Eugene died, and the confusion began.

LEGISLATURE CHOOSES HERMAN TALMADGE

The legislature chose Herman Talmadge as governor, based on the write-in vote. Governor Arnall said that Lieutenant Governor Thompson was the rightful successor. In the early morning hours of Wednesday, January 15, 1947, a group of Talmadge men broke into the governor's office, changed the locks on the doors, and readied themselves to run the state.

In turn, Ellis Arnall set up a temporary office at the capitol information counter. Three days later, with news cameras flashing, Arnall officially resigned. In the meantime Lieutenant Governor Thompson opened an office in downtown Atlanta and began legal proceedings to become governor. The government was in a state of total confusion.

Secretary of State Ben Fortson refused to give the official state seal used for legalizing documents to either man. No one was in a position to run the state. The national news media had a field day reporting Georgia's political chaos.

GEORGE SUPREME COURT RULES FOR THOMPSON

Finally, in March, the Georgia Supreme Court ruled that Thompson was the rightful head of state until a special election could be held in 1948 to fill the unexpired term of Governor-elect Eugene Talmadge. In that election, and in 1950, Herman Talmadge was legally elected as Georgia's governor. The "Three Governor Episode" would be remembered for years to come.

Do You Remember?

1. Why was it thought Eugene Talmadge would win the general election after the Democratic primary was over?
2. Who was Melvin Thompson?
3. In 1947, what group finally determined who Georgia's governor would be?
4. What role did Governor Ellis Arnall play in the "Three Governor" episode?

THE KOREAN WAR

After World War II ended in 1945, the Soviet Union and the United States became involved in a "cold war." This meant there was almost no positive political or economic relationship between the two nations. Each used a "sometimes real and sometimes perceived" threat of attack from the other country's military to keep national defense strong. At times, it seemed hostile words would lead to the use of weapons. However, as long as fighting did not break out, the war remained "cold."

At the end of World War II, Korea was divided along the thirty-eighth parallel of latitude. The United States supervised the government of South Korea, and the Soviet Union that of North Korea. On June 25, 1950, North Korea invaded South Korea, hoping to make one unified communist country.

Seventeen United Nations countries immediately sent troops to South Korea to stop invasion forces. These troops, led by divisions of American soldiers, which included 75,000 Georgians, pushed the North Korean troops back almost to the border of China. United Nations forces were not prepared when China joined the Soviet army to come to North Korea's aid. There seemed no way to avoid another world war.

After numbers of attacks and counterattacks, a battle line was drawn between the two countries in July 1951. Truce talks between the United States and the Soviet Union began shortly afterward, but the war dragged on for two more years. Peace was declared in July 1953, with no clear victor.

The Korean War was a costly one, with 2,500,000 killed or wounded. Of those killed, 25,000 were Americans and over 500 were Georgians. Today, Korea remains divided along the thirty-eighth parallel, and United States troops are still in South Korea to help with its protection.

The stark contrast of a country faced with a liberating army on one side and fleeing refugees on the other is a literal picture shown here during the Korean War. What do you think were the feelings of both sides?

Do You Remember?

1. Which troops occupied North Korea?
2. Who sent troops into Korea after the invasion of South Korea?
3. Who won the Korean War?
4. How many Georgians fought in Korea?
5. What is the status of Korea today?

THE FIGHT FOR CIVIL RIGHTS

African-American military men found little change in attitude toward blacks after World War II. Efforts to obtain civil rights became more organized. One of the first goals was to get blacks registered to vote.

In 1946, President Harry S. Truman set up the President's Committee on Civil Rights to study the problem of discrimination. Two years later, Truman, by executive order, outlawed racial segregation in the armed forces. The Federal Housing Act was passed in 1949. It did not allow racial discrimination in federally-financed housing. However, it was in the field of education that the most far-reaching change was felt.

THE SUPREME COURT AND EDUCATION

In 1883, the United States Supreme Court ruled against the Civil Rights Act of 1875 and legalized the **doctrine** of "separate but equal." This meant segregation was not against the law if blacks and whites were treated equally. In 1896, the Court upheld this decision in the case of *Plessy v. Ferguson*.

In 1935, the National Association for the Advancement of Colored People (NAACP) began the fight to end segregation in schools. Thurgood Marshall, who later became a Supreme Court justice, and Charles Houston, presented NAACP-supported cases in many of the twenty states where schools were still segregated.

Brown v. Board of Education

In 1950, seven-year-old Linda Brown, a black student, tried to enroll in an all-white school in Topeka, Kansas. When entry was denied, the NAACP helped her father sue the Topeka Board of Education. The case, referred to as *Brown v. Board of Education*, reached the Supreme Court in May 1954. After careful review, the Court said "separate but equal" schools were illegal. It ordered racial integration of schools "with all deliberate speed." States were slow to carry out the Court's orders.

President Eisenhower Sends Troops to Little Rock

In 1957, on September 4, nine black students tried to enroll in an all-white high school in Little Rock, Arkansas. They were

Opposite page: Jubilant attorneys capture a historical moment on the steps of the United States Supreme Court after the high court rules in their favor in Brown v. Board of Education *ending school segregation. Left to right: George Hayes, Thurgood Marshall and James Nabrit, Jr. Which attorney of this landmark case went on to become a Supreme Court Justice? Above: Although segregation had been outlawed, integration was far from peaceful. What type of courage do you think it took for the nine African-American students enrolling in Little Rock, Arkansas' all-white Central High School?*

Top: Feeling in Georgia ran high during the mid 50s and early 60s. Pro-segregation rallies like the one seen here in 1959 in front of the governor's mansion were commonplace. Above: Franklin county resident Samuel Ernest Vandiver was Georgia's governor from 1959-1963 during the most turbulent years of integration.

blocked by the Arkansas National Guard, which had been called out by Governor Orville Faubus.

President Dwight D. Eisenhower responded by sending 10,000 federal troops to enforce the court-ordered desegregation plans for Little Rock's schools. On September 25, after several tense days with both federal and state troops present, the nine students were admitted to Central High School.

GEORGIA RESISTS SCHOOL DESEGREGATION

In Georgia, most of the state's school systems refused desegregation. The general assembly voted in 1955 to cut off state funds to any system which integrated their schools.

Ernest Vandiver, who became Georgia's governor in 1959, was elected, in part, on his promise to keep Georgia's schools segregated. However, in 1960, the Georgia General Assembly recognized change was at hand. It organized a group to study the problem of integration. The fourteen member commission was headed by Atlanta banker, John Sibley.

The "Sibley Commission" held hearings all over the state to learn how the public felt about integration. Reaction was swift and direct. By a three to two margin, Georgians said they would rather close schools than integrate them. The commission recommended that local school systems be allowed to decide if they would abide by a probable court order to integrate public schools, or close them. In many communities, private schools were opened to avoid the issue.

University of Georgia Admits Blacks

The Supreme Court and United States district courts held their ground. On January 6, 1961, the University of Georgia admitted its first two black students: Charlayne Hunter who became a newspaper reporter and Hamilton Holmes who became a doctor.

Atlanta Begins School Integration

In was also 1961 when the largest school system in the state, Atlanta City Schools, began token integration by allowing nine black students to enroll in a formerly all-white high school. The peaceful integration of four high schools by the end of the year prompted President Kennedy to praise the system.

Court Orders All School Systems to Integrate

During the next three years, the courts ordered all systems in the state to integrate schools. After the Civil Rights Bill of 1964 passed, the federal government refused federal funds to those systems who did not end segregation. Some chose to take the cut in funding, but integration continued to come about across the state.

In 1969, the United States Department of Justice filed suit against the Georgia State Board of Education, demanding that the state withhold funds from systems which refused to follow court-

Charlayne Hunter and Hamilton Holmes leave campus at the end of their first day. After leaving the University of Georgia, Charlayne Hunter Gault went on to become a respected journalist, and is now national correspondent on the McNeil-Lehrer Report news program. Hamilton Holmes became a doctor.

Although the integration of Georgia schools was a slow process, it was, by and large, a peaceful process. Here you see counselor Dorothy Morrison showing Mary McMullen her new locker at Atlanta's Grady High School in 1961.

ordered desegregation plans. Communities moved to comply with federal laws and, by 1971, all Georgia's public schools were integrated. This made Georgia the first state with a large black population to have a statewide integrated school system.

THE MONTGOMERY BUS BOYCOTT

The successful desegregation of southern systems of transportation began at 5:30 p.m. on Thursday, December 1, 1955 and, along with it, a movement that would change America.

Rosa Parks' Bus Ride

Mrs. Rosa Parks, a middle-aged black seamstress was "bone weary" from a long day of work. She boarded a Montgomery, Alabama public bus, paid her $.10 fare, and sat down in the first empty seat. By custom and law, the section in which Mrs. Parks sat was for "whites only." At a theater, six white passengers got on the bus. The driver ordered all blacks to move to the back. Three rose to move, but Mrs. Parks stayed where she was. The driver called for a policeman. Rosa Parks was arrested, booked, fingerprinted, and briefly jailed. She had violated a city ordinance which stated that bus drivers had the right to decide where passengers would sit. Her trial was set for December 5.

A Boycott is Organized

Mrs. Parks was a former officer in the Montgomery chapter of NAACP. News of her arrest quickly spread among the 50,000-member black community. A group of black ministers gathered to talk about ways to support Mrs. Parks. They asked Atlanta-born Martin Luther King, Jr. to be their spokesperson, and agreed to hold a one-day bus **boycott** on the day of Mrs. Parks' trial.

On Sunday, December 4, black ministers and civic leaders asked that all blacks stay off the buses on Monday. Even though Mrs. Parks was found guilty, the bus boycott was ninety percent successful. The black community was encouraged to continue the boycott until the following demands were met: a) black passengers would be treated with courtesy; b) black drivers would be assigned to primarily black routes; and c) seating would be on a first come, first served basis.

Above: Frequently reporters have asked Mrs. Rosa Parks the origin of her bravery when she refused to give up her seat on a Montgomery, Alabama, bus. She replied that she was just tired. However, her simple gesture of defiance would ultimately change the civil rights struggle forever. Left: On December 5, 1955, Mrs. Parks entered the Montgomery courthouse.

Above: Today visitors can return to 522 Auburn Avenue N.W. in Atlanta to see the childhood home of civil rights leader, Dr. Martin Luther King, Jr. **Opposite page:** *This portrait of Dr. Martin Luther King, Jr. by George Mandus, hangs in the state capitol as a silent memorial to his civil rights leadership.*

A NONVIOLENT MOVEMENT IS BORN

Dr. Martin Luther King, Jr., leader of the bus boycott, began making speeches all over the city in support of peaceful protest. Car pools were formed in black neighborhoods, and black-owned taxi cabs charged only a dime for a ride to or from work. In a matter of weeks, the city's bus revenue fell by sixty-five percent.

Outdated Law Leads to Black Leaders Arrest

In March 1956, three months after the boycott started, Dr. King and eighty-nine other black leaders were found guilty of violating an outdated 1921 anti-labor law forbidding boycotts. They appealed their convictions. In November, the city went to court again, demanding an end to the car pools and asking to be paid for the money lost on bus service.

As the trial date approached, Dr. King was afraid a victory for the city would undo eleven months of progress made through peaceful protests. He entered the courtroom on November 13, to face the same judge who had found Rosa Parks guilty. About noon, a reporter handed Dr. King a teletyped message from one of the national news services. The United States Supreme Court had just upheld a district court ruling that made segregation on public transportation unconstitutional. When the court decision officially reached Montgomery on December 21, 1956, Dr. King and a white minister boarded a city bus and rode through the streets without incident. The Montgomery bus boycott was over, but the movement for civil rights was just beginning.

Martin Luther King, Jr.—A Tradition of Protest

The success of the Montgomery bus boycott thrust Martin Luther King, Jr. into the national spotlight. He was a third generation minister who had grown up in the tradition of protest. King was born on January 15, 1929, the second of three children. He lived in Atlanta and attended Booker T. Washington High School. The school was Atlanta's first black secondary school, and had been built largely because of the protest efforts of King's grandfather, A.D. Williams, and other black leaders.

In 1944. when he was fifteen, King entered Morehouse College as a special student. Morehouse president, Dr. Benjamin Mays, was among the men who influenced the young man. King was

Right: "Sit-ins" at store lunch counters were another type of non-violent protest during the early 60s when many of your parents were young children. *Below:* Before the Civil Rights Bill of 1964 was passed, African-Americans frequently had to drive miles out of their way to find a motel or hotel that would accept them. Sometimes they were forced to sleep in their cars if accommodations were not available. In 1963, one of the many non-violent protest demonstrations took place at Atlanta's Grady Hotel.

ordained to the ministry at Ebenezer Baptist Church in 1947, after which he enrolled at Crozer Theological Seminary in Pennsylvania. After graduating with honors from Crozer in 1948, King earned a doctorate in theology from Boston University. While in Boston, he met and married Coretta Scott from Marion, Alabama, who was studying at the New England Conservatory of Music.

During his years of study, King developed a philosophy of nonviolent approach to social change. He based his ideas on the writings of Henry David Thoreau, author of *On Civil Disobedience*, and the teachings of India's Hindu leader, Mahatma Gandhi. King first practiced non-violence during the Montgomery bus boycott. He was aided by other ministers and civic leaders, including Edward Nixon and the Reverend Ralph Abernathy.

King called the boycott a conflict "between justice and injustice." He believed in a four-pronged approach for gaining civil rights for all Americans: direct, nonviolent actions; legal redress; ballots; and economic boycotts.

King Heads SCLC in Atlanta

Encouraged by the success of the boycott, King carried his message of a nonviolent approach to social change to other parts of the South. He moved to Atlanta in January 1960, as head of the

Southern Christian Leadership Conference (SCLC), a group he helped form the year before. Dr King often traveled two or three thousand miles a week spreading the message of non-violence.

Protests Continue With Lunch Counter Sit-ins

During the early 1960s, King started lunch counter "sit-ins" to protest the segregation of department and chain store lunch counters in the South. Rich's department store was the site of the first Georgia sit-in, where King was joined by Julian Bond, Lonnie King, and other students from Morehouse College. Their efforts continued in spite of anti-trespass laws passed by the Georgia General Assembly making sit-ins illegal.

Albany Becomes Center of Civil Rights Activity

Albany became a center of civil rights activity in 1961. This primarily farming community had a population that was about

Albany, Georgia became the site of many protest demonstrations in the early 60s. Here police carry a demonstrator down the steps of the Albany Public Library. However, arrest or threats of jail did little to dissuade those protesting to gain their civil rights. Today, Albany continues to progress in maintaining positive race relations in the city.

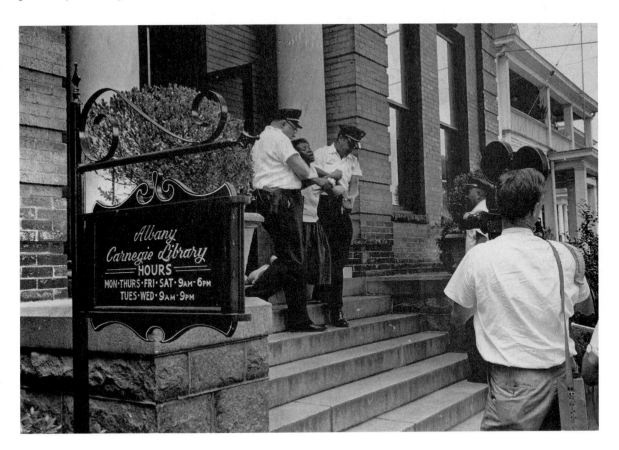

In April 1960, students formed the Student Nonviolent Coordinating Committee (SNCC). Leaders of the SNCC, like James Forman, used the "sit-in" strategy to integrate public facilities in over 100 cities. By the middle 1960s, the SNCC became known for more militant protest.

forty percent black. Six years after *Brown* v. *Board of Education*, Albany schools were still segregated. Only a small number of African-Americans were allowed to register to vote.

On November 1, 1961, the Interstate Commerce Commission backed the Supreme Court decision prohibiting segregation in interstate bus and train stations. Workers with the NAACP and Student Nonviolent Coordinating Committee (SNCC) decided to test the ruling by sitting in the "Whites Only" waiting room at the Albany, Georgia, bus station. They were quickly arrested. This prompted the black community to unite and form the "Albany Movement" led by Dr. William Anderson.

In December, black and white "Freedom Riders" arrived in Albany to support the Albany Movement. They were arrested at the Central Railway Terminal. The next day, SNCC organizer James Forman led a march of black high school students to the same train station. The students were arrested and jailed, while members of the national press watched. At one point during the months of protest in Albany, 500 people were either in jail or out on bond. Black leaders arrested included Dr. King and Reverend Abernathy, who had traveled to Albany to ask city officials for a meeting to resolve the dispute. Before the year's end, a biracial committee was formed to study concerns of the black community in Albany.

The United States District Court for the Northern District of Georgia heard the case of *Baker* v. *Carr* in May 1962. On May 25, the court ordered the state to redistrict and **reapportion** one house of the legislature, based on population. A called session of the Georgia General Assembly decided that the senate would be reapportioned. The state was divided into fifty-four districts. After the redistricting, Fulton County, where Atlanta is located, had seven senatorial districts. This change did away with the County Unit system. It also gave predominantly black population areas an equal opportunity to elect legislative representatives. In a 1962 senatorial election, Atlanta attorney Leroy Johnson became the first African-American senator in Georgia since Reconstruction.

Protest Moves to Birmingham, Alabama

In April 1963, Dr. Martin Luther King, Jr. began a campaign in Birmingham, Alabama, to end discrimination in all areas of that city's public life. For several nights, television news showed at-

The bombing of the Sixteenth Street Baptist Church in Birmingham, Alabama, on September 15, 1963, shocked the nation. The racial rioting that followed the bombing led to the deaths of two other young African-Americans in the streets of the stunned city. The mayor appeared on television and appealed to the entire citizenry to end "this senseless reign of terror."

tempts to control demonstrators with high pressure fire hoses and attack dogs. Over 3,000 persons, including Dr. King, were arrested.

On September 15, 1963, during Sunday School at Birmingham's Sixteenth Street Baptist Church, an exploding bomb killed four black children and injured fourteen others. Even though a riot followed the tragedy, many blacks and whites joined together to stop further violence in the struggle for civil rights.

President Kennedy Sends Strong Civil Rights Bill to Congress

President John F. Kennedy sent the strongest civil rights bill in history to Congress on June 19, 1963. It called for an end to discrimination in public facilities, assurance of fair employment and voter registration practices, withholding of federal funds from projects where discrimination was practiced, and the authority of the attorney general of the United States to file suit against school districts where desegregation had not been carried out.

"I Have a Dream"

Congress did not pass the bill quickly and, on August 28, 1963, over 250,000 people representing all races, creeds, and nationalities gathered before the Washington Monument to demonstrate for its passage. As they stood together, Martin Luther King, Jr. made one of the most remembered speeches of his career.

. . . . *I have a dream that one day this nation will rise up, live out the true meaning of its creed: "We hold these truths to be self-evident, that all men are created equal."*

I have a dream that one day on the red hills of Georgia sons of former slaves and the sons of former slave-owners will be able to sit down together at the table of brotherhood. I have a dream that one day even the state of Mississippi, a desert state sweltering with the heat of injustice, sweltering with the heat of oppression, will be transformed into an oasis of freedom and justice.

I have a dream that my four little children will one day live in a nation where they will not be judged by the color of their skin, but by the content of their character. . . . Let freedom ring from Stone Mountain of Georgia. . . . Let freedom ring from every hill and molehill . . . from every mountainside. Let freedom ring.

When we let freedom ring—when we let it ring from every village and every hamlet, from every state and every city, we will be able to speed up that day when all God's children, black men and white men, Jews and Gentiles, Protestants and Catholics, will be able to join hands and sing in the words of that old Negro spiritual, "Free at last! Free at last! Thank God almighty, We are free at last!"

Opposite page: On August 28, 1963, the largest crowd ever to assemble in front of the country's capitol came to demonstrate their commitment to the passage of the Civil Rights Bill. As blacks and whites stood hand in hand joining in song, Joan Baez led "We Shall Overcome" and the nation reached a turning point in the area of civil rights. ***Above:*** *People who had never met before the march on Washington suddenly found themselves closely linked in a common bond of brotherhood.*

Do You Remember?

1. When was racial segregation outlawed in the armed forces?
2. What Supreme Court case led to school integration?
3. Who is Thurgood Marshall?
4. Where were troops sent by President Eisenhower to enforce school integration?
5. What was the Federal Housing Act?
6. Why did Rosa Parks refuse to give up her seat on the bus?
7. What role did Dr. King play in the Montgomery bus boycott?
8. What did the Montgomery bus boycott accomplish?
9. Where was Martin Luther King, Jr. born?
10. What influenced Dr. King's non-violent approach to social change?
11. What four things did Dr. King believe would bring about social change?
12. How many people were a part of the march on Washington?
13. What was the Civil Rights Bill of 1964?
14. What was the SCLC?

THE ASSASSINATION OF JOHN F. KENNEDY

The morning of November 22, 1963, President and Mrs. Kennedy and Vice President and Mrs. Johnson attended a breakfast gathering in Fort Worth. Afterward, they flew to Dallas, an eight-minute plane flight, with the President and the Vice President, as was customary, flying in separate planes. At the Dallas Airport, President and Mrs. Kennedy joined Texas Governor John Connally, Jr. to begin the fateful drive into the city.

At 12:30 p.m. on November 22, 1963, President John F. Kennedy and his wife Jacqueline were riding in a motorcade through the streets of Dallas, Texas. Without warning, shots were fired. The forty-six-year-old President, with a massive head wound, slumped down in the seat of the open limousine. He was immediately taken to Parkland Hospital but, thirty minutes later, President Kennedy died without regaining consciousness. A little over an hour and a half later, on the presidential jet that carried Kennedy's body, Vice President Lyndon B. Johnson was sworn in as the thirty-sixth President of the United States.

A stunned and shocked nation mourned its tragic loss. Several days later, as millions watched on television, alleged assassin Lee Harvey Oswald was being moved from one jail to another. Jack Ruby, a Dallas Kennedy supporter, walked up to Oswald and shot

Left: Twenty-five people crowded into the cabin of the late President's jet as it stood on the runway of Love Field in Dallas ninety-nine minutes after President Kennedy was pronounced dead. The wife of the former President watched as Judge Sarah Hughes administered the oath of office to Lyndon B. Johnson, a onetime Texas farm boy, school teacher, and great-grandson of Georgian Jesse Johnson. *Below:* Georgia's Dean Rusk was secretary of state during the Kennedy and Johnson administrations.

him at point blank range. This ended any chance of knowing for sure why the President had been killed.

In a speech to Congress, President Johnson said, "No memorial or eulogy could more eloquently honor President Kennedy's memory than the earliest possible passage of the civil rights bill for which he fought.. . . We have talked for one hundred years or more. Yes, it is time now to write the next Chapter—and to write it in the book of Law."

A NOTE OF INTEREST—DEAN RUSK

The Georgian most closely associated with both the Kennedy and Johnson years was Canton native Dean Rusk, who served as secretary of state. Rusk was the second Georgian to hold that office. The first, John Forsyth, served under President Andrew Jackson.

Rusk joined the State Department as an assistant secretary following World War II. He believed United States intervention in Korea would slow communist aggression in the Far East. In 1952, Rusk was appointed president of the Rockefeller Foundation. There, he worked to distribute $250,000,000 for various projects, including foreign aid.

Kennedy named Rusk secretary of state in 1960. He was known

for acting behind the scenes with what **colleagues** called "quiet diplomacy." During the Johnson years, Rusk was criticized for backing a massive build-up of American troops in Vietnam. However, President Johnson supported his decisions.

Dean Rusk worked to help underdeveloped countries improve education, health, and economic productivity. He left his national position in January 1969 and returned to his native Georgia. In 1970, he became a professor of international law at the University of Georgia School of Law.

Do You Remember?

1. When was John F. Kennedy assassinated?
2. Who was the alleged assassin and what happened to him?
3. Who followed Kennedy as President? What were the new President's feelings toward the Civil Rights Act?

PRESIDENT JOHNSON PUSHES CIVIL RIGHTS ACT

Under President Johnson's leadership, and with the political pressure of both black and white supporters, the Civil Rights Bill of 1964 became law. This was the most far-reaching and important civil rights legislation since Reconstruction. Basically, the "equal protection of the laws" clause of the Fourteenth Amendment was given greater influence. It made segregation of all public facilities illegal. This included restaurants, theaters, hotels, public recreational areas, schools, and libraries. It also prohibited discrimination in businesses and labor unions.

In spite of the Civil Rights Act, blacks in many sections of the South still could not vote. Dr. Martin Luther King, Jr., who was awarded the Nobel Peace Prize in 1964, began to give attention to voting rights.

In the summer of 1964, "Freedom Summer," people from all over the country came to the South to help blacks register to vote. Much effort was made by the Student Nonviolent Coordinating Committee (SNCC). This group included Georgia's Julian Bond as one of its founders, and Georgian John Lewis as its national chairman.

During the voter registration drive, three young men, two black

President Lyndon B. Johnson's signing the Civil Rights Act of 1964 was a momentous occasion. It made the segregation of public facilities illegal and offered more equitable opportunities to the nation's 22 million African-Americans. President Johnson is handing one of the pens used to sign the bill to Attorney General Robert Kennedy in recognition of President John F. Kennedy's influence in passing the Civil Rights Act.

and one white, were killed in Mississippi. This again drew national attention to the South.

In March 1965, Dr. King met with civil rights leaders in Selma, Alabama, to plan **demonstrations** and marches in support of voting rights. As he led marchers to the Dallas County courthouse, King and over 500 students were arrested and jailed.

King planned a march from Selma to the state capital in Montgomery to call attention to his cause. On March 7, over 600 marchers approached the Edmund Pettus Bridge which spans the Alabama River. There, they met about 200 state troopers armed with billy clubs and tear gas. The marchers fell back into Selma, followed by the county sheriff's mounted posse.

King went to Montgomery to request a march permit, which was granted by a United States district judge. President Johnson

Above left: Georgia's John Lewis (seated center) leads a sit-in at the Mississippi state capitol in 1965. The hundreds of students who converged on Mississippi from all over the nation helped add more than 1,200 African-Americans to the voting rolls. Above right: The Selma to Montgomery March in 1965 is shown here. On reaching the capitol steps in Montgomery, King told the group of over 25,000 that, "We are on the move and no wave of racism will stop us."

activated the Alabama National Guard and sent army troops, federal marshals, and FBI agents to Selma to protect the marchers.

On March 21, more than 4,000 Americans of differing races, led by Dr. King and Rabbi Abraham Herchel, began the fifty-mile walk to Montgomery. About 25,000 others joined the group in Montgomery to complete the march in support of equal voting rights.

The march influenced Congress to pass the Voting Rights Bill of 1965. Within a year and a half, a million southern blacks were added to the registers of voters.

A SHIFT IN MOOD

After the march from Selma to Montgomery, the mood of many seeking equal civil rights changed. These left the moderate, non-violent approach of Dr. King and followed aggressive activists like Stokely Carmichael, H. Rap Brown, and Eldridge Cleaver. A new group called the Black Panthers emerged. In the summer of 1967, riots and burnings of black communities began in places like Watts in Los Angeles, Detroit, Michigan, and Newark, New Jersey.

Dr. King and his supporters urged an end to violence. On April 3, 1968, King was in Memphis, Tennessee, to organize support for 1,300 striking sanitation workers. There had been threats on King's life, but he said,

In 1965 the mood of the nation had begun to shift, as racial violence exploded in the Watts neighborhood of Los Angeles. Thirty-four people were killed, and hundreds were injured. Property damage was almost $40,000,000. By 1967, the violence had spread to other cities.

It really doesn't matter what happens to me now because I've been to the mountain top . . . and I've looked over and seen the promised land. I may not get there with you. . . . But we, as a people, will get to the promised land. . . . Like anybody, I would like to live a long life. Longevity has its place. . . but I'm not concerned about that now.

The next day, Thursday, the thirty-nine year old King was on the balcony of a Memphis motel talking with Jesse Jackson, standing below. A shot from a high powered rifle left Martin Luther King, Jr. dead at the hands of an assassin. His followers mourned the passing of their leader.

On March 11, 1969, James Earl Ray, a forty year old high school drop-out was tried and convicted for King's murder. He was sentenced to ninety-nine years in prison.

The movement toward civil rights for all Americans did not die

with Martin Luther King, Jr. It continued through the work of many others, including Mrs. Coretta Scott King, Dr. Ralph Abernathy, Reverend Jesse Jackson, and Georgia political leaders Andrew Young, John Lewis, and Julian Bond.

Do You Remember?
1. What did the Civil Rights Act of 1964 accomplish?
2. Who were three Georgians who played a role in the voting rights aspect of the civil rights movement?
3. What did the Voting Rights Bill of 1965 accomplish?
4. When was Dr. Martin Luther King assassinated? Where? By Whom?
5. Who were some of the leaders of the civil rights movement who continued the struggle after Dr. King's death?

In 1966, the Georgia House of Representatives votes to deny a seat to Julian Bond, because of his criticism of the war in Vietnam and his association with SNCC. The United States Supreme Court later ordered that Bond be reinstated to his representative's seat in the Georgia General Assembly. Two years later, Bond's name was placed in nomination as a Democratic vice presidential candidate, but he had to refuse because he was not old enough to qualify as a candidate.

*Above: After being elected to the Presidency in 1964, Lyndon Baines Johnson quickly found himself embroiled in the escalation of the Vietnam War. In this photograph, a reporter's question about anti-war demonstrators provokes an angry response. **Opposite page:** As American soldiers slogged through the rice paddies of Vietnam, the nation was split as never before in their feelings over America's involvement in the war.*

A NATION DIVIDED—THE VIETNAM WAR

When the Civil War was fought, the nation was split according to the part of the country in which one lived. The nation was divided again in the 1960s, but it was not geographic differences which separated Americans from each other. This time the division came from personal beliefs that led to demonstrations and violence at home, and the loss of over 50,000 American lives in a country thousands of miles from the United States.

VIETNAM—HOW IT ALL BEGAN

It began in 1954, a few years after the end of the Korean War. Indochina, a country in the Far East, had been governed for years by the French. In 1954, the people of Indochina had forced the French out and formed their own countries: Cambodia, Laos and Vietnam. Vietnam was divided into two separate countries: North Vietnam, controlled by a communist government, and South Vietnam, in the hands of an anti-communist government. The United States and other nations of the world recognized the legitimate status of these new governments.

Within a few years, communist forces of North Vietnam began to invade South Vietnam. They also provided arms and supplies to pro-communist South Vietnamese known as Viet Cong. At first, President Eisenhower sent military advisors and money to help the South Vietnam government withstand the challenges of the North Vietnam invaders. His successor, President Kennedy, continued aid to South Vietnam. He increased the number of military advisors and "armed observers." When United States planes or helicopters working in advisory or observer roles were shot down, more troops were sent to South Vietnam and more funds were provided to help its anti-communist government stay in power.

The Gulf of Tonkin "Incident"

In August 1964, North Vietnamese gunboats attacked an American destroyer in the Gulf of Tonkin, off the coast of Southeast Asia. In response, Congress passed the Gulf of Tonkin Resolution which gave President Lyndon Johnson the power to use whatever measures were necessary to "repel any armed attacks against the forces of the United States."

The initial philosophical differences which grew from the Vietnam War controversy gave way to anger, violence, demonstrations and the burning of draft cards and flags. On October 21, 1967, 50,000 anti-war demonstrators congregated around the Lincoln Memorial. Soon the demonstrators stormed the Pentagon across the Potomac, clashing with military police.

After winning the election in 1964, Johnson stepped up American involvement in Vietnam and, by the end of 1965, there were 185,000 troops fighting there. Americans at home were divided on our involvement in the war. Those who were opposed were called "doves," after the bird of peace. Those in agreement were called "hawks."

Television Changes the Face of War

Each night, millions of Americans watched news of the war on their television sets. It was the first time a nation had been able to see war events almost as soon as they took place. There were pictures of young soldiers dying, and of Vietnamese being killed and their villages destroyed. It was sometimes hard to tell enemies from friends.

In November 1969, 250,000 United States citizens staged a protest demonstration in Washington, D.C. Some riots on college campuses were violent confrontations between National Guard troops and student protestors. Both negative news coverage of the war and draft **evasion** increased.

Nixon Promises End to War

After his election in 1968, President Richard Nixon promised to bring the American troops home. He tried to force the communists to negotiate a peace by increasing bombings. As a result, thousands more were killed and injured.

Finally, in January 1973, a cease fire was declared, bringing America's involvement in the war to an end. More than 2,000,000 Vietnamese and 57,000 Americans had been killed. At least 1,200 Americans were missing. There was no clear victory, and neither Vietnamese government would cooperate to find missing Americans and return prisoners of war.

The United States spent over $100,000,000,000 on the war. Hawks and Doves were so divided that returning troops were hurt and confused by their reception. It was not until the late 1980s that Americans gave Vietnam veterans recognition for their part in a war few people understood.

Do You Remember?

1. What was Vietnam called in 1953?
2. Why was the Gulf of Tonkin Resolution important?
3. Which United States President sent the most troops to Vietnam?
4. When was the Vietnam cease fire declared?

Above: Wartime in Vietnam was an exhausting time for soldiers who knew that while they were fighting in the rice paddies of that foreign country, American citizens were fighting over the war in the streets at home. *Left:* Designed by Maya Yang Lin, a 21-year-old, Vietnamese-American woman, the Vietnam War Memorial in Washington, D.C. is a simple but powerful remembrance of the war dead.

THE WATERGATE SCANDAL

In November 1972, President Nixon was re-elected to a second term in a landslide victory. His popularity following the Vietnam conflict was at an all-time high. However, on June 17, 1972, shortly before the Republican Nominating Convention, five people were arrested in the headquarters of the Democratic National Committee in the Watergate Building in Washington, D.C. The five burglars, trying to learn Democratic strategy, carried money, cameras, film, and listening devices called "bugs."

During the investigation of this break-in, it was learned that three of the five lawbreakers were members of President Nixon's re-election campaign staff. More importantly, some members of Nixon's staff not only knew about the break-in, but tried to cover it up with lies and denials. Increasingly, suspicion fell on the President himself.

In the course of the investigation, Vice President Spiro Agnew was accused of tax evasion and of bribing a public official in Maryland. Agnew resigned from office, and was replaced by Congressman Gerald Ford from Michigan.

Other Nixon staff members admitted their role in covering up the Watergate break-in, and indicated the President was aware of their actions. Opinion polls showed the public favored impeachment proceedings against the President. Tape recordings of conversations between Nixon and top aides which might have shown the President either innocent or guilty were erased or withheld from the public. It was said "national security could be compromised" by revealing the President's private conversations.

House of Representatives Votes to Impeach Nixon

President Nixon refused to cooperate with the investigation of the Watergate incident. The House of Representatives voted to recommend impeachment of the President for: 1) blocking the investigation of the Watergate affair; 2) abusing presidential powers; and 3) failing to release the taped White House conversations. On August 5, under order from the United States Supreme Court, the tapes were turned over to a special prosecutor. They revealed that, in spite of his public denials, President Nixon was involved in the cover-up.

G. Gordon Liddy, a member of the Nixon re-election campaign, was arrested for his role in the Watergate break-in and subsequent cover-up. He was indicted and imprisoned along with other co-conspirators.

Nixon Resigns

On August 8, before a television audience of over 100,000,000 people, a solemn President announced his resignation from office, effective August 9, 1974. He was the first United States President to resign.

Ford Becomes President

His successor, Gerald Ford, at once granted a presidential pardon to Nixon for any crimes he might have committed. Ford argued that the pardon was necessary to end the Watergate scandal and allow the nation to resume business. President Nixon's term in office had included some major foreign policy accomplishments. However, it was badly marred by Watergate.

Do You Remember?

1. What was Watergate?
2. What were the Watergate burglars trying to do?
3. For what three charges was the President to be tried?
4. What was one of President Ford's first official acts when he assumed office? Why?

Above: Presidential aide and former legal counsel to Nixon, John Dean's testimony implicated the President during a Congressional hearing in the attempt to cover up the Watergate break-in. Left: A solemn President Richard Nixon addressed the nation on August 8, 1974. He told the television audience that "I have never been a quitter. To leave office before my term is completed is opposed to every instinct in my body. But the interests of America come first." It was the first time in the nation's 198-year history that an American President had resigned from office.

SPOTLIGHT ON JAMES EARL CARTER, JR.

James Earl "Jimmy" Carter, who followed Gerald Ford, was the first Georgian to become President of the United States. He was born in Plains on October 1, 1924, and grew up on his parents' southwest Georgia peanut farm. Carter attended Georgia Southwestern College and Georgia Tech before receiving an appointment to the United States Naval Academy. After graduation, he was assigned to the Pacific Fleet. Later, Carter went to Union College and studied physics.

When his father died, Lieutenant Carter left the Navy to run the family farm. His first venture in politics was as a member of the Sumter County School Board. In 1962, after winning a state senate race, he began the first of two terms in the Georgia legislature.

Carter Seeks Governorship

In 1966, Carter failed in a bid for governor. However, he began almost immediately to prepare for the next election. With his wife Rosalynn, Carter went from county to county, meeting voters and encouraging them to back a moderate for the state house. He was openly in favor of equality and the end of racial strife.

Carter won the 1970 election. His inaugural speech contained

Opposite page: The Plains, Georgia peanut farmer who served as Georgia's governor and then as the 39th President of the United States is also known for his concern, interest, and work for those in need.
Below: *With a population of less than 700, Plains, Georgia was suddenly thrust into the national spotlight as the election headquarters and hometown of presidential candidate Jimmy Carter.*

Right: During a debate with fellow Democratic candidates during the 1976 campaign, Jimmy Carter demonstrated his knowledge of, and sensitivity to, a variety of issues.

Below: When the work schedule would allow, the Carters, with their daughter Amy, would use the presidential helicopter to escape the pressures of Washington and spend some time at Camp David, outside Washington.

these words: "I say to you quite frankly that the time for racial discrimination is over." Indeed, it was a new day in Georgia politics. In 1972, black civil rights leader Andrew Young was elected to Congress and, the following year, the "city too busy to hate" elected Maynard Jackson as Atlanta's first black mayor.

Carter's Governorship

During his time in office, Carter reorganized the state's executive branch, cutting government agencies from about 300 to 22. He also began "zero based budgeting." This meant that, in deciding how much money would be spent for various state causes, the amount began at zero rather than at the spending level of previous years.

Carter spent a great deal of time working to enact legislation to protect Georgia **consumers.** Many of his efforts failed, however, due to strife between Carter and Lieutenant Governor Lester Maddox. By the end of his four-year term, Carter's popularity had declined greatly. Many Georgians were surprised when he announced his candidacy for the presidency.

"Jimmy Who?"

Carter began a grass-roots campaign, going back and forth across the country shaking hands, much as he had done during his campaign for governor. A campaign slogan was, "I will never lie to you." The national news media poked fun, calling him "Jimmy Who?" because of his lack of national exposure and experience.

Carter Wins Presidency

Americans upset by Watergate and Ford's pardon of Richard Nixon were searching for a leader who was honorable, hard working, and earnest. James Earl Carter fit that description. When the electoral votes were counted, Carter had defeated Ford 297 to 240. The unknown "Jimmy Who?" was the first President from the Deep South since the Civil War.

Most historians agree that it takes at least twenty-five years before the effectiveness of a major office holder can be rated. Therefore, it will be some time before history judges the Carter presidency.

During Carter's term in office, a severe oil shortage caused high gas prices and long lines at service stations across the country. Some said the President was not moving fast enough to find energy substitutes. A slow economy and high rate of inflation did not gain President Carter any popularity. However, the major criticism of Carter was his failure to win a quick release for fifty-

The most notable accomplishment of President Carter's term was the Camp David Summit in 1978. Egypt's President Sadat and Israel's Prime Minister Begin met with the President for thirteen days, hammering out a treaty between the two countries. At the conclusion of the Summit, Begin remarked, "He [Carter] worked harder than our forefathers did building the pyramids."

Jimmy Carter continues to serve the nation as a writer and unofficial foreign relations mediator. In this photograph he is shown as an active member of Habitat for Humanity, building low-cost housing for the poor in Tijuana, Mexico.

two American hostages held in Iran. His administration worked hard to get them released, but they were not given freedom until the day of President Reagan's inauguration.

Carter's Accomplishments

Carter will likely be best remembered for the Camp David Accords. This series of meetings was held at the presidential retreat, Camp David, between leaders of Israel and Egypt. These sessions, in which Carter acted as mediator, led to peace treaties between the two warring nations.

In addition, Carter developed a foreign policy emphasizing worldwide human rights. He appointed more women and minorities to federal judgeships and policy positions than any previous President. Carter signed the Panama Canal Treaty in 1977. The treaty will transfer ownership of the Panama Canal Zone from the United States to Panama in the year 2000, and calls for the permanent neutrality and operation of the canal. President Carter was also responsible for submitting a civil service reform package to Congress, which they made law in 1978. The legislation divided the Civil Service Commission into two agencies. One is an independent Merit System Protection Board to investigate grievances of civil service workers. The other is the Federal Labor Relations Authority, which oversees federal labor and management policies.

A Return to Private Life

When Carter was defeated for re-election by Republican Ronald Reagan, he returned to Georgia. He planned a presidential library and policy center near Emory University in Atlanta, and wrote his **memoirs**, *Keeping Faith*. Carter continues an active, though largely unofficial, role in foreign policy mediation and conflict resolution.

Do You Remember?

1. Where was Jimmy Carter born?
2. What did Carter accomplish as governor of Georgia?
3. What were Carter's major accomplishments as President?
4. Why didn't Carter get recognition for the release of the American hostages from Iran?

A CHANGING GEORGIA

Modern day Georgia's move from an agrarian to an industrial society is seen most clearly in population shifts.

ONE-THIRD OF GEORGIANS LIVE IN ATLANTA AREA

In 1980, a third of all Georgians lived in a seven county area around Atlanta: Fulton, Gwinnett, DeKalb, Cobb, Rockdale, Clayton and Douglas. 1990 statistics show a continuing trend toward urban living. If the next four most populous counties (Chatham, Richmond, Bibb and Muscogee) are added to the **metropolitan** Atlanta area, these urban centers contain over half of the state's population. Between 1980 and 1990, Georgia's population grew from 5,462,989 to 6,386,948, moving its national ranking from thirteenth to eleventh. During this same period, people continued to move from inner cities to suburbs. Atlanta's population fell from 425,000 to 384,153.

The growth in Georgia's population is important for a number of reasons. Federal monies **allocated** to the state increase with the population. Also, the state gained one new seat in the United States Congress because of the latest census figures.

The majority of Georgia's counties have less than 25,000 residents and income averages about $9,478 a person. In contrast, per capita income in the Atlanta metropolitan area averages about $13,848. However, people continue to move into the state to enjoy the mild climate, geographic diversity, and job opportunities.

The Atlanta metropolitan area is home to over two million Georgians, with the city of Atlanta serving as the focal point for business and industry. The face of the impressive skyline changes each year as more and more buildings are added to it.

Georgia Governor Joe Frank Harris and former State School Superintendent Charles McDaniel, pictured here, worked together to improve the state's educational system and pass the Quality Basic Education (QBE) Act.

SOCIAL AND CULTURAL CHANGES

There have been a number of social and cultural changes in Georgia during the modern period. Some of the most important of these have been in the field of education.

Progress in Education

Each weekday morning, close to 1,000,000 students begin another day of classes. School population varies from an average daily attendance of 300 in some counties to almost 68,000 in metropolitan Atlanta.

In 1947, a constitutional amendment added a twelfth grade to the state's secondary schools. By 1954, the addition had been made in all school systems.

The general assembly approved a Minimum Foundation Program in 1949, which established a nine-month school year. The act also provided that the same minimum amount of money would be provided to educate each student. However, both the legislators and Georgia's voters refused to raise taxes to fund the program. The Minimum Foundation Program was not implemented until the 1951-52 school year when Governor Herman Talmadge got the legislature to pass a three per cent sales tax for education. Even then, funding for black and white students was not equal. In 1953, Georgia allocated $190 for each white student and $132 for each black student.

Unequal funding ended with school integration, following passage of the Civil Rights Bill of 1964. By 1985, an average of $2,682 was spent for each student.

The next major piece of education legislation in Georgia came in 1974 under the direction of Governor Jimmy Carter. Carter had been a member of the board of education in a small, rural county. He knew some communities refused state and federal funds so they could keep small, local high schools. Carter wanted such schools combined with others to provide broader educational programs for all the state's students.

In 1973, the general assembly approved a blue ribbon committee to study the educational system and recommend improvements. The result was the Adequate Program for Education in Georgia (APEG), which was enacted in 1974. APEG was recognized around the nation as a model for state educational improvement. However, it suffered the same fate as some earlier Georgia legislation. It was never fully funded, so it could not be fully carried out.

The most recent educational improvement program in Georgia was called Quality Basic Education (QBE). This 1985 reform was led by State School Superintendent Charles McDaniel and Governor Joe Frank Harris. It was based on a standardized program and curriculum in all the state's schools, and on enough money to fund the program. Like improvement programs before it, QBE has not been fully funded by the legislature, so its effectiveness cannot be judged.

Georgia ranks third in the nation in the number of school dropouts, in spite of the efforts to improve education. In 1986, for example, 37.3 per cent of Georgia's students left school before graduation. These "at risk" young adults enter the job market with minimal educational skills and job training. Other areas of educational concern continue to be inadequate teacher salaries, funding for new programs, the acceptance of statewide standardized testing scores as a method for evaluating schools, and the equality of educational opportunity in every part of the state.

Governor from 1983 through 1990, Joe Frank Harris from Cartersville made educational reform the top priority of his administration.

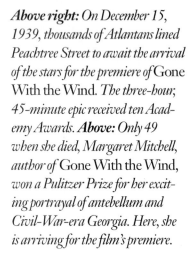

Above right: On December 15, 1939, thousands of Atlantans lined Peachtree Street to await the arrival of the stars for the premiere of Gone With the Wind. *The three-hour, 45-minute epic received ten Academy Awards. Above: Only 49 when she died, Margaret Mitchell, author of* Gone With the Wind, *won a Pulitzer Prize for her exciting portrayal of antebellum and Civil-War-era Georgia. Here, she is arriving for the film's premiere.*

THE FIELD OF ENTERTAINMENT

A major part of any state's heritage rests in its artists, musicians, writers, and performers. Georgia provides a rich setting for creativity. This has been particularly true for writers.

Georgia Authors

New South authors, including Sidney Lanier and Joel Chandler Harris, along with Progressive Era writer Erskine Caldwell (*Tobacco Road* in 1932 and *God's Little Acre* in 1933), set the stage for literary excellence. In 1949, however, an untimely death robbed the state of well-known author Margaret Mitchell.

Peggy Mitchell, as she was known to her friends, won the Pulitzer Prize for *Gone With the Wind* in 1936. The movie that followed is an American film classic. On August 11, 1949, as Peggy and her husband were crossing Peachtree Street on their way to see a movie, a speeding taxi hit her. Five days later, she died, leaving the state in mourning and the nation wondering what "other great American novel" had died with her. In 1985, Margaret Mitchell was named Georgia's "most famous citizen."

Georgia's first Pulitzer Prize winner was Caroline Miller for her novel *Lamb in His Bosom*. Carson McCullers' 1940 book, *The Heart Is a Lonely Hunter*, her 1946 *Member of the Wedding*, and *Reflection in a Golden Eye* became successful plays and movies. Eugenia Price wrote *Beloved Invader*, *Lighthouse*, and *New Moon Rising*, a trilogy about St. Simons Island. Joyce Blackburn is noted for her biographies and Suki children's books.

Eliot Wigginton, a Raburn County high school teacher, has worked with his students to produce a series of best-selling books entitled *Foxfire*. Each book provides a unique look at life in the North Georgia mountains.

Books by Atlanta newspaper columnist Celestine Sibley continue to delight Georgia readers, especially her unusual *Christmas in Georgia*.

A fellow columnist, humorist Lewis Grizzard, has published numbers of books, and his daily column appears in over 200 newspapers.

Flannery O'Connor wrote a collection of short stories in 1955, entitled *A Good Man is Hard to Find*. Caroline Lovell's *The Golden Isles of Georgia*, offers a descriptive view of the history and development of the state's coastal islands.

James Dickey wrote, among other works, *The Firebombing*, a poem describing his experiences as a combat fighter. Dickey also wrote *Deliverance*, a top-selling novel, which was made into a movie filmed in the North Georgia mountains around Tallulah Falls. In 1983, Spelman graduate Alice Walker was awarded a Pulitzer Prize for *The Color Purple*, her account of African-American life in the South. It has been made into a well-known movie. Another famous Atlanta author is Pat Conroy, who is known for *The Great Santini*, *The Lords of Discipline*, and *The Prince of Tides*.

African-American author, Frank Yerby, who did much of his writing in Europe, wrote twenty-six selections. Among those written by Yerby, a native of Augusta, were *Foxes of Harrow* and *The*

Atlanta poet and novelist, James Dickey, received acclaim for his book Deliverance, *which was made into a movie, filmed in the north Georgia mountains at Tallulah Gorge.*

Top: Eatonton-born Alice Walker received the coveted Pulitzer Prize for her novel, The Color Purple. *Above: Born in Albany, Georgia, Ray Charles' version of "Georgia on My Mind" was so successful it was made the state song.*

Golden Hawk. His first story, *"Health Card"* won the O'Henry Award for best short story. Still other notable Georgia writers include Lillian Smith who authored *Strange Fruit*, Margaret Long who wrote *Affairs of the Heart*, and Ware County's Ann Nichols who is known for *Abie's Irish Rose*.

Georgia Entertainers

The list of Georgia entertainers in modern times includes such well-known actors as Atlanta's De Forrest Kelley, who played Dr. McCoy in the "Star Trek" series, Claude Akins of "Sheriff Lobo" fame, and pro football player and actor Jim Brown. Waycross produced Pernell Roberts, who is best known for his roles in "Bonanza," and "Trapper John, M.D.," and movie and television star Burt Reynolds.

For years, audiences have laughed at the antics of comedian Nipsey Russell, born in Atlanta, and "Sanford and Son" star Desmond Wilson from Valdosta.

Up and coming new stars from the state include Kim Basinger from Athens who performed in "Batman," Julia Roberts of Smyrna, and Holly Hunter of Conyers who starred in "Broadcast News."

Well-known cartoonist Walt Kelly has entertained several generations of readers with his comic strip, Pogo. The strip shares the author's perception of current events through the eyes of Pogo, the Possum, and other Okefenokee Swamp characters.

Georgia Musicians

Georgians can boast of some well-known musicians, including Grammy winner Ray Stevens, who sang the hit, "Everything is Beautiful," Otis Redding, who made "Sitting On the Dock of the Bay" popular, and country and western stars Brenda Lee, Jerry Reed, and Kenny Rogers.

Augusta produced James Brown, and Little Richard is from Macon. Albany claims Gladys Knight and Ray Charles. Knight's group, "Gladys Knight and the Pips," had twenty-eight years of top forty hits. Charles performs the state song, "Georgia On My Mind."

Atlantan Mattiwilda Dobbs, has performed throughout the nation and in Europe as an opera star with the Metropolitan Opera.

Sports Stars

From the early 1900s, football, baseball, and basketball have been popular in Georgia. Fans support athletes at the high school, college, and professional levels. In the early 1900s, Ty Cobb, the "Georgia Peach," thrilled sports fans as a major league hitter and base stealer. He was joined in the Baseball Hall of Fame by Hank "The Hammer" Aaron, who holds twenty-one major league records, including Most Home Runs.

Georgia fighter, Evander Holyfield, is a former Olympic bronze medal winner. Herschel Walker is a native of Wrightsville, Georgia, and played college ball at the University of Georgia in Athens. "Rosey" Grier is a Georgia football great who went on to make a career in movies.

The first Heisman Trophy winner from Georgia was University of Georgia player Frank Sinkwich. The award itself is named for a former coach at Georgia Tech, John Heisman.

Georgia Entertainers—A Proud Heritage

These authors, musicians, and sports heroes, along with other Georgians like artist Lamar Dodd, actor Melvyn Douglas, Olympic track star Wyomia Tyus, former pro quarterback Fran Tarkenton, and popular music composer Johnny Mercer have provided untold hours of entertainment for people across the country.

Do You Remember?

1. Did the state's population increase or decrease between 1980 and 1990?
2. Where does a third of the state's population live?
3. How does Georgia rank nationally in terms of high school dropouts?
4. When was the school term increased to nine months?
5. What are some of Georgia's major educational concerns today?
6. Who was Margaret Mitchell?
7. What books did Pat Conroy write?
8. Who is in the Baseball Hall of Fame for hitting the most home runs?
9. What is Georgia's official state song and what Georgia-born musician performs it?

Top: Forty-year old "Hammering Hank" Aaron made baseball history when he hit his 715th home run to break Babe Ruth's major league record. Above: Evander Holyfield became the heavyweight boxing champion of the world when he defeated Buster Douglas.

CRISIS IN THE GULF

Iraqi President Saddam Hussein put the world community on alert in 1990 by ignoring the demands of a coalition of the United Nations and attacking neighboring Kuwait.

In the late 1980s, the Berlin Wall between East and West Germany was torn down, ending a separation which had existed since the end of World War II. In early 1990, the Soviet Union, Great Britain, and the United States signed the final accord to reunite the two Germanies, bringing a formal close to post-World-War-II occupation divisions. Several countries formerly under communist rule asked for and got a democratic government. Disarmament agreements had been signed between the United States and the Soviet Union, and the Cold War seemed at an end. Plans were in place to decrease national defense forces and budgets in both countries.

Then, in August 1990, the picture of world peace changed. The middle eastern country of Iraq, headed by President Saddam Hussein, swept into the neighboring Moslem nation of Kuwait. Both oil-rich countries have the power to influence the world economy. The United States alone imports millions of barrels of oil from Kuwait each year.

OPERATION "DESERT SHIELD"

To protect those oil fields, the United States government has a treaty with its middle eastern allies promising to assist them if the need arises. When Iraq took over Kuwait, the United States asked the United Nations for help. With United Nations backing, armed forces from the United States and a number of other nations began to move into the desert of Saudi Arabia. The military build up was called "Operation Desert Shield."

In Georgia, thirty-three percent of the population had an immediate family member in the active or reserve armed forces. Within a few months, hundreds of Georgia men and women were placed on alert because of the middle east crisis.

OPERATION "DESERT STORM"

"Desert Shield" became "Desert Storm" on Wednesday, January 16, 1991. One day after the United Nations' unmet deadline for Iraq to leave Kuwait, thirty-three allied nations declared war on Iraq.

For forty-three days, United States citizens watched the war on

television while it was taking place on the northeast side of the Arabian peninsula. People began using words like "sorties" (bombing missions), "scuds" (missiles from Iraq), and "patriots" (United States anti-missile missiles that sought and shot down Iraqi scuds). The scud missiles were aimed at Kuwait, Saudi Arabia, where most allied troops were based, and Israel, a long-time enemy of Iraq.

Television viewers learned that soldiers, marines, and fliers in the field were eating "MREs" (Meals Ready to Eat) which had replaced the K-Rations of World War II. They consisted of foods such as beef stew, chicken with rice, or meatballs and tomato sauce sealed in heavy plastic bags.

Americans also learned more about Iraq. Its major religion is Islam. Men in Iraq usually wear long, loose-fitting robes called Aba, and a Haik, or piece of cloth wrapped around the head for protection against sun, wind, and sand. Women dress in loose-fit-ting gowns and wear flowing, waist-length scarfs around their

The readiness position of United Nations coalition forces, led by the United States, for Operation Desert Shield quickly turned into active wartime as Operation Desert Storm began on January 16, 1991.

You can see the excitement and happiness on the faces of these families and friends as they welcome Georgia troops as they return home from Operation Desert Storm.

heads. Some cover most of their faces with veils, leaving only the eyes showing. Iraqis eat pita bread, rice pilaf, chicken, and some meats. Pork and alcoholic beverages are forbidden by religious laws.

On February 23, day thirty-nine of the war, after thousands of allied bombing attacks on Iraq, the land war began. Thousands of Iraqi troops surrendered to allied forces. Four days later, the allies marched into Kuwait City and Iraqi forces were defeated.

The war was short, but the damage to Kuwait was great. Iraqi troops had bombed over 500 Kuwaiti oil wells, destroyed millions of dollars in buildings and equipment, and left a huge oil spill in the Persian Gulf.

Troops not involved in the peace-keeping force returned to their countries. The first United States troops came back on March 8. Family and friends welcomed 763 members of the Twenty-Fourth Mechanized Infantry Division based in Fort Stewart, Georgia. For over a year, Georgia cheered its over 21,00 active duty military men and women, 775 National Guard troops, and 1,200 Army Reserve troops as they came home.

Do You Remember?
1. Why is Kuwait important to the United States?
2. Who invaded Kuwait?
3. What was the United States military build-up in Saudi Arabia called?
4. How many days did Operation Desert Storm last?
5. How many allied countries declared war on Iraq?

LOOKING AHEAD TO THE FUTURE

A CHALLENGE TO GEORGIA'S STUDENTS

There have been many developments from the beginning of Georgia's history to the present. The first Georgia settlers stepped off the ship *Anne* at Savannah in 1733. From that time forward, each event in history was the result of people's ideas and actions. When the next Georgia history textbooks are written, the last chapter will show how you are helping to determine Georgia's future history. Among the things you can do are:

a) register to vote when you become eighteen, then use that vote to influence the direction of the state by casting it for the elected officials of your choice;

b) work actively to care for our environment through recycling efforts, energy conversation, protection of the soil from erosion, guarding plant and animal life from extinction, and preserving our historical landmarks and rich cultural heritage;

c) understand how to become a mature adult member of society. This includes:

1) accepting responsibility for and helping others, regardless of social, racial, cultural, or economic backgrounds;

2) being part of a healthy and drug-free environment;

3) doing your part to end the spread of AIDS and other life-threatening diseases; and

4) recognizing that by being a lifelong learner and taking an active part in your children's education, the future will be built on each person's ability to think critically and solve problems.

Meeting these and other challenges will ensure that the state and nation will continue to progress and be able to provide for generations still to come.

The future will be built on each person's ability to think critically and solve problems.

THE DISPUTE OVER AN IRON HORSE

In 1953, Chicago sculptor Abbott Pattison came to the University of Georgia in Athens as a visiting artist. He sculpted several works for the college, including an abstract of a mother and child carved from an eight-foot high, five-ton chunk of white marble from the Tate, Georgia quarry.

The following year, Pattison returned under a Rockefeller Foundation grant to work on several other selections for the campus. One was a horse welded from sheet steel.

The giant abstract horse was finished in two months and stored behind the school's fine arts department building. Some time later, workers loaded the three-ton horse on a flatbed truck and moved it to the grass area in front of the freshman dormitory. Students gathered to watch the workers putting the sculpture in place. By early evening, the crowd had grown to several hundred.

The students threw confetti on the sculpture, painted the underside yellow, stacked bales of hay around its head, and scratched derogatory remarks along the sides. Throughout the night, cries of "Burn that horse" could be heard. Mattresses and old tires were piled up and burned around the sculpture.

Worried that the pranks would become more serious and someone would be injured, University President O.C. Aderhold ordered the horse moved from the campus. Maintenance foreman C.M. Thompson loaded the sculpture on a truck and took it to his farm in Madison County, about ten miles outside of Athens, and hid it behind a barn. After a tornado destroyed the barn, the horse was moved to nearby woods and was all but forgotten except by occasional hunters.

Three years later, L.C. Curtis, a professor in the University's agricultural department, asked school officials if he could have the "art work." Permission was granted and, once again, the horse was loaded and moved. It had become known as the "iron horse" because of its weight and appearance.

In 1954 the University of Georgia was the site of a dispute over an iron sculpture of a horse.

The iron horse was located in the middle of a field between Greensboro and Athens just off of Highway 15. After students discovered the horse's location, they planned occasional trips to visit the horse at night and, when possible, tip it over. The sculpture was placed in concrete to prevent future vandalism. For years, cows slept at its feet and passing drivers slowed down or stopped to look at the huge sculpture standing alone in a field of tall grass.

Thirty-three years later the fate of the iron horse again made headlines. In 1990, University alumni and some school officials tried to relocate the sculpture to its original home, the grounds of the University. It was decided, after much discussion, that such a move would not be fair to the Curtis family or to the many Georgians who protested moving the horse from its safe site overlooking Highway 15 just past the Oconee River. It is a fair guess that there are not many farms in the United States where one can find a three-ton steel sculpture of a horse standing peacefully in the middle of a field, maintaining a silent vigil for passers-by to see.

The iron horse finally found a home in the middle of a field between Greensboro and Athens just off of Highway 15, where it has become a familiar site to passers-by.

CHAPTER REVIEW

Summary

As World War II ended in 1945, Georgia was experiencing an economic boom as a result of wartime industries. Many Georgians had left farms to find work in the cities, and population studies began to favor urban areas over rural.

Those remaining in rural areas also saw changes in postwar Georgia. New farm machinery and a new emphasis on row crops like corn, soybeans, and peanuts are examples of changes in agriculture.

In 1950, the nation went to war again, this time in Korea. During the same period, there were many involved in a struggle for civil rights in Georgia and throughout America. In 1954, the United States Supreme Court ordered the integration of public schools. Seven years later, in 1961, the first black students were admitted to the University of Georgia and the schools in Atlanta were fully desegregated. Within the next ten years, all schools in Georgia were integrated.

During the late 1950s and early 1960s, civil rights struggles took the nation's attention. Dr. Martin Luther King, Jr. became a national leader in a movement of nonviolent protests against discrimination. The movement included bus boycotts, protest marches, sit ins and, finally, a "Freedom March on Washington" in 1963 to call for freedom from discrimination and demand passage of the Civil Rights Act.

Shortly after the march on Washington, the nation was stunned when President John F. Kennedy was killed by an assassin's bullet on November 22, 1963.

The Civil Rights Bill was enacted by Congress in 1964, but the late 60s continued to be a time of racial violence and tension.

Dr. Martin Luther King, Jr. was assassinated in Memphis, Tennessee in 1968.

The late 1960s found the nation increasingly drawn into the conflict in Vietnam. This involvement resulted in a bitter and violent division among the population of the United States. More than 57,000 American soldiers were killed in this conflict.

Vietnam was followed by a period of political scandal and distrust best symbolized by Watergate, a burglary by some staff members of President Nixon's Re-election Committee who broke into the Democratic headquarters seeking campaign information or plans. What began as a burglary led to the resignation of an American President.

Georgian James Earl Carter, campaigning for the presidency, capitalized on slogans suggesting that Americans wanted honest, hard-working officials and were tired of the political insiders' ways of doing business. Despite limited political experience and little national exposure, Carter was elected President in 1976.

Carter had little success in domestic policies and his presidency is best judged from the successes of the Camp David Peace Accords, a series of peace treaties between Egypt and Israel which Carter mediated. Increasing international terrorism, including the kidnapping of fifty-two American hostages by Iran, marked the Carter years. President Carter served only one term in office. He was succeeded by Ronald Reagan.

On January 16, 1991, thirty-three allied nations, including the United States, declared war on Iraq. Iraq had taken over neighboring Kuwait, a small Muslim country with only 2,000,000 people, on August 2, 1990. After forty-three days of bombing and about four days of land attacks, the war was over and allied military forces began returning home.

People, Places, and Terms

Identify, define, or state the importance of the following.

1. November 22, 1963
2. Jackie Robinson
3. Alice Walker
4. Operation Desert Storm
5. Watergate
6. Jimmy Carter
7. Margaret Mitchell
8. *Brown* v. *Board of Education*
9. Carson McCullers
10. Dalton
11. Civil Rights Act of 1964
12. Dr. Martin Luther King, Jr.

The Main Idea

Write a short paragraph to answer each question.

1. How has life changed since the early 1950s?
2. Considering current state population trends, will the state continue to grow? Why or why not?
3. Which Georgia governors promoted the cause of education? How?
4. What events led to the passage of the Civil Rights Act of 1964?

Looking Ahead

The next chapter looks at Georgia's diverse economy. Georgia plays a vital role in the economy of the nation. It is among the leading states in several categories of our national economy. You will learn:

➤ about Georgia's service industries;
➤ about Georgia's manufacturing industries;
➤ about Georgia's agriculture;
➤ about the 1996 Olympics coming to Atlanta.

Extend Your Thinking

If you were in charge, based on text information, decide how you would improve each of the following areas?

1. Education in our state
2. Equal Opportunities for all Georgians
3. Expansion of Georgia's economy

DID YOU KNOW . . .

. . . In 1990 Life magazine listed 100 of the most influential Americans in the twentieth century? Among such names as Martin Luther King, Jr., Billy Graham, and Henry Ford are those of Wallace Carothers, who invented nylon, Frank McNamara, who gave us credit cards, and Willis Carrier who invented the air conditioner.

. . . As they had in World War II, the Coca-Cola Company gave free Cokes to the armed forces stationed in the Saudi Arabian desert during the Persian Gulf Crisis?

. . . The average American needs eight eight-ounce glasses of water each day, while troops stationed in Saudi Arabia need ninety six eight-ounce glasses a day to remain healthy?

. . . The chairman of the Joint Chiefs of Staff, General Colin Powell, was the first black and youngest officer ever to lead the nation's armed forces?

. . . Jack Ruby, who killed Kennedy assassin Lee Harvey Oswald, died of cancer in January, 1967, while awaiting the result of an appeal of the death sentence for his crime?

. . . Girls were first allowed to play on a Little League baseball team in 1974?

CHAPTER SIXTEEN

GEORGIA'S ECONOMY

Economics is the science that deals with the production, distribution and use of goods and services. It includes the study of such matters as money, wages and taxes.

— *School Dictionary*, 1985 Harcourt, Brace, Jovanovich, Inc.

KNOWING THE DEFINITION of the word "economics" is necessary to understanding this chapter. Economics has been important to all cultures in recorded history. Metal was first used as currency in the middle east in about 2,000 B.C. Before that, goods and services were obtained through a system known as bartering. For example, a furniture maker might have given a table to a cobbler in exchange for a pair of sandals. The practice of bartering is still

*The Atlanta Olympic Organizing Committee including (left to right) mayor Maynard Jackson, former mayor Andrew Young and the chairman, Billy Payne, jubilantly returned to the city after Atlanta had been named the site of the 1996 Summer Olympics. **Left:** Fireworks celebrate the Olympic news.*

Above: Banking is one of the cornerstones of the state's economy. Citizens and Southern Bank, better known as C & S, was one of the first chartered banks in the state (1887). Opposite page top: Few Georgians thought that when the 1988 closing ceremonies were being celebrated in Seoul, Korea, there was a possibility that Atlanta would become an Olympic host city. Opposite page bottom: Atlanta will be host to the Super Bowl in 1994.

used today by some people. Two current economic terms are "inflation" and "recession." Inflation occurs when income has greatly increased or money is easy to borrow. Consumers are willing to pay higher prices to buy services and manufactured goods. To meet consumer demand, businesses step up production and, eventually, overproduce.

Sometimes, in the economic cycle, a recession occurs. The increase in income slows, and banks lend less money at higher rates of interest. It becomes more difficult to buy such items as houses and cars. Consumers also purchase fewer goods and services not considered necessary for basic living. When there is less demand for goods and services, some businesses and factories either close completely or use fewer workers to produce what consumers can buy. Many people may find themselves unemployed.

A recession usually continues until banks lower interest rates and it becomes possible for consumers to borrow money easily again. The purchase of goods and services increases. Businesses and factories expand, and the need for workers increases.

The economic figures in this chapter may be different from those in current newspapers. Prices, and available goods and services, are influenced by demand and, therefore, change often.

GEORGIA'S ECONOMY— A DIVERSIFIED ECONOMY

In the 1800s, Georgia was mostly a one-crop agricultural state. Today, it has a strong and diversified economy. Diversity means "variety." Thus, a diversified economy is one in which there are a number of different businesses or industries in which people work. Economic diversification and interdependence go hand in hand with each other. For example, on a given street there may be a factory that makes parts for airplanes next to a fast-food restaurant. Across the street, there might be a bank, a flower shop, and a public library. All these places depend on each other for success.

Factory workers might eat lunch at the restaurant, or deposit their paychecks at the bank. On the way home from work, they may buy flowers for a friend, or check out a book at the library.

In addition to handling checking accounts, the bank may lend money to the florist for building a greenhouse. The florist pays the

bank a fee, called interest, for borrowing the money to expand.

Georgia's present-day diversification and economic development is fairly new. There was a short period of economic growth during and after World War II. Then the state experienced a slow-down until the late 1970s and early 1980s, when **per capita** income began to increase.

Georgia may not suffer as much as some other states from the recession of the early 1990s. This is due, in large part, to an increase in foreign investments, and the selection of Atlanta as the site of the 1994 Super Bowl and the 1996 Olympic Games. The Super Bowl and Olympic Games will pump millions of dollars into the state through construction needed to host the events, and the money spent by those who attend them.

An economic picture of the state can be seen by looking at various types of employment. However, the number of people employed and the amount of money made changes every day. The most important thing to consider is the Gross State Product, or GSP, which is the total of all goods and services provided.

GEORGIA'S LARGEST INDUSTRY—THE SERVICE INDUSTRY

Seventy-five percent of Georgia's GSP is in the area of service industries.

Retail and Wholesale Trade

Selling is the state's number one economic activity, employing over 648,000 people. It includes everything from clothing, furniture, household appliances, and grocery stores, to automobile and sports equipment dealerships. There is usually a place to buy anything a consumer wants.

Wholesale and retail trade accounts for about $26,500,000,000 a year, or an average of $4,850 per person. Increasingly, shopping malls are becoming the center of the retail industry. In the metropolitan Atlanta area alone, there are over sixteen major shopping malls.

Top and above: One of the biggest retail areas in Georgia is Lenox Square in Atlanta. It attracts visitors from all parts of Georgia and the southeast.

Finance, Insurance, and Real Estate

The finance, insurance, and real estate industries employ about 137,000 Georgians. In 1887, the state's first bank, Citizens and Southern, was chartered in Savannah. Today, over 383 banks hold deposits of $31,000,000,000 and **assets** of over $40,000,000,000. Four hundred Georgia banks closed in the 1920s, due to the decline of "King Cotton," but no state bank shut its doors during the Great Depression.

Closely related to banking is the real estate industry. In 1990, the average cost of a home in Georgia was $84,000. This was very different from the 1889 national average of $2,300 for a three-bedroom house.

Both banking and real estate influence the insurance industry. For example, to secure a loan for a house, the buyer must have insurance to cover the cost of the loan in case of fire or other loss. One must show "proof of insurance" on an automobile in order to buy a tag in Georgia. In addition, most Georgians have some medical and life insurance.

Above: The Coastal States Insurance Building in Atlanta. Left: The sale of homes in this multi-million-dollar industry is an indicator of economic growth. A sluggish housing market is a sign of an overall weakened economy, but the reverse is also true. When bank mortgage loan interest rates are at a low level, "Sold" signs indicate a booming economy. Today, the average price of a home varies from $65,000 to $100,000. What are some things a homeowner can do to increase the value of his property?

*Above: Every year over 39 million people travel to or through Atlanta. Delta Airlines uses Atlanta as its southeastern hub. **Opposite page top:** Media magnate Ted Turner founded the Cable News Network, headquartered in Atlanta. **Opposite page bottom:** 1200 miles of interstate highways connect Georgia with its neighboring states. The interchange at I-85, and I-285, shown here, is one of the busiest in the state.*

Transportation, Communications, and Utilities

Together, transportation, communications, and utilities make up another major portion of the state's service industry. They employ over 162,400 persons. The state's outstanding ease of transportation is one of the main attractions for new businesses and industries. Atlanta's Hartsfield Airport is the second busiest in the world. Only Chicago's O'Hare Field handles more passengers. Hartsfield is the southeastern hub for Delta Airlines, and over 39,000,000 people a year change planes there for other destinations. In addition, 25 airlines operate 224 direct international flights to 14 countries from Hartsfield. There are 121 other public, 142 private, and 6 military airports in the state.

Georgia has 1,200 miles of interstate highways, 17,800 miles of state highways, 87,000 miles of paved city and county roads, and 5,400 miles of railroad track. In Savannah and Brunswick, the state's two major seaports, millions of tons of soybeans, winter wheat, a clay product called kaolin, cherries, and forest products are exported each year. Ships bringing sugar, heavy equipment, and steel arrive daily at the two ports.

The communications industry includes publications, radio, and television. The state has over 29 major daily newspapers with circulations ranging from 5,271 in Cordele to 400,000 in Atlanta. A total of 180 newspaper and 155 magazines are published in Georgia.

Television began in the state in 1948 with the introduction of WSB-TV. Today, Georgia's electronic broadcasting field includes twenty-five commercial stations. There are 310 radio stations which carry everything from "hard rock" music to twenty-four-hour news.

Georgia is so dependent on its utilities, which include electrical and gas energy, that, without them, the state would come to a standstill. An abundance of electrical power has been the most important factor in Georgia's growth. Eighty-seven percent of the

state's power is generated by plants that burn coal, oil, or natural gas. Seven percent comes from nuclear energy, and six percent from hydroelectric sources (water power). Plant Hatch at Baxley was Georgia's first nuclear-powered plant. Hydroelectric plants include Clark Hill and Hartwell dams on the Savannah River, Allatoona Dam on the Etowah River, and Buford and Walter F. George dams on the Chattahoochee River.

Professional and Personal Services

Several hundred thousand doctors, attorneys, repair persons, garage attendants, barbers, beauticians, home cleaners, and theater employees are considered part of the service industry. Such businesses and professions are for the purpose of making life healthier, more secure, and more enjoyable.

Tourism

Tourism is increasing in importance to Georgia's economy. There are 225,000 employees in the motel, hotel, restaurant, recreational, and tourist businesses. In 1988, 1,700,000 visitors spent $2,500,000,000 in Atlanta's convention industry, and $8,000,000,000 elsewhere in the state.

Movie and Television Productions

Another growing part of the state's economy is the production of movies and television programs. In the early 1970s, the movie *Deliverance*, based on the novel by James Dickey, was filmed around Tallulah Falls in North Georgia. Since that time, several

Top: *Over fifty two power plants in Georgia provide needed electricity to homes and businesses. The Scherer coal-powered plant pictured here is located in Monroe and Jones counties.* **Above:** *Money from tourism and business travel accounts for an important percentage of state income. One of the best-known hotels in the Atlanta area is the Ritz Carlton. The hotel has played host to presidents, foreign dignitaries, movie stars and rock 'n roll groups.*

successful movies, including *Roots*, *Smokey and the Bandit*, and *The Prize Fighter*, have been partly or totally filmed in Georgia. A number of television series, including "In the Heat of the Night," are filmed here each year. Today, Georgia ranks third, behind California and New York, as a site for motion picture and television filming.

In 1989, actress Kim Basinger purchased part of the town of Braselton for $30,000,000, with plans to build a major studio for movie productions. Due to its mild climate, diverse geographic locales, few labor restrictions, and Southern hospitality, Georgia's future in the movie industry looks secure.

Government

Government is a major link in the economic chain. It regulates businesses, builds roads for transporting goods, educates workers, and provides other needed services. Over 447,000 workers keep the state operating. Close to half that number are employed in the state's schools. Georgia is home to about 67,000 civilian employees of the federal government. The state's major military installations include Dobbins and Warner Robbins Air Force Bases, and Forts Benning, Gordon, and McPherson. Naval bases and ports in Savannah, Brunswick, Kings Bay, and the lower coastal area continue to expand.

Do You Remember?

1. What is the definition of "diversity"?
2. What are Georgia's major service industries?
3. How many Georgians are employed in tourism?
4. How many passengers change planes in Atlanta each year?

*Top left: Each morning approximately 60,500 educators begin the invaluable process of teaching Georgia's future leaders, citizens and consumers. **Top:** Paratrooper training at Fort Benning in Columbus, one of eleven military installations in Georgia. **Above:** Secretary of State Max Cleland gives an Outstanding Georgia Citizen award to actress Kim Basinger for her investment in Braselton.*

MANUFACTURING

Manufacturing is the second most important industry in Georgia. It accounts for over 550,000 jobs and 19 percent of the GSP. There are numerous industries associated with manufacturing.

TEXTILES

The manufacture of carpets, rugs, fabric, yarn, and thread makes Georgia a leader in textiles. The industry employs 107,000 in cities like Dalton, Griffin, Columbus, Thomaston, and Dublin. It produces a third of the world's carpets. Dalton, where more carpet is made than in any other United States city, is known as the "Carpet Capital of the World."

West Point Pepperell is Georgia's textile pioneer. Another early giant is the Bibb company, with headquarters in Macon. This company, founded in 1876, employs 5,600 people in 9 Georgia plants. Principal products include yarns for carpet and clothes, and items such as sheets, comforters, blankets, bedspreads, and draperies. The company is probably best known for juvenile lines such as Strawberry Shortcake, Annie, and the Dukes of Hazard.

The textile industry in Georgia accounts for well over one billion dollars a year in revenues and employs more than 100,000 workers.

CLOTHING

Georgia's clothing industry is located in 122 of Georgia's 159 counties and employs over 78,000 workers. There are over 458 firms manufacturing wearing apparel ranging from T-shirts to men's suits.

FOOD PRODUCTS

About 56,000 employees work in a variety of food plants which produce such items as poultry, eggs, soft drinks, canned fruit, bread and pastries, peanut butter, fruit cakes, pickles, barbecue, candy, and seafood. From Claxton, which is known for fruitcakes, to Gainesville, noted for poultry and eggs, to Brunswick, famous for seafood, food production is important to Georgia's strong economy.

Probably the most famous Georgia food production company is the Atlanta-based Coca-Cola Bottling Company. In 1990, their products accounted for 41.1 percent of the world's soft drink market. In 1990, each percentage point of the market was worth $444,000,000 in retail sales.

Each day, in sixty-seven counties, Georgia produces over 6,000,000 pounds of chicken, 16,000,000 eggs, and 84 tons of turkeys. Fifteen percent of the nation's frying chicken comes from Georgia. The poultry industry employs about 9,000 people.

Castleberry Foods cans such items as barbecue, chili, corned beef hash, and beef stew. The company produces over 450,000 pounds of food each day. Harris Foods, headquartered in Marietta, oversees Wendy's franchises. Marietta is also home to Georgia Mountain Water, which distributes spring water. For a sweet tooth, Bobs Candies in Albany is well known for their popular peppermint candy canes.

Tom's, based in Columbus, first packaged Tom's Roasted Peanuts for five cents a bag. Today, the company has 360 snack products and, with over 150,000 machines, ranks first in national vending.

In the early 1950s, Pennsylvanian Nick Pascarella and his wife were driving north from Florida, where they had tried to find a suitable place for a steak house restaurant. A tire blew out on his

Top and above: *Over fifteen percent of the nation's poultry comes from Georgia, and the state is second only to California in the number of eggs produced each day.*

car, and Pascarella was advised to go to a store on Walton Way in Augusta for a replacement.

While in the store, he told of his failure to find a restaurant site. The manager encouraged him to look no further. A year later, Pascarella opened his first Western Sizzlin down the street from the tire store. It was an immediate success. One of the early visitors to the restaurant was Athenian Jim Maupin. He was so impressed with the quality of food and service that, in 1965, he purchased a franchise to open an Athens Western Sizzlin. Today, there are over 650 Western Sizzlin steak houses in the United States.

Transportation Equipment

Over 50,500 Georgians work to produce transportation vehicles and equipment. Lockheed-Georgia in Marietta is the state's number one manufacturing employer with over 14,000 workers. This company builds the C-130 Hercules, a cargo carrier, and the world's largest airplane, the C-5A Galaxy.

Formerly the Bell Bomber factory in World War II, Lockheed-Georgia in Marietta is essential to the national economy and defense. The 76-acre facility is one of the largest in the world. What type of planes are made at Lockheed and why are they important to the national defense?

Left: In more crowded population areas like Atlanta, condominiums are becoming increasingly popular. Why do you think this is true?
Below: Close to 15,000 construction workers in Georgia depend on good weather, a solid housing market, and increasing population to make a living. Their specialized skills are essential to a growing state.

The Blue Bird Body Company in Fort Valley is another major transportation company. Blue Bird sells one out of three, or 12,000, school buses bought in the United States each year. It also makes the Wanderlodge, a luxury camper home that sells for about $200,000.

Both Ford and General Motors have assembly line plants in Atlanta.

Chemicals

There are 371 chemical plants in Georgia. Most are located in Fulton and DeKalb counties. These chemicals are used in medications, polishes, soaps, and detergents. In 1990, 21,748 employees worked in this industry.

Electrical Equipment

Companies like Scientific-Atlanta and General Electric employ 23,953 Georgians. They make such items as household appliances, batteries, communication cables, transformers, and video games.

Construction

The construction industry accounts for only five percent of the GSP. However, without it, other industries could not build or expand. Close to 147,000 workers are employed in construction. They include contractors, carpenters, electricians, painters, and people with other related skills.

Mining

Mining is the smallest manufacturing employer with 8,000 workers. However, it is important to larger industries. Georgia ranks first in the nation in the mining of granite and marble, and first in the world in the production of kaolin.

Crushed granite, used mainly for highway construction, is produced in forty quarries located in the Piedmont and Eastern Highlands area of the state. Elberton is known as the "Granite Capital of the World." Here, 1,800 persons make over 150,000 granite monuments, markers, and mausoleums each year.

Marble is located in small areas around Tate in southeast Pickens County. There is enough marble at Tate to last for the next 3,000 years. Large blocks are used for carvings like the Lincoln Memorial. Crushed marble is put in roofing and agricultural lime. It is also a filler for over 2,000 products, including toothpaste and poultry feed.

Kaolin, found along a narrow band from Macon to Augusta, is a fine white clay used mainly as a coating for paper. It gives magazines and books a shiny look. Kaolin is also used in making china, paints, rubber, plastic, cement, many detergents, and fertilizers. Ninety percent of the nation's exported kaolin comes from Georgia.

Above: More granite monuments and markers are made in a twenty-mile radius of Elberton than any other location in the nation. Ninety percent of the output of the thirty-five quarries are cemetery memorials. *Right:* Georgia granite on the docks at Savannah waits for shipment overseas.

Georgia also has rich deposits of **bauxite**, **manganese**, fullers earth, limestone, and phosphate. Until 1849, when large amounts of gold were discovered in California, Georgia was the leading gold-producing state. There were mines throughout North Georgia, particularly near Dahlonega. Today, gold is scarce and the cost of mining it high. It is now found by running water through a trough to separate the gold from sand, or in dredging operations. In Lumpkin County, tourists sometimes pan for gold.

There is a strong likelihood that the page you are touching and reading right now was coated with kaolin, a fine white clay mined in Georgia. The industry is worth over 500 million dollars a year.

Do You Remember?
1. Where is the granite capital of the world?
2. How many Georgians are employed in manufacturing?
3. Where is the C-130 Hercules manufactured?
4. Who ranks number one in the nation in the number of snack vending machines?
5. What Georgia business got started because of a flat tire?

As Georgia's leading cash crop, the peanut harvest varies from 1.5 to 2.16 billion pounds of peanuts a year. The state leads the nation in the production of this popular food. The next peanut butter and jelly sandwich you make could have been made from peanuts grown right here in southwestern Georgia.

AGRICULTURE

Agriculture, including farming, fishing, and forestry, accounts for one percent of the GSP.

FARMING

Before World War II, Georgia was primarily an agrarian state. Today, Georgians work on 49,600 farms which utilize only 4,761,250 acres to raise crops or poultry, or provide grazing for cattle. The state ranks first in the nation in the production of peanuts and pecans. Apples, tobacco, peaches, watermelons, and soybeans are other important crops. Cotton accounts for less than two percent of the agricultural production of the state. Farmers raise over twenty types of vegetables, and corn is grown on nearly every farm. Two of the most valuable crops are sweet potatoes and Vidalia onions.

By far the leading farming activity in Georgia is the production of poultry. There are a large number of poultry processing plants located in the state.

Few areas in Georgia are not involved in some type of agriculture. The chart below shows farm production by leading counties.

Farm Product	County
Corn	Grady County
Wheat	Sumter County
Vegetables	Decatur County
Broilers	Barrow County
Turkeys	Oconee County
Cattle	Mitchell County
Apples	Gilmer County
Pecans	Dougherty County
Soybeans	Burke County
Peanuts	Worth County
Tobacco	Colquitt County
Hogs and Pigs	Colquitt County
Dairy Farms	Morgan County
Peaches	Peach County

Below: Once only a late spring and early summer delicacy for Georgians, today the sweet, "no tears" Vidalia onion is shipped throughout the country. In 1990, Vidalia onion farmers in the Toombs county area found a way to preserve the onion so it could be sold year-round. **Bottom:** *Third nationally in the production of peaches, Georgia first started cultivating this delicious fruit in 1899. During the summer it is difficult to drive more than a few miles without seeing a familiar roadside peach stand.*

One of Georgia's oldest towns, Darien was first settled in 1736 and became a post-revolutionary port of entry in 1816. Today many residents in this small picturesque community depend on the shrimping industry for their livelihood.

FISHING

In 1986, Georgia's commercial fishing industry was valued at $24,500,000. Shrimp is the most important catch, crab is second, and finfish third. Darien, Savannah, and Brunswick are the leading commercial fishing ports.

A fairly new fishing enterprise is **aquaculture**, where ponds are built to raise trout or catfish. The fish are fed until they are large enough to harvest and sell commercially.

FORESTRY

Forests cover 70 percent of Georgia with 250 types of trees. Cut, they would make a 569-feet-high stack across all four lanes of Interstate 75 from Tennessee to Florida.

The state's 24,000,000 commercial forest acres rank it first in the country. Georgia has many forest-related industries which employ about 80,000 people and contribute $8,600,000,000 to the economy each year.

Georgia has a long history of producing "naval stores" or "pitch" (resin) from slash or longleaf pines. This resin is used to fill the seams of wooden ships. Tar, also produced, is used to coat the wood in ships to prevent rotting. Today, "gum naval stores" include turpentine, which is used as a paint thinner or solvent, and rosin. Rosin is the yellowish to dark brown resin used on violin bows. Gum naval stores now produce only about $3,000,000 in income each year. The leading forest products today are pine pulpwood and saw timber. Pulpwood is worth $386,000,000 a year, and saw timber is valued at $288,000,000.

Eight out of every ten trees harvested in Georgia are southern yellow pines. Much of the success of Georgia's forest industry is due to the efforts of Milledgeville native Dr. Charles Herty. He showed that pine pulp could be processed and bleached easily for a variety of uses. Today, Georgia leads the nation in the production of pulp. Each time you read a newspaper, magazine or book, load groceries in a paper bag, or write a letter, there is a strong possibility that the paper came from a Georgia pulp mill.

Union Camp, located in Savannah, is the world's largest pulp and paper mill. Each day the mill manufactures 2,850 tons of paper. Neighboring Savannah box plants produce an average of 4,000,000 boxes a year.

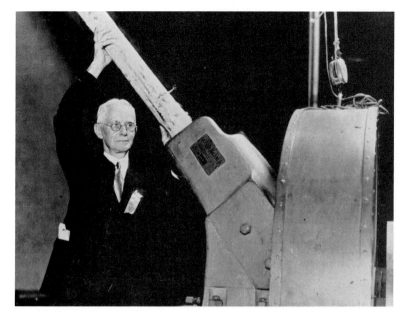

Left: Dr. Charles Herty, a chemistry professor at the University of Georgia, found an efficient way of removing turpentine from trees that led to an increase in Georgia's production of naval stores. He later discovered a way for paper pulp from pine wood to be used in newsprint and paper products. *Below:* Since it takes 15 to 45 years for a tree to grow from a seedling to harvest size, attempts are being made to carefully supervise the hardwood logging industry to avoid stripping the land of its most valuable renewable resource.

Lumber and plywood are also important forest products. Related industries employ about 16,000 workers. Such items as houses, cabinets, and flooring are made from Georgia's pine and hardwood trees. Furniture and mobile home industries employ over 9,000 Georgians.

Another major forest industry is firewood production, valued at $136,000,000 a year. Trees used for firewood are usually hardwoods, such as oak, birch, or hickory.

Forest-related industries are important to Georgia's economy because of the large number of products used daily made from trees. Forests are a renewable resource. Each time a tree is cut, another can be planted. Depending on its type, it takes fifteen to forty-five years for a tree to grow from a seedling to a size for harvesting.

Do You Remember?

1. What is the leading farming activity in Georgia?
2. What Georgia county leads the state in the production of peanuts?
3. What is aquaculture?
4. What is the value of Georgia's forest-related industries?
5. What are two leading forest products? How is each used?

Thousands of Georgians took a day off from work on September 18, 1990 in anticipation of the announcement naming a host city for the 1996 Summer Olympics. When Atlanta was given the nod, the celebration started in full force and continued for several days.

THE SUMMER OLYMPICS FORMALLY MAKE ATLANTA AN INTERNATIONAL CITY

On Tuesday, September 18, 1990, at 7:45 a.m., many Georgians were packed into Underground Atlanta. People there, and almost everywhere else in the state, were tuned to radios or television sets waiting for the "big announcement." In Tokyo, Japan, Atlanta Olympic Organizing Committee head Billy Payne was joined by Andrew Young, Mayor Maynard Jackson, Vince Dooley, and 300 Atlanta boosters, which included middle and high school students.

For three years prior to this date, groups in Atlanta and Savannah had planned, talked, hosted parties, and taken International Olympic Committee members around the state, in an effort to gain the bid for the 1996 Summer Olympics. When the president of the committee stood in front of the microphone, fingers were crossed, stomachs were filled with butterflies, and mouths were dry from nerves and stress. The time for the announcement had arrived! "The International Olympic Committee has selected to host the 1996 Summer Olympics, the city of ...... Atlanta!"

There were shouts of joy as thousands of Georgians celebrated their instant transition into an international state. Journalists and tourists from all over the world will come for the games.

The cost for hosting the Olympics is expected to be well over $1,000,000,000. Half of this will come from corporate sponsors and ticket sales, and the rest from radio and television broadcasting rights. No Olympic expenses are to be met by taxpayers.

It will be necessary to build stadiums for the games and housing for the athletes, so there will be an estimated 44,895 jobs in construction. About 38,860 people will work in service industries providing transportation, hotel accommodations, and food. At least 70,000 volunteers will serve as unofficial hosts and hostesses. It is expected that 625,000 visitors will spend about $568,000,000 at the Olympics.

It is estimated that, during the two weeks of the games, $86,000,000 will be spent on souvenirs alone. After the games, the 9,500 units of Olympic housing on North Avenue in Atlanta will be used as dormitories for Georgia Tech, the Atlanta University Center, and Georgia State University.

O F • S P E C I A L • I N T E R E S T

GEORGIA, A STATE FOR FOREIGN INVESTORS

Foreign investments are playing an increasingly important role in Georgia's economy. For example:

➤ A sixth of Georgia's farm products are exported.

➤ Forty-one countries operate foreign consulates or trade offices in the state.

➤ In 1988, Georgia schools enrolled over 13,000 students who spoke one of seventy languages other than English.

➤ Japan has 316 companies operating in Georgia, Great Britain has 201, West Germany has 161, Canada has 137, and the Netherlands has 116.

➤ Georgia ranks ninth in the nation in the number of employees working in foreign-owned plants (about 82,000). Japanese sites in Georgia employ 10,900 persons.

➤ Georgia ranks sixth in the nation in the number of foreign-owned acres (709,000).

➤ In terms of capital investment, Canada has $1,400,000,000 invested in the state, followed by the United Kingdom with $1,300,000,000, and Japan with $875,000,000.

➤ Foreign investors like Georgia because it is close to markets, suppliers, and key industries, has ample air transportation, good living conditions, a mild climate, strong regional growth, and a good quality, moderately-priced labor market.

WHAT'S IN A DOLLAR?

The Great Seal of the United States, in the right-hand circle above, has its own intricate symbolism. The bald eagle, our national bird, holds a scroll in its beak. In its feet the eagle holds an olive branch and 13 arrows. The olive branch has 13 leaves and 13 fruits for the 13 original colonies. It also symbolizes the power of the nation to make peace. The 13 arrows indicate the power of the nation to make war. Above the eagle's head is a crest containing 13 stars, also representing the original colonies.

1. Circle on left: The motto Annuit Coeptis means "He has favored Our Undertaking" and symbolizes the religious faith of the founding fathers.
2. The bright triangle around the eye was an ancient symbol standing for the total knowledge of humanity.
3. The unfinished pyramid signifies a nation yet unfinished. The pyramid also stands for strength and endurance. On the base are the Roman Numerals for 1776.
4. The caption Novus Ordo Seclarum meaning "A New Order of the Ages" describes the revolutionary eighteenth century concept of the rise of a new nation founded on the belief in freedom.
5. Circle on right: The group of 13 stars formed into 1 star stands for the U.S. motto—"E Pluribus Unum" or, "out of many, one". The light around it stands for a new nation that is taking its rightful place among the nations of the world.
6. The American bald eagle is the national bird and symbolizes power. The shield, with 13 stripes on a blue background represents the 13 original states that became one under the United States Congress.

CHAPTER REVIEW

Summary

In the last half of the twentieth century, there have been significant economic changes. Georgia's economy was strong after World War II because of the large number of wartime industries in the state. Today, the state has a very diversified economy.

Service industries account for seventy-four percent of Georgia's Gross State Product. Services industries include wholesale and retail trade, finance, insurance, and real estate, transportation, communications, utilities, tourism, the motion picture industry, and personal services.

Manufacturing industries are ranked second, and account for nineteen percent of the GSP. These industries include textiles, clothing, food production, transportation equipment, and mining.

Agriculture is ranked third in Georgia's GSP. Georgia is the nation's leading producer of peanuts and pecans. It is the nation's third largest producer of corn. Forest-raised products and naval stores are still vital to Georgia's economy, and are a major international export item. Georgia is the world's major exporter of kaolin.

Increasingly, foreign investments in Georgia have added to the strength of the state's economy. Economists predict that the upcoming 1996 Olympics in Atlanta and Savannah will boost the state's economy by approximately $80,000,000.

People, Places, and Terms

Identify, define, or state the importance of each of the following.

1. Dalton
2. naval stores
3. Elberton
4. Atlanta Olympic Organizing Committee
5. goods
6. services
7. diversification
8. Gilmer County
9. Vidalia onions
10. barter

The Main Idea

1. Name the industries in which Georgia ranks first in the nation.
2. What is Georgia's largest industry?
3. How does the federal government contribute to Georgia's economy?

Extend Your Thinking

Write a short essay to answer each question.

1. If you were elected governor of Georgia, what would you do to expand the state's economy?
2. If you were head of the Atlanta Olympic Committee, what are some of the things you would do to help Georgia's economy over a long-term basis?

DID YOU KNOW . . . ?

. . . One of Georgia's millionaires, Herman Russell, owns H.D. Russell Construction Company which is the fourth largest black-owned company in the United States?

. . . Eleven of the top one hundred black-owned businesses in America are located in Atlanta?

. . . Some experts predict that by the year 2000, the average work week will be 25 hours rather than the current 40 hours?

CHAPTER SEVENTEEN

THE PROCESS OF GOVERNMENT

Let us say this much to ourselves, not only with our lips but in our hearts. Let us say this: I myself am a part of democracy — I myself must accept responsibilities. Democracy is not merely a privilege to be enjoyed — it is a trust to keep and maintain."

— Stephen Vincent Benet

THE UNITED STATES OF AMERICA is a republic. A republic is a political order which has an elected head of state instead of a king or queen. The United States is governed as a constitutional democracy. A democracy is "a form of government in which power is in the hands of the people either directly or through elected representatives."

When George Washington became the first President of the United States on April 30, 1789, the new Constitution went into effect. Article VI of that document states that the Constitution, and laws and treaties made under the authority of the United States, shall be the supreme law of the land. At that time, the nation's population was about three million. Today the federal government must protect the rights and provide for the welfare of over 246,000,000 people. As our population grows and the needs of citizens change, it is necessary to add to the Constitution. Such additions are called amendments.

Coated with gold leaf from Dahlonega, the impressive Georgia State Capitol in Atlanta houses the General Assembly, the State Museum of Service and Industry, the Hall of Flags, and the governor's office.

LEVELS OF GOVERNMENT

Government is carried out at three levels: federal, state, and local. Each level is separate, but their duties often overlap. The chart below is an overview of our political management system.

Agencies	Elected By	Functions
FEDERAL		
Legislative Senate House of Representatives	Popular vote in each state	➤ Makes laws for the nation
Executive President Vice President	Electoral vote	➤ Approves laws ➤ Commander-In-Chief of armed forces ➤ Makes treaties
Judicial Supreme Court Court of Appeals District Courts	Appointed by President	➤ Interprets laws and United States Constitution
STATE		
Legislative Senate House of Representatives	Popular vote in state districts	➤ Makes laws for state
Executive Governor Lieutenant governor	Statewide popular vote	➤ Can veto state legislative bills ➤ Heads state militia
Judicial State supreme court Superior court State court	Generally elected by popular vote	➤ Interprets state laws ➤ Passes sentences
COUNTY/CITY		
County commissioners	Popular vote in county districts	➤ Provides services to county residents (i.e. police, fire, sanitation, schools, etc.)
Mayor and city council	Popular vote of residents of city (mayor sometimes elected by city council or commisssioners)	➤ Provides services to city residents (i.e. police, fire, sanitation, schools, etc.)
City council and city manager (city manager appointed by council)	Council elected by popular vote of residents of city. City manager appointed by Council	➤ Provides services to city residents (i.e. police, fire, sanitation, schools, etc.)

By 1990, there were twenty-six amendments to the original Constitution. The first of these reads:

Congress shall make no law respecting an establishment of religion, or prohibiting the free exercise thereof; or abridging the freedom of speech, or of the press; or the right of the people peaceably to assemble, and to petition the Government for a redress of grievances.

These rights, commonly called the Five Freedoms, belong to citizens of the United States under our democratic form of government.

THE DUTIES OF GOVERNMENT

In a democracy such as ours, the government has many tasks. Most of them are part of three main duties: 1) to protect individual freedom; 2) to provide for the common welfare of the citizens; and, 3) to regulate the nation's commerce.

Do You Remember?

1. What is a democracy?
2. When did the United States Constitution go into effect?
3. By 1990, how many amendments were there to the original Constitution?
4. What is the definition of the term "amendment"?
5. What are the Five Freedoms?
6. What is one of the duties of government?
7. What was the population of our nation in 1789?

The United States Capitol in Washington, D.C. was designed by amateur architect Dr. William Thornton, who received $500 and a lot in the city for his work. The building was begun in 1792 but was burned by the British in the War of 1812. By 1863, the capitol had been rebuilt and included the present House and Senate wings.

THE FEDERAL GOVERNMENT

The federal government is divided into three branches: **legislative, executive,** and **judicial.** The Constitution gives different tasks to each of the branches. There are fifty-seven federal agencies within the three branches. Between 2,900,000 and 3,200,000 people are employed by the United States government.

THE LEGISLATIVE BRANCH

The legislative branch of the federal government is called Congress. Congress has two parts: the Senate and the House of Representatives.

The swearing-in ceremony for newly-elected United States congressmen is a distinguished and solemn affair as our representatives promise to uphold the Constitution of the United States and to pass laws that are for the benefit of all American citizens.

Senators are elected by popular vote to serve six year terms of office. Each state elects two senators.

The number of representatives for each state is decided by that state's population. Representatives serve two year terms and, like senators, are elected by popular vote. Georgia sends eleven members to the House of Representatives.

The expressed powers of Congress are stated in the United States Constitution. Congress also has implied powers, allowing it to make any laws needed to carry out its expressed powers.

THE POWERS OF CONGRESS

Expressed Powers

Congress can:
1. regulate commerce with foreign nations and among the states;
2. levy and collect revenues or taxes;
3. coin and issue money;
4. borrow money on the credit of the United States;
5. establish bankruptcy rules;

6. establish naturalization processes for citizenship;
7. establish post offices and post roads, or routes used for the delivery of the mail;
8. issue copyrights and patents which protect the rights of authors and inventors;
9. regulate weights and measures;
10. establish federal courts, to define and punish piracy on the high seas, to define and punish offenses against the law of nations (to punish for treason);
11. punish counterfeiters of federal money and securities;
12. legislate for territories of the United States, such as the District of Columbia, and to provide for and maintain national parks, federal buildings, and other federally owned lands;
13. declare war and make rules for warfare and the operation of the armed services.

Implied Powers

Congress has the authority to make all laws necessary to carry out the expressed powers granted in the Constitution. One important example is that Congress has the implied power to set penalties for the breaking of any federal law.

*Below: Sixth Congressional District, Republican Newt Gingrich serves as the House Minority Whip in 1992. **Bottom:** As one of Georgia's two U.S. Senators, Democrat Sam Nunn serves as chairman of the Armed Forces Committee, one of the most influential positions in Washington.*

Elected as the nation's forty-first president in 1988, Texan George Bush carried forty of the country's fifty states. He ran on a platform of stabilizing the economy, improving education and waging war on drugs. Bush received worldwide recognition in 1991 for his leadership of the coalition of nations involved in the Persian Gulf War.

THE EXECUTIVE BRANCH

The executive branch of the federal government is made up of the office of President, the office of Vice President, cabinet departments, and agencies such as the National Security Council, Council on Environmental Quality, and the Council of Economic Advisors.

The Constitution provides that electors chosen by the people shall elect the President and Vice President. An 1845 act of Congress called this body the "college of electors." It is commonly known as the electoral college. Today, a vote for a presidential candidate is also a vote for his electors. Therefore, the candidate who wins the popular vote in each state also wins that state's electoral votes. Each state has the same number of electors that it has members in Congress. However, no member of Congress or any other federal employee may be an elector. Georgia has 13 of the 538 electoral votes. It takes 270 electoral votes to elect the President and the Vice President.

The President is the head of the executive branch of government. It is his duty to see that the Constitution, laws and treaties, and decisions of federal courts are enforced. To make this possible, the President has executive powers.

THE POWERS OF THE PRESIDENT

The President can:

1. appoint and dismiss thousands of federal employees including ambassadors, federal judges, judges of the Supreme Court, ministers and consuls, cabinet officers and those who serve under them. Major presidential appointments are made with the consent of the Senate;
2. act as commander-in-chief of the nation's armed forces;
3. call extra sessions of Congress;
4. recommend legislation;
5. veto bills;
6. sign legislative bills into law;
7. receive diplomatic representatives;
8. enter into treaties or compacts with foreign governments, with the approval of the Senate;
9. issue proclamations, such as recognizing a sports team, honoring astronauts, or congratulating a 4-H group;
10. pardon all offenses against the United States except in cases of impeachment, where a pardon can never be granted.

Above: Two men that President Bush relied on heavily during the Gulf War crisis were Secretary of Defense Dick Cheney and Secretary of State James Baker. *Left:* Former United States Senator and current Vice President under George Bush, James Danforth "Dan" Quayle of Indiana is shown here conferring with the Emir of Kuwait during the Persian Gulf crisis.

Since its inception in 1778 and confirmation the following year, the United States Supreme Court has been the highest court in the land. Members are appointed by the President and confirmed by the Senate to serve lifetime terms of office. This group portrait shows the 1991 Supreme Court, led by Chief Justice William Rehnquist (seated center).

THE JUDICIAL BRANCH

The third branch of the federal government is the judicial branch. Its duties include deciding on the meaning of the Constitution and laws. It also sees that people receive fair treatment "in accordance with . . . law." The judicial branch protects individual citizens from any ill treatment by the other branches of government. The Supreme Court and all lower federal courts make up the judicial branch. The Supreme Court has a chief justice and eight associate justices. These men and women are appointed by the President with the consent of the Senate. Congress authorizes the Supreme Court to review decisions of all lower-ranking federal courts and to review the decisions of the highest-ranking state courts. When the Supreme Court decides a case on constitutional grounds, that decision becomes the guideline, both for all lower courts to follow and for laws that deal with similar issues.

The greatest power of the Supreme Court is that of judicial review, or the ability to set aside the actions of the legislative or executive branches of any government agency. The Court can declare laws or presidential acts unconstitutional. The chief justice of the Supreme Court presides over impeachment proceedings against a President. The Court can prevent executive action through injunctions, or court orders, which forbid such action.

The middle level of the judicial system is the court of appeals. Congress divided the nation into twelve judicial circuits, and each circuit has a court of appeals. A court of appeals may have from four to twenty-four judgeships, depending on the work load in a given circuit.

Courts of appeals are called appellate courts. This means they review cases tried in lower courts, or the judgments of administrative agencies. There are no juries or witnesses in appellate courts. They only hear appeals of decisions made by trial courts, which do have juries and witnesses.

There are ninety-four district courts that rank below the courts of appeals. They hear cases of civil and criminal violations of federal laws. District courts are the only federal courts which use juries and witnesses in trials.

The final part of the federal judicial system is a series of courts created by Congress to deal with special kinds of cases. The United States Tax Court hears disputes between citizens and the Internal Revenue Service. The Court of Military Appeals reviews military court-martial convictions. The Court of International Trade decides civil suits against the United States involving trade with other countries. The United States Claims Court handles suits against the United States because of acts of Congress or contracts with the government. There are also bankruptcy courts that operate under the supervision of United States district courts.

For the first 145 years, the Supreme Court had no permanent home and was moved from building to building. It was not until 1935 that the Supreme Court had its own building.

SEPARATION OF POWERS AND THE SYSTEM OF CHECKS AND BALANCES

The men who wrote our Constitution did not want any one branch of government to become more powerful than the other two. They divided the functions of government among the three branches. The writers also provided for checks and balances to keep the branches of equal importance. For example, the power to pass a bill was given to the legislative branch, but the executive branch must either sign the bill into law or veto it so it does not become law. The judicial branch cannot write bills or sign them into law, but it can declare a law unconstitutional. In that way, each branch of government has a check on the power of the others.

LEGISLATIVE CHECKS ON THE EXECUTIVE AND JUDICIAL BRANCHES

Executive
1. Congress must approve presidential appointments.
2. Congress controls the budget and money appropriations.
3. Congress can impeach and remove a President from office.
4. Congress can pass laws over the President's veto.

HOW FEDERAL LAWS ARE MADE

1. A bill can be suggested by anyone, including special interest groups, the President, a member of Congress, or a government agency. It is written in special legal language.
2. A Congressman introduces the proposed bill. If the bill originates in the House of Representatives, it is placed in a container called a "hopper" on the House clerk's desk. In the Senate, the bill is handed to the Senate clerk. The bill is read and given a number. For example, HR 125 would be the 125th bill introduced during that session in the House of Representatives.
3. The bill is referred to a committee. The legislators on the committee study the bill. They may hold public hearings where people can speak for or against the bill. After they study the bill, the committee may decide to send it to the House or Senate as it is, rewrite it, or "kill" it. Killing a bill means it is not voted out of committee.
4. If the committee so decides, the bill is "reported out" favorably or unfavorably to the full House or Senate for a vote.
5. The bill from the committee is scheduled on the calendar for discussion in the House or the Senate.

6. The bill is read and debated. During debate the bill can be amended or changed.
7. The bill is read a third time and put to a vote. There are several ways a vote can be taken. One is a voice vote where "aye" or "nay" is shouted out by the members of the House or Senate. If a division vote is taken, members stand and are counted for or against the bill. A record vote is by roll call. Each member's name is called and his vote recorded.
8. Once a bill passes either the House of Representatives or the Senate, it is sent to the other group. There the same steps to passage are repeated.
9. If the House and Senate pass different versions of the same bill, a conference committee of members from both houses is appointed to combine both versions into a single bill. When the conference committee members agree, the bill is sent to the House and Senate to be passed.
10. Finally, the bill goes to the President. If he agrees with the bill, he signs it into law. If he does not agree, he vetoes it and returns it to Congress. Congress can overturn a presidential veto by a two-thirds vote in both houses. If a veto is overturned, the bill becomes law.

HOW THE U.S. CONSTITUTION IS AMENDED

There have been twenty-six amendments to the original Constitution since it was adopted by the thirteen original states in 1788. The Constitution can be amended by following one of four different routes.

Route One

1) An amendment to the Constitution is proposed by a two-thirds vote of both houses of Congress.
2) A proposed amendment is ratified by the legislatures of at least three-fourths of the states.
3) The Constitution is amended.

Route Two

1) An amendment to the Constitution is proposed by a two-thirds vote of both houses of Congress.
2) Special conventions are held in the states. At least three-fourths of them must ratify the proposed amendment.

3) The amendment is added to the Constitution.

Route Three

1) An amendment is proposed by a national convention called by the Congress at the request of two-thirds of the state legislatures.
2) Special conventions are held in the states. Three-fourths of them must ratify the proposed amendment.
3) The amendment is added to the Constitution.

Note: Route 3 was used in the adoption of the original United States Constitution.

Route Four

1) An amendment is proposed by a national convention called by the Congress at the request of two-thirds of the state legislatures.
2) The proposed amendment is ratified by at least three-fourths of the state legislatures.
3) The amendment becomes part of the Constitution.

Judicial

1. Congress must vote to confirm the President's judicial appointments.
2. Congress can impeach and remove federal judges from office for wrongdoing.
3. Congress can change laws overturned by the courts, or initiate a constitutional amendment.
4. Congress can restrict the jurisdiction of courts to deal with certain types of cases.
5. Congress can create more court systems or do away with existing ones.
6. Congress can determine the times and places where federal courts hold sessions.

President from 1901-1909, Teddy Roosevelt, the first president to ride in an automobile, tried in his own unique way to circumvent the system of checks and balances. After reading the text to find out what Roosevelt said, decide the message he was trying to give Congress.

EXECUTIVE CHECKS ON THE LEGISLATIVE AND JUDICIAL BRANCHES

Legislative
1. The President can veto congressional legislation.

Judicial
2. The President has the power to appoint or remove federal judges.

JUDICIAL CHECKS ON THE POWERS OF THE LEGISLATIVE AND EXECUTIVE BRANCHES

Legislative
1. The Supreme Court can declare laws unconstitutional.

Executive
1. The Supreme Court can declare presidential acts unconstitutional.
2. The Supreme Court can prevent executive actions through injunctions.
3. The chief justice of the Supreme Court presides over the impeachment proceedings of a President.

Checks and balances are meant to keep branches of government equal, but sometimes people find ways around them. For example, it is said that President Teddy Roosevelt wanted to send the United States Navy around the world. He wished the sailors to gain experience, and also to let other nations see the strength of our forces. Congress did not like Roosevelt's plan, and refused to provide the money. Roosevelt is said to have replied, "Very well, the existing appropriation will carry the navy halfway around the world and if Congress chooses to leave it on the other side, all right."

Do You Remember?
1. Which federal government branch has the power to declare war?
2. How many ways are there to amend the Constitution?
3. How many electoral votes does Georgia have?
4. What check does the judicial branch have over the executive branch?

HOW THE FEDERAL GOVERNMENT HELPS GEORGIA

Georgians, like other Americans, pay taxes to the federal government. In turn, the federal government uses part of this money to help the state. Georgia receives about $2,830 federal dollars per capita (each head or person) each year. Even though some states receive larger amounts, Georgia gets more federal dollars than her citizens pay in income taxes.

How does federal money come back into the state? The federal government builds and keeps up the interstate road system and all other federal highways in the state. About $5,333,000 comes into Georgia each year as social security benefits and federal and military retirement payments. The federal government makes sure we have postal service and the service of federal courts. It takes care of the national forests and parks, such as Oconee National Forest and Chattahoochee National Forest. Your own school may receive some federal money. About ten percent of what is spent by most public school systems comes from the national government.

The military presence in Georgia takes a large number of federal

Georgia can boast of nine national parks and eight national wildlife refuges. One of the most famous is the largest national wildlife refuge in the eastern United States, the Okefenokee Swamp. Why is it important for the government to offer a refuge area to endangered and threatened species?

Georgia's 1200 miles of interstate highway allows travelers to drive from the Florida border to the Tennessee border without ever leaving an expressway. Interstate highways in the state include I-16 shown here, I-20, I-75, I-85, I-285, and I-475.

dollars. Georgia is home to eleven military bases. They employ over 120,000 civilian and military personnel who are paid over $2,000,000,000 a year. The state's newest military facility is the Naval Submarine Base at Kings Bay in Camden County. It cost over $1,500,000,000 to build the base, making it the most expensive peacetime building project in the Navy's 216 year history. Industries in Georgia receive close to four million dollars a year for military contracts, mostly to build aircraft. Because of the defense department dollars, Georgia ranks tenth in the nation in the amount of federal money received.

Several of the major tourist attractions in the state are maintained by the federal government. Visitors can drive through the 396-acre Okefenokee National Wildlife Refuge and Wilderness Area watching for wood ducks, storks, alligators, and hundreds of flowering plants and trees. They can wander along the beaches and marshes of Cumberland Island National Seashore and photograph a bald eagle, or picnic in the maritime live oak forest.

Tourists interested in military history can visit the sites of Civil War battles at Chickamauga-Chattanooga National Military Park in northeast Georgia. They can also visit Kennesaw Mountain National Battlefield Park north of Atlanta. Along the state's coastline, visitors can tour the site of James Oglethorpe's fortified town, Fort Frederica, or touch cannon fired during the Civil War at Fort Pulaski on Tybee Island.

Those interested in the Georgia Indians who lived 8,000 years ago can view artifacts at Ocmulgee National Monument in Macon. There are over forty-two national historic landmarks in the state. One of Georgia's newest national historic sites is the home of Dr. Martin Luther King, Jr. in Atlanta. Visitors can tour the twenty-three acres that include Dr. King's birthplace, boyhood home, church, and memorial gravesite.

Do You Remember?

1. How many military bases are located in Georgia?
2. About how much money does Georgia receive per capita each year?
3. What military historical sites in Georgia are maintained by the federal government?
4. Where does Georgia rank in terms of federal dollars received?

GEORGIA'S GOVERNMENT

Georgia was one of the thirteen colonies which became states after the American Revolution. These states were governed under the rules and laws of the new United States of America.

Georgia adopted its first state constitution in 1777. In 1983, Georgians approved the state's tenth constituion. Even though there have been changes in the bodies of the constitutions, their purpose has remained the same. The constitution states:

To perpetuate the principles of free government, insure justice to all, preserve peace, promote the interest and happiness of the citizens and of the family, and transmit to posterity the enjoyment of liberty, we the people of Georgia,

Sworn in as Georgia's 79th governor in 1991, Zell Miller served as Georgia's lieutenant governor longer than anyone in the state's history—from 1974 until his election as governor. In what ways could Miller's tenure as lieutenant governor help him succeed as governor?

One of the governor's main duties is to sign or veto bills passed by the state legislature. Here, Governor Joe Frank Harris signs a bill in the capitol rotunda.

relying upon the protection and guidance of Almighty God, do ordain and establish this Constitution.

Georgia's constitution claims, "All government, of right, originates with the people, is founded upon their will only, and is instituted for the good of the whole. Public officers are the trustees and servants of the people and are at all times amenable to them." In other words, any power the government has is given by the citizens, and is for the good of everyone. Persons elected to public office in state government work for the people, and are accountable to the voters for their actions.

The constitution further states: "The people of this state have the inherent right of regulating their internal government. Government is instituted for the protection, security and benefit of the people; and at all times they have the right to alter or reform the same whenever the public good may require it." Therefore, Georgia's government is meant to serve the people, and the constitution allows the people to change the government when it fails to serve their needs.

The constitution gives voters the right to control state government by electing state officials. Citizens also may suggest laws which might improve the way the state is governed.

Georgia, like the nation, has three branches of government: executive, legislative, and judicial. The tasks of these branches are, in many ways, like those of the federal branches.

THE EXECUTIVE BRANCH OF GOVERNMENT

The largest branch of state government is the executive branch. The governor is the chief executive officer of the state. Since the end of Reconstruction, Georgia's governors have been members of the Democratic party.

The governor is elected by a majority popular vote for a four-year term. The law allows governors to serve two consecutive terms, so it is possible for one person to be the state's chief executive officer for eight years. After a second term, an individual may wait four or more years, then be elected again.

The governor's salary was $88,872 in 1990. The state also pays for the governor's travel, and for the expenses of the executive mansion.

The Georgia Constitution describes the governor's formal powers. They can be classified in three ways.

Executive powers include the right to appoint state officials, and the right to see that civil and criminal laws are enforced.

Legislative powers include the right to send requests and messages to the legislature, and the right to veto bills so they do not become laws. The governor may also call special sessions of the legislature.

Judicial powers include the right to pardon persons convicted of crimes, and the right to appoint state justices in the event of unexpired terms.

Other formal powers include:
a) managing the state's budget;
b) directing the attorney general to act as a representative of the state in lower court cases involving state law;
c) presenting annual "State of the State" addresses to the legislature;
d) preparing budget bills for consideration by the house of representatives;
e) acting as commander-in-chief of the Georgia National Guard;
f) heading the state's civil defense units;
g) sending Georgia Highway Patrol officers and the Georgia Bureau of Investigation into communities in times of danger.

The first governor's mansion in Milledgeville cost $50,000 although in 1935, the Georgia General Assembly had appropriated only $10,000. Today the home of the governor is located on West Paces Ferry Road in Atlanta. It serves a double function as the official residence of the governor and as a center for public functions such as state dinners and receptions.

One of the primary duties of the lieutenant governor is to preside over the state senate. Here, Lt. Governor Pierre Howard (third from left) discusses the 1991 state budget with (left to right) Speaker of the Georgia House of Representatives Tom Murphy, Senator Don Johnston and Representative Terry Coleman.

Georgia's governor has many informal powers. Some are the result of tradition and custom, and some are necessary to enforce formal powers. The informal powers of the chief executive include:

a) communicating to the public a personal position on issues of interest to all Georgians;

b) acting as honorary head of the political party which elected him or her to office;

c) issuing proclamations to honor individuals, holidays, or special events and, with the legislature's approval, adding new state symbols.

d) representing the state in meetings with other state officials, federal officers, or foreign dignitaries;

e) meeting with business and industry leaders from other states or nations to encourage them to expand their businesses into Georgia;

f) working with members of the legislature to get laws passed;

g) guiding state agencies.

Sometimes the informal powers of a governor may seem more important than the formal powers. However, a governor's greatest influence is through his power to appoint individuals to boards and executive offices. For example, Governor Joe Frank Harris, who served from 1983 to 1990, appointed all fifteen members of the board of regents (the board which controls the University System of Georgia and all public colleges and universities). He named all ten members of the state board of education (the board which controls public elementary and secondary schools of the state). He also selected a state superintendent of schools needed to complete an unexpired term of office.

Governor Harris appointed a panel of business leaders, legislators, and citizens to write a legislative package called Quality Basic Education (QBE). When this package became law in 1985, it affected all public school students in Georgia. For example, an eighth grade student in Ocilla has the same study objectives an an eighth grade student in Columbus. In several grades, all students take a state-prepared test during the spring. First-time Georgia teachers must pass tests during their first three years of teaching to show they are able to instruct students. This legislation also changed the way school systems are funded. In these ways, Governor Harris made an effort to improve education all over the state.

The executive branch of state government also includes the office of lieutenant governor. The lieutenant governor is elected by popular vote. However, unlike the governor, this official can serve an unlimited number of consecutive terms in office.

The lieutenant governor is the presiding officer of the senate. The lieutenant governor makes senate committee appointments, assigns senate bills to committees, and recognizes members of the senate who wish to speak. Because of these powers, the lieutenant governor may affect the passage or failure of some senate bills.

In the event of a governor's death, resignation, or impeachment, the lieutenant governor becomes the state's chief executive. He also serves as the chief executive officer when the governor is out of the state.

The executive branch of Georgia's government employs approximately 67,000 people. They fill jobs ranging from teaching in one of the state's colleges to protecting state-maintained roads or forests.

Georgia has 159 county school systems and 28 independent school systems. Here you see a classroom at Spalding Elementary School in Sandy Springs. Major changes in Georgia's education system were made during Governor Joe Frank Harris' terms in office.

Do You Remember?

1. What are some of the formal powers of the governor?
2. How many consecutive terms can a Georgia governor serve?
3. What are the major duties of the lieutenant governor?

THE LEGISLATIVE BRANCH OF GOVERNMENT

On the second Monday of each January, 180 members of the house of representatives join together in the house chamber for the start of the 40-day legislative session. The senate has a similar but smaller chamber for their 56 members. As a result of the 1990 census, the makeup of the Georgia General Assembly will change. How does the census influence the membership of the general assembly?

Amendment X to the United States Constitution states: "The powers not delegated to the United States by the Constitution, nor prohibited by it to the States, are reserved to the States, respectively, or to the people."

State constitutions grant the reserved law-making power to the legislatures. An exception has to do with amending the constitution. The legislature may propose an amendment, but it must be approved by the voters before it becomes law.

The legislative branch of Georgia's government is officially known as the Georgia General Assembly. It was formed in 1777 as a one-house legislative body and is older than the Congress of the United States. In 1789, the Georgia General Assembly was reorganized as a two-house, or bicameral, legislature, with a senate and a house of representatives.

In addition to numerous committee meetings, visits from constituents and lobbyists, and legislative debates, members of the state senate must confer with each other about local and statewide needs. Shown here, Senators Cathy Steinberg and Nathan Deal are discussing upcoming legislation.

The house of representatives and the senate operate in similar fashion except for two major differences. Only the house of representatives can write appropriations bills. Only the senate can confirm appointments of the governor to executive offices. Either group can propose and pass bills, and all bills must be approved by both houses before being sent to the governor.

Members of the legislature are elected by popular vote to two-year terms of office. There is no limit to the number of terms a representative or senator can serve. There are 180 members of the house of representatives and 56 members of the senate.

The Georgia General Assembly meets each year for a forty-day session, beginning on the second Monday in January. Breaks and recesses do not count as part of the forty days, so the sessions usually last until the middle of March.

The lieutenant governor presides over the senate. The representatives elect a speaker as their presiding officer. The speaker, like the lieutenant governor, appoints committees and their chairmen, and assigns bills to those committees. A presiding officer has the power to:

1. determine the order of business in his house
2. control debate

Representatives Denmark Groover, Thurbert Baker, Calvin Smyre and Mary Margaret Oliver discuss a bill pending before the House.

3. rule out proposed amendments to bills
4. enforce rules of procedure for the general assembly
5. control meeting times and recesses of the general assembly
6. order a roll call vote on any issue.

The lieutenant governor does not have a vote in the senate, but the speaker of the house votes when it is necessary to break a tie.

Members of the house and senate are organized into committees. Some are permanent, lasting during a session and from one session to the next. Others are appointed for a special task and last only until their work is completed. All proposed legislation is reviewed by a house or senate committee before being presented for a vote to the whole body. Some of the standing committees include the Ways and Means Committee, which handles bills involving taxes; the Appropriations Committee which works on the budget; and the Judiciary Committee which deals with bills concerning the state's laws and court system.

A member of the Georgia General Assembly may serve on several committees. Committee chairmen decide when their committees will meet. They choose the order in which assigned bills will be discussed, and when they will be voted on. The committee system makes it possible for proposed bills to be studied closely. There would not be time for such study if each bill were discussed only by the entire house.

After a committee studies a proposed bill, it may take one of three actions. It can decide to pass the bill as written to the house or senate for a vote. It can make changes in the wording of the bill before sending it to the legislature. The committee may also keep the bill in committee, thus killing the bill. When presenting a bill to the full body, both house and senate committees may recommend either a favorable or unfavorable vote. In the house, a bill can also be presented with no commitee recommendation.

Examples of special committees are those which work on assigned issues and concerns between sessions of the legislature. These are known as interim committees. A conference committee is appointed when the house and senate pass different versions of a bill. This committee takes the two bills and tries to write one which can be passed in both houses. A committee of the whole is made up of members of both houses and works on an assigned topic or issue.

TYPES OF LEGISLATION

The Georgia General Assembly can pass laws on any matter not denied them by the United States Constitution. They can amend state laws or do away with them. The general assembly can pass legislation on such matters as taxation, educational improvement, contracts, and real and personal property. Other subjects they deal with include inheritances, mortgages, corporations, and marriage and divorce. The legislature makes laws concerning fines, im-

One of the most important functions of the members of the Georgia General Assembly is to serve on legislative committees. These committees can determine whether or not proposed bills make it to the house or senate floor for a vote. Here you see the House Industry Committee discussing the controversial parimutuel betting bill. After defining the term "parimutuel betting," how would you have voted?

During a regular legislative session, thousands of bills can run from one or two pages in length to the size of a small book. It is the role of men and women like Jimmy Vining at the Capitol Print Shop to see that the bills are printed and put together correctly for members of the house or senate to read and study before making final votes.

prisonment, or death in criminal matters. They also consider "public regulation," such as morals, public health, business or professional regulations, or any general welfare rule which restricts personal property.

HOW STATE LAWS ARE MADE

Any citizen may suggest an idea for a law, and any senator or representative can propose a bill for consideration. All bills which affect how the state raises or spends money must come from the house of representatives. Bills about anything else may begin in either house.

Bills in the Georgia General Assembly go through almost the same steps as those in the United States Congress before they become law.

1. A proposal is written in legal language and turned in to the clerk's office. There it is given a name and number. For example, the twelfth proposal turned in to the house of repre-

sentatives' clerk during a given session will be H.R. 12. After the proposal is given a number, it is called a bill.

2. Copies of the bill are made for members of the house which is to consider it. The bill is assigned to a committee.

3. The committee to which the bill is assigned may have public hearings so interested persons may speak for or against the bill. They may also ask legislative staff members to gather information about the bill. The committee studies the bill and talks about its good and bad points.

4. The committee assigned to handle the bill can do several things:
   a) it can hold the bill and not release it to the house or to the senate;
   b) it can vote the bill out of committee and recommend that it be passed;
   c) it can vote the bill out of committee and recommend that it not be passed;
   d) it can make changes in the bill and vote the new version out for consideration by the house or senate;
   e) in the house only, the bill can be voted out of committee with no recommendation. If a bill is not voted out of committee, it is "killed" unless the full house votes to take the bill from the committee and assign it to another one.

5. A bill sent to the full house or senate can be discussed, debated, and amended. A majority vote is required to pass a bill.

6. When a bill is "certified," or passed, by one house of the general assembly, it is carried by messenger to the other house for consideration.

7. Again, the bill is assigned to a committee. As before, the bill may be kept in committee, changed, or voted out as it is to be handled by the entire house.

8. If both houses pass a bill, it is signed by their presiding officers and clerks before being sent to the governor.

9. The governor can handle a bill in one of three ways. He can sign it into law. He can take no action and let it become law automatically. He can veto it and return it to the house where it originated. If a bill is vetoed, the general assembly can override the veto by a two-thirds vote of both houses. The bill then becomes law.

Pages to serve both the Georgia House of Representatives and the Georgia Senate come from all areas of the state. Their job is to deliver messages, distribute bills, and perform other errands for the members of the Georgia General Assembly. The job provides invaluable experience and insight into the workings of government.

At the end of a legislative session, the Speaker bangs the gavel for the last time and shouts out "sine die," the signal for adjournment. Instantly, throughout the legislative chambers, thousands of sheets of paper are thrown into the air officially marking the end of another forty-day term. The Latin term "sine die," means without a day, or there is no additional date for convening, thus the session is ended.

WHEN THE HOUSE AND SENATE DISAGREE?

Remember that for a bill to become a law, the exact same version of the bill must be passed by both the house of representatives and the senate. Many times, one house will pass a slightly different version of a bill than the other house adopted. When this happens, the amended bill must be sent back to the other house to be reconsidered for a vote there. If the two legislative groups cannot agree to pass, or adopt, identical versions of a bill, a "conference committee" is appointed. The conference committee is made up of three senators and three representatives. Their job is to work out a compromise bill that both houses might accept. The compromise bill must be passed by both the senate and the house of representatives before it is sent to the governor.

Do You Remember?

1. What are some of the powers of the presiding officers of the house and senate?
2. What is a conference committee? When is it used?
3. Why is the committee system important?

THE JUDICIAL BRANCH OF GOVERNMENT

The highest-ranking court in the Georgia court system is the state's supreme court. The seven supreme court justices are elected by majority popular vote to six-year terms. If a supreme court justice resigns or dies before the end of a term, the governor may appoint a justice to complete that term of office.

Supreme court justices elect the chief justice from among the seven members. The supreme court is an appellate court, which means it only reviews cases on appeal from lower-ranking courts. There are no witnesses and juries as in lower-ranking trial courts.

Another responsibility of the supreme court is to interpret both the state and federal constitutions. It may review cases involving treaties, the constitutionality of laws, titles to land, equity, wills, capital felonies, habeas corpus, extraordinary remedies, divorce, and alimony. It may outline a code of judicial conduct for the judges of the state, and regulate the admission of attorneys to practice law in Georgia. The supreme court automatically reviews all Georgia cases involving the death penalty.

Decisions of the supreme court are binding. This means they

Justices of the Georgia Supreme Court frequently deliberate for hours in committee, debating the pros and cons of a law as it applies to an individual or to the state. Here, Chief Justice Thomas O. Marshall conducts a committee meeting of the 1989 court. What are some of the characteristics which a person would need to become a Georgia Supreme Court Justice?

have the final authority in matters of law at the state level.

The second highest ranking state court is the court of appeals. Nine judges serve on this court, and they elect one of their members to serve as the chief judge. The judges are elected to six-year terms by a majority popular vote.

The court of appeals, like the supreme court, is an appellate court. It hears cases appealed from lower ranking courts.

Below the appellate courts are the trial courts of Georgia. The trial courts hear original cases, such as civil cases involving disputes between private parties, and criminal cases involving violations of laws or commission of crimes. Trial courts include the state superior courts, state courts, probate courts, juvenile courts, magistrate courts, municipal courts, and justice of peace courts.

Each court has a special jurisdiction (the range of actions over which the court has control or influence). For example, the juvenile court handles cases involving persons under the age of seventeen. The probate court deals with the wills and estates of deceased persons. Magistrate courts can only hear cases involving sums under $3000.

The role of the judicial branch of Georgia's government is to protect citizens from abuses by government by providing each citizen with "due process of law." The United States Constitution says no state can deprive any citizen of life, liberty or property without "due process of law." This means a person arrested for a crime has the right to have a lawyer present during questioning in court. He must be given a speedy, public trial before a fair judge and jury. He may face and question witnesses, or remain silent so as not to incriminate himself.

The courts also protect citizens from each other by handling civil cases (disputes that are not crimes), and criminal cases.

THE SEPARATION OF POWERS AMONG THE BRANCHES OF GEORGIA'S GOVERNMENT

The Georgia Constitution, like that of the United States, provides separate powers for each branch of government. It also provides for checks and balances so each branch of government can prevent the other branches from having too much power.

The executive branch can veto bills passed by the legislature, and can call special sessions of the legislature. It also has some appoint-

In 1974, the Georgia Supreme Court held an extradition hearing to determine whether white supremacist J.B. Stoner would be returned to Alabama to stand trial for 16th Street Baptist Church bombing (see page 475). Stoner was subsequently extradicted and convicted of the crime.

ment powers when officers of the court resign or die.

The legislative branch can impeach government officials. It can override a governor's veto of bills to make them into law. It must confirm appointments made by the governor. It can also propose constitutional changes.

The judicial branch determines whether or not laws are constitutional.

Each branch of government is responsive to the citizens of Georgia since most officials in each branch are directly elected by the voters.

LOCAL GOVERNMENT IN GEORGIA

Local governments are the most numerous of all governments in the United States. Georgia has 159 counties and each of these counties has a governmental organization. In addition to the counties, there are many cities in Georgia and each of them also has a government.

Not only are local governments the most numerous forms of governance, they are also the closest to the people and the most likely to affect people directly. Local governments get their powers and their right to exist from the Georgia State Constitution.

THE COUNTY AS A POLITICAL UNIT

Counties are set up by the state government to carry on certain governmental functions. In Georgia, county powers are limited by the purposes for which the counties may tax. These purposes are listed in the state constitution. They include the power to tax to cover the cost of: county administration; police (sheriff) and legal systems; construction and maintenance of roads and bridges; public health; medical care for people who cannot afford to pay; assistance to dependent children; parks and libraries; and public education.

County Government

County governments are required by the state constitution to be uniform except for the following instances: The Georgia General Assembly may, in any county, establish commissioners of roads and revenues, consolidate the offices of tax receiver and tax collector into the office of tax commissioner, and abolish the office of

This is the impressive granite county courthouse in Elberton, Georgia. At one time, the town was actually called Elbert Court House.

treasurer. Since all county governments are similar, we will examine the governmental structure of Fulton County, to show both the operations of a county, and how cities and counties cooperate in sharing services.

Fulton County is the most populous county in Georgia. It was originally created in 1853 by the Georgia General Assembly. It was enlarged in 1931 when Milton and Campbell counties merged with Fulton County.

Fulton County covers 523 square miles. Atlanta occupies about 117 square miles, or 22 percent, of Fulton County. Atlanta accounts for approximately 62 percent of Fulton County's taxable property and approximately 73 percent of its population. Nine other incorporated cities are also located within Fulton County: Alpharetta, College Park, East Point, Fairburn, Hapeville, Mountain Park, Palmetto, Roswell and Union City.

A board of commissioners governs Fulton County. The board consists of seven members elected to four year terms. Four commissioners are elected from geographic districts and three are elected from the county at large. The chairman of the board

Pictured below is the Charlton County Courthouse, located in Folkston. The county was created in 1854 with land taken from Camden County. The county includes a sizable portion of the Okefenokee National Wildlife Refuge and Wilderness Area known as the Okefenokee Swamp.

The Atlanta City Hall is located on Mitchell Street between Central Avenue and Washington Street. Built in 1929, at a cost of more than one million dollars, the multistoried terra cotta (a hard waterproof ceramic clay) exterior is an impressive sight to the thousands of visitors who conduct their city business each day. Perhaps the most discussed and admired part of City Hall is beyond the front entrance. Here one finds four massive bronze elevators. Inscribed into each of the reddish-brown glossy metal doors is the seal of Atlanta bearing a phoenix and the words "Resurgens 1847-1864, Atlanta, Georgia."

Eatonton, the county seat of Putnam County, is home for the Putnam County Courthouse shown above. Putnam County was created in 1807 with lands from Baldwin County. The county is named in honor of General Israel Putnam who served in the French and Indian War and the revolutionary war.

was elected by a majority of its members until 1990 when, for the first time, the office was filled directly by the voters.

The board of commissioners sets levels of services to be provided by each department of county government when it approves each annual departmental budget.

In Fulton County, the board of commissioners appoints a county manager as its chief executive officer. The county manager, with the commission's approval, appoints all department heads except those department heads who are elected officials or whose appointments are specifically provided for in the law. The county manager's chief function is to carry out policies set by the county commission.

Through contract agreements, the county provides financial support to shared ventures, including the Fulton-DeKalb Hospital Authority and the Atlanta and Fulton County Recreation Authority (Atlanta Stadium and the Omni). Public hospital facilities are administered by the Fulton-DeKalb Hospital Authority which operates Grady Memorial Hospital. Property zoning is a joint function of the county and Atlanta. Library services to residents of Fulton County are provided by Atlanta in a contract between the two governments.

The school system for the county, including all nine incorporated areas outside the city limits of Atlanta, is operated by the Fulton County Board of Education, which is elected by the voters and which appoints a superintendent of schools. The elected Atlanta Board of Education appoints a superintendent of schools for the city.

Atlanta operates with an elected city council and an elected mayor form of government. Municipal court judges, city traffic court judges, and the chief solicitor of city court are elected. All other officials or department heads are appointed.

THE CITY AS A POLITICAL UNIT

A city with its own government is called a municipality. The city can exist as a political unit when it is given a charter by the state legislature. A city government can do only what the charter authorizes it to do. For example, most city charters allow cities to provide police protection, license businesses, maintain streets and sidewalks, control traffic, and provide water and sewerage services.

Other services to the citizens may be provided if they are included specifically in a city's charter. Atlanta and some other cities in the state, for example, operate their own school systems because that power is granted in their charters from the state.

City Government

The most common forms of city government are called the mayor-council form, the council-manager form, and the commissioner form. In the mayor-council style of government, the elected city council is responsible for making the laws. An elected mayor acts as the city's chief executive officer with the responsibility for seeing that the laws are carried out and that city agencies do their jobs. The role of mayor in such a form of government may be a weak position or a strong position, depending upon the amount of power and authority given to the mayor's job.

In the council-manager style of government, the voters elect a city council which appoints a city manager. The council establishes laws and policies, and the city manager is responsible for appointing the heads of city governments and for seeing that they carry out their jobs.

In cities with a commissioner form of government, the voters elect commissioners. Each commissioner is the head of a department within the city government and the mayor is elected by the commissioners from among themselves.

City-County Government

Some counties also provide services outside of incorporated municipalities for things such as water, sewage, sanitation, and fire protection.

As long as city and county governments provide distinctive types of services in the same area, they do not get in each other's way in providing good services to the people. However, when a county becomes more largely urban, city and county governments may provide the same services to the same people.

One way to avoid this duplication is for city and county governments to form a single government. Two such mergers have taken place to date. The city of Columbus and Muscogee County merged in 1971. Athens and Clarke County formed a single government unit in 1990.

The Wilkes County Courthouse, pictured above, is located in Washington. Wilkes County was created in 1777 with lands acquired through the Cherokee Indian cession and the Creek Indian cession of 1773. It is named in honor of John Wilkes, a member of the British Parliament who opposed England's treatment of the colonies.

Two of the many people who cast their votes during the 1990 primary in Marietta are shown here. They joined thousands of voters throughout the state in exercising the most fundamental right of any Georgian or American citizen— the right to vote to choose those who will represent them. Sadly enough, only about forty percent of those Georgians who were eligible to vote took advantage of that right. Why do you think it is important to vote? Will you take the time to vote?

THE VOTER'S ROLE IN GOVERNMENT

Georgia citizens take an active part in state government by voting. Voters select persons to fill some government offices, and decide major questions and issues.

To register to vote in Georgia, a person must be at least eighteen years old, and a citizen of the United States. An individual must also be a legal resident of Georgia and the county where registration takes place.

Voting in national, state, and county elections is managed according to the Georgia Election Code. The secretary of state is the chief election official. He makes sure candidates meet the qualifications to run for office. He also schedules elections, prints ballots, and provides all election materials to Georgia's counties. After an election, the secretary of state checks the results in each county and publishes them.

A general election is held in November, at least every even-numbered year. This is when major federal and state officials are selected. Other elections are held as needed to select public officials at all levels of government: national, state, county, or city.

Voters select the most important state officials. These officials, in turn, appoint others who work for and with them. Therefore, a citizen can, by voting, influence all of state government.

Voters also have the right and responsibility to decide some issues. Since it requires a vote of the people to change the state constitution, proposed amendments sometimes appear on the ballot. Another item voters decide is a "bond issue," in which some level of government asks permission to raise money for a public project. For example, some schools, libraries, and hospitals have been built with public money approved by the voters on a bond issue.

GEORGIA'S CAPITAL AND CAPITOL

Atlanta, once a crossroad for Creek and Cherokee Indians, is now home to over half a million people. It is also the capital, or seat of government for the state of Georgia. Each January, several hundred legislators arrive from all over the state to open the annual session of the Georgia General Assembly. Senators and representatives work in the gold domed **capitol,** which also houses offices for the governor, lieutenant governor, and other state officials.

Building the capitol took five years. Its exterior walls are Indiana limestone. Inside, the walls, floors, and stairs are polished Georgia marble. When the **capitol** was dedicated in 1889, it was the state's tallest building. Today, its seventy-five foot round dome is highly visible on the Atlanta skyline. The dome is covered with sixty ounces of gold mined in Dahlonega. A statue called "Miss Freedom" stands on top of it with her arm stretched skyward holding a torch of liberty and freedom.

Over 9,000 employees work in the government office buildings located near the capitol. These buildings range from three-story marble structures to the twenty-story brick and glass "twin towers" of the James H. Floyd Veteran Memorial Building. With the exception of the State Forestry Commission, which is located in Macon, every state department is headquartered in Atlanta.

The gold-plated dome of Georgia's state capitol in Atlanta brings together the old Georgia of 1889 with the new 1990s city of great skyscrapers. "Miss Freedom" sitting atop the capitol dome welcomes Georgia citizens and visitors.

Do You Remember?
1. How many justices are elected for the Georgia Supreme Court? How long are their terms of office?
2. What court handles cases involving persons under seventeen years of age?
3. What are the requirements for voting in Georgia?

GEORGIA STATE SYMBOLS

You can learn much about where you live by examining the symbols selected to represent the state.

The term symbol is defined as something that represents another thing. For example, a ring can be a symbol of love or friendship. An anniversary symbolizes an important event such as a wedding or birthday. States also have symbols to remind us of important events, valuable resources, or significant ideals. The Georgia Legislature officially names a state symbol by majority vote to identify something representative of the state. Each time you see one of Georgia's state symbols, it can be a reminder of your home and heritage.

The State Bird

The brown thrasher (page 34) officially became Georgia's state bird in 1970, although Governor Eugene Talmadge had issued a proclamation naming the brown and white songster a symbol of the state in 1935. Farmers, in particular, like to see the long beaked bird nesting in low bushes on their land, because the thrasher diet includes grasshoppers, worms and caterpillars that can be destructive to farm crops.

During the same period that the brown thrasher was named the state bird, the 1970 Georgia House of Representatives selected the second bird, the bobwhite quail, as the official game bird of the state. This quail is best known for its distinctive "bob-bob-white" call and as a sports bird for game hunters. Georgia is known as the "Quail Capital of the World" and has several plants which process and ship the delicacy throughout the country.

The State Flower

Georgia's state flower, the Cherokee rose, was adopted by the Georgia Federation of Women's Clubs and confirmed by the state legislature as a state symbol in 1916. The rose came from China and was introduced into the new world by Spanish settlers who brought it to Florida. Its American name came about because the rose was a favorite of the Cherokee Indians, who spread it throughout Georgia. The plant is high climbing, excessively thorny, and has vivid green leaves. The flower has waxy-white petals with a velvet texture, and a large golden center. Because of its hardy nature, the plant was once used as a hedge throughout the state. It is not seen as often now due to ever expanding highways and housing developments.

The State Tree

The live oak (page 36) was adopted as Georgia's state tree in 1937. It is found primarily along the coastal plains and on the islands where settlers first made their homes. The majestic tree sometimes has a trunk twenty five feet in diameter. It can grow more than forty feet high and have a limb span of more than a hundred feet in diameter. A live oak tree often lives for several hundred years, and is a host for clinging Spanish moss which, during the early settlement days, was used for stuffing mattresses and chairs.

The State Flag

Long the topic of debate because of the background of the Confederate battle flag, the present-day Georgia flag was adopted in 1956. The current flag replaced the original state flag which had been adopted in 1879. The state pledge of allegiance reads: "I pledge allegiance to the Georgia flag and to the principles for which it stands: Wisdom, Justice, and Moderation." The latter section of the pledge is also the state motto: Wisdom, Justice, and Moderation.

Other State Symbols

The state fish, the largemouth bass, is found mostly in warm water steams and lakes. Georgia boasts one of the world's records for the biggest largemouth bass ever caught. The bass was adopted as a state symbol by the Georgia House of Representatives in 1970.

The state insect is the honeybee. It is an aid to agriculture, and is responsible for the cross-pol-lination of more than fifty different crops. Honey produced by the bees is a valuable commodity in Georgia's economy.

In 1976, the Georgia House of Representatives recognized three other state symbols: the official state gem, the state mineral and the state fossil. Staurolite, found in old crystalline rocks was designated the official state mineral. The popular names of staurolite crystals are "Fairy Crosses," or "Fairy Stones." These minerals are abundant in north Georgia and have been collected for generations as good luck charms. The state gem is the second most abundant mineral on earth: quartz. It can be seen in a wide variety of colors in Georgia. Quartz is most commonly recognized as the amethyst, often used in jewelry, and the clear quartz which resembles a diamond when it is faceted, or has many small flat surfaces.

The shark tooth, Georgia's state fossil, is a common fossil in the coastal plain region. In fossil form, the shark tooth can be traced back 375 million years. Fossilized shark teeth are found in a variety of colors ranging from the common black and gray to white, brown, blue, and reddish brown.

In 1989, the gopher tortoise became Georgia's newest symbol. It is the official state reptile.

Each of these symbols is a reminder of the wealth of natural resources throughout the state of Georgia.

APPENDIX II

GEORGIA COUNTIES

County	Date Founded	County Seat	Named For
Appling	1818	Baxley	Col. Daniel Appling
Atkinson	1917	Pearson	William Yates Atkinson
Bacon	1914	Alma	Augustus Octavius Bacon
Baker	1825	Newton	Col. John Baker
Baldwin	1803	Milledgeville	Abraham Baldwin
Banks	1858	Homer	Dr. Richard E. Banks
Barrow	1914	Winder	David Crenshaw Barrow
Bartow	1832	Cartersville	Gen. Francis Stebbins Bartow
Ben Hill	1906	Fitzgerald	Benjamin Harvey Hill
Berrien	1856	Nashville	John MacPherson Berrien
Bibb	1822	Macon	William Wyatt Bibb, M.D.
Bleckley	1912	Cochran	Logan Edward Bleckley
Brantley	1920	Nahunta	William G. Brantley
Brooks	1858	Quitman	Preston Smith Brooks
Bryan	1793	Pembroke	Jonathan Bryan
Bulloch	1796	Statesboro	Gov. Archibald Bulloch
Burke	1777	Waynesboro	Edmund Burke
Butts	1825	Jackson	Capt. Samuel Butts
Calhoun	1854	Morgan	John Caldwell Calhoun
Camden	1777	Woodbine	Sir Charles Pratt, Earl of Camden
Candler	1914	Metter	Gov. Allen Daniel Candler
Carroll	1826	Carrollton	Charles Carroll

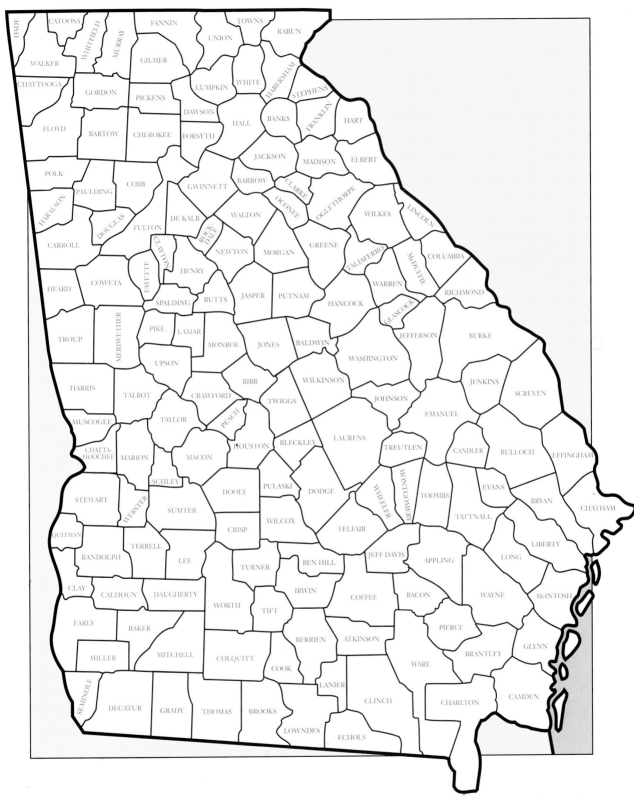

GEORGIA COUNTIES   571

County	Year	Seat	Named For
Catoosa	1853	Ringgold	Cherokee Indian Word
Charlton	1854	Folkston	Robert Charlton
Chatham	1777	Savannah	William Pitt, Earl of Chatham
Chattahoochee	1854	Cusseta	Chattahoochee River
Chattooga	1838	Summerville	Chattooga River
Cherokee	1831	Canton	Cherokee Indians
Clarke	1805	Athens	Elijah Clarke
Clay	1854	Fort Gaines	Henry Clay
Clayton	1858	Jonesboro	Augustin Smith Clayton
Clinch	1850	Homerville	Gen. Duncan Lamont Clinch
Cobb	1832	Marietta	Thomas Willis Cobb
Coffee	1854	Douglas	Gen. John E. Coffee
Colquitt	1856	Moultrie	Walter Terry Colquitt
Columbia	1790	Appling	Christopher Columbus
Cook	1918	Adel	Gen. Phillip Cook
Coweta	1826	Newnan	Coweta Indians
Crawford	1822	Knoxville	William Harris Crawford
Crisp	1905	Cordele	Charles Frederick Crisp
Dade	1837	Trenton	Maj. Francis Langhorne Dade
Dawson	1857	Dawsonville	William Crosby Dawson
Decatur	1823	Bainbridge	Commodore Stephen Decatur
DeKalb	1822	Decatur	Johann DeKalb
Dodge	1870	Eastman	William Earl Dodge
Dooly	1821	Vienna	Col. John Dooly
Dougherty	1853	Albany	Charles Dougherty
Douglas	1870	Douglasville	Stephen Arnold Douglas
Early	1818	Blakely	Gov. Peter Early
Echols	1858	Statenville	Gen. Robert M. Echols

Effingham	1777	Springfield	Francis Howard, Earl of Effingham
Elbert	1790	Elberton	Gov. Samuel Elbert
Emanuel	1812	Swainsboro	Col. David Emanuel
Evans	1914	Claxton	Gen. Clement Anselm Evans
Fannin	1854	Blue Ridge	Col. James Walker Fannin
Fayette	1821	Fayetteville	Marquis De Lafayette
Floyd	1832	Rome	John Floyd
Forsyth	1832	Cumming	Gov. John Forsyth
Franklin	1784	Carnesville	Benjamin Franklin
Fulton	1853	Atlanta	Robert Fulton
Gilmer	1832	Ellijay	Gov. George Gilmer
Glascock	1857	Gibson	Thomas Glascock
Glynn	1777	Brunswick	John Glynn
Gordon	1850	Calhoun	William Washington Gordon
Grady	1905	Cairo	Henry Woodfin Grady
Greene	1786	Greensboro	Nathaniel Greene
Gwinnett	1818	Lawrenceville	Gov. Button Gwinnett
Habersham	1818	Clarkesville	Joseph Habersham
Hall	1818	Gainesville	Gov. Lyman Hall
Hancock	1793	Sparta	John Hancock
Haralson	1856	Buchanan	Gen. Hugh Anderson Haralson
Harris	1827	Hamilton	Charles Harris
Hart	1853	Hartwell	Nancy Morgan Hart
Heard	1830	Franklin	Gov. Stephen Heard
Henry	1821	McDonough	Patrick Henry
Houston	1821	Perry	Gov. John Houstoun
Irwin	1818	Ocilla	Gov. Jared Irwin
Jackson	1796	Jefferson	Gov. James Jackson

Jasper	1807	Monticello	William Jasper
Jeff Davis	1905	Hazelhurst	Jefferson Davis
Jefferson	1796	Louisville	President Thomas Jefferson
Jenkins	1905	Millen	Gov. Charles Jones Jenkins
Johnson	1858	Wrightsville	Gov. Herschel V. Johnson
Jones	1807	Gray	James Jones
Lamar	1920	Barnesville	Lucius Q. C. Lamar
Lanier	1920	Lakeland	Sidney Clapton Lanier
Laurens	1807	Dublin	Col. John Laurens
Lee	1826	Leesburg	Gen. Richard Henry Lee
Liberty	1777	Hinesville	concept of freedom and liberty
Lincoln	1796	Lincolnton	Gen. Benjamin Lincoln
Long	1920	Ludowici	Dr. Crawford Williamson Long
Lowndes	1825	Valdosta	William Jones Lowndes
Lumpkin	1832	Dahlonega	Gov. Wilson Lumpkin
Macon	1837	Oglethorpe	Gen. Nathaniel Macon
Madison	1811	Danielsville	James Madison
Marion	1827	Buena Vista	Gen. Francis Marion
McDuffie	1870	Thomson	George McDuffie
McIntosh	1793	Darien	William McIntosh, Creek Chief
Meriwether	1827	Greenville	Gen. David Meriwether
Miller	1856	Colquitt	Andrew Jackson Miller
Mitchell	1857	Camilla	Gen. Henry Mitchell
Monroe	1821	Forsyth	President James Monroe
Montgomery	1793	Mount Vernon	Maj. Gen. Richard Montgomery
Morgan	1807	Madison	Gen. Daniel Morgan
Murray	1832	Chatsworth	Thomas W. Murray
Muscogee	1826	Columbus	Muscogee Indians

Newton	1821	Covington	Sergeant John Newton
Oconee	1875	Watkinsville	Oconee River
Oglethorpe	1793	Lexington	James Edward Oglethorpe
Paulding	1832	Dallas	John Paulding
Peach	1924	Fort Valley	Georgia Peach
Pickens	1853	Jasper	Gen. Andrew Pickens
Pierce	1857	Blackshear	President Franklin Pierce
Pike	1822	Zebulon	Gen. Zebulon Montgomery Pike
Polk	1851	Cedartown	President James K. Polk
Pulaski	1808	Hawkinsville	Count Casimir Pulaski
Putnam	1807	Eatonton	Gen. Israel Putnam
Quitman	1858	Georgetown	Gen. John Anthony Quitman
Rabun	1819	Clayton	Gov. William Rabun
Randolph	1828	Cuthbert	John Randolph
Richmond	1777	Augusta	Charles Lennox, Duke of Richmond
Rockdale	1870	Conyers	Rockdale Church
Schley	1857	Ellaville	Gov. William Schley
Screven	1793	Sylvania	Gen. James Screven
Seminole	1920	Donalsonville	Seminole Indians
Spalding	1851	Griffin	Thomas Spalding
Stephens	1905	Toccoa	Gov. Alexander H. Stephens
Stewart	1830	Lumpkin	Gen. Daniel Stewart
Sumter	1831	Americus	Gen. Thomas Sumter
Talbot	1827	Talbotton	Gov. Mathew Talbot
Taliaferro	1825	Crawfordville	Col. Benjamin Taliaferro
Tattnall	1801	Reidsville	Gov. Josiah Tattnall
Taylor	1852	Butler	President Zachary Taylor
Telfair	1807	McRae	Gov. Edward Telfair

Terrell	1856	Dawson	Dr. William Terrell
Thomas	1825	Thomasville	Gen. Jett Thomas
Tift	1905	Tifton	Col. Nelson Tift
Toombs	1905	Lyons	Robert Toombs
Towns	1856	Hiawassee	Gov. George Washington Towns
Treutlen	1917	Soperton	Gov. John Adam Treutlen
Troup	1825	LaGrange	Gov. George Michael Troup
Turner	1905	Ashburn	Captain Henry Gray Turner
Twiggs	1809	Jeffersonville	Gen. John Twiggs
Union	1832	Blairsville	Union loyalty
Upson	1824	Thomaston	Stephen Upson
Walker	1833	LaFayette	Maj. Freeman Walker
Walton	1818	Monroe	Gov. George Walton
Ware	1824	Waycross	Nicholas Ware
Warren	1793	Warrenton	Gen. Joseph Warren
Washington	1784	Sandersville	President George Washington
Wayne	1803	Jesup	Gen. Anthony Wayne
Webster	1853	Preston	Daniel Webster
Wheeler	1912	Alamo	Gen. Joseph Wheeler
White	1857	Cleveland	David Thomas White
Whitfield	1851	Dalton	Reverend George Whitfield
Wilcox	1857	Abbeville	Maj. Gen. Mark Wilcox
Wilkes	1777	Washington	John Wilkes
Wilkinson	1803	Irwinton	Gen. James Marion Wilkinson
Worth	1853	Sylvester	Gen. William James Worth

GOVERNORS OF GEORGIA

TRUSTEE

James Edward Oglethorpe, Trustee 1733-1743

William Stephens, President 1743-1751

Henry Parker, President 1751-1752

Patrick Graham, President 1752-1754

ROYAL GOVERNORS

John Reynolds 1754-1757

Henry Ellis 1757-1760

James Wright 1760-1776

PROVISIONAL GOVERNORS

Archibald Bulloch (President, Safety Council) 1776-1777

Button Gwinnett (President, Safety Council) 1777-1777

STATE GOVERNORS

John Adam Treutlen 1777-1778

John Houstoun 1778-1779

John Wereat (President, Executive Council) 1779-1780

George Walton 1779-1780

Richard Howley 1780-1780

Stephen Heard (President, Executive Council) 1780-1781

Nathan Brownson 1781-1782

John Martin 1782-1783

Lyman Hall 1783-1784

John Houstoun 1784-1785

Samuel Elbert 1785-1786

Edward Telfair 1786-1787

George Mathews 1787-1788

George Handley 1788-1789

George Walton 1789-1789

Edward Telfair 1789-1793

George Mathews 1793-1796

Jared Irwin 1796-1798

James Jackson 1798-1801

David Emanuel (President, State Senate) 1801-1801

Josiah Tattnall, Jr. 1801-1802

John Milledge 1802-1806

Jared Irwin (President, State Senate) 1806-1809

David Brydie Mitchell 1809-1813

Peter Early 1813-1815

David Brydie Mitchell 1815-1817

William Raburn (President, State Senate) 1817-1819

Matthew Talbot (President, State Senate) 1819-1819

John Clark 1819-1823

George Michael Troup 1823-1827

John Forsyth	1827-1829
George Rockingham Gilmer	1829-1831
Wilson Lumpkin	1831-1835
William Schley	1835-1837
George Rockingham Gilmer	1837-1839
Charles James McDonald	1839-1843
George Walter Crawford	1843-1847
George Washington Towns	1847-1851
Howell Cobb	1851-1852
Herschel Vespasian Johnson	1852-1857
Joseph Emerson Brown	1857-1865
James Johnson (Provisional)	1865-1865
Charles Jones Jenkins	1865-1868
Thomas Howard Ruger	1868-1868
Rufus Brown Bullock	1868-1871
Benjamin Conley	1871-1872
James Milton Smith	1872-1877
Alfred Holt Colquitt	1877-1882
Alexander Hamilton Stephens	1882-1883
James Stoddard Boynton (President, State Senate)	1883-1883
Henry Dickerson McDaniel	1883-1886
John Brown Gordon	1886-1890
William Jonathan Northen	1890-1894
William Yates Atkinson	1894-1898
Allen Daniel Candler	1898-1902
Joseph Meriwether Terrell	1902-1907

Hoke Smith	1907-1909
Joseph Mackey Brown	1909-1911
Hoke Smith	1911-1911
John Marshall Slaton (President, State Senate)	1911-1912
Joseph Mackey Brown	1912-1913
John Marshall Slaton	1913-1915
Nathaniel Edwin Harris	1915-1917
Hugh Manson Dorsey	1917-1921
Thomas William Hardwick	1921-1923
Clifford Walker	1923-1927
Lamartine Griffin Hardman	1927-1931
Richard Brevard Russell, Jr.	1931-1933
Eugene Talmadge	1933-1937
Eurith Dickinson Rivers	1937-1941
Eugene Talmadge	1941-1943
Ellis Gibbs Arnall	1943-1947
Melvin E. Thompson	1947-1948
Herman E. Talmadge	1948-1955
S. Marvin Griffin	1955-1959
Samuel Ernest Vandiver, Jr.	1959-1963
Carl E. Sanders	1963-1967
Lester Maddox	1967-1971
Jimmy Carter	1971-1975
George Busbee	1975-1983
Joe Frank Harris	1983-1991
Zell Miller	1991-

GLOSSARY

This glossary contains many of the important or useful words used in this textbook. Many of these words appear in **boldface** in the textbook. Remember that many words have more than one meaning. The definitions given here are the ones that will be most helpful in reading the textbook.

abolish do away with, or put an end to

abolitionist person who wanted to abolish or do away with slavery

academy private school for special instruction

activist a person who believes in or takes part in direct action to bring about changes in government, social conditions, etc.

aggressive quick to attack or start a fight

allege declare to be true without offering proof

allegiance loyalty to a person, ruler, nation or cause

allocate to set aside for a particular purpose

ally friend or close associate, or friendly country

amendment statement added to change the Constitution or to make it clearer

ammunition bullets, gunpowder, grenades, etc.

annals historical records

ancestry people who make up a line of descent; ancestors

antebellum period before the Civil War

anthropology scientific study of human beings

antisemitic against or opposing someone who is Jewish

appropriate set aside public funds for a specific purpose

aquaculture art or science of growing fish or other sea life commercially

archaeology scientific study of past human activities, life, and customs as they are shown by the tools, monuments, and pottery remaining from past societies

architect person who designs buildings and oversees their construction

armistice temporary stop in fighting agreed on by the two sides; truce

arsenal store or supply of weapons

artisan worker skilled in making a particular product

assets all the property owned by a person or an organization

authority right and power to control persons or things

ballot written or printed paper used to cast or register a vote

biracial involving members of, or relating to, two races

blockade close off a city, coast, harbor or other area to prevent passage or traffic

boycott refuse to buy, sell, or use an item or service in order to force a change

candidate person who seeks or is put forward by others for an office or honor

canister a metallic cylinder, filled with shot or tear gas, that bursts and scatters its contents when fired from a gun

cantata choral composition for a story to be sung, but not acted

capital city where a state or national government is located

capitol the building where a state or national legislature meets

cerebral hemorrhage a condition in which a blood vessel in the cerebrum breaks and releases blood into the nearby tissue; a stroke

ceremony formal act or set of acts performed appropriate to a custom or ritual

cession act of giving up something, such as land

chaff husks of grain remaining after being separated from the seed during harvesting

charter written paper from a nation or state giving certain rights and privileges to a particular group of people

civil of ordinary citizens or ordinary community life, as set apart from military or religious life

clan tribe or group of people tracing descent from a common ancestor

climate weather, including the degree of coldness and hotness and the amount of rain, snow, and wind that occurs in an area over time

colleague a fellow member of a profession, staff, or organization; an associate

colony area that is ruled by another country

commissary store where food and equipment are sold,

such as on a military base

compromise settle an issue by each side giving up some demands

concentration camp a large fenced-in prison area for prisoners of war or those regarded as undesirable by a government

confederacy alliance of groups, tribes or states

conscription being forced or drafted into military service

constitution basic law and plan for governing a country or state

consumer someone who buys and uses goods and services

crematorium a furnace for burning the bodies of the dead; a building in which such a furnace is housed

cultivation process of cultivating the soil or a crop

culture way of life of a group of people, including their beliefs, art, skills, and daily way of life

currant small, sour, red or blackish berry that grows on a prickly shrub

decade period of ten years

delegate person named or elected to act for others

denomination name for a group, particularly a religious body having the same beliefs

demonstration a display of public feeling, as in a rally or parade

deny declare to be not true

depression period of drastic decline in the national economy

diplomacy the art or practice of managing relations between nations without use of warfare

discrimination act of making or noticing a difference; often, mistreatment of people based on prejudice

disenfranchise take away a legal right, especially the right to vote

distillery establishment or plant for distilling, especially alcoholic liquors

diversity difference or variety

doctrine a principle, belief, or teaching, as of a church, that is held to be true

domain territory under control or rule of a person or government

draft choose, especially for required military service

economic management of money

economy system of producing or selling natural resources, goods and services

emigrate leave a country or region to settle in another

enlist join or convince someone to join a group, such as the armed forces

episode event or series of events in a person's life

escalate increase or grow rapidly

establish begin or create

estate all of one's possessions; all the property and debts left by a deceased person

evacuation removal of troops from a dangerous area

evasion act of avoiding, escaping or dodging

excavation uncover by digging

executive branch of government with the responsibility to see that the laws and affairs of the nation or state are carried out

exhibition show or display for the public

expel force out

exploration searching or looking for something, often in unknown or little-known areas

explorer one who searches or travels in a little known region

extinct no longer existing in living form

fascist person who advocates a government led by a dictator who requires complete devotion to a nation which opposes progress or liberal ideas

federal relating to a central government

finance management and use of money, especially by government, banks, and businesses

finished product something that is completely processed

foundry place where metal is cast

frontier part of a country that has not yet been settled

garrison military base

generation group of people who grew up at about the same time; the average length of time between the time of the birth of parents and the birth of their children

geography study of the earth and its plant and animal life

geology scientific study of the origin, history, and structure of the earth

grist grain or a quantity of grain for grinding

harquebus heavy portable gun invented during the 15th century

history continuing events of the past leading up to the present

horticulture art or science of growing flowers, fruits, and vegetables

horticulturist a person who specializes in growing flowers, fruits, and vegetables

immigrant person who moves to another country

impeach charge a public official with misconduct

imply say or mean something without expressing it directly

inaugurate place into office by a formal ceremony

incandescent providing visible light as a result of heating

independence state of being free

independent free from the influence or control of others

indentured servant person who agrees to work for another in exchange for specific goods or services

indigo various plants which produce a violet blue dye

industrial related to industry, or the making of goods on a large scale

industry making or producing of goods on a large scale

inflation continuing rise in the prices of goods and services

inflationary unusual increase in prices, wages, or circulating currency

institution established behavioral pattern of importance in the life of a community or society

integrate open to all people without regard to race

integration process or result of opening to all people without regard to race

investment act or process of investing, money that is invested

journalist person who collects and writes news stories or articles for a newspaper or magazine

judicial relating to courts of law or the administration, or management of a system of justice

jurisdiction control or authority

kaolin fine white or grayish clay used in porcelain or china, and as a coating for paper and textiles

lancer cavalryman (soldier on horseback) armed with a spear

legislation act of law making

legislative having to do with the making of laws

levy impose or collect a tax

lien claim on someone's property in order to make sure payment of a loan is made

litigation legal action or process

magnanimity act of being generous in forgiving

majority greater number or part

manufacture make, especially by using machinery

martial law temporary military rule

materiel supplies, such as guns and ammunition of an army or military force

memoirs an account of experiences that the author has lived through

menial appropriate for a servant

mercantilism system of economy prevailing in Europe at the time America was being settled. It was based on establishing colonies and developing industry and mining to gain a favorable balance of trade.

metropolitan relating to a large city

migrate move from one country or region to another

migration act or an example of moving from one country or region to settle in another

military relating to soldiers, armed forces or war

militia organized group who receive military training outside the regular armed forces and who are called to serve in an emergency

minimum smallest possible quantity or degree

minstrel show variety show, once popular in America, in which performers sang, danced, read poetry, and told jokes

missionary person sent to do religious or charitable work

moat deep, wide ditch, usually filled with water, around a castle or fort

nation group of people organized under a single government

national of, having to do with, or belonging to a nation

naval stores products, such as pitch and turpentine, obtained from trees and used primarily for shipbuilding

neutral not taking sides in a war, quarrel, or contest

nominate propose as a candidate for a public office

offense violation of a moral or social code

ordinance law or regulation, usually one made by a city or town

paleontology the scientific study of fossils and ancient forms of life

palisade row of large pointed stakes forming a fence to protect an area

pardon forgive an offense without punishment

parish political district corresponding to a county

per capita per person; of, for, or by each individual

plurality number by which the vote of a winning candidate is more than that of his closest opponent

policy general plan that is chosen to help people make present or future decisions

political dealing with the structure or affairs of government, politics, or the state

poll casting or registering of votes in an election

popular sovereignty pre-Civil War doctrine, or belief which allowed a new territory to decide whether or not slavery would be allowed in its territory

poultry birds, such as chickens, turkeys, ducks, or geese, that are raised for their eggs or meat

prehistory time before people began to record events in writing

principal first in importance or most important

prohibition the act of forbidding by law or authority

proprietary owned by an individual or a group. In the case of a colony, this ownership was given by the King of England.

proposal plan or scheme that is proposed for others to consider

provisional temporary, awaiting permanent arrangements

radical one who favors basic change of a social or economic system

ratify consent to officially, or to make valid

ration fixed amount or portion, especially food

raw material any product or material that is changed into another product or material by processing or manufacturing

reapportion to distribute anew

recession usually, temporary slowing down of buying and selling goods, construction, and other economic activities

redeem buy back

regulation rule or law

reveille sounding of a bugle early in the morning to awaken persons in a camp or garrison

sacred set aside for worship of a god or deity

sanitary free of dirt and germs; clean

sanitation disposal of sewage and wastes

scandal act or set of acts that offends moral feelings and leads to disgrace

secession act of withdrawing from a state or nation

secede withdraw formally, such as a group from an organization or country

segregate separate or keep apart people of different races

segregation act of segregating or the condition of being segregated

servitude condition of being a slave

settler person who makes a home in a new region or country

sheath case for the blade of a knife or sword

siege surrounding or blockading of a town or fort in an attempt to capture it

skirmish minor fight between small bodies of troops

slave person who is owned by and forced to work for another person

slavery condition of being a slave or the practice of owning slaves

social having to do with people in their living together or an informal gathering of people, such as a church or neighborhood group

solvency ability to pay all legal debts

species distinct kind or sort

speculator one who buys and sells a commodity with a chance for great profit

stockade enclosure or pen made with posts and stakes

suburb town or district that is close to a city

suffrage right to vote

supplies materials or provisions stored and dispensed when needed

system group of structures for travel, communication, or distribution

tariff tax on imports and exports

temperance totally refrain (do without) alcoholic beverages

textile cloth or fabric, usually one that is woven or knitted

thatch plant stalks or foliage used for roofing

treaty formal written or spoken agreement, usually between nations

tribal belonging to a certain tribe or group

tribe group of persons or clans descending from a common ancestor, language, culture, or name

tributary stream or small river that flows into a larger river

troops armed forces, soldiers

truce temporary stop in fighting

trustee person legally responsible for a property, territory, or for another person

unanimous having the agreement of all

utopia imaginary, ideal place

veto keep from becoming law

vocational relating to a specific trade or skill

volunteer give or offer one's service, such as in the military or community

welfare health, happiness, or prosperity; well being

INDEX

AKNOWLEDGMENTS

SPECIAL CONSULTANT: Gladys Twyman, Atlanta City

READERS: Richardean Anderson, Fulton County; Elaine Bailey, Dodge County; Alan A. Barge, Clayton County; Joan P. Barker, Cobb County; Wiley R. Barker, Dougherty County; Sharon Beavers, Whitfield County; Tom E. Brackett, Fannin County; Jacquelyn C. Brandon, Clayton County; Brenda E. Bryan, Muscogee County; Janet Byars, Cobb County; Gary Cochran, Whitfield County; Albert DeVencenzo, Chatham County; Susan R. Ethridge, Chatham County; Victoria Goon, Bibb County; Nellie M. Graham, Atlanta City; Max Griffin, Decatur County; Carole Jacobs, Fulton County, Mark Jones, Chatham County; Walter E. Harrison III, Colquitt County; Deborah Jan Holmes, Ware County; Madge H. Kibler, Clarke County; Jane P. Layfield, Gwinnett County; Harriet R. Madison, Fulton County; Rickey A. Martin, Cherokee County; Mary McKinney, Richmond County; Regina Tucker Montgomery, Cobb County; Richard Muska, DeKalb County; Vera C. Phillips, Dougherty County; Catherine S. Pittman, Glynn County; Mary H. Pounds, Cobb County; Penny Ratliff, Decatur City; Nancy Reimer, Dougherty County; Barbara Rogers, Stephens County; Marialaine H. Scott, DeKalb County; Patricia G. Smiley, Chatham County; Virginia P. Stanley, Atlanta City; Philip Stephens, Toombs County; Julie A. Yost, Fulton County; Gerald Lee Zeigler, Dougherty County

SURVEY PARTICIPANTS: Joy Autry, Hall County; John Barnett, Floyd County; Tom E. Brackett, Fannin County; Jacquelyn C. Brandon, Clayton County; Josephine G. Briese, Camden County; Sadie B. Brooks, Atlanta City; Helene Brown, Gwinnett County, Tomilea L. Hall-Burnham, Decatur County; Michael D. Chuites, Muscogee County; Robert S. Codner, Heard County; Lynn Coker, Floyd County; Anita G. Cole, Gwinnett County; Peggy O. Compton, Cobb County; Jan Cook, Bulloch County; Sonja Gail Cook, Marietta City; Vicki J. Day, Chattooga County, Gale B. Dopson, Dodge County; Beth W. Drake, Hogansville City; Karen W. Dykes, Dodge County; David Lyman Edgy, Appling County; David A. Edmondson, Dekalb County; Lois J. English, Upson County; Mark R. Fried, Glynn County; Beth Futch, Bulloch County; Carole E. Grace, Bibb County; Judieth Groves, Columbia County; Willie D. Hill, Bibb County; Delories Epps Horton, Cherokee County; Gail Broome Jackson, LaGrange City; Nina P. Jarrell, Taylor County; Kathie L. Johnson, Richmond County; Thomas M. Kemp, Grady County; Ted W. Key, Clayton County; Wilma B. Kimbrough, Whitfield County; Joan C. Laframboise, Cobb County; Rob Lauer, Atlanta; Linda Ann Lee, Fulton County; Vance F. Lusk, Jr., Fayette County; Ken Taylor, Jr., Bryan County; Marthell S. Miller, Paulding County; Marsha M. Moore, Laurens County; Elaine W. McCaw, Vidalia City; Helen McClellan, Bremen City; James C. McGilvray, Colquitt County; Michael G. Nance, Dekalb County; James H. Paschal, Columbia County; William R. Pass, Oglethorpe County; Jeaneen Phillips, Paulding County; Elizabeth Pierce, Clayton County; Michael E. Ray, Bulloch County; Virginia Rushing, Walker County; Marialaine H. Scott, DeKalb County; Dr. Robert L. Scott, Brooks County; Brenda A. Smith, Waycross City; Rhonda M. Stephens, Carroll County; Grady Trussell, Jr., Macon County; Gerald A. Tuck, Liberty County; E. C. Walker, Baldwin County; Dorothy V. Williams, Atlanta City; Larry F. Woodard, Doublin City; James A. Zoll, Fulton County.

PICTURE CREDITS: Cover Robin McDonald. i Georgia Department of Industry, Trade, and Tourism. ii Robin McDonald. iv Robin McDonald. vii Georgia Department of Industry, Trade, and Tourism. viii-ix (top left) Robin McDonald; (top all others) Georgia State Department of Industry, Trade, and Tourism; (below left) Robin McDonald; (below right) Georgia Department of Industry, Trade, and Tourism. Back cover: Robin McDonald.

UNIT I: x-1 Robin McDonald. **CHAPTER ONE** 2 (all) Robin McDonald. 3 Robin McDonald. 5 Robin McDonald. 6 (both) Robin McDonald. 7 (both) Robin McDonald. 9 Georgia Department of Industry, Trade, and Tourism. 10-11 Robin McDonald. 12 (above) Georgia Department of Industry, Trade, and Tourism; (right) Robin McDonald 13 Georgia Department of Industry, Trade, and Tourism. 14 (both) Robin McDonald. 15 Robin McDonald. 16-17 Robin McDonald. 17 (top) Georgia Department of Industry, Trade, and Tourism. 18-19 (spread) Georgia Department of Industry, Trade, and Tourism. 19 inset Georgia Department of Industry, Trade, and Tourism. 20 (above) Georgia Department of Industry, Trade, and Tourism; (right) Robin McDonald. 21 (left) Georgia Department of Industry, Trade, and Tourism. 22 Georgia Department of Industry, Trade, and Tourism. 23 Robin McDonald. 24 Robin McDonald. 25 (above left and left) Georgia Department of Industry, Trade, and Tourism; (right) Robin McDonald. 26-27 (both) Robin McDonald. 28 Robin McDonald. 29 Robin McDonald. 31 Georgia Department of Industry, Trade, and Tourism. 32 The Bettmann Archive. 33 (both) Robin McDonald. 34 (both) Robin McDonald. 35 Robin McDonald. 36 Robin McDonald. 37 (above) photo copyright Peter Bergh, (below) Georgia Department of Industry, Trade, and Tourism. 39 Georgia Department of Industry, Trade, and Tourism. **CHAPTER TWO:** 40-41 Georgia Department of Industry, Trade, and Tourism. 43 Red Mountain Museum. 44 (both) Red Mountain Museum. 45 Red Mountain Museum. 46 Tennessee State Library and Archives. 47 The Bettmann Archive. 48 Atlanta Historical Society. 49 (top) Red Mountain Museum; (above) Tennessee State Museum. 50 (right) Alabama State Museum, (below) Tennessee State Museum. 51 (right) Alabama State Museum; (below) Tennessee State Museum. 52 (top) Alabama State Museum; (middle bottom) Red Mountain Museum. 53 (above) Tennessee State Museum, (below) Red Mountain Museum. 54 Georgia Department of Industry, Trade, and Tourism. 55 Georgia Department of Industry, Trade, and Tourism. 56-57 (spread) Robin McDonald. 57 (bottom) Georgia Department of Industry, Trade, and Tourism. 58 (above) Tennessee State Library and Archives, (right) Georgia State Archives. 59 The Bettmann Archive. 61 (both) Robin McDonald. **CHAPTER THREE:** 62-63 Georgia State Archives. 64-65 The Bettmann Archive. 66 The Bettmann Archive. 67 (above) The Bettmann Archive, (left) Georgia Historical Society. 68 Georgia State Archives. 69 (above) Georgia State Archives, (left) The Bettmann Archive. 70 The Bettmann Archive. 71 (left) The Bettmann Archive. 72 (both) Georgia State Archives. 73 Georgia State Archives. 75 (left) Georgia Historical Society, (above) Smithsonian Institute. 76 (above) Georgia State Archives, (left) Georgia Historical Society. 77 Special Collections, University of Georgia. 78 Georgia State Archives. 79 (both) Georgia Historical Society. 80-81 Henry Francos duPont Winterthur Museum. 82 Georgia State Archives. 83 Georgia State Archives. 84 Georgia Historical Society. 85 Georgia State Archives. 86 Georgia State Archives. 87 (both) Georgia Historical Society. 88 (both) Georgia Historical Society. 89 Robin McDonald. **CHAPTER FOUR:** 92 Georgia State Archives. 93 (top) The Bettmann Archive, (above) Atlanta University Special Collections. 95 Georgia State Archives. 96 (above) The Bettmann Archive, (right) Tennessee State Museum. 97 Robin McDonald. 98 Robin McDonald. 99 Georgia Department of Industry, Trade, and Tourism. 100 Georgia State Archives. 101 Georgia State Archives. 102 (above) Atlanta University Special Collections, (right) The Bettmann Archive. 103 (left) The Bettmann Archive, (below) Georgia State Archives. 104 The Bettmann Archive. 105 (left) Robin McDonald, (above Georgia State Archives. 106 Georgia State Archives. 107 The Bettmann Archive. 108 (both) Georgia State Archives. 109 Georgia State Archives. 110 Georgia State Archives. 111 Georgia State Archives. 112 Georgia State Archives. 113 (both) Georgia Historical Society. 114 Robin McDonald. 115 (both) Georgia State Archives. 117 (top right) Georgia State Archives, (bottom left) The Bettmann Archive. **UNIT III:** 118 Georgia State Archives. 119 The Bettmann Archive. **CHAPTER FIVE:** 120 Georgia State Archives. 121 The Bettmann Archive. 123 (left) Georgia State Archives, (top) The Bettmann Archive. 124 The Bettmann Archive. 125 (both) Georgia State Archives. 126 The Bettmann Archive. 127 The Bettmann Archive. 128 The Bettmann Archive. 129 (both) Georgia State Archives. 130 (both) Georgia State Archives. 131 Georgia State Archives. 132 Alabama Department of Archives and History. 133 (left) Georgia Historical Society, (top and above) Alabama Department Archives and History. 134 (both) The Bettmann Archive. 135 (left) Georgia State Archives. 137 The Bettmann Archive. 138 Atlanta University Special Collections. 141 (top) Georgia State Archives. 142-143 (spread) Georgia Historical Society, (inset) Robin McDonald. 144 Tennessee State Museum, (right) Robin McDonald. 145 Georgia State Archives. 146 (above) The Bettmann Archive, (right) Georgia State Archives. 147 (both) Robin McDonald. 148 (above) Georgia State Archives, (right) Atlanta Historical Society. 149 Georgia State Archives. 151 Georgia Historical Society. **CHAPTER SIX:** 152-153 Georgia State Archives. 155 Tutwiler Collection, Birmingham, Alabama Public Library. 156 Tennessee State Museum. 157 (above) Robin McDonald, (left) Georgia Department of Industry, Trade, and Tourism. 158 Atlanta Historical Society. 159 Tennessee State Library and Archives. 160 Robin McDonald. 161 Robin McDonald. 162 Atlanta Historical Society. 163 Gilcrease Institute. 164 New Echota State Historic Site. 165 New Echota State Historic Site. 166-167 Robin McDonald. 167 (inset) Robin McDonald. 168 Georgia Department of Industry, Trade, and Tourism. 169 (both) New Echota State Historic Site. 170 Georgia State Archives. 171 Museum of City of Mobile. 172 (right) Alabama Department of Archives and History, (below) Horseshoe Bend National Military Park. 173 Horseshoe Bend National Military Park. 174 (both) Georgia State Archives. 175 Tennessee State Museum. 176 (both) Georgia State Archives. 177 (top) The Bettmann Archive, (above) Robin McDonald. 178 (both) Tennessee State Museum. 179 The Bettmann Archive. 180 (top) Tennessee Historical Society, (above) Tennessee State Library and Archives. **CHAPTER SEVEN:** 184-185 The Bettmann Archive. 186-187 Georgia Department of Industry, Trade, and Tourism. 189 The Bettmann Archive. 190 Georgia State Archives. 191 (both) Georgia State Archives. 193 The Bettmann Archive. 194 (top) The Bettmann Archive, (above) collection of Bob Womack. 195 Robin McDonald. 196 Georgia State Archives. 197 Alabama Department of Archives and History. 198 Atlanta Historical Society. 199 Georgia State Archives. 201 Georgia Department of Industry, Trade, and Tourism. 202 Robin McDonald. 203 (top) Robin McDonald, (above) Georgia Department of Industry, Trade, and Tourism. 204 Atlanta Historical Society. 205 Robin McDonald. 206 Georgia State Archives. 207 Georgia State Archives. 208 Georgia State Archives. 209 The Bettmann Archive. 210 Robin McDonald. 211 Georgia State Archives. 212 (both) William S. Hoole Special Collections Library, University of Alabama. 213 (both) The Bettmann Archive. **CHAPTER EIGHT:** 216-217 Robin McDonald. 219 Atlanta Historical Society. 220 Atlanta Historical Society. 221 The Bettmann Archive. 222 collection of Bob Womack. 223 Atlanta Historical Society. 224 Atlanta Historical Society. 225 Atlanta Historical Society. 226 The Bettmann Archive. 227 The Bettmann Archive. 228 Atlanta Historical Society. 229 (both) Georgia Department of Industry, Trade, and Tourism. 230 (both) William S. Hoole Special Collections Library, University of Alabama. 231 Atlanta Historical Society. 232 Atlanta Historical Society. 233 Atlanta Historical Society. 234 (above) collection of Bob Womack, (right) The Bettmann Archive. 235 The Bettmann Archive. 236 (both) collection of Bob Womack. 237 collection of Bob Womack. 238 The Bettmann Archive. 239 The Bettmann Archive. 240 Tennessee State Library and Archives. 241 Atlanta Historical Society. 242-243 Kennesaw Mountain National Military Park. 244 Atlanta Historical Society. 244-245 (spread) Atlanta Historical Society. 246 (both) Atlanta Historical Society. 247 Atlanta Historical Society. 248 Georgia Department of Industry, Trade, and Tourism. 249 collection of Bob Womack. 250 (both) The Bettmann Archive. 251 The Bettmann Archive. 252 Georgia Department of Industry, Trade, and Tourism. **CHAPTER NINE:** 256-257 Georgia State Archives. 259 (above) William S. Hoole Special Collections Library, University of Alabama, (left) Georgia State Archives. 260 (top) The Bettmann Archive, (above) Atlanta University Special Collections. 261 The Bettmann Archive. 262 (both) Middle Tennessee State University. 263 Library of Congress. 264 (both) Georgia State Archives. 265 (both) The Bettmann Archive. 266 (top) Georgia Historical Society, (above) Georgia State Archives. 267 (both) Georgia State Archives. 268 Atlanta Historical Society. 269 Georgia Department of Industry, Trade, and Tourism. 270 Georgia Historical Society. 271 (both) Atlanta Historical Society. 272 Atlanta Historical Society. 273 Georgia State Archives. 274 (right) Atlanta University Special Collections, (below) Georgia State Archives. 275 (top) The Bettmann Archive, (above) Atlanta Historical Society. **UNIT III:** 278 Atlanta Historical Society. 279 Robin McDonald. **CHAPTER TEN:** 280 Atlanta Historical Society. 281 Atlanta Historical Society. 283 The Bettmann Archive. 284 The Bettmann Archive. 285 Atlanta Historical Society. 286 Georgia State Archives. 287 (both) Georgia State Archives. 288 Georgia State Archives. 289 Georgia State Archives. 290 Georgia State Archives. 291 Georgia State Archives. 293 (right) Robin McDonald, (below) Georgia State Archives. 293 Atlanta Historical Society. 294-295 Robin McDonald. 296 Atlanta Historical Society. 297 Atlanta Historical Society. 298 *Atlanta Journal and Constitution*. 299 Georgia State Archives. 300 The Bettmann Archive. 301 The Bettmann Archive. 302 Atlanta Historical Society. 303 (left) Georgia State Archives, (below) The Bettmann Archive. 304 Georgia State Archives. 305 Georgia State Archives. 306 Robin McDonald. 307 The Bettmann Archive. 308-309 (all) The Bettmann Archive. 311 The Bettmann Archive. **CHAPTER ELEVEN:** 312-313 Atlanta Historical Society. 314 The Bettmann Archive. 315 (left) Georgia State Archives, (below) The Bettmann Archive. 317 Robin McDonald. 318 Atlanta Historical Society. 319 Atlanta Historical Society. 320 Atlanta Historical Society. 321 Atlanta Historical Society. 323 Georgia State Archives. 324 Georgia State Archives. 325 Atlanta Historical Society. 326 (both) The Bettmann Archive. 327 The Bettmann Archive. 328 The Bettmann Archive. 329 (left and above) The Bettmann Archive. 330-331 (both) Atlanta Historical Society. 332-333 (above and left) Atlanta Historical Society. 334 (both) Georgia State Archives. 335 Georgia State Archives. 336 Georgia State Archives. 337 Robin McDonald. 338 (both) Atlanta Historical Society. 339 Georgia Historical Society. 340 (above) *Atlanta Journal and Constitution*, (right) Atlanta Historical Society. 341 Atlanta Historical Society. 342 (both) Coca-Cola Company Archives. 343 (both) Coca-Cola Company Archives. 344 Coca-Cola Company Archives. 345 (both) Coca-Cola Company Archives. **CHAPTER TWELVE:** 348 Georgia State Archives. 349 The Bettmann Archive. 351 Georgia State Archives. 352 Atlanta Historical Society. 353 The Bettmann Archive. 354 Alabama Department of Archives and History. 355 The Bettmann Archive. 356 Atlanta Historical Society. 357 The Bettmann Archive. 358 Atlanta University Special Collections. 359 Atlanta University Special Collections. 360 Atlanta University Special Collections. 361 Atlanta University Special Collections. 362 Atlanta Historical Society. 363 Atlanta University Special Collections. 364 Atlanta University Special Collections. 365 (both) Atlanta University Special Collections. 366 Atlanta University Special Collections. 367 Atlanta University Special Collections. 368 (both) Atlanta University Special Collections. 369 *Atlanta Journal and Constitution*. 370 *Atlanta Journal and Constitution*. 371 The Bettmann Archive. **CHAPTER THIRTEEN:** 374-375 Atlanta Historical Society. 376 The Bettmann Archive. 377 The Bettmann Archive. 378 The Bettmann Archive. 379 The Bettmann Archive. 380 The Bettmann Archive. 381 Georgia Historical Society. 382 Georgia State Archives. 383 Atlanta Historical Society. 384 *Atlanta Journal and Constitution*. 385 The Bettmann Archive. 386 Atlanta Historical Society. 387 (left) The Bettmann Archive, (above) Atlanta Historical Society. 388 (right) Atlanta Historical Society, (below) Georgia Historical Society. 389 (above) The Bettmann Archive, (left) Georgia State Archives. 390 (both) Georgia Department of Industry, Trade, and Tourism. 391 Girl Scouts of the U.S.A. 392 Girl Scouts of the U.S.A. 393 Georgia State Archives. 394 Atlanta Historical Society. 395 Georgia State Archives. 396 Robin McDonald. 397 Robin McDonald. 398 (both) The Bettmann Archive. 399 The Bettmann Archive. 400 The Bettmann Archive. 401 The Bettmann Archive. 402 The Bettmann Archive. 403 The Bettmann Archive. 404 The Bettmann Archive. 405 (above) The Bettmann Archive, (left) Georgia State Archives. 406 (both) The Bettmann Archive. 407 The Bettmann Archive. 408 (right) Atlanta Historical Society, (below) Georgia State Archives. 409 (both Atlanta Historical Society. **CHAPTER FOURTEEN:** 412-413 Atlanta Historical Society. 414 (above) The Bettmann Archive, (right) Atlanta University Special Collections. 415 (top) Atlanta Historical Society, (above) The Bettmann Archive. 416 Georgia Historical Society 417 The Bettmann Archive. 418 (both) The Bettman Archive. 419 (above) The Bettmann Archive, (left) Georgia Historical Society. 420 Atlanta Historical Society. 421 (above) Georgia Department of Industry, Trade, and Tourism, (left) *Atlanta Journal and Constitution*. 422 (top) The Bettmann Archive, (below) Atlanta Historical Society. 423 (top) The Bettmann Archive, (above) Atlanta University Special Collections. 424 Atlanta University Special Collections. 425 Atlanta University Special Collections. 426 (all) The Bettmann Archive. 427 (both) The Bettmann Archive. 428 Georgia State Archives. 429 Georgia State Archives. 430 *Atlanta Journal and Constitution*. 431 *Atlanta Journal and Constitution*. 432 (both) *Atlanta Journal and Constitution*. 433 Georgia State Archives. 434 (both) The Bettmann Archive. 435 The Bettmann Archive. 436 The Bettmann Archive. 437 The Bettmann Archive. 438 The Bettmann Archive. 439 The Bettmann Archive. 440 Georgia Department of Industry, Trade, and Tourism. 441 The Bettmann Archive. 442-443 (top) Atlanta Historical Society, (left) Georgia State Archives. 444 Georgia Historical Society. 445 The Bettmann Archive. **UNIT VI:** 448-449 *Atlanta Journal and Constitution*. **CHAPTER FIFTEEN:** 450-451 *Atlanta Journal and Constitution*. 452 The Bettmann Archive. 453 (all) The Bettmann Archive. 454 (above) *Atlanta Journal and Constitution*, (right) Georgia State Archives. 455 *Atlanta Journal and Constitution*. 456 Atlanta Historical Society. 457 (both) *Atlanta Journal and Constitution*. 458 (both) *Atlanta Journal and Constitution*. 459 Atlanta Historical Society. 460 *Atlanta Journal and Constitution*. 461 The Bettmann Archive. 462 The Bettmann Archive. 463 The Bettmann Archive. 464 (top) *Atlanta Journal and Constitution*, (above) Georgia State Archives. 465 *Atlanta Journal and Constitution*. 466 *Atlanta Journal and Constitution*. 467 (both) The Bettmann Archive. 468 Atlanta Historical Society. 469 Georgia Historical Society. 470 (both) *Atlanta Journal and Constitution*. 471 The Bettmann Archive. 472 Atlanta University Special Collections. 473 Birmingham Public Library Archives. 474 The Bettmann Archive. 475 The Bettmann Archive. 476 The Bettmann Archive. 477 (both) The Bettmann Archive. 478 The Bettmann Archive. 479 (both) The Bettmann Archive. 480 The Bettmann Archive. 481 *Atlanta Journal and Constitution*. 482 The Bettmann Archive. 483 The Bettmann Archive. 484 The Bettmann Archive. 485 (both) The Bettmann Archive. 486 The Bettmann Archive. 487 (both) The Bettmann Archive. 488 Georgia State Archives. 489 Georgia State Archives. 490 (both) The Bettmann Archive. 491 The Bettmann Archive. 492 The Bettmann Archive. 493 Georgia Department of Industry, Trade, and Tourism. 494 *Atlanta Journal and Constitution*. 495 *Atlanta Journal and Constitution*. 496 (both) Atlanta Historical Society. 497 The Bettmann Archive. 498 (both) The Bettmann Archive. 499 (both)The Bettmann Archive. 500 The Bettmann Archive. 501 The Bettmann Archive. 502 *Atlanta Journal and Constitution*. 503 Georgia Department of Industry, Trade, and Tourism. 505 courtesy Carolyn Smith. **CHAPTER SIXTEEN:** 508-509 *(both) Atlanta Journal and Constitution*. 510 Georgia Department of Industry, Trade, and Tourism. 511 (both) The Bettmann Archive. 512 (both) Georgia Department of Industry, Trade, and Tourism. 513 (both) Georgia Department of Industry, Trade, and Tourism. 514 Georgia Department of Industry, Trade, and Tourism. 515 (above) The Bettmann Archive, (below) Georgia Department of Industry, Trade, and Tourism. 516 (both) Georgia Department of Industry, Trade, and Tourism. 517 (top both) Georgia Department of Industry, Trade, and Tourism; (bottom) The Bettmann Archive.518 Georgia Department of Industry, Trade, and Tourism. 519 (both) Georgia Department of Industry, Trade, and Tourism. 520 Georgia Department of Industry, Trade, and Tourism. 521 (both) Georgia Department of Industry, Trade, and Tourism. 522 (above) Robin McDonald; (right) Georgia Department of Industry, Trade, and Tourism. 523 Georgia Department of Industry, Trade, and Tourism. 524 Georgia Department of Industry, Trade, and Tourism. 525 (both) Georgia Department of Industry, Trade, and Tourism. 526 Robin McDonald. Georgia Department of Industry, Trade, and Tourism. 527 (left) Georgia Historical Society, (below) Georgia Department of Industry, Trade, and Tourism. 528 *Atlanta Journal and Constitution*. **CHAPTER SEVENTEEN:** 532-533 Georgia Department of Industry, Trade, and Tourism. 535 Robin McDonald. 536 *Atlanta Journal and Constitution*. 537 (below) *Atlanta Journal and Constitution*, (bottom) The Bettmann Archive. 538 The Bettmann Archive. 539 (both) The Bettmann Archive. 540 The Bettmann Archive. 541 Robin McDonald. 544 The Bettmann Archive. 545 Robin McDonald. 546 Robin McDonald. 547 *Atlanta Journal and Constitution*. 548 *Atlanta Journal and Constitution*. 549 Georgia Department of Industry, Trade, and Tourism. 550 *Atlanta Journal and Constitution*. 551 *Atlanta Journal and Constitution*. 552 Georgia Department of Industry, Trade, and Tourism. 553 *Atlanta Journal and Constitution*. 554 *Atlanta Journal and Constitution*. 555 *Atlanta Journal and Constitution*. 556 *Atlanta Journal and Constitution*. 557 *Atlanta Journal and Constitution*. 558 *Atlanta Journal and Constitution*. 559 *Atlanta Journal and Constitution*. 560 *Atlanta Journal and Constitution*. 561 Robin McDonald. 562 Robin McDonald. 563 *Robin McDonald*. 564 Robin McDonald. 565 Robin McDonald. 566 *Atlanta Journal and Constitution*. 567 Georgia Department of Industry, Trade, and Tourism.